Rings of Truth

Rings of Truth

Jim Britt

with Eve Eschner Hogan

Health Communications, Inc.
Deerfield Beach, Florida

www.hci-online.com

Library of Congress Cataloging-in-Publication Data

Britt, Jim

Rings of truth / Jim Britt with Eve Eschner Hogan.

p. cm.

ISBN 1-55874-724-9 (trade pbk.)

I. Hogan, Eve Eschner. II. Title.

PS3552.R49718R5 1999 99-40759

CIP

ISBN-1-55874-724-9

Publisher: Health Communications, Inc.
3201 S.W. 15th Street
Deerfield Beach, Florida 33442-8190

Cover design: Peter Quintal and Lex Munson
Book design: Dawn Grove

To my mother and father, who gave me the gift of life
and who are now both watching over me.

To my dear wife, Joanna, who loves me unconditionally
and gives me the freedom to be myself.

To my six sons, Jeff, Jim, Warren, Weston,
William and Walker,
who chose me as their father and student.

To Alea, who began as a figment of imagination,
but whose insights proved her real.

To all those who are seekers of Truth.

Contents

Acknowledgments

It would be impossible to name all the people who have influenced this book, but I want to express my deepest appreciation to:

My family and friends, for their support and love; their stories are written into these pages. I appreciate each and every one of them, individually and collectively, for their encouragement and support of my work and this project throughout the years.

Eve Eschner Hogan, for her love and dedication to this work, her imagination, superb creative writing skills and the many contributions woven throughout, without whom this book would not have been possible.

Rosemarie Evans, whose contribution and support in getting this work out to the public has truly made a difference.

And a special thanks for the workshop participants who trusted me and had the courage and willingness to open their hearts and minds to experiencing a better way of life.

Author's Note

It is my wish to express to you the grace through which this book was written. It would almost require another book just to tell the story of the many coincidences and the mystical unfolding that took place during its formation. There is no doubt of the Divine Guidance that led the way for its creation.

I also wish to impress upon you as you read this text that while parts have been fictionalized, it is based on true events. In some instances the events have been compressed so as to move the story along, but the essence of the lessons learned and truths realized has been retained in full. Any references to teachings, processes and examples of letting-go experiences are actual accounts, virtually word for word, of real people who have attended my seminars and workshops. While some may seem "too good to be true" or "too easy to be true," they *are* true stories. It is my hope that knowing this will help you to understand and assimilate the principles and processes more readily.

I invite you to soak up the following story as entertainment for your mind, nourishment for your heart and a wake-up call for your soul.

Jim Britt

Preface

She watched him closely as he slept, aware that Matt couldn't see her or feel her presence. It was hard to see him in so much pain and not be able to simply "fix it" or show him the way. Yet she knew that she had to let him take each step on his own. She could not interfere by helping him until he was ready. She could help him become aware of what he already knew and that was all. Anything else he was not ready to understand. He would not be able to see or hear her until then anyhow, so all she could do for now was love him and watch. She knew he would come around, and when he did, she would be there.

She watched him sleep alone in the huge bed, in the huge room, in the huge house, reminiscing about all the nights she had watched over him, longing for him to know her.

When Matt was young, his family had continually moved from town to town in the constant search for work, often as laborers in the cotton fields. She remembered the many nights he had cried himself to sleep in the depths of loneliness, not realizing that he wasn't alone. Able to receive his feelings, she recalled the exhaustion and pain his young body had endured from picking cotton for hours on end, with the sun's intensity bleaching his reddish brown hair and burning his face. He and his brother and sisters had helped their mother, endlessly pulling behind them the sacks of cotton that year after year grew bigger as they did, matching them in size. Their father did whatever he could to bring in some meager income, despite a back injury that severely limited his earnings.

Matt's loneliness and hardships were so painful in those years that he had begun to shut out his feelings, which unfortunately excluded her as well. All these years she had waited, knowing him better than he knew himself. She shared each pain and every happy moment, appreciating each fully. She was unknown, unseen. Still, she knew her time was coming as she watched him sleep. Patience was her virtue, which she shared with him whenever she could. In it, she knew his soul's mission and what a timeless thing it was.

Her thoughts turned to the mother and father who had raised him. The life they led was hard and deserving of respect, particularly in light of the compassion they always had for others. His father was stoic, yet kind, a skilled tinkerer who took great pleasure in buying old cars and fixing them up. His mother had always been a hard worker who demonstrated endurance and strength with grace. She had done what she had to do to care for her children, not an easy task in the depths of Oklahoma in the 1940s.

Reviewing Matt's life was like watching a silent movie: The hot dusty fields, the rundown homes with outhouses in back, the bloody fingers from picking cotton, the constant moves from town to town. These all passed by without words; his parents, though kind, had not been much for talking. "Time to get up." "Go wash at the pump." "Please pass the potatoes." "How many bags did you pick today?" "Well, I guess it's time to go to bed. . . ." The art of conversation was a luxury precluded by exhaustion.

Remembering his wedding day, she smiled as she thought about how he had looked as if he were playing "dress up" in his borrowed suit, all six feet four inches of him. In the early sixties in Oklahoma, many people married young, and he was no exception. At seventeen he had believed he was ready for adulthood. In love with Sarah, he couldn't wait to marry her. Sarah was in love with him, too, but was no more prepared for adulthood than he. With a hint of amusement, she remembered their youthful, romantic ideas of marriage.

When his first son, Jerry, was born, Matt was barely more than a babe himself—eighteen and becoming a father. Seven years later, his second son, Tim, was born. The two boys were precious to him, but he was never really sure how to be a dad. He hadn't experienced much of a childhood himself, what with the realities of being poor from birth. Naturally, he had believed that making enough money and being a good provider was equal to good fathering.

Matt's intense desire to break out of pain and poverty had caused him to work hard, first in a gas station, then in a factory and finally in his own businesses. He had sought answers to his questions about life and spent hours on end contemplating and studying ways to find both wealth and happiness. Going from rags to riches, he had eventually begun sharing his discoveries and successes with others.

She was impressed with how far he had come. He had evolved into a powerful seminar facilitator who could move people to action, through teaching them to pull themselves up and make the most of their lives, no matter what their circumstances. Over the past fifteen years, he had transformed from a new, hopeful speaker into a seasoned, dynamic one and had made a difference in the lives of hundreds of thousands of people. He had taught them what it takes to be a success, to build a business, to set goals and to reach them, in no small part through the example of his own life. He had given them hope.

Matt was an honest, kind man and a master at the external affairs of life, a motivated soul who was excellent at motivating others. She treasured him for his genuine desire to help people be happy, and she looked forward to the day when he would transcend being simply a motivational speaker into being a truly inspirational one instead. The transformation would occur in the substance of what he taught and the long-term effects of those teachings. She knew the time was nearing for this metamorphosis to begin.

She laughed lightly, causing a ripple of happiness and love to emanate from her presence and reverberate throughout the room. Matt didn't yet know who he was and how he would impact the world, but she did. She blew a gentle kiss to the sleeping man and wove a prayer around him as she watched him wake.

1

The Awakening

The wind chimes tolled softly like temple bells as they blew in the gentle breeze. My home, on a hilltop in Sedona, was surrounded by natural beauty and was as peaceful as a monastery. Lying there, just waking up, I enjoyed the sounds of morning as I watched the day begin. The bright Arizona sun rose over the majestic red rock cliffs just outside my window. Their strength, their solidity, their evidence of enduring power always took my breath away and left me feeling blessed. Thinking about how fortunate I had been, I gave thanks for all I had achieved.

From the vantage point of my bed, I looked at my surroundings. My clothes were hanging neatly in the closet. Southwestern art that Sarah and I had picked out at the Sunday afternoon art festival years ago still decorated the room. Pictures of the kids, taken several years earlier, were hanging on the wall.

My eyes came to rest on the computer patiently waiting for my words of wisdom. Today I would finish writing my personal growth book. My agent had been waiting for the finished manuscript for weeks, and finally I would have something in hand for all those who had been asking for it.

I took the moment to review, with some amazement, all I had done while en route from virtually nothing to virtually everything. My dad used to say, "It doesn't matter what you do, just do it well." He was good at most things he did—whether working odd jobs or playing pool. I had followed his advice my whole life, giving my best shot to everything I did, and it had paid off. I had run large companies and addressed thousands of people, teaching them how to pursue the "American Dream" of acquiring all the things that would make them happy. I taught them, too, to do their best at everything they did, passing on to thousands the one thing I remembered my dad teaching me. It had been good and lasting advice. I laughed as I remembered my friends remarking about how successful I was and how I must be the "happiest man in the world." If they could only have seen the dusty fields where I had grown up.

I remembered the time my little sister twisted her ankle in the field when we were picking cotton. I hated seeing her get hurt. I wanted to protect my family, although there usually wasn't much that I could do. I took my sister's sack and filled it along with mine, as if getting her work done would somehow make up for her pain. Hard work was the common thread that ran throughout my life.

My gaze turned to the pillow next to me, now noticeably empty instead of full of life as it once had been. How long had it been since Sarah and the boys left? It must have been a couple of years already, as Jerry was nearing seventeen now and Tim was turning ten. Seeing them a few times a year never seemed like enough.

The divorce replayed itself in my mind as tears stung the corners of my eyes. I thought of how beautiful Sarah had looked on our wedding day. We were both so full of love and faith. Who would ever have thought that we would end up divorced? I had promised that when we had all these things, a beautiful home, new cars and plenty of money, we would be truly happy. I had worked hard to get them, not realizing that all the time away from home would end up putting a fatal distance between us.

As I thought of the boys and Sarah, guilt and emptiness invaded me. Here I was with all these things in a beautiful home, with everything except happiness. The house was full of objects that recalled the past, but it held no life to create any future memories. The silent room only emphasized the question that suddenly struck me: *If I have achieved so much, why am I hurting so much inside?*

I felt numb as my lack of happiness revealed itself. How could I not be happy? I had everything. I taught people the secrets of happiness. I lay there in bed and felt my perfect world crumbling around me. Why hadn't I noticed this deep pain before? The answer was obvious: I had kept myself too busy to notice. The very work that had kept me from seeing my marriage dissolving had kept me from feeling the pain of it, too. Focusing on outer success had kept me from feeling my inner failure.

Questions pounded the shores of my mind like crashing waves: *Was anything I taught true? What is truth? If this isn't happiness, what is? How did I get this way? What am I here for? Who do I think I am, to be doing this work?* One after another the doubts rolled in, bit by bit eroding the tattered shoreline of my beliefs. Tears streamed down my face as I realized that most of what I had taught, and all I had stood for, no longer seemed true. Had I led all those people astray?

Wondering what had gone wrong, I looked around the room at all the things I had gathered in my effort to be happy. A fine collection of forty-seven designer suits hung in my closet, along with sixty shirts and twenty pairs of perfectly polished shoes. Similar trophies surrounded me everywhere—yet held no happiness. I clearly saw what I had done. I had taught the *pursuit* of happiness, rather than the *experience* of happiness. I had been blinded by the chase, not comprehending that, while in pursuit, one never really arrives. *Things* were not the answer. They could help to *celebrate* happiness, but they could not *deliver* it.

Still numb, I rolled out of bed and turned on the computer, thinking that perhaps I could put this feeling to use and inspire a creative finish to the already overdue manuscript. Perhaps I could simply revise the parts that no longer felt right. Staring at the blank computer screen, fingers poised on the keys, I waited, hoping perhaps for some sort of automatic writing to take over and offer me an opening thought, but my hands hovered over the little plastic squares, immobilized. Not a word presented itself. Instead, the emptiness of the screen created a glow that spotlighted me as the star of the show that was beginning to play out before me. Not recognizing the character, I slowly typed, *Be careful of who you become, in the search for what you want.*

I sat there for what felt like hours, waiting, thinking and wanting to find the words to finish the manuscript, but my thoughts were totally preoccupied with my discovery of unhappiness. The comment I had typed haunted me. Who had I become? I had become a loner. I dated fairly regularly but made no commitments or promises to anyone; in truth, I kept the women I dated at a safe, though occasionally intimate, distance. I had male friends, but none whom I considered "best friends" or confidants. I justified this as merely an effect of my high value on privacy. Now I wondered if I hadn't just used "privacy" as an excuse for not getting involved, for not feeling. How could I have failed to notice being so alone, so isolated, so—*unsuccessful* in the midst of so much "success"?

I realized in that moment that I hadn't suddenly become this way; I had been this way all along. I tried to remember a time when it wasn't so, but I could not. Certainly I had felt happy at times in the company of others, like my wife and kids, but an overriding sense of loneliness now invaded even the memory of those times. A picture of myself as a boy, alone, flashed before my eyes. He was not happy, had few if any friends and had learned to avoid friendships so as not to get hurt. Moving as often as the family had, friendships never stood a chance. The only difference between "him" and me was that young Matt had had no material goods, no money and no influence. I, on the other hand, had somehow managed to acquire a fortune, all the goods I could want, people valuing my advice and paying money to hear what I had to say.

I did not like where these thoughts were leading. This was no way to end my book. Finally, I abandoned the computer and attempted to do something else with my day, hoping perhaps to distract myself and thus avoid the tremendous discomfort I felt.

I thought of running errands, but lethargy overwhelmed me. I couldn't force myself to go out the door. Thinking that reading might open up an avenue of inspiration, I chose a book and tried to concentrate on its message. Soon I realized that my eyes had scanned the same paragraph at least twenty times with no comprehension, and it became apparent that the turmoil was not going to submit meekly to being drowned. It demanded my attention by sheer sabotage of all else I tried to do.

This must be depression, I analyzed, then lectured myself that I had no right to be depressed. Attempting to "think positive," as I had taught others countless times, I wrote down all the reasons I had for being thankful and came up with quite a lengthy list, including the standbys of "health" and "wealth." But no matter how many items I listed, "happiness" refused to be included. No matter how much positive thinking I forced upon myself, the dark cloud did not lift. The feelings only seemed compounded by "The List," as it offered proof that I didn't deserve to wallow, and self-judgment began to pile up on top of the depression.

I had already wasted most of the day, not accomplishing anything I set out to do. A blanket of tiredness draped itself over me, inviting me to sleep. I held out as long as I could, trying various tasks around the house to snap me out of it, but nothing worked. By late afternoon I fell into bed, telling myself that a little nap would cure whatever was ailing me.

What started as an afternoon siesta lasted well into the night, completely throwing off my internal clock. Somewhere around midnight, I began an hourly vigil of checking the clock and getting angry at its evidence that I was missing the sleep I still desperately wanted even though my body was no longer tired. Tossing and turning, my restless movements pulled the corner of my sheets loose, and I woke up lying partly on sheets and partly on the bare mattress. By five o'clock, not only could I not sleep, I could no longer stay in bed. The night had proven to be more tiring than restful.

Feeling a strong need to do something—anything—I considered various possibilities, and a sudden urge to get rid of all that was meaningless came over me. I went to the closet and pulled out all but a few of the thousand-dollar suits, the freshly pressed shirts, and the soft leather shoes and dumped them in a pile. The wrenching feeling in my stomach brought back an all-too-familiar memory. Staring at the bundle on the floor, my mind wandered back to when I was twelve, to a day when my mother and I were in the department store picking out school clothes. It was a special day each year when we were allowed to pick out two new shirts. I took this task seriously, because I needed just the right ones. The smell of new clothes surrounded me and the colors bombarded my senses. Which two? My adolescent image depended on this important decision! Searching the racks, I finally found one that was perfect, blue with a green pattern. My heart raced as I imagined how good I would look on the first day of school, each hair in place, meeting all the kids. I held the shirt carefully, searching the store for another that I liked as well. It was futile. None of the other shirts compared to the perfection of the first one. Using the logic that if one was good, two were better, I chose a shirt just like the first, only with the pattern reversed. Instead of blue with a green design, it was green with a blue design. Two perfect shirts! Mom let me proudly pay the lady at the counter with the money we had earned picking cotton that summer. Walking out of the store, excited about starting school, I knew that I had chosen well.

The first day of school was just as I had imagined it. I looked fine and everyone told me so. Comments like, "Great shirt!" "You sure can pick 'em!" and "The shirt's cool!" poured over me, feeding my pride. This year was going to be the best year yet! While I had noticeably grown a couple of inches over the summer, with each compliment I felt myself get even taller! The next day, I put on the second shirt and received similar rave reviews. Though I was careful to alternate, never wearing the same shirt two days in a row, the comments changed after a few days. Within a week I heard, "Are you ever going to take that shirt off?" "Don't you think it might need washing?" and "Don't you have any other clothes to wear?" My efforts to explain that I had *two* shirts, one blue with green and one green with blue, were useless. The days wore on and the comments got worse. A song was even written and slung at me on the playground. What began as the pride of my existence turned into my very enemy, separating me from the other kids.

The last day of school, with barely an ounce of self-worth left in me, I fled from the school bus to the tune of "my song," tearing the buttons off as I ran. Ripping the shirt from my back, I ran into my room and wrenched the second shirt from its hanger. Wringing and pulling at the fabric on the way to the backyard, I furiously dug a hole for the funeral of my pride. I threw in the shirts, shredding them for good with the shovel. Tears poured from my eyes as I yelled out my vow, pounding on the side of the house, "When I grow up, I'm never going to live like this!" As I covered the shirts with dirt, my tears watered the seed that had grown over the years into the pile on my floor. Sitting in my empty house, looking at what had grown from my childhood planting, I painfully realized that having or not having made little difference in being happy or unhappy. I wished silently that true happiness could have been as simple as that twelve-year-old had believed. As I gathered up the harvest of years of false beliefs, tears once again watered my future.

If *having* things was not happiness, and *not having* things was not happiness, then just having what I needed and used would suffice. I stuffed my car with everything that no longer was of use and headed off in search of a charity. I glanced at my watch and was surprised at how much time had passed while I had sorted through my things and my memories. Pulling out of the driveway, I was caught up again by the majesty of the red rock walls that surrounded me. I paused and allowed their beauty to fill me, as if doing so might help heal the hole I felt inside, feeling thankful that I was still able to see beauty. Basking in that moment left me believing that there really was a God, which I hadn't questioned until this day. I took in a deep breath of hope as I drove the short distance to the local Goodwill. Perhaps my act of "good will" would help me discover what action needed to be taken next.

The musty smell of the large thrift store, so reminiscent of childhood shopping trips, struck me as soon as I opened the door. As I handed over the piles, the volunteers thanked me warmly but looked at me a little oddly. They must have done the mental math that told them they could buy a house with the money spent on these clothes. I didn't explain and they didn't ask, though the questions hung silently between us. The air in the store felt thick with ghosts and stories, and I walked away feeling lighter as I added mine to the mix. I prayed that my throwaways would add to someone else's life, someone who knew that things were tools, not solutions. Turning my back on what had once seemed so important, I breathed a sigh of relief and left the relics of my past behind.

Confusion surrounded me like a thick fog during the drive home. Thoughts about my unresolved book and the things I had taught rolled through my mind. The frustration I had felt sitting at the computer, unable to write, had left me disconcerted. I asked myself: *Can I really finish my book? Do I want to finish it? Is any of it valid? If it hasn't worked for me, how can I expect it to work for others?* Part of me felt as if no meaning remained in my life, for everything and everyone was gone and I no longer knew what I believed. I was tempted to drive over the edge of the cliffs—taking the "easy" way out. Another—wiser? more hopeful? more gullible?—part of me felt excited, that perhaps out of this "emergency" something wondrous, something new, something real might emerge.

Fear jumped in as I pondered my options. *Should I cancel all my speaking engagements? Do I have anything of value to say? What about my book? Should I call my agent? What will I do with my life, if I have nothing left to teach?* All I knew was that if I wanted different results, I would certainly need to take different actions.

I surfaced from my thoughts to find myself pulling back into my driveway. Thankful that some unconscious part of me always knew the way home, I took solace in the hope that it would also find my way out of the turmoil into which I had thrown myself. I returned to my computer and reread chapter after chapter of my manuscript. The truth I had seen in it only days ago was erased by my new realization of its superficiality and emptiness. Without the slightest hesitation, I dragged the entire document and years of research into the miniature trash can on the screen. I laughed aloud at the thought that such a small trash container could hold so much garbage. File after file disappeared. Fifteen years, hundreds of hours of research, interviews, time away from my family—almost half my life—thrown out with the flick of a finger into the world's tiniest garbage can. Then I emptied the trash! For the moment, I felt emptied, too.

My body ached as much as my soul. Dazed, I went outside and

climbed into the hot tub. The colors of the sky gilded the ledges of the red rock wall, and I took a deep breath as the sun set before me. Fear gripped me again as I realized what I had done. I had destroyed the past, purposefully letting it go, without having a picture of what the future held. The transition from day to night, light to dark, was all too pat a metaphor for my own transition. I quickly reminded myself that the sun would rise again, as always, and that the night held beauty and value, too. I thanked God that the teacher in me, though not always right, was always present.

I laughed out loud to think of myself as a teacher. I had always disliked teachers, most of them anyway. Watching the sky get darker, I found myself reliving the darkness of my education. I sat in class, surrounded by the faces of my tenth-grade classmates, feeling so distant, knowing none of them and none of them knowing me. The room was quiet, with each of us left to our own thoughts as we studied verbs for the tenth year in a row. I then made the fatal mistake of my academic career: I unconsciously chewed the gum that had been carefully stored behind my molars, saved for later. My English teacher, who cared more about the gum rule than about the students, stormed across the room. Gripping my hair with her chalk-covered fingers, she threw me out of class in front of everyone. Years of rejection and disrespect overwhelmed me. Frustration won out over reason as I grabbed her arm and pushed her to the floor, yelling, "Don't ever touch me again!" I walked out of the school system forever, with the stone-silent class sitting in judgment behind me, or so I thought. Now, from my hot tub vantage point on a crystal clear night, I wondered what that high school dropout would have thought if someone had told him then that he would grow up to be a teacher, or funnier yet, a "teacher of teachers." I held my breath and went under the water to let the images of my past swirl and wash away.

Wiping the water from my eyes, I surfaced from my cleansing dive to the vision of a beautiful woman standing at the edge of the tub! For a brief moment, the surrounding water reminded me of a pond in the woods long ago, rather than a Jacuzzi on the deck of my home. I was so awestruck by the woman's finely sculpted features and the essence of her presence that I almost forgot to wonder who she was, why she was there, and how she had gotten onto my deck. Maybe I had stayed underwater too long! Was I seeing things? I was sure that her absolute beauty was the only thing that kept me from reacting normally to the presence of a stranger in my home. The woman smiled, melting my heart, assuring me of her reality and her gentleness. All I wanted to do was look at her. I was afraid to speak for fear she would vanish, but in my nakedness I thought it might be wise to ask a few basic questions. Before I could ask, I heard her words in my head, though her mouth never moved, no sound ever came out. The internal whisper urged, *"Don't think, just feel."*

As she slipped into the water directly across from me, the water line rose with the addition of a second person. Still, I couldn't help wondering if I was imagining her. Without words we looked into each other's eyes. Her presence was compelling; I felt suddenly and completely *different,* quite apart from the obvious strangeness of her being there at all. Her gaze held me mesmerized as a wave of unconditional love washed over me. As if time had stopped, I never wanted this moment to end. I saw my own life flash before me as I sat entranced, facing love. As she looked into my soul, I knew that she knew *everything* about me, had seen everything I had ever done and had heard everything I had ever said. Never before had I felt so accepted, so known. My eyes began to water as I wished that I deserved the love I was receiving, which she continued to pour into me, despite our shared vision of my mistakes and failures. I squirmed at this, knowing she knew everything and seemed to love me anyway.

I wondered if this was what happened when someone died. All the pieces were in place—except that in this case God was a woman, but I could handle that—the life flashing by, the visions, the judgments. I suddenly realized that the judgments weren't coming from her at all. All the judgments of my "failure" were emanating from me! I silently prayed that should I ever be blessed with being in the presence of this Goddess again—for what else could she be—that I would deserve the shower of love she bestowed upon me.

Seemingly hours passed in what was likely only moments. I finally asked aloud, shattering the silence, "Who are you and why are you here?"

Her voice sang sweetly in my head, *"I am here to honor your growth."*

"My growth?" I croaked in disbelief. "This has been one of the hardest days of my life. I have thrown away years of work and thousands of dollars. I have been in a complete state of confusion over what is true and what isn't. I don't see much honor or growth in that. What do you mean?"

Her voice was love itself with a trace of amusement as she replied, *"Those are just the outer effects. Look again from the inside and tell me what you have discovered. Close your eyes and look within."*

Reluctant to close my eyes, wanting neither to lose sight of her nor risk her disappearing, I forced myself to follow her directions. As I did, I replayed the events of the day, this time as an observer rather than a participant, managing to separate myself somewhat from the conflict and emotions I had been feeling.

Watching, I reported, "I learned that most of what I have believed in, stood for and taught wasn't real. I have spent my life looking for happiness outside of me—in things, in books and in possessions. Today I discovered that none of these things bring happiness."

"And what did you do about it?"

"I threw away all that I saw as untrue, all that was not working, and gave away some of the outer trappings of my supposed happiness."

She encouraged me by asking—again by some marvelous kind of telepathy—how that made me feel. Surprised by a suddenly peaceful feeling, I answered, "I feel relieved, like I no longer have to hold onto what isn't real or useful. I feel as if my hands are now free to create something new, to embrace what is ahead."

Her thoughts merged into mine and directed me to summarize the gift of my day into one or two simple words. In my heart I felt her smile as I uttered the word, *"Surrender."*

Goose bumps crawled up my skin as they so often do when truth is spoken. Along with them came a resurgence of the waves of unconditional love that I had felt while looking into this mysterious woman's eyes. Longing to gaze into them again, I opened my eyes slowly, not wanting to break any "rules." Surprisingly, no woman was to be seen: no Goddess, no eyes, no smile. Questioning the reality of what had just apparently happened, I looked around, hoping she had simply gotten out of the tub and was still nearby. Out of the corner of my eye, on the floor where the wondrous woman had originally stood, something golden flashed in the moonlight. Moving through the water, I reached out and picked up a circle of gold the size of a bracelet, wondering whether it belonged to the mysterious woman or if it were some remnant of a past hot tub date that I had never noticed before. Examining the ring more closely, my eyes rested on the word *Surrender* engraved inside. A now-familiar wave of pure love washed over me. I held the moment as long as I could, then popped the bubble with more mental questions. While my mind was busy asking, my heart was full of knowing. While I could not see her, I was sure that she was still there.

She watched as Matt slept more soundly than he had in weeks. As she reviewed the evening's encounter, she was pleased that it had gone so well. She was happy for his willingness to see his learning.

The golden ring she had left him rested on the nightstand. She knew he did not yet understand its significance, but was confident that he would keep it safe until he had attained the others. Of course, he thought it was only a bracelet. Little did he know the importance and honor of the earning. All in good time, all in good time. She smiled again in her patient way.

Matt's act of surrender was just the beginning. Much like the moment of free fall before a parachute opens, leaving the past behind before the future has unfolded is both exhilarating and frightening. Just the decision to move forward is a step of trust, faith in the unknown processes of life—surrender. She knew Matt would never be the same. Growth had occurred and more changes were imminent.

She wished him to understand that giving away his possessions was not as important as his realization that the things were not necessary. They were not him. Perhaps he had gone a little overboard by throwing and giving everything away, but that was just his way. It was typical of the zest with which he was ready to let go of that which was not working, to surrender, and in so doing, to embrace what was meant to be.

As Matt rolled over, she was aware that her thoughts might be interfering with his restful sleep. She offered a prayer of thanks and asked that protection surround him always.

2

Aloha Spirit

When I woke the next morning, I scanned the room skeptically. My eyes came to rest on the golden circlet next to the bed. My mind sprang into a lineup of prudent questions: *What had happened last night? Who was that woman?* The inquisition paused only long enough for me to wonder whether I would ever see her again, then continued. *What did all this mean? What should I do now?* The confusion from the day before began to return as my stomach churned with uncertainty. The question, *What should I do now?* gnawed at me. I breathed in deeply to calm my nerves.

With each new breath, visions began to dance in my mind of tropical islands, placid bays with calming turquoise water, sandy beaches and the caress of an ocean breeze. Within minutes I booked a flight to Kauai, rationalizing my escape with the hope that a change of scenery would help me clear my mind and come up with a new plan.

Soon I sat on a Hawaii-bound plane, listening to bits and pieces of conversations going on around me in an attempt to avoid the ones going on inside me. The woman to my right gripped the armrest in terror as we took off. While I was not afraid of flying, her outward expression of fear seemed to mirror my inner turmoil. I looked away.

The man in the seat ahead of me was talking with his two-year-old. "See how small everything looks from up here?!" It struck me as odd to look down on all the people, cars, and houses and imagine the drama going on in each. I silently wished I could always see things from this perspective—observing without being involved.

I tried to sleep but woke to find my mouth wide open and my neck kinked on one side. Giving up, I watched the movie, *Being There* with Peter Sellers, wondering why they were showing a movie that was nearly twenty years old. Everyone in the movie kept treating the main character as if he were a god, when in actuality he was just a simple gardener. He never said anything of importance or great significance, but those around him took his every word and turned it into some vital message about the meaning of life. I couldn't help but think about how people process information through the filters of their own beliefs. We make people what we want them to be. We hear what we want to hear. The question, *Just what is real?* passed through my head. *Is anything real or is everything just our own story projected onto a screen we call "reality"?* I wondered about what people heard when I spoke. If people could take simple, meaningless information and turn it into economic and political statements as shown in the movie, what did they do with the things I had taught? I thought for a moment that it didn't even matter what I said; people would hear what they wanted to anyway. I wasn't sure whether I felt relieved or discouraged.

I was eager to arrive in Hawaii, yet at the same time felt apprehensive about the decisions I needed to make. What appeared small on the horizon loomed larger as we approached, and the specks quickly grew into trees, hotels and beaches. My anxiety grew with them as the plane landed.

The humid warmth wrapped itself around me as soon as I stepped off the plane. I silently wished that one of the beautiful island girls handing out flower leis to the tour groups would hand one to me, too, as the scent of Plumeria filled the soft air. I thought for a moment of the woman in my hot tub and how beautiful the flowers would look on her. My heart ached slightly, as an unfamiliar yearning burned at my soul. I swallowed an antacid, pretending the pain was physical, as I headed for the baggage claim.

Kauai looked much as I remembered it. The small airport made me feel as if I had flown backward in time, and I almost wished I had, as if to erase all my past mistakes. Hoping it would allow me to take in the expansive scenery without barriers, I rented a convertible and drove through Kapa'a out to the north shore. I barely noticed the tropical landscape as my past continued to replay itself in my mind. I might as well have been looking into the rearview mirror the whole time, since all I saw was what was behind me.

Finally, the scenic lookout at Princeville captured even my bemused attention. Few other places in the world could claim to be so beautiful. The view extended from the mountains full of waterfalls that feed the Hanalei River, past the small village of Hanalei to the ocean. I counted at least twenty waterfalls and watched long enough to see cloud shadows change the very shapes of the mountains as they passed overhead and transformed outcroppings into valleys, valleys into ridges. Rainbows materialized and disappeared, shredded into colored mist by the winds that whipped the ocean water. The beauty born of the interaction of so many elements transfixed me.

I looked down on Hanalei Bay, where the color of the water varied from brilliant turquoise to deep navy blue. Ripples from the trade winds blew across the surface, reminding me that the scene was real, rather than a perfectly painted backdrop for a movie. As I gazed, I deeply felt the magic of this place and found myself humming "Puff the Magic Dragon," as I searched the mountain range behind the bay for the shape of this giant. Making out his head at the end of the road near Bali Hai, I wondered why the song proclaimed that the dragon "lived by the sea in a land called Hanalee," instead of "lived by the bay in a land called Hanalei." I took it as a good sign that my thoughts had turned to such trivia.

Carefully dodging frogs on the road, I made my way to the bed-and-breakfast where I planned to stay. I crossed the old bridge over the river, along the only route in and out of Hanalei. My eyes followed the river up toward its source near Waialeale, the rainiest place in the world. Clouds gathered there, concealing the mountain peaks. In the valley before me, two horses, tied in the grass, grazed between the river and the road. A couple of white cattle egrets, with long legs and long necks, stood atop the horses while others walked in their hoof-trails searching for upturned bugs. Now and then, one would fly to the other horse to see if the bugs were better over there. They seemed in no hurry as they watched the world go by.

Hanalei was a peaceful little town with not much more than a wooden-stepped general store, a museum with a small cafe that had great local-style plate lunches, a post office, an old school and a church built in the 1800s, a prominent symbol of missionary influence. The irony struck me that few such spiritual places existed on the planet. The beauty here, as in Sedona, just oozed with God's presence, and I wondered why the missionaries couldn't see it, thinking they had to bring the presence with them. They must not have realized that the local folks already knew all about it.

Taro fields stretched from the river to the foot of the mountains. Their elephant-ear leaves looked like millions of green hearts spread across the land. The Hanalei River was the perfect place for the outrigger canoe team to practice. The rhythm of their paddles was the only thing here keeping time. The river flowed out to the bay, unmatched for its serenity. The lineup of ironwood trees, black lava rocks, red dirt, white sand and turquoise blue water was sliced through by a thin line of horizon, capped by the powder blue of the sky and white puffy clouds.

Sitting outside on the lanai of my room, overlooking the water, I planned my time as I watched the sun set in brilliant hues of orange and pink, touched with gold and that special pearly effect that seems to happen only in the tropics. I thought about why I was here and was determined to work out every detail before leaving the islands. I listed the things I wanted to do: beach time for a day or two, backpacking trip to Kalalau Valley for a couple of days, then back for some serious contemplation and more planning. Every time I thought about the future, a boa constrictor of anxiety gripped me somewhere around the thorax, making breathing a suddenly conscious effort. I would wrestle it off and win for the moment, knowing that the snake-like fear was off regaining its strength and would be back. I felt as if it had laid eggs in my stomach, and that any sense of victory at having won the battle would be short-lived. I sighed heavily and yawned as I added sleep to my list of goals.

I slept that night surrounded by a mosquito net that reminded me of romance. The white gauzy drapings held a feeling, as if I had been here before—with someone—but who? Searching my memory for a clue, I could find no reminders and I drifted off to sleep. Dreams wove themselves around me, as indistinct as the netting. I knew I was dreaming, but the images weren't clear, except for a place with white gauze tenting that I didn't recognize. A sense of love and safety hung around me like a mist. The mysterious woman seemed to dance through my dreams, though tangible evidence escaped me. I slept soundly, enjoying a gentle yet ambiguous sense of union.

A rooster's crowing jolted me awake with the awareness that I was no longer at home. As I prepared for the beach, the essence of the dream haunted me. It felt like an ancient memory, but I couldn't make it clearer. Warmth and familiarity, as if I weren't alone, invaded me. While she had eluded me in my sleep, I now looked about hopefully to see if the mystery woman was near. Instead, I found myself wrapped in wishful thinking. Taking a deep breath, allowing the mood from my dreams to clear, I questioned "reality" once again.

Carefully baking both sides of my body equally, I soaked up the tropical sunshine, not being able to remember the last time I had allowed myself to rest like this. It had been years since I had lain on a beach without a book, phone, wife and kids. The thought of the boys stung me. I had done such a good job of ignoring my pain over their absence, focusing instead on my career. I could see them in my mind's eye, catching crabs and riding waves in the gentle surf. They would love it here. Sadness again overtook me.

I looked out on the boats that were gathered in the bay and marveled at the freedom their captains must feel. For a fleeting moment I considered renouncing the rest of my belongings and taking up a life on the sea, but just then a gusty trade wind struck the side of the boats, bouncing them like Ping-Pong balls in the waves. I settled back into the thought that I could admire them without following their lead.

I took out pen and paper and tried to design a life plan. Using every lesson I had ever taught on goal setting, I busily started by mind-mapping. The two areas of my life that needed my attention most, or so I thought, were career and family. I jotted these down, then added health, for balance. Focusing first on my career, I began to write more of a journal entry than a list or a mind map: *If much of what I have been teaching isn't working, and if I am going to continue to teach, I either need to teach something different or only teach the "How-to" sales and financial tips that I know so well. What I can't teach is about personal growth and happiness—at least not until I fully know how they work.*

Rereading my words, I couldn't get too excited about spending my life only teaching people how to make money—especially since they would believe that money would make them happy, and I now knew that wouldn't be so. So I turned my thoughts to teaching something new.

My writing continued: *If I want different results, then I need to do something different.*

Pause, nothing, stare. . . .

Obviously, in order to do something different, I need to learn something else.

This thought made my stomach churn even more. Why did I feel so agitated? I had always been a seeker of knowledge and open to learning. Why was I so bothered about having to learn something new?

The answers flowed out onto the page before me: *I have read over four thousand books in the search for truth and reality. While many of these books held great ideas, as anyone could see by the underlined passages and dog-eared corners, either the secret on how to apply them is not in the books, or they do not provide the ultimate answers.*

I thought about how many times I had underlined a passage with the full intent of practicing the teaching, only to find the book years later, without having applied it at all. Then I wrote the real source of my discomfort:

If the answer is not in books, where am I going to find it?

This sure seemed complicated. There had to be a simpler way to figure all this out. I felt as if I was trying to put together a jigsaw puzzle without the benefit of the picture on the box. I barely noticed the dolphins leaping from the water in front of me or the butterfly that landed on my towel. I shook the sand off of my things and headed back to my room with deeply furrowed brows.

Another day passed by with memories from my past and fears about my future consuming all my thoughts. The Na Pali coast was calling to me, so I prepared for my backpacking trip. The journey I was about to take was an eleven-mile hike along the cliffs of the northwest shore. This area was unreachable by car, so in order to see it one had to take a helicopter, a boat, or, as I was about to do, walk. Hiking it alone might not have been the wisest choice, but lacking better alternatives, I decided to do it anyway. After all, I had dug my old backpack out of the garage and bought brand-new hiking boots for the occasion.

I asked the man running the bed-and-breakfast for information about the hike. He explained, "Just follow the only road to the end, down near Ke'e Beach. The trail starts right there, you can't miss it. Make sure you have plenty of water with you. It's eleven miles into Kalalau, and they can be hot ones."

I asked, "What is Kalalau like? Is it worth the effort?" I had heard that Kalalau was like the Garden of Eden, but wanted some confirmation from the local knowledge.

He smiled and answered, "It depends on what you like. Waterfalls, streams, fruit trees, a beautiful beach and naked people enjoying it are all you'll find there. If you're looking for nightclubs, it isn't the place for you."

We both laughed as I made my way out the door. If all of this were true, it certainly had the potential of taking my mind off my concerns and giving me a mental rest, which I dearly needed. I envisioned the beach and valley joyfully as I set foot on the rocky trail.

The trail went steadily up for the first quarter mile. Breathing heavily as I reached the first lookout point, I was glad that this trail was so close to sea level, as more elevation might have done me in. I stopped there to look toward my destination. My eyes followed what looked like a goat trail along the cliffs to Kalalau Valley. The path wove in and out of valleys and ravines, punctuated by lookout points. The sun beat down on parts of the trail with an intensity that made me apprehensive. I focused my sights on the valley and beach eleven miles in the distance, and with determination began again. Stepping over roots, rocks and streams, I made my way toward my goal, thankful that this part of the trail was mostly shaded. I reached another lookout point and again set my sights on the valley, which now appeared only slightly closer than the last time I had looked.

The first resting place was a beach two miles in along the trail. I took off my pack and boots and put my feet in the stream. My heels were a little red, but I didn't think much about it. Snacking on dried fruit, I envisioned the beauty of the valley where I was going. Imagined feelings of the peace and joy I would experience once I arrived motivated me to continue. With all the pieces back in place, boots and backpack on, I continued on my way after only twenty minutes. I looked up to find the trail and saw that the pleasant path in the shade would fast become a series of switch backs in full sunlight. Glad that I had started relatively early, I again envisioned my goal and continued on.

This section of the trail was back and forth, up and hot. The sun beat down harshly, treating me no differently than the rest of the landscape, and I wondered if I had been fooling myself. At one point, I looked straight down to see the surf crashing on the rocks below, which caused me to gasp for just a moment, as my heart and stomach suddenly tangled in a battle to occupy the same space. A gust of wind pushed against my pack, blowing me slightly off balance. Simultaneously, adrenaline rushed through my veins and paralyzed me as I held on for dear life to the hot, rocky slope.

Just then, two naked hikers waltzed around the next bend. My mind turned from my fear to a new dilemma. How were we going to pass each other? The trail was only wide enough for one with a backpack, with a steep upward slope leading to a knife-edged ridge on one side and a steep downward slope leading to crashing surf on the other. At best we would have to turn sideways and carefully pass, which fully clothed would have been challenging enough. I looked back to see if there was a wider space anywhere in sight behind me, but there wasn't, and no wider place appeared beyond them, either.

As the couple neared, I tried to look less frightened and more like a happy hiker. The effort of trying to look calm while at the same time appearing to ignore their nakedness as we met on this treacherously narrow trail suddenly struck me as incredibly funny. I feared they would think I was laughing at them, so in addition to my other efforts, I tried to quell the belly laughs that were building up inside me.

Imagining what I must have looked like to them, I nodded a hello, afraid to speak lest the laughter escape.

We stood facing each other for a moment, assessing the passing problem. Not getting much help from me as I battled with conflicting emotions, they elected to turn sideways with their backpacks to the ocean and sidestep past me. I followed their lead by turning sideways as well, flattening my back to the wall. I stood still as they edged their way by, thinking that I had never been so close to a naked man before. The morbid thought crossed my mind that with one push, his naked girlfriend could be mine. I must have been watching too much TV! Having a thought so far out of character broke the dam that held the laughter back. Here I was, face to face on the edge of a cliff, brushing past two naked people, risking my life and theirs, thinking absurd thoughts and laughing hysterically while clinging to the cliff at the same time. They looked at me, startled. After they passed, I held still against the slope until the laughter calmed. I looked in the direction of the hikers; all I could see were their butts walking away under their packs, which caused me to start laughing all over again. I watched as they looked over their shoulders a little nervously and then picked up their pace to move away from me. Welcoming the comic relief in my day, I let go of my death grip on the wall and resumed my quest.

I safely reached the next lookout point and again allowed my eyes to journey the distance ahead of me to gauge my progress. I wished then that I had managed to ask the hikers how much farther it was. Smiling at the thought of them, I forgave myself for not asking. My attention now focused on the uncomfortable rubbing sensation on both heels, and I silently cursed myself for not breaking in the boots before taking on a trail like this one. I marched on in anticipation.

I stopped for a break at Hanakoa Valley, the nine-mile point. A small cabin stands here for hikers to camp in, and I wondered whether to stay the night and carry on the next day or just continue on in the remaining daylight. The cabin was set back in a narrow valley. The shadows of large mango trees combined with the stream made it dark and damp. My eyes followed the small creek down to the ocean. Water-tumbled boulders the size of elephants filled the opening of the valley, where a beach normally would be. I tried to imagine the force required to smooth the edges of rocks that size. The ocean looked so calm and gentle from here; it was hard to imagine that it could muster the energy required to make such changes. I thought of my own rough edges and wondered what would be required for smoothing my human imperfections. What ocean did I need to wash my jagged spots away? I sensed that there was a message to be gained from the calm strength of the sea and its ability to transform, but for now the full meaning eluded me.

I stepped inside the cabin and allowed my eyes to adjust to the darkness. It was small and empty. The wooden walls were covered from floor to ceiling with messages from campers who had passed by. As I ate a cookie, I found myself reading everything from *Kanani waz hea* to *Live long and prosper—Spock.* For some reason, I couldn't pull myself away and wondered if this was more of my effort to seek answers.

The door opened and a blinding light streamed in, lighting up the words *BE HERE NOW* on the cabin wall.

I turned to see a woman walk in. The backlighting concealed her face, as my heart skipped, hoping it was the mystery woman. As my eyes adjusted to the light, I tried to hide my disappointment when I didn't recognize the woman standing before me. I was thankful to see that she was fully clothed and, as I slapped at a mosquito, thankful I was as well.

She seemed a bit surprised to see me, but calmed immediately as our eyes met. She was about thirty-five, with an earthy, grounded feel about her; she had the appearance of kindness. She took off her pack and introduced herself.

"Hi, I'm Nan. How are you?"

"Hi, I'm Matt. Just enjoying the reading material," I said, pointing to the walls.

She smiled and joined my wall-gazing as she asked, "Are you coming or going?"

I explained that I was hiking in and hadn't decided yet whether to continue on or stay the night here. I shared my concerns about the blisters on my feet. She explained that she was on her way out but had gotten a late start, so she was staying in the cabin and continuing on in the morning. She kindly offered me some moleskin for my heels and began to dig in her pack to get it.

I asked, "How much farther is it?"

"Only a couple more miles, but they aren't easy ones. It will probably take you another hour and a half to get to the beach. Then you'll still need to find a spot to camp. By then it will be getting late."

Enjoying the company of another person for the first time in what seemed to be weeks, I asked if she minded sharing the cabin. She looked at me penetratingly, assessing me through and through. The moment of silence made me shift uncomfortably, until her smile and nod eased the tension. She said she would be honored.

The evening was quickly approaching, so we collected wood and set up camp. The mosquitoes were gathering by the thousands, detracting considerably from the comfort of the place. We decided to build a fire, even though the Hawaiian air was plenty warm, and we settled beside it and began to talk.

"What do you do?" I inquired.

"I'm an art teacher and a counselor, of sorts," she replied. "I make stained glass windows and teach children how to develop their creativity. I live in Santa Barbara."

I asked, "What does 'counselor of sorts' mean?"

"People come to me for guidance a lot. I guess there is something about me that people trust," she said with a smile.

I could see why people trusted her. She had an easy, honest way about her. She seemed to have the same calm strength as the ocean—I could sense that she was very powerful when focused. She went on to tell me, "Actually, I'm psychic, although I think we all are. I just seem to know how to access my intuition better than most. People come to me when they have questions about their lives, and if I can, I help them gain clarity."

Just as I was thinking I might take advantage of the opportunity to find some answers to my own questions, she asked me, "So, what's your story?"

I wondered briefly, if she was so psychic, how come she didn't know, but then answered myself by figuring that psychics probably don't do readings constantly; besides, that would take the fun out of meeting people.

After explaining my recent situation, I asked her advice. "I'm a motivational speaker. Or rather, I was. I'm not sure anymore."

I paused in thought and added, "I woke up a few days ago counting my blessings, and the next thing I knew, I was feeling so unhappy. I had achieved the success I had been seeking, but had lost my family in the process." I went on to tell her about giving away my things and destroying my manuscript and research.

"My priorities suddenly seem to be mixed up. Now I am wondering what I should be doing and what is really true. I came here hoping to clear my head and find some answers."

I left out the part about the beautiful woman, not wanting to risk sounding too crazy. After all, she had agreed to share the cabin with me, and I wanted her to know I was harmless.

"What are the exact questions you would like to find the answers to?" she asked.

"What should I be doing with my life? What is truth? What is real?" I paused, then added, "Also, I want to know whether I should continue teaching, and if so, what?"

She looked at me with a depth that I had seldom felt, particularly on such short acquaintance, and then closed her eyes. I watched as her face relaxed. When she opened her eyes, she smiled, as if she had seen something beautiful. I waited for her to say something, but she just kept looking at me and smiling.

Finally, I asked, "Well?"

She took her time to answer, her face looking more thoughtful. "I was told that I can't tell you—that you must figure it out for yourself. Until then, you aren't ready to know. What I can tell you is that you will touch millions of people in a very deep way before you are through here." She sat in contemplation, then added, "From what I have seen, my personal opinion is that you should keep teaching."

"But what?" I asked.

"That is the part you have to discover. All I can add is that if you treat the discovery a little more like a treasure hunt and a little less like the burden of your existence, you'll have a lot more fun. Ultimately, you can't avoid what you are here to do, so you may as well just relax and do it." Her eyes caught mine once again as she smiled a knowing smile.

We talked well into the night before drifting off to sleep. Between the mosquitoes, the humidity, the hard wooden floor and the thoughts running through my head, the night seemed to last forever. Nan and I had become great friends during the course of the evening. Lying there, unable to sleep, I wondered what the chances were of two people coming together at the exact same remote place on the planet, at the exact same time, and sharing an experience that was meaningful to both. At least, meaningful for one, and hopefully for both, I amended. I caught a few more minutes of sleep before turning over again in search of comfort.

As the sun made its way over the mountains behind us, we made tea, ate breakfast, and exchanged itineraries and phone numbers. I carefully put the information in a zippered pocket as I bid Nan good-bye. As she started to walk away, she stopped and turned.

She smiled and said, "You might try not thinking so much, but rather *feeling* more. All the answers are in you already; you just need to get out of the way so they can come out. This is not a small life for you. Remember to enjoy the journey! Aloha."

With that, she was off. *Think less, feel more?* I began to sense a theme emerging, as those were the same words the goddess had said. As I thought of *her*, it occurred to me that I didn't even know her name. I made a mental note to ask, if I ever saw her again.

Preparing to continue my hike to Kalalau, I reflected on Nan's words: *"I can't tell you, you have to figure it out for yourself. . . . You'll touch millions. . . . You can't avoid what you are here to do. . . . Get out of your own way. . . . Enjoy the journey."*

I thought about adding these words of wisdom to the wall of the cabin and wondered if that was how all the others got there. Did they all emerge from wonderful encounters with other passersby? Since Nan had already left with the only pen between us, I etched them in my mind instead and continued on my way.

The remainder of the trail was hot, dusty and relatively uneventful. My mind was full, my feet were sore and the beach ahead grew larger with every step. I chuckled slightly as I realized that I was thinking about how I shouldn't be thinking so much—and then switched to *thinking* about how I *felt.* It was easier said than done. The concentration this required felt almost like meditation, which was a little hard to do while walking on a narrow trail with thirty pounds on my back. I decided to try again when I reached my destination.

Finally, the beach stretched out before me. I took off my boots and walked the remaining quarter-mile barefoot. The sand was hot, but it felt good compared to the burning of my heels when my boots were on. I paused for a moment to breathe in the fresh, salty air and take in the scene unfolding before me. At last I had reached my destination! The valley opening up before me displayed a series of pinnacles and ridges that had been carved by the artistry of time. Misty clouds hung around the top of the valley, providing a mystical, enchanted appearance. My senses were treated to cascading waterfalls, soaring Tropic Birds with long white tails, the smell of sun-baked fruit, and the sound of lapping waves on an empty, pure white beach, framed in turquoise tranquillity. This had to be heaven. Now I could *feel*! Peaceful, honored, humbled and joyous were the sensations running through me in a direct current, no intellectualizing needed.

I worked my way to the waterfall that provided a shower right on the beach. Although I felt as if no one else were here, a few tents and other signs of occupation began to emerge as my eyes scoured my surroundings. I absorbed every detail like a sponge, so that I could return here in my mind whenever I wanted. I noticed that the campers seemed to be divided. The cave dwellers were down on the beach, while the tree dwellers favored being just inside the vegetation line. I was sure there were also valley dwellers, but they were well concealed. Then the question popped into my head, *"Which one am I?"*

I had never really had the opportunity to explore this part of my identity before, so I of course set about the decision rationally. I considered location in terms of convenience, such as accessibility to the waterfall. I considered the mosquito situation of the night before and the softness of the ground. I considered incoming waves and morning light. Each place had its pros and cons, making it very difficult to decide.

The words, *Don't think, just feel!* meandered through my head.

Leaving my pack leaning against the rocks, I walked to the different camping spots to see how I felt about them. I sat in a few before settling on a clearing under a tree, right on the edge of the beach, which felt perfect. Proud of myself, I set up camp. The blisters on my heels had grown to the size of quarters. I reluctantly imagined hiking out the next day, not ever wanting to put on my boots again.

It was still early, not yet noon. After setting up my tent, I went exploring. Glad that so few people were here, I felt like I was on a bit of a vision quest that required a certain degree of solitude. After picking some mango and papaya for my lunch, I wandered back down toward the waterfall on the beach. Rock walls and terraces were reminders of the ancient Hawaiians who once lived here. I sat on a boulder and envisioned what life would have been like then. Suspecting that it was more difficult than one might think, I offered thanks for the opportunity to be here now.

I took advantage of the quiet moment to see how I was feeling. Closing my eyes, I looked inside. I felt happy! It seemed as if it had been ages since I had felt truly happy. I thought how ironic it was that I was so happy with only the things that I was able to carry with me, which then reminded me of giving my things away and the despair I had been feeling just days earlier. This triggered my fears and confusion over what I was going to do next, and suddenly I wasn't happy anymore. How had I managed to go from happy to miserable in such a short time?

I spent the rest of the afternoon alternating between heating up in the sun and cooling off in the waterfall, consumed with thoughts about what I was going to do with my life. Nan had said I should continue teaching, and somehow that felt right, but what should I teach?

Late in the afternoon, an inflatable raft motored up to shore and off-loaded two people and some camping gear. As I watched, I considered the blisters on my feet again. Motivated by a sincere desire not to put on my boots ever again, I got up from my towel and inquired about boating out the next day. The captain explained that he came every day, and for forty dollars I could ride out on the raft. Glad to find an alternative to hiking out, I made a reservation. I returned to my resting place near the rock walls, relieved.

I didn't move from that spot until well after dark. Just before sunset, a handful of campers gathered on the beach to see the green flash that sometimes happens at the moment the sun sinks beyond the horizon. They explained that it only happens on perfectly clear evenings when the sun sets over water, and even then it is not guaranteed. Meeting all the criteria, this evening seemed perfect, and a flash was a real possibility. We waited in a sort of laid-back anticipation as the sun neared the horizon.

Seabirds were returning to the shore for the evening, silhouetted by the setting sun. My eyes followed them toward land and were treated to the sight of the valley lit up in all its majesty. The golden hour of sunset spotlighted God's finest work. Shadows danced off the pinnacles, making one look like an ancient pyramid and another like a person trapped in stone; others were like pillars of strength supporting the soft and gentle beauty that lived upon them. A wave of peace washed over me as I wondered if I had ever seen a more beautiful sight. I almost missed the setting sun while I soaked up the changing shadows of the land and turned just in time to catch "the flash." Justly named, it was a quick flash of green light, so quick that I wondered whether I had just stared at the sun too long, but magical nonetheless. Satisfied, the happy campers returned to their evening preparations.

I simply sat without moving, as if in meditation, drinking in the beauty that surrounded me. I let the sand run through my fingers and felt thankful for each grain. I watched the phosphorescence sparkling in the placid slap of the waves. As the night grew darker, I laid back and experienced the stars emerging. First one, then another, then millions. I felt small. Millions of grains of sand below me, millions of stars in the sky above me, millions of people sandwiched in between. *Who am I? What is my place in all of this?* These questions lapped at my mind as I fell asleep, serenaded by the ocean's lullaby.

I woke the next morning in my tent, with only a vague memory of having moved there in the night. After packing up my belongings, I headed for the waterfall. Standing there with the endless stream of water pouring down on me, I felt refreshed and better able to tackle my future. As thoughts emerged, I allowed them to wash away. As fears bubbled up, the water diluted them and carried them out to sea. I enjoyed the thought of something big out there, gobbling up each fear and swallowing them whole.

I held my breath and went underwater, hopeful that when I surfaced the goddess-woman would be in front of me, just as she had appeared by my hot tub. All I saw when I emerged were a couple of campers waiting their turn for the waterfall. I got out and dried off, wondering again who *she* was and if I would ever see her again. I have to admit that by this time I was also wondering whether I ever actually had. If it weren't for that golden ring, I would long since have dismissed her as a delusion brought on by emotional stress.

The surf was up as the boat neared the beach. The captain dropped off his passengers in the water and had them swim their gear in, as the waves required that he anchor slightly offshore. He signaled me to swim out, as his passengers handed me a Boogie board and plastic trash bags to waterproof my things.

I stepped into the water, then stopped at the edge, paralyzed. Fear gripped every ounce of me. The pounding of my heart transported me to another place and time. Instead of there in Kalalau Valley as an adult, I stood on a beach near Monterey, California, as an eleven-year-old with my friend John. We had spent the night on the beach and woken up as explorers. The beach was covered with driftwood for as far as we could see, unimaginable treasures to the eleven-year-old eye. After literally leaving no stone unturned, John suggested that we make a raft. Following my instantaneous agreement, we carefully tied together pieces of driftwood and topped it all with a slab of plywood. We nailed the deck in place and stood back to admire our work. A perfect fishing raft! We grabbed our poles, T-shirts, lunch sacks, and bait and headed out into the bay.

The water was clear and calm as we rowed off shore with our homemade oars. The clarity enabled us to see every fish passing below as we made our way to deeper waters. We had built a magic carpet, and magical it was turning out to be! It transported us to a great fishing spot, and we were reeling them in one after the other. All was going well until we were about a mile or two offshore. Then we noticed the raft floating a little lower in the water than it had been, but with the excitement of fishing, neither of us became too concerned. Within a matter of minutes, though, we found ourselves standing ankle-deep in water. Before we could even think about what to do, the entire raft sank beneath us! At first we treaded water, upset because we'd lost our fish and fishing gear; then we looked toward shore. Realizing how far out we were, we were overcome by the conviction that we were about to drown. We started swimming madly for the beach, hearts pounding. Encouraging each other, we took turns yelling out, "I can't make it!" to which the other would yell back, "Yes, you can! Keep swimming!" We traded back and forth, alternating between confidence and mortal fear.

As we swam, we looked up frequently to gauge the distance. Then we saw them—first one fin, then another and another! Knowing we were in Great White waters, adrenaline pumped through our bodies. We paused for only a moment's watching; then, with more motivation than ever, we swam as fast as we possibly could, fear rushing through our veins. No longer able to distinguish between reality and imagination, we regularly saw dark shapes passing below us. All we knew was that the circling fins were getting closer and closer. We each kept a nervous eye on the sharks, each other and the shore. Undoubtedly our fear kept us alive, as the speed with which we were swimming stopped us from noticing how blue our skin had turned from the cold. Certain that we were either going to drown or be eaten, we splashed, screamed, swam and encouraged each other to shore. Our lower halves ran and our top halves swam as soon as we touched bottom. I wasn't sure at first if I felt sand or shark beneath my feet. Crawling up the beach in exhaustion, we were still too scared to realize we were safe. We flopped onto the warm sand to thaw our bodies out and watched the fins swim back and forth, searching for us just outside the breakers.

Now as I stood on the beach of Kalalau Valley, preparing to swim toward the rubber raft in front of me, it all came back, paralyzing me in my tracks, almost as if I could still see the ominous fins searching me out. The boatman waved to me again, signaling me to cross over. I forced myself to put my gear on the Boogie board and take a few steps into the water. With a deep breath, I rationalized that if I had made it a couple of miles years ago as a boy, with sharks circling me, certainly I could survive swimming forty feet in crystal clear water as an adult. The thought didn't help much, though; adrenaline flowed through me, thicker than blood.

I half dog-paddled, half breast-stroked toward the boat, pushing the board carrying my belongings while scanning the water for signs of danger. The fins of the past were as clear as if they circled me now, and dark shapes seemed to swirl gracefully below, full of menace. Though swimming as quickly as possible, I felt convinced that at any moment I would be consumed. The delay getting into the water, compared with the speed with which I swam the distance to the boat, must have been a strange sight. The boat captain eyed me with an odd look as he helped me on board, as I was breathing heavily and fear hung in my eyes.

Gaining composure with a deep breath, I settled onto the rubber boat, thankful to be alive rather than grated by the jaws of a shark. Once completely safe, I realized that I had been consumed after all—not by the shark, but entirely by the fear I had created. It seemed to me that to be ruled by fears was just as bad as facing an actual object of fear itself, for I had been eaten by the shark again and again in my mind. The actuality of it happening or not was a mere technicality.

As we lifted anchor, my eyes made one last panoramic sweep of the valley and I felt a little sad to be leaving. Kalalau seemed even more beautiful from this distance. I silently said good-bye as we began bouncing over waves, splashing our way back to Hanalei.

As we moved along the shoreline, I was overwhelmed by the scenery that stretched out before me. How had I missed the thousand-foot waterfalls, rock archways, trees, lush plants and clouds mirroring the peaks and ridges as I had hiked in? I picked out the spot where I had clung to the cliffs when the naked hikers had passed me by, but this time I drank in the beauty of where I had been standing. I identified each lookout point where I had stopped, marveling at the magnificence surrounding them.

How had I missed the wonder of this coastline as I passed through it the first time? I reviewed my hike, searching for an answer to this question. As I "looked," I saw that my entire journey had been spent looking forward to where I was going and backward to see how far I had come. I never once saw where I was! I had missed it completely. In fact, most of my vacation had been that way. With a sinking feeling, I had to admit that I had spent most of my life that way, too.

My thoughts turned to the highlights of my trip—the time spent talking with Nan, the golden hour on the beach at sunset followed by the night under the stars. At those times, I wasn't looking forward or backward, but rather being where I was in that moment. I squeezed my eyes together to fight back the emotion of realizing that I had bypassed most of my life by missing so many present moments. The lit-up words on the cabin wall, *Be Here Now,* flashed on my closed eyelids, and I finally understood their meaning. I wondered if they had been written there just for me.

Determined to change the way I had been living, I focused my attention on the boat ride, taking in every detail. I watched as sea turtles appeared and disappeared after quickly taking a breath. I breathed in the salty air and tasted the water that splashed in my face. I moved to the bow of the boat for the bumpiest ride, wanting to take in as much sensation as possible, trying to make up for lost time.

As we arrived in Hanalei, I experienced the place anew, as if I had never been there before. Wondering what was different, as I had always appreciated the peaceful perfection of this place, the answer suddenly came—this was *feeling* instead of *thinking*!

I put down my pack on the beach and laid out a towel. Using my gear as a headrest, I laid down and felt the day. A bird glided gracefully in search of its afternoon meal as I fell asleep.

A light breeze blew over me, waking me up from my nap. I opened my eyes, and—*she* was there, the mysterious woman, smiling as she gazed at me with those incredibly clear eyes that seemed both to penetrate and welcome my soul! I was sure she could hear how loudly my heart was pounding as I smiled back. She took my breath away. All questioning of her reality melted instantly. It occurred to me that if God would simply show up in person from time to time, he would have no trouble in finding believers. If his intention was to send *her* as a representative, then he could count me among the most devoted.

I heard her speak, as if her words were my thoughts. She greeted me with, "*Aloha.*"

I listened as she continued. "*The Aloha Spirit is the union of the heart and mind within each individual. It is a heartfelt expression of love.*"

We sat in silence, just looking at each other and enjoying the moment. I thought of the many questions I should ask, about who she was, where she came from, how she had found me—and why, but I didn't want to ruin the feeling of just being with her. As it turned out, she had a few questions of her own.

"What have you discovered since you saw me last?" she inquired without words.

I replied out loud, hesitant to think, lest it dispel the feeling of being with her. I was still balancing thinking and feeling and hadn't mastered it yet. As I formulated my words, I drank in all her features. "I found that I have missed most of my life by either looking forward or backward. I have spent so much time thinking about the past and planning for the future that I haven't truly enjoyed where I was."

She congratulated me. *"Once again, I honor you for your growth. What are you doing with your newfound awareness?"*

I thought for a while, then answered, "I am paying more attention to each moment and appreciating them as they happen."

I felt her praise and added, "I'm also feeling more and thinking less. I sense this has a lot to do with fully experiencing the moment." Her smile felt almost as if it were my own.

She stood up and held out her hand; as she did so, I understood an invitation to cool off in the bay. I took her hand, feeling almost shy as it occurred to me that I still did not know her name. As we walked to the water's edge, I was about to ask, when I heard her voice say sweetly, *"You know my name; you know me well. You just don't remember. Ask yourself the questions you wish for me to answer, and all this will come back to you."*

Our eyes met and held as we slowly sank below the surface. The water felt cool and refreshing. Still holding hands, we surfaced and looked up toward the mountain range. Waterfalls were everywhere. I could hear her silently counting them as I glanced around me, watchful for lurking dark shapes, still not feeling completely comfortable in the water. She stopped and looked at me intensely, saying, *"Let's talk about fear. What have you discovered about that?"*

I explained my thoughts from earlier. "I know now that fear itself can be as terrifying as the thing you are afraid of. I scare myself unnecessarily, but I'm not sure what to do about it."

Then I added, "I imagine that if I could truly be in the moment, experiencing what is really happening now, then I wouldn't be afraid. The fear of the sharks was so real, though. They really did circle me, and in that moment I had a good reason to be afraid! Three good reasons!"

"When was that fear real?"

"When I was eleven, swimming to shore in California." Reliving it yet again, I instinctively looked around me in the water.

She squeezed my hand gently, bringing me back into the moment with her. *"Since the fear was real then, what is it now?"*

Clearly, the only answer I could give was, "Imagined."

She smiled and looked back to the mountains, continuing her waterfall count, leaving me a few moments to fully digest the lesson.

Then she resumed the conversation. *"When do you anticipate experiencing that which you feared, then?"*

"In the very immediate future!" I answered quickly. I smiled slightly, beginning to see the absurdity.

She stayed intent, asking, *"And when do you experience the fear?"*

I replied just as intently, "In the present moment." A light went on in my head as I spoke. "Fear is a feeling from the past that is projected into the future with the anticipation of it happening again, and then experienced in the moment! You can experience real fear in the moment, as I did when the sharks presented a real danger, but the fear I have been experiencing here is imagined—it is *not real.*" The statement sounded more like a question, as I explored these newfound beliefs.

She looked at me with a love that filled my whole being. *"If you were to summarize all that you have found, what would you say?"*

"All that is real is in the moment," I replied. Then, as the learning penetrated more deeply, I added, "True happiness is in the moment, as well." I stood silently as I allowed the awareness to fully sink in. The happiness I had spent my life seeking was *here, now.* I surprised myself as I looked at her and said, "The message is to live each moment."

She let go of my hand and placed one of hers on my shoulder, the other on the top of my head. I felt, in the absence of words, that she was blessing me. I breathed in the blessing and silently thanked her. In the humility of the moment, I lowered my eyes and bowed my head. My gaze was caught by something shiny at my feet. I looked up and caught her eye as she dropped her hands and looked into the water with me. Holding my breath, I dived under the surface to see what was reflecting the sun's light and came up with a golden ring in my hands.

I stood there in the water, alone. I felt as if she had become a part of all that surrounded me; she was nowhere, yet her beauty was everywhere. I felt fully alive as I read the inscription in the circle, *Live Each Moment.*

Carefully holding the cherished gift, both in my hand and in my heart, I swam reverently to shore.

Although he didn't know she was there, she sat with him as he meditated on the beach, cradling the second ring of the Master's Key in his hands. From their separate vantage points, they both enjoyed his new appreciation of the moment.

She was glad Matt was opening up to her, that he was feeling her in his life more. His heart was beginning to open, and the open heart was her domain.

She rejoiced in his discovery that the happiness for which he had searched his entire life could be found only in the present moment. He would never find it in the past; searching there would only bring remorse over what had been done or left undone, or yearning for what was no longer. He would never find it looking to the future, since looking there creates only desire, leaving the present moment unfulfilled. Here, now, is the only place wherein happiness can be experienced.

How much happier he would be when the present moment was emptied of the fear he'd brought forward from the past. When the fears from his past were no longer projected into the future, it, too, would look more promising.

She focused on him the energy of her conscious support, as his reflections led him to the knowledge that it is necessary to have goals and to plan for the future, but that one must always be careful not to miss the journey. Life does not "begin" when we reach our destination, it is in process all along the way. It is in process now.

She sat quietly nearby, not wanting to disturb him. Placing her hand on Matt's heart, she offered a prayer that he would soon be able to see just who he really was. She smiled, enjoying his unfolding and their entwining.

3

Gaining Perspective

Bidding Hawaii good-bye was never easy. Even those who lived there, surrounded daily by its beauty never seemed to take it for granted, perhaps because the scenery was constantly renewed by the shifting clouds and changes of light. I reluctantly packed my bags and went for a final walk on the beach before my flight. Being more fully present, I reveled in the sensation of the sand beneath my feet, the wind in my hair and the sun on my skin. After dipping my toes in the turquoise water, I took in a deep breath of soft, fresh tropical air and ambled slowly down the beach. I experienced a feeling on this island that I had felt nowhere else in my life; its essence was peace and connectedness.

I found myself wondering again, *What is going on? Who is this woman, and why is this happening to me?* Whenever she was with me, I accepted her presence and love as complete reality, but when she was gone, I became filled with a mixture of doubt and yearning. Slipping my hand into my pocket, I gripped the golden rings that verified her existence. Only the tangible nature of the rings and the value of the truth each one carried reassured me of my sanity. The concepts symbolized by the rings were becoming such a part of me that I could not imagine how I had lived without them, and the possibility—no, make that *certainty*—that more rings were to come was both terrifying and exhilarating. I knew that the puzzle wasn't complete yet.

I pulled the circlet from my pocket and reread its simple message, *Live Each Moment.* In *this* moment, I wished to be with *her, now.* My rational mind insisted that it was absurd to want to be with a woman who appeared and disappeared, especially one whose name I didn't even know! Rings or not, I couldn't be totally sure that she wasn't just some self-produced effect of my overly vivid imagination. Yet, the warmth I felt when I thought of her was genuine and the things she was showing me were powerful.

Taking a moment to sit in the sand, I reviewed the changes that had occurred so quickly in my life. Thinking about happiness, I wrote in the sand with a stick, *Happiness is what is happening now.* As I studied them, a wave washed up and gently erased some of the words, leaving only *Happiness . . . happening,* just long enough for me to see the similarity of the two words before the next wave washed them away, too.

Even my confusion must be happiness, I concluded, since confusion was the overriding experience of the moment. Rather than focusing on what I didn't know about this intriguing woman, I turned my attention to what I did know, to see if any clearer pictures would emerge. I listed in my mind everything I had observed or heard. She was beautiful and gentle. She seemed wise and loving. Until this moment, it had never occurred to me that she matched me in height, a rare event in the life of a six foot four man! Her long hair was flowing and thick, her smile magnificently bright. She claimed to be in my life to help me grow, and she brought me specific acknowledgment of my inner progress. She appeared to know everything about me, all my thoughts, experiences and feelings. Her intuition was very clear. Somehow, I sensed that she deeply appreciated beauty. In human terms, if that's what she was, I guessed that she was very creative and would enjoy artwork and painting, although she had never said so. I could imagine her holding a child or a kitten with a nurturing quality that would be precious to behold. I didn't know where my perception of these qualities came from, but the more that I listed, the more the sensation of appreciation grew.

Was I just projecting what I wanted to be true—or did I know more about her than I suspected? She was the very essence of "woman"—of that I was positive. I felt reassured that she had now emerged twice in conjunction with my growth and increased understanding, so if I continued to focus on learning, perhaps she would appear again. Enjoying this vision as long as I could, I walked to my car and began the journey home, determined to learn quickly.

As I drove, I realized that of the long list of qualities I had associated with this woman, few of these same characteristics were inherent in me. I was more intellectual than artistic, more of a thinker than a feeler, and hard working rather than playful or nurturing. I sensed there was something to be learned from my admiration of her qualities, but for now I opted to stop thinking for a while and just enjoy my last few hours in Hawaii.

After checking in at the airport and settling into the front row of the small inter-island plane, I listened as the pilots performed their instrument check. One explained to the other that a red light was on, indicating a clogged fuel line. The flight attendants huddled and were told to prepare the passengers for a delay. Rather than becoming upset, I was thankful that the red light had warned us now rather than later, over the Pacific Ocean. My imagination carried me away as I tried to visualize what I would have done if the lead pilot had simply said, "Aw, just turn off the light; we can make it!" Would I have gotten out of the plane or just sat there, trusting? Would I have insisted that someone do something, or would I have been satisfied with ignoring the red light, too?

This led me to wonder about the "red lights" in people's lives. Surely mechanical devices weren't the only things warning us of impending danger. I felt sure that we all received warning signals, both internally and from our surroundings, just as the pilot did by observing the instrument panel. Our "instrument panels" were our individual worlds—not only our bodies, our thoughts and our feelings, but everything in our lives. Ill health, broken relationships, arguments, money problems, anger, fear—weren't these all warning signs that something needed readjustment or repair?

If we didn't pay attention to the "red lights," our lives would get stuck or even fall apart. If we kept on the same course without making adjustments, we would always get the same results, without improvement, perhaps even ultimately "crash and burn." People I had known throughout my life passed before my mind, as I clearly saw how they had gotten stuck in despair or unhappiness because they didn't accept the events and emotions of their lives as signs to adjust or to repair and realign. I wondered how many times I had done the same thing. I forced myself to ask, *What were the red lights in my life?* I saw that pain, aloofness and confusion had been some of my past signals. In hindsight, I could now see those flashing indicators and how they had preceded the divorce.

I carried the question into the present: *What are my red lights now?* Regretfully, I watched the same signals—pain, aloofness and confusion—blinking at me, trying to get my attention. It struck me that it was easy to see exactly what someone else was doing "wrong" and what they needed to do differently, but when it came to seeing our own lives, we didn't recognize the signs so easily. Rather than seeing events and upsets as universal feedback or warning signs, we tend to feel blame or anger without seeing that we can take a different action and create different results. I vowed to look for and pay attention to all the "red lights" in my life from that moment on, just as the announcement came that the flight was finally ready for takeoff.

I barely had time to jot down my thoughts for future reference, as the short inter-island hop lasted only a few minutes. Changing planes in Oahu, I settled into a bigger airplane, still deep in thought. A young man sat down beside me, and we buckled ourselves in for the journey to the mainland.

We introduced ourselves. His name was Ed, and he was going to the mainland to visit his sister for a week. He was a scuba diver and led tourists on daily dives of the reefs. "My parents wanted me to do something more traditional with my life, but I love what I do," he confessed.

Intrigued, I asked, "What do you love most about it?"

"This may sound funny, but I love how it puts me in the present moment. I mean, well, it isn't possible to think about anything else for very long without coming back to what is happening right then. Have you ever dived?"

"No. I have snorkeled, though." I began to wonder if the people around me had always reinforced the lessons in my life, but I had just never noticed before.

Looking thoughtful, he said, "Diving is a lot like meditation. You know when you snorkel, how rough it can be on the surface with the wind and the waves?"

I nodded as he continued.

"Did you know that no matter how rough it is up there, when you drop down just a few feet, it gets calm? The farther down you go, the more peaceful it gets. There you are, breathing slowly and deeply, surrounded by tranquillity, and at the same time you can look up and see the turmoil on the surface. You can observe it without being a part of it. You can see the raindrops or the breaking waves without feeling them. You can even watch fish pass by, like thoughts, but you seldom stay with the same fish for the duration of your dive. You are truly an observer. Yeah, it is a lot like meditation; that's what I like about it—that plus all the creatures I get to see. There is always something new, no matter how many times I dive."

Ed then picked up a book, and with a smile that signaled an agreeable end to our conversation, immersed himself in reading throughout the rest of the flight, leaving me to ponder his comments. I took out my journal to continue recording the events, thoughts and discoveries of the past two weeks.

The announcement that we were preparing to land in Los Angeles pulled me away from my writing. Opening my window shade to look outside, I was treated to a spectacular display of city lights. I found myself trying to identify different parts of the city. I looked down on a stream of lights that had to be a freeway and marveled at how beautiful the traffic was from up high. Ribbon-like streamers of red and white light wove and intersected with other ribbons, forming an intricate pattern throughout the city, connecting it all together. I watched as everything grew from miniature to life-size.

After renting a car, I headed for a hotel in Santa Monica. Now the traffic somehow appeared bigger than life. One guy cut me off and another almost rear-ended me. I sat in the same place for what seemed to be fifteen minutes before giving up and searching for a way to get off the freeway. How did the traffic go from being so beautiful to being so chaotic and frustrating? Ed's words about diving flashed through my mind: *"When you drop down a couple of feet, it gets calm; you can observe it without being a part of it."* I clearly saw the difference between observing the chaos and being in it. It was as different as standing in the middle of the freeway as traffic zooms by or standing on the side watching the traffic pass from the safety of the curb. I began to see that observation was the means by which one could get that perspective. Arriving at the hotel, I put my thoughts on hold while I checked in.

Since I planned to stay in the Los Angeles area for a couple of days before returning to Sedona, I decided to call Nan in Santa Barbara to see how the rest of her trip had gone, hopeful that perhaps we could get together. As I dialed the number, I became aware of how much stronger I felt compared to when I had met her. Had it only been a matter of days? It felt as if a lifetime had passed. Her voice was pleasantly familiar as she answered the phone.

"Hello?"

"Hi, Nan? This is Matt—from the cabin on the Na Pali—on Kauai."

"What a nice surprise! Where are you?"

"I'm in Santa Monica for a couple days—just got back from Hawaii. I was wondering if you wanted to meet for a late dinner somewhere between L.A. and Santa Barbara."

"I'd love to—when and where?"

We made plans to meet and I quickly hit the road. Within an hour we were sitting down to dinner. She told me about the rest of her trip, and I shared the highlights of mine. I told her about the rest of my journey into Kalalau and about the awareness I had gained taking the boat out. I teetered on the edge of telling her about the rings and the mysterious woman but couldn't quite imagine how to explain them, so I held off.

I shared the newest of my thoughts. "I have been thinking a lot about observation, or rather self-observation. It's so easy to just go through life without ever really taking a look at what you are creating. Unless you observe, you don't really know what you are doing."

She agreed, "If you don't look at how you're showing up in the world, then you're likely to miss the whole point in being here, which, in my opinion, is to self-correct, grow and evolve. Being aware is half the battle."

I replied, "I used to think that awareness alone was the answer, but today I saw it all differently. Awareness is certainly an aspect, but simply being aware isn't enough."

She asked, "What do you mean?"

"Well, when you are aware that you are doing something or feeling something, you may be still emotionally involved in doing it or feeling it. Let me rephrase that. Okay, take today for instance. When I observed the traffic from the plane, I wasn't involved. After I landed and got caught in it, I was *aware* of the traffic but was also *a part of* the traffic. I got caught up in it and bothered by it. I think our emotions are like that. When we are *aware* that we are angry, we are still feeling anger. We identify with *being* angry.

"But when we *observe* ourselves being angry, we don't identify with the aspect of ourselves that is angry. Instead, we are somehow separate from the anger. The observer isn't angry; the *observed* is angry. We all have the ability to observe 'ourselves' from 'outside' ourselves, as it were, and we are able to see ourselves as more than just the one being observed. Am I making any sense?"

"Perfect sense, I think," as she smiled. "What you are saying is that when we see what we are doing from another perspective, we become objective observers instead of subjective participants—yes?"

"Yeah, I think so," I answered, still thinking it through. "But also, the objective observer sees the observed, the situation *and* itself—and therefore, that part of us sees a much bigger picture."

Without hesitation she continued, "You know, I had an experience like that once when my old boyfriend and I broke up. It was really strange. I remember lying on my couch crying—you know, those deep, deep sobs. Well, anyhow, I was crying really hard, and at the same time I heard a voice, a part of myself, saying, 'Listen to that crying! Isn't it amazing that I am sobbing like that; I haven't cried like that since I was a little girl—hmmm!' It was like a part of me was watching what was going on without being involved. I remember thinking what a strange experience that was, to be so detached and at the same time so involved. It actually gave me hope, even though I thought I might be a little crazy, because I could see that a part of me was strong, no matter what. Have you ever had that happen?"

"I'm not sure, but I can imagine it clearly. Actually, I do think I have experienced something similar. When Sarah and I split up, a part of me was depressed and another part was okay with it all, although I'm not sure it was quite as vivid for me as your experience. I think, though, that if we practiced that kind of a detached view of our lives every day, rather than just when we were in crisis, what a lot we would learn! Then, if we made decisions from that strong, knowing place, rather than the weak, confused place—it would be powerful, wouldn't it?!"

Nan agreed, and we both committed to taking closer, or rather, more distant looks at our lives. She added, "In some ways, that kind of self-observation takes the 'Being in the Moment' thing one step further—to *observing* where you are in the moment. Uh, that didn't come out too clearly. I mean, it is like being in the moment and knowing you are in the moment at the same time—kind of like lucid dreaming—when you are dreaming and yet you know you are dreaming."

I continued her thought. "You know, when you are sitting in a movie theater, watching a scary movie from right up close? You can't help but be scared! But if you focus on the edges of the screen, the scariness loses some of its impact—and if you stand at the back of the theater and watch over everyone else's heads, it isn't nearly as scary. If you stand out in the hallway and watch through the doors, it becomes even less engaging. I suspect that if we viewed our lives in the same way, we could truly *see* them so much more clearly."

We laughed and philosophized well into the night, reminiscent of the first time we met. I felt a deep kinship with Nan and wondered why it seemed so natural to tell her everything I was thinking—well, almost everything. She reminded me in many ways of the mysterious woman, for she was intuitive, kind and warm. We parted ways with promises to stay in touch.

As I drove back to my hotel, my mind wandered again to the woman with the golden rings. I wondered whether I would see her again, or rather, *when* I would see her again. I wanted to share my new revelations with her, too. I was hopeful that my new discoveries would bring her back to me.

Back in the hotel room, I went into the bathroom to brush my teeth. Standing there in front of the mirror, my own eyes caught my attention. I wondered if I had ever really looked into them before. Certainly I had looked at everything else: my mustache, my reddish-brown hair . . . but my eyes? I didn't think so, and tonight they demanded my full attention. Something almost confrontational in them made me want to look away, but still they held me mesmerized. I felt exposed and realized that I had nowhere to hide. I was truly facing myself. The question, *Who are you?* echoed through my mind as I stared more deeply into the reflected image.

My pupils seemed to become a passageway to the universe, almost like something out of *Star Trek*, leading me toward unexplored territory. I felt a depth to myself that I had never really noticed before. I had heard that "the eyes are the windows to the soul" and had always felt more connected to other people when I looked into their eyes, but I had never truly connected with my own. The more I gazed, the more my face seemed to change, almost as if viewing a slide show of emotions. I saw pain and sadness. I saw joy and laughter. I saw myself young and old. For a glimmering moment, I saw love. The more I looked, the more I saw the real me. Overwhelmed, I wanted to turn away and squeeze my eyes closed before returning to those in the mirror.

I began to ask myself some questions, starting out as silent wonderings, then progressing to spoken inquiries: *What is it like to live with me? What must it have been like for my wife and kids?* I suddenly saw, from what felt like their perspective, what it was like to live with one so driven to achieve, to make money and to be "successful." The lack of time spent on fun and recreation hit me as I was forced to admit the truth. I saw how private I had been, keeping most of my thoughts and feelings to myself. I realized that I had never really allowed them to truly know me.

My questions continued. *What is it like to wake up with me?* I clearly saw how quiet I am in the morning and how unavailable for conversation. I recalled how Sarah had been the opposite, waking up wanting to talk right away, and how I had responded only with one-word replies to her commentary.

What is it like to be a participant in my seminars? I saw myself as very knowledgeable, yet somehow distant from the people. I cared about them but didn't know them, and they didn't know me.

I continued through at least a half-dozen questions: *What is it like making love with me? . . . What is it like to have a father like me? . . . What is it like to have a friend like me? . . . What is it like to have a neighbor like me? . . . What is it like to work for me? . . . What is it like to have a son like me? . . . What is it like to have a brother like me? . . . What is it like to get consultations with me?* The barrage of questions ended with the awareness that I needed more balance in my life. I was all work and no play. Clearly I needed to spend more time taking care of my body, my relationships and my spirituality—which could simply mean spending more silent time in nature. Other than this Hawaii trip, that aspect had received very little time at all.

The word *recreation* popped into my mind. I could certainly use more of that! I then saw the word as *re-creation,* and it dawned on me that *recreation* was a tool for *re-creating* one's family, one's peace of mind and one's relationship with oneself. I promised myself more balance and recreation.

Examining the life I had lived before Kauai, I once again saw how much time I spent reliving the past or preparing for the future and how little time I spent fully present with myself or other people. This presented itself as a lack of connection in my life, which went far in explaining the pain of feeling so separate and alone. I had filled my time with work, just as others filled theirs with radio, TV, alcohol or drugs. Whatever the method, the effect was the same: stay busy and fill the silence so you can't hear or see how unhappy you are, how alone you are nor the changes you need to make.

It came down to balance. Each area of life interacts with the other areas, either supporting or taking away from them. They can either work together to create a wonderful quality of life or work at odds, creating imbalance and eventually discomfort. I had pulled vital energy away from certain valuable aspects of my life, and now I silently vowed to pay more attention to all aspects, balancing them rather than emphasizing one or another while neglecting the whole.

While proceeding through this self-observation, I was amused by how clever the human ego was at avoiding taking responsibility. I understood why most of us don't look closely at ourselves, since the process isn't exactly painless. At the same time, I experienced a strange sort of relief from facing myself honestly. I felt as if I now had some control over my circumstances, once I had honestly identified my part in it all. I contrasted this with how powerless I felt when blaming someone else for my troubles, much less when assigning the blame to "circumstances" or even "fate."

Having undergone all the self-observation I could stand for one night, I took a deep breath, headed off to bed and quickly fell asleep. I found myself in the midst of a dream, sound asleep yet knowing I was dreaming. I was in a large palace or temple with stone steps and carvings in the rocks. People were in the distance, but none were recognizable. Incense burned nearby, and I felt a great sense of honor and awe with each breath of the scented air. I felt someone's presence and looked around but could see no one. A fog of some sort seemed to cloud my vision. Then a form began to emerge through the veil of gray. A woman draped in a white gown descended the steps toward me. While I still could not see her clearly, I felt a strange familiarity, then a deep love for her. As she neared, I recognized her and woke suddenly, sitting up and uttering the name, *"Alea!"*

I sat in my bed for several moments, trying to realize where I was and which experience was real—sitting here in my bed or standing there at the steps of the temple with the mysterious woman. *"Alea."* I repeated the name several times, *"Alea, Alea,"* letting the familiar sound of it roll off my tongue. The beauty of the name matched her. Looking at the clock, I saw that it was still four hours before my wake-up call. I jotted the name down on the pad by my bed and went back to sleep.

I didn't move an inch until the phone rang at seven, jarring me awake. Turning on the light and answering the phone, I listened politely to my summons to wake, even though it was only a recording. It wasn't until I hung up the phone that my eyes lit on the name I had written on the paper next to my bed. As I read the name out loud, *"ALEA,"* the dream suddenly came rushing back to me.

"You remembered!" a feminine voice said sweetly from the shadowed corner across the room.

Startled, I jolted upward, almost hitting my head against the headboard. The woman stood there in white, just as in the dream. *"I knew you would,"* she added, with her brilliant smile.

Overwhelming joy flooded through me as I saw her. I hardly knew this woman, yet felt so close to her, as if she were my best friend. I regained my composure and exclaimed, "I'm so happy to see you! Where have you been?" Then I managed to ask, "Who exactly are you?"

She came and sat down on the bed. I wondered about the tremendous respect I felt for her, as she answered, *"Your questions will be answered in time. For now, it is enough to say that I am always here."*

My inner voice demanded that she answer them now. She smiled as if she had heard my thoughts and I felt myself blushing slightly, embarrassed by my impatience.

It was all I could do to utter politely, "Who are you? Please tell me."

Changing the subject as if she hadn't heard, she said, *"You have been busy! Tell me what you have discovered."*

I hesitated only long enough to wonder whether I had really asked her. "I have always taught that self-awareness was the first step toward change, but now I see that simple awareness is not enough. With awareness, you can still think you *are* the drama that you are aware of, but with *self-observation,* you can separate yourself from the drama and are better able to make choices—and changes."

"And how does this apply to you?"

"I saw that I wasn't paying attention to who I had become. I was so focused on making money that I had overlooked my health, family and relationships. I wasn't even observant enough to notice that what I was teaching wasn't working. I have decided to take a regular look at myself and my life, as objectively as possible, and make adjustments."

Alea ceremoniously handed me another golden circle with the words *Observe Yourself* etched in it. She said, *"You have earned this, and I again honor you for your growth."* She paused long enough for me to feel the sacredness of the moment, then continued, *"It is time for me to tell you something very important. Please listen very carefully."* She looked deep into my eyes, and I felt as if the secrets of the world were hiding in hers, about to be revealed. I felt strangely vulnerable yet honored at the same time.

"I know you have many questions, but I cannot answer them at this time. You simply must trust me. You have a very important mission on the planet. I can tell you this only because you already have a sense of the truth of it. The lessons you are learning now are critical aspects of what you must master in order to fulfill your purpose here. These gifts may not be easy, but they are all wonderful. The rings are more than mere symbols to remind you of your growth. I cannot reveal their larger meaning to you now. Just know that you must keep them safe. All together there are twenty-one, all of which you must earn in order to truly blossom, but the first seven make up the seed. I will guide you as much as I can, but you are the one who must do the work. I cannot reveal anything to you that you have not yet discovered for yourself. I can merely ask the right questions. Above all, you must trust yourself and your own inner knowing to find the answers—and earn the other rings."

Alea was right about the multitude of questions I had, but I didn't bother to ask. We sat in silence as I attempted to assimilate all she had shared. Then she said, *"Look into your heart, and tell me what you want."*

I paused, then responded, "I want to discover the meaning of life and how to be happy."

"Why?"

"So I can teach other people how to be happy."

Again, she responded, *"Why?"*

"Because I want to make a difference on the planet."

"Why?"

Surprising myself, I said, "Because that is what I was born to do."

"Why?"

"Because the planet needs more love."

With a sweet smile she again asked, *"Why?"*

Tears welled up in my eyes. "Because I need more love."

One last time she asked gently, *"Why?"*

Slowly I whispered, "Because I need to be more loving." I saw what she was doing—facilitating my self-observation so I could clearly know my deepest motivations, my "compelling *why's*" in life.

"So, what do you really want?"

Breathing in the revelation, I answered with the obvious: "Love."

She then suggested, *"Now think about the material things that you used to want. Take any one of them, for starters."*

I didn't know why, but the first thing that popped into my head was a limousine, so I said, "A white limousine."

"Perfect. Why did you want it?"

With a laugh, I admitted, "Because I would look good—and successful—in it."

She smiled. *"Yes, you would. Why do you want to look good and successful?"*

I responded intently, "So that people will be impressed and take me seriously."

Her mood matched mine. *"Why do you want people to take you seriously?"*

"Because I want them to listen to me."

"Why?"

"Because I have something of value to say, and I think I can help them."

"Why do you want to help them?"

"So that they will be happier—and so that they will like me."

"And why do you want them to like you?"

"So that I will have more friends."

"And why do you want more friends?"

My answer was surprisingly serious. "Because I am tired of being alone."

Yet again she asked, *"Why?"*

I then saw that the line of questioning had come full circle. "Because I want more love, and I want to be more loving."

"Why?"

An image flooded into my awareness. "Because I remember being held by my mother as a baby, and how safe and warm—and complete I felt."

I sat in silence as the impact of this self-observation sank in.

Alea simply said, *"Now that is a far cry from wanting a limousine to look good."*

She sat quietly to allow me time to absorb, then continued, *"What do you suppose the rest of the people on the planet want?"*

Pulled away from my thoughts, I said, "I know the obvious answer is love, but I am not sure that love is what motivates everyone."

"Oh? And who is not motivated by love?"

Taking a bit of a stand, I said, "Well, murderers and violent people, or terrorists. Take gang members. They aren't motivated by love; they are motivated by power and greed."

"Why do you suppose they are greedy and want power?"

Immediately I saw the same cycle of answers lining up. "So that the other gang members will like them." As I spoke, I saw that gangsters didn't hurt others simply because they liked to hurt people, but rather to meet needs of their own, such as being noticed and heard. They needed a sense of belonging, a sense of personal power and capability in the world. What they did, they did in order to feel loved.

Alea nodded all the while, as if listening to the rest of my thoughts. I took a deep breath as I profoundly felt a new understanding of human beings—myself included.

I asked, "Are we all born simply to love and be loved?"

Sweetly, she asked, *"What do you feel?"*

The reply resonated all the way through my soul. "We are all born to love and be loved."

She smiled and touched my cheek softly, wiped away a tear that had escaped, then gently closed my eyelids.

She asked a final question. *"What is love?"*

Before I could open my eyes or answer the question, I knew that she had disappeared. Holding the ring of *self-observation* in my hand, I knew that the answer to this last question was a crucial step in my unfolding. I lay there thinking about the changes I needed to make in order to bring my life into better balance and, for a fleeting second, I felt a wave of fear. I clearly needed courage to embrace the tasks and challenges that lay ahead and felt excited at the prospect of discovering and earning the rest of the "gifts." It was somewhat like living in a scavenger hunt.

Holding up the golden circlet in a silent salute between both hands, I breathed a silent "thank you" to Alea, wishing I had thanked her while she was here. I distinctly heard her reply, soft but audible in the room, *"You are welcome, Dear One, you are welcome."*

Invisibly and lovingly keeping watch over Matt in his reverie, Alea wished she could just hand him all the remaining rings, the entire Master's Key, in a desire to relieve him of the growing pains. Yet all was perfect as it was.

He had discovered the value of self-observation most quickly. Self-observation was more important for growth than he knew, yet she was sure he was seeing clearly and well on his way to understanding.

She followed Matt's thoughts and musings as to how people pay immediate attention to physical pain as a "red light," warning sign or call to action. They spend hundreds or even thousands of dollars to get well, take medication, change their diet, exercise, put on casts, go into physical therapy or get physical adjustments to straighten things out—all to be relieved of pain. She wondered why they don't put the same kind of energy into relieving emotional pain; most do not even recognize it, too, as a call to action—or how their physical pains relate to their emotional and mental pains.

People live their dramas without realizing that "they" are not the drama, and that they actually have full control over the dramas they are living. Only through self-observation can they gain a perspective that will allow them to see they are not the small self, caught in the waves on the surface, but rather the deeper Self, grounded in calm and serenity, able to observe all that is taking place. From this perspective, one can choose a different drama or no drama at all—but without self-observation one cannot see the difference between reality and drama. Without observation, there is no reality, only drama. Once distinguished, choice is possible, and choice is power.

Even though he hadn't yet formulated the thought into words, Alea knew that Matt understood that if he called someone to ask for directions, the first thing they would need to know would be, "Where are you now?" In order to answer, he would have to stop and observe his location. Simply answering, "Lost," would not help. He would need to locate the signposts, which in life are often the "red lights" and warning signs that we are gifted with along the way.

Alea sensed that Matt was a mere hair's breadth from being able to state that anything that did not feel "based in love" nor "feel loving" would qualify as an excellent "red light," and if observed, could be appreciated as a gift of guidance rather than some sort of divine punishment.

If we would only realize that love is our only true motivation, our true desire, then choices about what to do, which way to turn and which signs to pay attention to would become so much easier. Self-observation allows us to see where we are now, to clearly envision our destinations and to plot courses for manifesting those visions.

Since Alea knew where Matt was heading, she knew how vital it was that he observe himself to know where he was each moment and realign his steps with love. She rejoiced in his unfolding wisdom. She rejoiced for him. She rejoiced for herself. She rejoiced for the whole planet.

4

Inner Resources

Two days in Los Angeles were just enough to make me ready to return to the peacefulness of my home and the red rock walls of Sedona. Much like the sea, they were always the same yet constantly changing as the sunlight and clouds moved over them. The various shades of reds and browns struck a brilliant contrast to the multiple greens of the tropics. I couldn't claim to prefer one over the other and counted my blessings for having the experience of both.

Once in the familiarity of my home, I couldn't resist looking in all the corners of my house to see if any goddesses were hiding there. I was determined not to be caught by surprise again. A little disappointed at finding no one, I sat alone on my deck. This was the exact same place I had sat a few weeks ago, and yet now everything looked different. Before, the world around me—or rather within me—had seemed stale, old, outdated. Now adventure seemed to loom everywhere, and even my indecisive turmoil excited me. I still sought a million answers, but now the questions had changed. Now, I was asking, *What is love? . . . What is real?* along with the all-consuming questions: *Who is Alea, really?* and even more important, *Who am I?*

It didn't make much sense to me. My logical mind struggled with the whole situation, but my heart was happy, happier than it had been in years—perhaps ever! I ran Alea's words through my mind, which just created more to wonder about. What was this "purpose" she claimed I was here to fulfill? What kind of "important mission" was she talking about? Part of me wanted to laugh at the very idea, which rang of fairy tales or the legends of King Arthur or other mythical heroes. *That couldn't possibly relate to me,* commented a cynical inner voice, and yet I felt an inner knowing of the truth of her words. I felt challenged to discover this personal mission—whatever it turned out to be—and to fulfill it.

I had originally entered the personal growth arena out of personal interest and need, then continued out of a knowing that I had to help others. Even as a child, I had suddenly stopped my work in the cotton field one day, looked around at all the others stooped over in the sun, and imagined that I was talking to them all, telling them that we didn't have to live like this. It wasn't the work that felt wrong, it was the despair and hopelessness with which we were *doing* the work. I wanted to see happy people in the field instead of poor-spirited, broken people. I couldn't imagine, though, why they would listen to me, since I was as unhappy as they were. Now, in the solitude on my deck, I realized that this had been the birth of my drive to make a difference, to help people be happier. At age ten, I had had no idea how to go about it, but I became determined to begin my search. In hindsight, I guess I had known on some level that I had "an important mission" to fulfill. Maybe that was why the recent sense of being "wrong" had been so disconcerting. Sitting there on my deck, I suddenly knew that I had to continue teaching.

Immensely relieved by this decision, I was now ready to take on some more immediate tasks. I checked my messages and returned a multitude of calls. One message invited me to speak at a corporate sales seminar, to motivate a sales force and share some success tips. A twinge of insecurity churned in my stomach. I had spoken to thousands and thousands of people, but now, for the first time in years, I felt unsure, almost fearful about speaking. The relief of my moments-before decision was short-lived; the throes of discomfort concerning the path of my life again disturbed me.

I observed myself going into the fear and took a deep breath. Immediately, I felt more relaxed. I then asked myself my specific concerns in regard to speaking, quietly observing my answers. My fear was about teaching the same material I had taught before, that I might lead people astray. At one time I had believed everything I taught. Now I had discovered that some of the teachings were not effective—or at least not completely. I didn't ever want to be wrong again with something that I considered so important.

I just needed to be sure I was teaching the right material. Which parts of the program worked, and which didn't? How could I be sure? The ten-year-old within me again wondered why people would ever want to listen to me.

Obviously, I needed to spend more time thinking—and feeling—my way through all my material, discriminating between what I knew to be true and what might not be. Decisions would have to be made. Until then, the thought of speaking to an audience made me feel uncomfortable.

A loving voice whispered in my mind, louder than the other self-talk. It simply said, *"What you taught wasn't wrong, Matt, it was just incomplete. Be gentle with yourself. You have always been on the right track; the track was simply wider than you could see at the time. Now you can broaden your scope!"* It was as if Alea were standing in the room, but she was nowhere to be seen.

I tried to dismiss what I had just heard as a rationalization of my mind. The loving, peaceful feeling that persisted after the thought had gone could not be ignored and offered evidence of Alea's invisible presence, or so I interpreted it.

I took another deep breath and decided to focus on what I knew and felt comfortable with, instead of what I didn't know. From this perspective, I knew I could teach success skills easily, as I knew for sure how to make money and to be entrepreneurial. There was absolutely no question about my ability to teach *that* material. I made the decision to accept the speaking engagement and teach how to be successful in business.

My thoughts returned to the discoveries of the last few weeks. I could share with audiences what I was learning now and relate it to the good parts of my old material. I would no longer focus on the pursuit of happiness, but rather *living in the state of happiness!* I could teach people to go ahead and set goals, but to stay in the present and enjoy the journey. I could tell them that happiness is what is *happening now* in the present moment. I could share about fear and self-observation—from my own experiences—as a powerful tool for gaining perspective and making changes. As I became more adept at identifying the red lights in my life, I could help others learn to do the same. The more I focused on what I knew, the more comfortable I became and confident that I could soon create a new program for personal growth seminars.

My only concern was that it was all so new to me that I didn't feel as if I had achieved mastery—not enough to truly guide others through the process, not to mention field all their inquiries. As I imagined their continuous flow of questions, fear surfaced again, which required me to stop, breathe and bring myself back to the present moment again—and remind myself that none of this mental scenario was happening to me now! I took another deep breath and observed myself. It became obvious that all I needed was a little more courage and practice of the concepts. I had good material, speaking opportunities and plenty of experience as a speaker. All I needed was the courage to create a new program—one that truly worked—and to share it with the world. I also needed to continue applying these discoveries to my own life, as I knew that this was the way to attain true mastery and earn the right to teach others.

Another thought gnawed at the back of my mind. Eventually I would have to get up the courage to talk to Cindy, my agent, and confess to having thrown away my manuscript, the one for which she was so anxiously waiting. I still knew I had done the right thing and sensed that I had a far better book within me; I just needed to state my new discoveries in writing. This, however, was small comfort, considering what I expected Cindy's reaction to be.

Feeling relieved at having narrowed my "to do" list, I booked the speaking engagement and tackled the tasks of unpacking, laundry and playing "catch up." I spent the next few weeks committing my new thoughts to paper and organizing them in a concrete manner that could be communicated to others. For the most part, I planned to stay away from sharing the ideas with anyone until I was more confident, but I wanted to have it prepared and well thought out as that time approached. I wasn't sure exactly when or how I would deem myself "ready," but I assumed I would know when the time arrived.

Cindy's dreaded phone call finally came. I had been meditating and felt peaceful and centered when I answered the phone.

"Hi, Matt? This is Cindy."

"Hi."

"How is it going? I heard you took a trip. Where did you go?"

"I went to Kauai. I needed some time away to sort out some things, but I'm back at it now."

"Well, that's good. I'm glad you had a good time. Did you get in any writing?"

Cringing slightly, I answered honestly, "Yeah, a little. I spent more time thinking through my material, though."

"Well, how is it coming? When do you think you'll be done?"

Figuring I had better just come out and tell her rather than make things worse, I said, "I have made a few changes." I cleared my throat and added, "Actually, I'm making some major changes. I'm starting all over again." I thought I may as well go the distance. "In fact, I threw the whole manuscript away."

I could tell by the silence on the other end that she was trying to gauge whether I was serious.

"You're joking, right?" she gasped.

"Actually not. Listen, Cindy, I woke up one day before my trip, realizing that what I was teaching and writing didn't work. The reason I was having such a hard time finishing the book was because it wasn't the right book—it wasn't meant to be finished." I assumed from her silence that she wanted me to continue. "I have been working on some really great new material, though. I'm sure you will like it, but it's still in the research phase, so it will be a while before it is ready to share."

"I'm sorry Matt, I'm just sort of in shock here. You were so close to being finished. Can't you just complete that book and then write another one with your new material?"

"Cindy, you don't understand. It wasn't any good. It wouldn't have worked for people. I was teaching them how to acquire things and to pursue happiness—not how to *be* happy. Material things don't do the trick. I had a house full of things, and I wasn't happy. If it didn't work for me, why would it work for the readers? Not only that, but I really threw it away—all of it. I put it in the little computer trash can and dumped it."

"You really threw away your manuscript?! Oh, Matt! What has gotten into you? All that work!"

"Don't worry Cindy, I'm going to write a new book—a better one—one that will truly work for people."

"You don't get it, Matt. You had a virtually finished manuscript and a publisher who was interested. Do you know how much time and money you just threw away?"

"Money isn't the point here, Cindy. I can't publish a book I know isn't the truth, just for money."

"What is the truth anyway, Matt? How will you know when you have discovered it?"

"I'll know by the quality of my life. If it works for me, it will work for others."

"I hate to say this, but it could take you years to find your truth. In the meantime, the book you had was good enough. Do you know how few books would be written if every author tested out and mastered every one of his or her concepts? So tell me, what is the new book about?"

Up until now I had felt strong and confident, knowing I was right not to publish the old book. Now, however, my courage was failing me. Uncertain, I pondered my options. Do I tell her about Alea? NO. Well, *that* was a clear response. I almost laughed as I thought about how quickly, once you start this self-observation stuff, you can get responses from your core self. Do I tell her about living in the moment? NO. Do I tell her about self-observation? NO. I tried to buy some time by offering to put together a proposal and outline and send it to her.

She didn't let up. "When? What is it about?"

"It is basically about the same thing, just a better approach." I imagined what telling her the truth would sound like: *"Well Cindy, it's like this. I woke up one morning and realized that my life wasn't working. I took thousands of dollars worth of clothes and other items to the thrift store and came home and threw away my manuscript. Then this beautiful woman materialized in my hot tub, told me I was on the right path, and has been turning up in my life every so often since then with a new concept to share. I am going to write about what she teaches me. The only problem is, Cindy, that I don't know who she is, and she only shows up when she wants to—so the book might take a while."* I nearly laughed aloud at the thought but said instead, "I'm writing about success and happiness and personal growth, just like the other book, but this time I am going to be sure that the material is based in truth and love."

"Love? You aren't getting airy-fairy on me, are you? People buy success books to have more money and the dream house they always wanted. People want Rolex watches and Bally shoes—image and comfort, not love! We got enough of the love stuff in the sixties! Come on, Matt! What did you do, fall in love or something? Is that what brought all this on?"

Immediately I thought of Alea and suddenly felt protective of her. "No, Cindy, that's not it. Look, trust me. The new book will be great, honest."

"Uh huh. So, what do you want me to tell the publisher?" she asked sarcastically.

"Tell them I am revising the book with some new material I have recently, uh, stumbled upon and that I will keep them apprised of my progress."

"This time keep me apprised, too, will you? For that matter, as your agent, I am requesting that you don't do anything without checking with me first, okay?"

"Okay, I will keep you posted."

"Good, I will talk to you soon."

"Cindy?"

"Yes?"

"I love you."

"Oh shut up, Matt. Bye."

I chuckled as I heard the line go dead. Well, that was relatively painless, but it probably wouldn't be the next time, unless I made some progress. I wished I had just a little more courage when it came to talking about the new material. I wondered what I needed to do to feel stronger and more courageous. I thought about how easy it was to talk to some people about these things, like Nan and Alea, while with others it just didn't feel safe. I wondered whether I would ever feel confident enough to cover all this in a seminar.

The next morning I awoke from an intense dream. In it, I stood in a high school courtyard full of teenagers. One came running over to me, right after being stabbed. Hurt, he pointed toward a gang and the young man who had harmed him. I made sure he would be okay, then faced the gang members, who brandished knives and garden shears and made taunting threats. I felt no fear but simply held up my hands, saying, "Look, I am not going to get you into trouble. I am not going to do anything at all except talk to you." I singled out the apparent gang leader—the same young man who had stabbed the other boy—and began talking to him about love. He tried to move away from me, in order to still look cool to his friends, but I knew he was listening. Whenever he put up resistance, I agreed with him, then sent my message out to him again. I told him I understood that he had to fight for his place among his peers. I explained that fighting was not the answer, that it only perpetuated more fighting.

"If you look into your heart and the hearts of your friends, none of you really want to live this way. I know you don't. You just want to know your place in the world and to be respected. You can gain respect in other ways than physical power, but someone has to take the lead. I think it can start with you."

"But I *am* the leader!" he said proudly, still trying to maneuver away from me.

"Yes, you are the leader, and that means you are the one to show these other young men where true power comes from. It comes from strength within, not strength on the outside. Anyone can build up their muscles. Anyone can use weapons to hurt and to kill, but true strength comes from love. Loving your enemy requires more power than any weapon can provide you, and it achieves greater results. If you depend on just your physical power, you are easily replaced when someone stronger comes along. A leader built of true inner strength and wisdom, one who earns the respect of his peers out of love instead of fear, now *that* leader cannot be replaced. You can be that kind of leader!" I managed to get close enough to put my arm around his shoulder as I spoke, and then I began to cry.

I felt as if a hole had opened up in my heart, and that all the beings of the universe were crying through me. They wept for the pain of generations, of desperate efforts to find their places in the world, to love and to be loved—to love themselves. Sobbing, I felt the pain of the entire world in that moment.

Thinking that I was truly sobbing, I woke up, reaching to wipe the tears away. Finding none, I realized that it had only been a dream. I lay in bed, thinking. It had been so intense, so real. I tried to imagine myself really having the courage to talk like that to gang members about love. *Not yet,* I thought, *not yet.* I wondered how I could gain that kind of inner strength.

As I lay there, I began to see a string of desire that had run through my life. I had always wanted to bring more love and joy to others—from the field workers of my past to the teenage gang members in my dreams. For some reason, I felt the despair in people's hearts as if the anguish were my own. *When,* I wondered, *would I be able to help them?* I knew that I had done it to a superficial extent with the thousands I had already spoken to, but now, I wanted the love and happiness to be real, deep and everlasting. I wanted it to be worldwide and universal.

The day of the seminar finally approached. I drove to the hotel feeling clear and strong, resolved to speak only about what I knew hands down—business. People filed into the room as I pondered how each and every one of us has a story, a drama. I prepared to share my story with them—part of it, anyway.

I welcomed them all to the seminar and diligently gave them my best tips for success, sharing my first experiences in my own business. "I had a wife and child at home, was working in a factory, hadn't graduated from school, had no money and no business experience, when an opportunity to start my own business came along. After attending an introductory meeting, I quit my job the next day, much to the dismay of my family, and started distributing soap for a living.

"Actually, it wasn't quite that simple. I needed four thousand dollars to buy the soap and get qualified. I proceeded to go to twenty-two different loan companies, and they all said no. I was determined, though, as I walked into the twenty-third company. The gentleman at the desk asked me to fill out an application, and I said, 'No. Not until you tell me whether I am going to get this loan. I have filled out enough applications. I am going to start this business one way or another. Are you going to help me?' He must have seen the determination in my eyes, because he agreed to loan me the money—and soon I was in business, with eight thousand bottles of soap in my garage.

"After a couple of weeks in my new business, the company called and notified me that I would qualify for a higher level of pay if I invested another four thousand dollars. I convinced my father-in-law to put his dairy farm up as collateral, and a few days later the truck arrived with eight thousand more bottles of soap, bringing my total up to sixteen thousand bottles.

"The first person I introduced to the business, who had also bought four thousand dollars worth of soap, called me after his shipment arrived. He explained that upon seeing all the boxes, his wife had threatened, 'Either the soap goes or you go.' So he gave me all eight thousand bottles of his soap at no cost. There I was, with twenty-four thousand bottles of soap and all the determination in the world. As I saw it, success was right around the corner.

"What I found instead was that product and determination weren't enough—a strategy and some skill were also needed. Within one year, I lost virtually everything. The house was being taken away, the cars and the furniture had been repossessed, and my father-in-law was on the verge of losing his farm. I still had the soap, though!

"I was determined and didn't give up. At the most desperate moment of my life, the guy who brought me into the soap business dropped out, and the man who had introduced him started working with me. He showed me exactly what I needed to make it work. He explained, 'The secret of the business is to work with the people you introduce to the business instead of leaving them on their own. Help them build their business, and build yours at the same time. After all, when the distributors you introduce to the company make money, you make money too, so why not help them?!'

"I immediately started implementing the things he taught me, and within six months my soap business was bringing in a substantial income. Within a year, I had literally gone from being in debt and on the edge of being homeless to making several times my yearly salary at the factory every month! The key here is that I never lost faith; I never lost sight of making it go. You must have that kind of commitment to your business, and if what you are doing isn't working, do something different! Talk to the people who are making it work and ask them to help you, then turn around and help others to do the same. Helping each other and looking out for the other person's interest and well-being is a philosophy that all businesses should implement! This is called enlightened capitalism—working together in cooperation instead of competition."

I could feel the desire to talk about love creeping up on me. I tried to push it away, but it sprang out of its own accord. "The bottom line here, folks, is that what we all truly want is to feel love, support and a sense of belonging. We don't really want to be in business or to buy a product. We want love; we want a sense of connection. Being in business is about connections. It's about building emotional bonds with your clients and your representatives, and that starts with love. Lasting relationships, ladies and gentlemen, are about love and feeling connected. This is the greatest of all human needs. When a client calls with a problem, all they are saying is, 'Please reconnect me to the value of your product and the value of our relationship.'

"When one of your representatives is not performing the way they have in the past, all they are saying is, 'Please reconnect me to the opportunity, to the vision of the company, to my own vision and to my relationship with you.' If you can provide that connection for your customers and your representatives and teach your people to do the same, well, then you will truly be successful." I blushed a little as they gave me a standing ovation. I took a deep breath, realizing, *I talked about love, and they liked it!*

A woman came up to me afterwards and shared how moved she was by the presentation. She thanked me, explaining that it had given her an entirely new outlook on her business. Before walking away, she remarked, "You sure had a lot of courage. I hope if I am ever in that kind of situation, that I have as much courage as you!" I smiled and thanked her.

As I looked across the room, I thought I saw Alea among the crowd leaving the hall. My heart skipped a beat. Just then, the woman turned around, and I could see that it wasn't her at all. I slowly packed up my things, wishing that she had been Alea, for I really wanted to talk to her.

Walking out to my car, I felt a little stunned, almost as though recovering from a shock, a sudden fall or some other minor trauma, yet the feeling was not at all unpleasant. I couldn't quite identify why I felt so different, but I did. Talking about love had left me with a warm feeling. As I reached out to unlock my door, I was startled to see that someone had beaten me to it. Alea sat in the passenger seat, flashing her brilliant smile! I was beginning to think she liked to see me jump. I greeted her and jokingly asked if she needed a ride. She gave me a look that warmed my heart and said, *"That wasn't so bad, was it?"*

"Actually, it was a lot of fun! I didn't think I had it in me."

"Tell me what you discovered."

"Well, I didn't think I had the courage to talk about love in a seminar of business people—or with anyone for that matter. The funniest thing happened, though—I couldn't *not* talk about it. It was almost like I *had* to bring it up."

"That is the nature of love."

I mentioned the woman who had come up at the end and how she had admired my courage. "I guess I have been fairly courageous all my life, though I didn't realize it."

Laughing, I explained, "I just saw how I have been wandering around like the Cowardly Lion in *The Wizard of Oz,* wanting courage to be handed to me from the outside. I even wanted you to give it to me." We both laughed as I continued, "Now, just like in the story, I discovered that I have had courage all along! Courage is an inside thing, not something someone gives you." In my best Cowardly Lion voice, I said, "I've got courage!!"

Alea teasingly said, *"Well, here is your badge of courage—just for good measure."* She handed me another golden circle, this one with *Be Courageous* engraved upon it. We both giggled, sharing the joy of the moment.

After a few minutes of silent pleasure in her company as we drove through the countryside, I commented, "I used to think that courage was the opposite of fear, but I think right now that without fear, courage doesn't exist. If we weren't afraid to do something, how could an act be called courageous? Without the fear, it would just be a normal action. I suspect that fear always comes up when we are taking risks and doing something new. Taking a deep breath with self-observation helps us gather the courage to take the risk. Otherwise, we can get paralyzed by the fear."

Alea listened carefully, then asked, *"When you are in fear, what do you see when a new opportunity comes along?"*

I thought for a moment. "The risk; you see the danger."

"And when you are in courage, what do you see when the same opportunity comes along?"

"You see the advantages! Basically, in fear, you look for the risk in the opportunity, but in courage, you look for the opportunity in the risk!"

"What if you had courage, took a risk and it didn't work out. What would you gain?"

"Well, experience. You also have the possibility that it would have worked."

"And if you didn't have courage, and didn't take the risk, what would you gain?"

"Nothing, not even a chance at success. I guess having courage is really about having faith, trusting that everything will unfold perfectly. I suppose courage is really a trust in our inner abilities. We actually don't need to hesitate; what to do will become obvious."

"Matt, you will never be expected to do something or handle something that you aren't fully capable of doing," Alea assured me. *"We are all born with the resources we need for the task of living out our purpose. Our main job is to have the courage to take on our tasks, to look for our inner resources and to use them for the highest good of all."*

With that, she disappeared, leaving me to finish the drive home alone. As I drove, the many questions I had about her once again pummeled me. My head threw the questions like stones and my heart warded them off with a shield. At the same time, our conversation on the nature of courage filled me with excitement. One thing was for sure—I was getting more accustomed to her; a woman vanishing from the front seat before my very eyes hadn't even caused a swerve.

I felt different, excited about the path ahead, as I delved more deeply into the concept of courage. I wondered what the word actually meant. Upon arriving home, I got out my old dictionary. Among several in my house, this one was my favorite, because it explained the origins and meanings of words and their roots. Discovering the meanings of words was almost a hobby, certainly a passion, of mine.

"*Courage,* from *cor,* the heart. That quality of mind which enables people to encounter danger and difficulties with firmness." Courage was ultimately strength of heart—a quality from the core of one's being. I looked again at the latest golden ring from Alea and felt the warmth of my own core, as I committed to being courageous throughout my life's journey.

If Matt was the Lion, did that make her the Wizard? Alea laughed out loud at the thought. As Matt's happiness grew, so did her own—she felt more vibrant with the lightening of his spirit. She had waited an eternity for him to know her, and now, not only did he know her, but he was embracing her presence in his life with love!

Matt had found access to his inner resources, but she sensed that he still wasn't completely convinced that they were true and constant, available for the asking. His courage would grow as he experimented with this newfound power. At the same time, he didn't yet fully recognize the true value of courage. Courage is one of the first steps—a core step to be sure—toward self-mastery. Though he wouldn't have thought so, it was courage that allowed Matt to surrender and also to observe himself. Most people never truly look at who they are and what they are creating in the world, because they allow fear to paralyze them rather than lead them into accessing their courage—their strength of heart—and transforming the fear into a courageous act.

She actually knew very little of Matt's future, for many possible futures could take shape from this moment forward. Among them all, courage would be required. Nothing was predestined. Matt had absolute free will and could change the outcome at any time through his choices. All she truly knew was what he had been born to do, his mission, and his capacity for accomplishing it. Her job was to help him to be fully conscious of the things he was remembering. This knowledge would enable him to make the choices that would lead him to his purpose.

She could also respond in the realm of feeling—for love was her domain. As Matt opened his heart to love, she felt him become more whole. Along with "feeling whole" came a sense of being holy, of being one with the divine plan that was operating for the benefit of all.

5

Three Magic Words

I climbed a steep staircase that pointed straight up to the sky. Looking around, I wondered what I was climbing. The stone steps were vaguely reminiscent of a pyramid. Once on top, my heart and stomach met in a spasm as I caught sight of a straight vertical drop, just past the treacherously narrow top step. Teetering there, my only options were to fall off the back side or return down the dangerously steep stairway. I lay down on the top step in total fear of moving, choosing neither option for now. I was terrified, afraid even to look at my choices. I lay there, not knowing what to do. Suddenly I became aware that this was a dream and that I was asleep—what a relief! I felt such freedom, knowing it didn't matter what I chose to do! I took a deep breath, observed my situation with the new information and considered my options. I chose to take my chances and rolled right over the edge, waiting to see what would happen. I wasn't sure whether to be disappointed or pleasantly surprised, as I merely hovered there as if still on the step! I awoke, fully aware of my dream, and lay in bed thinking about how lucid it had been.

The dream made me realize that it had been several weeks since I had experienced anything "unusual." I was actually thankful that nothing of great importance had happened for a while, for I had just let the realizations of the previous month sink in while I restored some semblance of order and routine into my life. I had relaunched my speaking career without anyone else even realizing it had ever been in question. My confidence in teaching was regaining strength, although I still focused mainly on business and entrepreneurial information. I injected the new material whenever possible, stretching my previously perceived limits as often as I could.

Did the dream represent something big looming ahead—a risk or challenge? Wondering, my thoughts turned to the immediate future. The next day, my boys would arrive for a week. Still feeling guilty about the divorce and only seeing them a couple of times per year, I wanted the week to be perfect. I went to the garage and pulled out the sleeping bags, tent, cooler and fishing poles. I loved fishing with the boys. Sitting on a boulder surrounded by beautiful trees and rock walls, the sound of rushing water smoothing out the wrinkles in my soul, the smell of the red earth, and the fresh afternoon breeze all combined to make the number of fish caught or lost insignificant by comparison. The anticipation I felt about spending time together was at a depth that only my kids seemed able to touch.

I picked them up the next day in Phoenix. I couldn't believe how much taller they had both gotten in the months since I had seen them last. It was a little awkward when we first got together after not seeing each other for a while, an uncomfortable mixture of being strangers and being family. I always dreaded the beginnings of these visits. I just wanted to skip that part and get right into familiarity and comfort, but a little trust-building was always needed first.

It seemed as though that awkward stage passed quickly this time; we hadn't been in the car more than fifteen minutes before Tim, my younger son, began telling me everything. I listened as he told me all about school, his friends and the general details of his life. I looked in the rearview mirror at my oldest son, Jerry—now almost a man himself. I knew his adjustment to being with me would take a little longer than his brother's. Wishing for a way to speed things up, I imagined what it must be like for him to be yanked out of his reality and away from his friends. I imagined that he felt some anger toward me for the divorce, too. Being the oldest son, he undoubtedly got the brunt of the man-around-the-house responsibilities. As these thoughts passed through my mind, my heart was simply thankful that the boys were here. I looked forward to reestablishing our relationship.

I soon discovered that Tim was excelling in sports and dreamed of being professional one day. He hadn't yet developed an interest in girls and it was refreshing to hear the contentment in his voice. Loneliness did not seem to be part of his experience. Jerry, on the other hand, seemed to withdraw into music and silence. I could only imagine what was going on in his head. While I didn't think that he had a girlfriend yet, I was sure that the absence of one was weighing on his sixteen-year-old mind and spending a week away with his father was probably not helping his social life at all.

Being a father was not my area of expertise. I loved my boys and wanted to have a relationship with them, but I didn't know exactly how to do it. I was determined to observe myself throughout their visit and continually imagine what the experience of being with me was like for them. I hoped that even in some small way I would be able to begin the healing process with them.

We stopped by the house only long enough to pick up the things we needed, then immediately headed for Oak Creek Canyon—one of their favorite places. I didn't want to face any silent time in the house of "there's nothing to do." I put a high priority on keeping the boys busy. My former wife's complaints passed through my mind. She hated the fact that when the boys came to see me, they had "all fun and games" rather than the day-to-day reality of chores and homework of her life with them. I empathized with her but wasn't willing to change the way I spent our time together. After all, she had opted to move to another state, making my time with them rare. She also had the advantage of having their friends, their "toys" and other personal belongings around to keep them occupied. Our limited time was far too precious to spend on discipline, homework and chores. I hoped that Sarah would understand when they came home with tales of camping, fishing and going to the movies.

We set up camp and made dinner. Sitting around the campfire roasting marshmallows, I watched the reflecting light dance off the boys' faces, changing their appearance from one moment to the next. I wondered who they really were and who they would become. Tim pointed up and we turned our attention toward the firelight dancing with the trees. All at once a star streaked across the sky, bringing that special delight of a shared moment that could so easily have been missed. He looked up at me and asked, "Dad? Do you still go to church?"

"No, Son, I don't. Why?"

"Because we go to church every Sunday with Mom just like we used to. How come you don't go anymore?"

The last thing I wanted to do was interfere with their mother's desire for them to go to church. "Well, I guess I don't go because I haven't found a church that I really like." I waited to see if he wanted to know more, recalling that sometimes when a child asks where babies come from, the parent answers in great detail, while the child would have been satisfied with the simple answer of, "From mommy's tummy."

Tim looked thoughtful, then said, "Why don't you go to the same church we used to go to when we were all together?"

I was painfully aware of my other son's silence, knowing he was also listening for my answer. "I haven't found a church that makes me feel closer to God. I feel close to God sitting out here, watching shooting stars, sitting around the fire with the two of you. I don't mean to say that the two of you shouldn't go to church; I think you should. I just think that when you get older, you may want to go to different churches and listen to the messages of each, so you can choose the one that feels the best to you. I am simply still looking for the one that feels the best." *That was fairly diplomatic,* I thought to myself.

Then Jerry spoke up. "How many churches have you tried?"

I wasn't going to get out of this easily. I thought about all the churches and temples I had gone to, listening intently, wanting to find something to believe in. I remembered all the ministers, reverends, priests and rabbis of whom I had asked questions, in search of answers that made sense to me. I asked, "Who is God?" and had not yet gotten an answer that convinced me. They offered things like, "You just have to believe," or "When you are ready, you will know God."

I had asked, "Where is hell?" figuring that if a place of fire really existed, it ought to have a location, but no one could tell me where it was. Also, no one had yet satisfactorily answered my question as to why I needed to go to church. My questions were simple, yet seemed unanswered.

I responded to my son, "Oh, maybe twenty or so."

They both gasped audibly at the thought of my going from church to church without finding one I liked. Now their curiosity was getting the best of them. I don't think they had ever thought of questioning what was said at church. I am sure they never recognized that they had a choice about what to believe, especially when it came to things like God and the Truth—how could you choose whether or not to believe that? I could hear in my mind my former wife's anger if the boys returned home questioning God and church.

Figuring I had better elaborate, as I saw the boys exchanging looks for reassurance, I said, "I will share my beliefs with you two, but I want you to know that I am glad you go to church and want you to continue. It's just that I have seen a lot of people use religion as a reason to hate other people and judge other people. Wars even take place in the name of God. I prefer to have a private relationship with God, separate from the church—at least until I find a church that makes sense to me."

Jerry asked, "What would make sense to you?"

"Well, that's a good question. I always thought I would know it when I found it, but now that you ask, I guess it would be a church that *loves* God instead of *fears* him. I think people should do good things out of love instead of fear. Like with the two of you—I want you to respect me and do the right thing because you love me—and your mother—not because you are afraid of us or of getting punished. I think God feels the same way about all his children." I surprised myself with this answer, as I truly hadn't thought it through.

Alea's question, *"What is Love?"* crossed my mind, and I hoped that they didn't ask me that as well. I wondered whether Alea was God, or rather, Goddess. I knew this was more than I could discuss with the boys. Telling them that I was wondering if God was a woman—and that I was on a first-name basis with her—would probably destroy the remains of our relationship. I suddenly felt as if I were on that top step of the pyramid, trying to decide whether to roll off or carefully climb back down the steps I had ascended thus far. I chose to lie still for now.

The boys looked thoughtful. We went on with marshmallows in silence for a while, each absorbed in his thoughts, then one by one retired to our sleeping bags.

The week passed quickly, full of hiking, fishing and playing cards. In the middle of a hand of cards on the day before they left, Jerry asked, "Do you believe in God, Dad?"

My heart skipped a beat when he called me "Dad"—he said it so rarely. I answered, "Yes, I do. I'm just not sure exactly what I believe about him." He gave me a look that said, "That is exactly how I feel," but all he did was smile slightly and nod, then turn back to his cards. I was hopeful that all this talk about God would inspire them to seek out the truth and answers to their questions, rather than not believe at all.

We broke camp and returned to the house for their last night with me. We washed clothes, took hot showers and went to the movies. I figured I could soften the difficulty for their mom if I sent them, and their things, home clean.

At the airport, the awkward feeling returned, not the feeling of family reuniting as strangers, but rather as family dreading the upcoming estrangement. None of us said it, but all of us felt it. We knew it would be several months before we saw each other again. I felt as if my heart was being ripped from my chest as I said good-bye to each of them.

I pulled away from the airport thinking of the boys and our conversations of the week. I wondered whether the things I shared with them about God and religion would confuse them or serve them over time. My thoughts lingered on God, and all my questions again surfaced. I heard my son's voice in my mind asking if I believed in God. I had told him that I did, but did I even believe that? How can you believe in something when you don't know what it is? All I really knew was how much I wanted to believe in God and how much I hoped that God was real.

As I wondered, I pulled up to a stoplight. A bumper sticker on the car ahead of me caught my eye, and I read it out loud: *"Let Go and Let God."* I wondered exactly what that meant. *Let Go of what. . . ? Let God what. . . ?* The car pulled away, revealing a second bumper sticker: *God Is Love.* A light bulb went on in my head as I repeated over and over, *"God is Love, God is Love!"* I'm not sure what caused me to connect it all together, as this certainly wasn't the first time I had heard that simple phrase, but it all suddenly made sense to me. *God is Love, Love is God. It is that simple!* A laugh of discovery and understanding surged within me.

I thought of all I had been told about God throughout my life and how so many people fear God. Replacing all I had previously heard with the thought that God is Love, I suddenly saw that what people fear is love. How could this be? Why would people fear love? Was it because they didn't feel worthy? For whatever reasons, people don't believe that they deserve to feel love, and so they are afraid to let God, or Pure Love, into their lives. Perhaps they felt that Pure Love could not love *them*?

I then remembered the first time Alea had appeared to me. She had looked into my eyes with a clarity of love that I had never experienced before. Even though I sensed that she knew everything about me, I still felt her love. Even though it was wonderful, it felt uncomfortable to face myself in the presence of love like that. It is hard for people to believe that others will still love them if they know who they really are—which is why so many people play games and put on a facade that isn't real. I thought how different the world would be if everyone just simply loved everyone else. In order for that to happen, they would have to love themselves first. Otherwise they couldn't receive the love coming toward them; it would be too uncomfortable.

I thought about being judged by God when we die and wondered how we would live differently if we knew that we were being judged by *love!* It would be so simple and clear: Did our actions in life lead toward love or away from love? When you die, you get to review your life in the presence of unconditional love and squirm only in your own assessment of whether or not you deserve love—either way, love just keeps loving you! I then wondered what would happen if you didn't think you deserved this love. This instantly gave me a new definition of hell: Hell is sitting in the presence of total unconditional love and hating yourself because you don't feel you deserve the love—feeling that you are not worthy. It then dawned on me how many people experience hell in varying degrees all the time—through not loving themselves. Self-hate is true hell.

I played with the *Let Go and Let God* statement, replacing "God" with "Love," resulting in *Let Go and Let Love.* I suddenly saw a glimmer of all the things that we let stand in the way of feeling love, of feeling God, and wondered whether that was what we were supposed to "let go" of.

God is Love. I shook my head in amusement at the way truth revealed itself—and hid itself—in simplicity, as I pulled up to the office where my afternoon meeting was scheduled. I had arranged this meeting in advance, since I knew I would be in town, but now my thoughts were not at all on business. I took a moment to get my mind ready for my meeting, then went into my friend's office.

I greeted Tom and went with him to have a late lunch. We ate and handled our business. After our meeting, as we climbed back into his car, out of the blue he asked, "Do you read much?"

I responded, "Yes, I read quite a bit, why?"

"In the glove compartment is a book I think you will really like. You ought to read it."

I reached into the glove compartment and pulled out the book, *Three Magic Words,* by U. S. Anderson. The hair on my arms raised as I skimmed the first page. I knew this book held some of the answers I had been searching for; I could just feel it! I couldn't wait to read the book to find out what the three magic words were. I thanked him, assuring him I would read it right away. We shook hands and parted ways. I then headed back to Sedona with the book on the seat beside me.

I went out on my deck to enjoy the evening and opened the book that intrigued me so. At times like this I was glad I had studied speed-reading, as I felt impatient to learn the three magic words. However, once I started, I found that I wanted to hold onto everything the author said, so I read more slowly. The book held me spellbound as it explained the power of our minds and our ability to create our experience. It spoke of the control we have over our lives and our health.

It held everything I had wondered about; it spoke of evil and illusion, freedom and faith, creativity and intuition. And it spoke of love. It all made perfect sense to me. As I read, I thought surely it held more than *three* magic words—since I treasured each word as sacred. I read into the late hours of the night, mesmerized. This book held what I had searched for in all those churches.

Saved until the last chapter, the three magic words were finally revealed to me. "Chapter Twelve: YOU ARE GOD." I stopped right there and took in a deep breath, then read them again. *"You Are God."* I looked up from the book and out across the night sky. It all made sense. *"God is Everything. God is Love. Let Go and Let God. You are God."* These truths all came into sharp focus, including, "When you are ready, you will know God," which suddenly seemed absolutely true. *All of us are God! All of us are Love!*

My thoughts returned to my new theory on hell and self-hate. If we are God and we hate ourselves, are we hating God? If *God is Love,* then are we hating love? If someone doesn't believe in God, does that mean they don't believe in themselves, and vice versa—if they don't believe in themselves, then they don't truly believe in God? I quietly thought about how I had questioned myself and questioned God, and wondered about this newfound correlation. It seemed clear and simple: *God is Love* and *hell is hate,* whether it is self-hate or hate toward someone else. Judgment against people of other religions is not an act of love, but rather the opposite—a nonloving act. Judgment is *not* an act of God.

I sat outside through the night, putting these thoughts together in my mind. While looking at the stars, I felt connected—to everything and everyone! Almost as if in a daydream, I felt the vastness of the universe—I felt eternity. As if experiencing the entire universe in layers, my attention kept moving in closer to each successive layer, then to the one within that, and then to the one within that one, until my attention moved all the way down to the size of an atom within my own body. I clearly saw an entire solar system in every atom within me—and saw all of it as God, from the most distant of stars in the universe to the tiniest atom, and everything in between. *All of it is Love.*

I felt inspired. I felt clear and strong, loved and loving. It didn't surprise me at all when Alea appeared. I looked into her eyes and saw the universe there as well. I saw Love, I saw God, I saw myself. She smiled and said nothing. Nothing needed to be said.

I woke up the next morning still outside on my deck. I looked around. Alea was nowhere to be seen. I simply beheld the beginning of the day in reverence. I contemplated the night before and how vivid my experience had been. Now, looking out on the sky without the stars adding depth, it seemed closer, smaller, not as expansive, as if the daylight had placed a ceiling on the sky, a limit. I knew I was only viewing one of the many layers that I had "seen," and I wondered whether our awareness was like that, too. We have moments of clarity that allow us to see the whole picture and the immensity of it all, but in our normal state it is veiled from us, so that we don't get caught up in the incomprehensibility of it all—which could take up all our time in trying to make sense of it—like understanding infinity or the system inside an atom. Just as the stars are always in the sky, but we can't see them during the day. They come out at night to remind us that there is more out there than we can see. They are a great reminder; they cause us to think and to wonder.

As I dressed and got ready for the day it occurred to me that meditation is a lot like that, too. It allows us a perspective that reveals our own depth, or rather our limitless nature, which is veiled from us in our normal state.

I had an invitation to join some friends for a late afternoon gathering, so I used my morning wisely, recording everything I had experienced the night before. The day passed quickly as I entered thought after thought in my journal.

I showed up right on time at Jane and Patrick's house. They lived in a beautiful home overlooking Sedona's glorious rock formations. We watched the clouds gather for an afternoon thunderstorm in the distance, a spectacular sight. Five adults, two little girls and an infant *oohed* and *aahed* with each flash of light and clap of thunder. We laughed as the baby's eyes widened with each passing rumble. We then ate dinner on the deck while the girls went into a bedroom to play, taking the infant with them.

I was talking with Patrick about his business when he suggested that we go check on the girls. I joined him, continuing our conversation as we walked down the hall to the oldest girl's room. As we walked in Patrick said, "Hi girls, what are you doing?"

The girls, four and six, held the baby, feeding her with a bottle. The older of the two looked up and answered matter-of-factly, "We are feeding God."

Surprised by the answer, Patrick asked, "What?"

"We are feeding God."

"Feeding God?"

In amazement, the girl looked up at her father and said, as only an innocent child can, "You don't get it, do you, Buster?" She pointed to herself and her friend saying, "This is God." She held up the bottle and pointed to it saying, "Feeding God," and then pointed to the baby and said, "To God! Get it?"

Patrick and I looked at each other in amazement, then at the girls who were now completely back into what they had been doing before we had interrupted.

In light of the past twenty-four hours, it was all crystal clear to me. I was willing to bet that children have less of a "veil" between them and the truth than we have. I was sure that by observing our children, we could more easily discover our own true nature.

I said to Patrick as we went back down the hall, "Out of the mouths of babes! I wonder if we are all born with such wisdom and have forgotten it, or if we've just buried it over time."

Still surprised by his daughter's words, Patrick replied, "It's beyond me! We probably hide it in one of those really safe places. You know, the ones we can't find later!" We both laughed in amusement at human nature.

For the rest of the evening, I shared with him some of the "coincidences" and insights I had been experiencing over the past few weeks. He was a good friend, and I felt comfortable opening up to him. It turned out he had been seeking the same answers I had, which didn't really surprise me. The children had innocently given us the space to talk honestly with each other about our inner lives. However, I still kept Alea to myself.

I returned home to find Alea sitting in my living room. As she greeted me, I realized how much I enjoyed coming home to a companion and wondered whether I would ever get married again. Visions of my previous marriage flashed through my brain, and I immediately pushed the thoughts away. I sat down with Alea and told her about my new understanding of love and God, and my sense of connection.

"I have always heard, 'We are all One,' but I never really understood it until last night, when I actually experienced feeling connected to everyone else. We are all parts of God and God is simply love." I told her about the little girls and how they knew this already. "They saw everything and everyone as God, from each of them to the baby and even the bottle and the milk; they saw those as God, too!"

Alea smiled knowingly and said, *"God is the worshipped, the worshipper and the flowers offered in the worship."*

I nodded thoughtfully, then asked, "Alea—who are you? I mean really, who are you to me?"

She simply smiled again and handed me another golden ring. As I looked for the inscription, she spoke the words, *"Remember You Are God and I Am You,"* and once again disappeared.

She knew he was still confused about who she was in his life, and yet he had to discover that himself, as he must know by now.

She replayed the sequence of recent events in Matt's life, starting with his sons' visit and the questions they had asked, the bumper stickers, the book Matt had been given and his experience with the little girls. She reveled in the synchronicity with which Spirit worked when trying to get a message across. All those things lining up during the course of twenty-four hours were no mere coincidence. The cosmic sense of timing in such matters always delighted her, and she offered thanks for this assistance in Matt's life.

The world is truly a mirror for where we are and what we are going through. She knew that if he had not been ready, he wouldn't have seen the bumper stickers, read the book nor understood the significance of the girl's comments—even if they all had surrounded him, just the same. That was indeed the veil that

Matt had intuited. Our own ignorance veils our sight; our own level of willingness veils our ability to see.

People hold such varying beliefs about religion and God. It is all so much simpler than we have created it. We have brought our egos into a realm where ego does not belong. We judge each other's beliefs and practices, saying, "My way is better than your way," when there truly is only one way—God is love and we are all God. All life is one life. When we hurt someone else, we hurt ourselves. When we help someone else, we help ourselves. When we love someone else, we too, are loved.

She wished that people could see that their true nature is love, for that is why we all are motivated by it, why we all seek it. We are seeking to know our True Selves.

Alea whispered, "I Am Love, I Am Love," over Matt, and felt the warmth and fullness of meaning. We have all come here to discover this truth, to see through the veil. She knew Matt was well on his way; his understanding of this was her mission here.

6

The Illusion

"Thank you! Thank you very much!" I stood looking around as the audience gave me a standing ovation. I had just completed the first day of a two-day seminar and again had touched on love and the importance of connecting people. The participants seemed hungry for this information, and many came up to me afterward to share experiences in which they didn't feel loved or loving. Before, when I had focused only on success and happiness without the spiritual overtones of love, I hadn't realized so many people were in pain. Now I was apparently pushing their buttons, and they all came to talk to me about it. I felt helpless at processing them through their emotions. Something was getting in the way of their feeling loved and loving. I wondered exactly what that "something" was. Was it different for everyone, or could there be some common principle that could help them all? I wished I knew.

After the hall cleared out, I stood there alone, thinking about people and their problems. I thought about the stories they had told me; some were recent, some were stories from their childhood, and some were stories from ten and twenty years before. It astonished me that we could hold onto problems for so long, not realizing their detrimental effect. I considered how a good story had a beginning, a middle and an end. Each of these people's upsets also had a beginning and middle, but not all of them had an end—yet. The phrase, "Forgive and Forget," so commonly heard while I was growing up, rolled through my mind, but now it seemed that people were not able to forgive and forget very well. It was more as if they stuffed their anger and hurt into some kind of holding area, and those repressed feelings got in the way of feeling loving and loved.

I sat in the empty room, thinking about everyone else and all their problems, masterfully avoiding looking at myself. A wave of self-observation washed over me, and I dived in to watch myself from the calm waters below. I asked myself what stood in the way of my feeling love—and why I was so alone. Taking a deep breath, I watched how I kept myself distant from others. In reviewing my life, I saw how reserved I was, letting in only a select few. I thought about Sarah and how she never really knew who I was, even after fifteen years of marriage. In the past, I might have blamed this on her, but now I saw my part in it. I had never *let* her know me. I forgave myself a little with the awareness that I hadn't truly known myself.

I thought about the beginning, middle and end of my problems with Sarah. I could fairly well identify the beginning, although they had built up slowly over time. No single event caused our problems. The "middle" had taken place over about a nine-year period, when I wasn't really happy in the relationship. I sighed heavily at the thought of spending nine years in a relationship that didn't work for either of us. I then tried to identify the "ending" of our problems. I remembered Sarah asking me which choice I would make if I were forced to choose between her and "all this personal growth stuff." Letting her know that I would choose my personal growth over her—if I were offered such an ultimatum—was a definite catalyst to the ending of our marriage. I then realized that the end of the marriage wasn't the end of our problems; we still had challenges to face over the raising of the boys and I obviously was still upset by the whole thing. I guessed that she was, too. I shuddered at the realization that we were still in the "middle." I wanted the "story" to end, at least the painful part.

I slipped out of observation and slid right into feeling sad. Tears welled up in my eyes as I thought of my marriage, my family and my self-created distance. Sensing movement, I looked up to see Alea walking toward me. I preferred it when she caught me in a good mood, so I quickly wiped away my tears. She walked right up and sat down next to me. I was so absorbed in my feelings that I forgot to concern myself with who she was and why she kept coming into my life. In fact, I no longer felt a strong need to know. I was simply glad she kept returning.

Putting her arm around my shoulder, she said, *"Hi."*

I sniffled and returned, "*Hi.*"

"So, what's going on?"

"All this self-observation is kind of painful; I don't always like what I see."

"That's why you needed courage! It's not easy to look at oneself, which is why most choose not to. The idea is not to give you more ammunition for self-hate, but rather to help you see what has gotten in the way of feeling love, and what you can adjust to attain more self-love, more closeness to God." Her voice was gentle as she reached for my hand and held it.

"I know, I should probably just think positively and move forward, but the pain just seems to hold on."

"What are you thinking now?"

"I'm thinking that it's my fault that my marriage didn't work and my family is living in two states. Maybe if I had done something differently, my family would still be together."

"Uh huh, and what are you feeling?"

I took a moment to become aware of what I was feeling. "I'm feeling guilty and sad. My chest is all tight and my throat is constricted."

"So, if you were to 'think positively,' what would you be thinking now?"

I wasn't sure where she was going with all of this, but from past experience, figured I would understand before too long. "I guess I would think that everything is always perfect, and as long as I learned from the experience, it would all be okay."

"Okay, now think those positive thoughts and tell me how you are feeling again."

I concentrated on thinking positively, then checked in with my feelings. "I am feeling the same—only now my stomach is churning."

"So, what does that tell you about merely thinking positively?"

"Well, it doesn't make me feel a whole lot better—in my body, anyway. The feeling is still there. In fact, the feeling intensified, because I added in guilt about feeling this way when I 'should' be feeling like everything's okay. My thoughts no longer line up with what I'm feeling."

"When someone tells you to 'cheer up' when you are sad, it doesn't work—because the effort to change is in your head, but the feelings are in your body. Based on this little experiment, what do you suppose gets in the way of people being more loving—and loved?"

I still wasn't completely sure what she was leading to, but after a moment said, "I guess the feelings themselves."

She nodded.

"So, what do you do about that? You can't just change your feelings like you change your thoughts."

"Why not? What are thoughts made of?"

"Energy, I guess."

"Well, what are feelings made of?"

"I guess they're energy, too."

"Feelings and thoughts are made up of the exact same stuff, Matt. Feelings are simply trapped energy, as tangible as this pen." She held up a pen as she continued to explain. *"All we have to do to feel closer to God, closer to Love, is to let go of the feelings that are in the way. If you just 'think positively' without releasing the pent-up or stuck feelings, then all you are really doing is suppressing them. It's guaranteed that when you suppress your feelings, they will resurface later."*

The bumper sticker, "Let Go and Let God" emerged in my thoughts, and I wondered whether this was what it meant.

Alea added, *"Think of all the stories you have heard about people's problems. What are the common feelings or needs that get in their way?"*

I reviewed story after story in my mind, seeing that acceptance was a big one, as almost everyone wanted others to like and approve of them—be it their parents, their spouses, their children or perfect strangers. I then saw that people also seemed to have a need to approve of others. Either they wanted people to approve of them, or they wanted to approve of what other people did, which expressed itself as wanting to control what others did.

I said, "It seems as if people either have a need for acceptance or a need to control the people and situations around them."

"Exactly! These two needs, the need to be accepted and the need to be in control, form the basis for all conflicts, whether internal or external, for all individuals. Try to think of any upset that cannot be traced back to the need for acceptance or control."

I ran a few scenarios through my head and found, indeed, that they all boiled down to the need for acceptance or control—or both. It seemed fairly reasonable to want both of them, so I asked Alea, "Isn't it somewhat prudent to want control and acceptance?"

"The problem lies in the need, Matt. When people need acceptance from others, they are like vacuum cleaners sucking up attention. Of course it varies in degree, but when it's there, these people are often very wearing to be around. They are almost impossible to accept when they are so needy of validation, especially because they aren't accepting of themselves. When one doesn't accept oneself, it's impossible to hear someone else's approval. People seek acceptance from the outside world but can't receive it until their inside world feels it. It's a vicious cycle. When you need acceptance, you seldom have it.

"The same goes for those who need to be in control. When people need control, they very seldom are truly in control. The more they exert their will on others, the more resistant others become to them. They often match up with acceptance-needing people, because those people want to please and so are more easily controlled. However, acceptance-hungry people often still do whatever they want—but behind controllers' backs, so that they don't lose the acceptance. Consequently, controllers aren't really in control at all, but only have the illusion of control. They are really seeking acceptance and expressing it in their controlling behaviors.

"It sounds complicated but is really quite simple. When people let go of the 'need' for acceptance, they gain the acceptance of others. When they let go of the 'need' for control, they gain true power. By letting go, they inherit the freedom of the present moment, a freedom to choose and act from a place of certainty and confidence rather than fear. This freedom is quite literal, for—when freed up from the mental, emotional and physical energy that has been bound up by the ego-needs—one's actions and surrounding events, and one's perception of those

events, take on an 'effortless,' almost magical quality—a flow. The need for acceptance and the need to be in control are ego-driven. When you really look at this, you see that what everyone wants is to either be approved of or to approve of others—otherwise stated, to be loved or to love. Love is not an ego issue, however, so when we approach it from an ego-driven state, we actually block love rather than realize it. Self-realization, knowing our divine nature, is the solution at the root of this paradox."

I tried to make sense of all she was saying, but could only assume that it would all become clearer to me as we proceeded.

She went on, *"So let's get back to your feelings. Do you still feel them?"*

"Yes." I still felt constriction in my chest and throat.

"Do you like feeling that way?"

Surprised by her question, I answered, "No."

"Do you think this is about your need to be in control or your need for acceptance?"

I decided that guilt was undoubtedly about a need for acceptance. I wanted Sarah and the boys to forgive me. I wanted to forgive myself. "Acceptance," I answered.

"Do you want to let it go?"

"Yes."

"Are you willing to let it go?"

I wanted to say "yes" right away but found myself a little hesitant. Feeling guilty and sad had served me in some ways. For one, it had protected me from getting involved with someone else, from risking hurt and pain again. I suddenly saw that guilt and sadness gave me a reason for staying alone. If I let these go, I wondered, what would happen to me? I concluded that whatever happened could not be worse than what I was already going through.

Alea gave me the few seconds I needed to think it through, then asked again, *"Are you willing to let it go?"*

This time I answered, "Yes."

"When are you willing to let it go?"

All the possibilities for when I might be ready to let the feeling go passed through my mind. Unable to identify any time better than the present, I answered, "Now."

She instructed me to close my eyes, focus on the feeling in my body, take in a deep breath, then release it.

I followed her instructions, taking in a deep breath and letting it go. I felt the constriction in my throat and chest lessen.

"What are you feeling now?"

Observing myself, I said, "Lighter, less constricted, but I still feel tightness in my throat."

"Good, let's do it again. Close your eyes, focus on the feeling, take a deep breath and release it."

Again, I followed her instructions. This time, the tightness dissipated completely. I no longer felt sad or guilty. In fact, I started to laugh. I couldn't believe how much lighter I felt!

After a moment of enjoying the absence of the feeling, I asked, "So what just happened?"

"As I already mentioned, feelings are just energy. What happens when we have an upset or conflict is that the energy gets trapped in our body, and we feel it as pain or discomfort. No matter how much we 'think positively,' it doesn't go away until we consciously let the feeling go and return to our natural state—which is one of love. You see, Matt, 'thinking negatively' comes from feeling negatively. If we change the way we feel, our thoughts will automatically change, as a reflection of what we feel."

I asked hesitantly, "Will it come back?"

"Probably not, but if it does, just observe it and let it go again—and again if necessary, until it is gone for good. It's like peeling away the layers of an onion. Simply observing what you are feeling peels away a layer, in and of itself. Just keep peeling away the layers, until you get to your core—love. Then, once you let go of the feelings that have gotten in the way of love, you will be able to respond with love in the present moment, from a state of full awareness. In this state, you can more easily observe yourself, interpret the warning signs and guideposts along the path, clarify your intentions and put love into action. This ability to respond is immensely different from merely reacting to situations out of unconscious, ego-protective needs.

"Letting go requires three things, Matt: intention, willingness and commitment. The three questions I asked you stated those requirements: 'Do you want to let it go?' 'Are you willing to let it go?' and 'When?'"

Her eyes crinkled as a little laugh escaped her. *"What do you suppose is required to hold onto the feelings that get in the way of love?"*

After a moment, I realized that she was laughing because letting go and holding on required the exact same things. "Intention, willingness and commitment!"

"Yes. However, holding onto them requires a lot of energy, while letting go requires no energy at all, only choice. Funneling one's energy into holding onto all the upsets takes so much energy that one ends up having little left for creating loving feelings in new situations. To return to our natural state of love, to who we really are, all we need to do is let go of the non-loving feelings we have stored over time, or that we create in the moment. Love is our natural state, Matt—everyone's natural state. There is no way to 'get' love. The only way is to 'be' love. Love is not an emotion; it is a state of self-awareness, an understanding of our true nature and the true nature of others. The way to have more love is to reveal your true nature, by discovering who you are not and letting that go."

I remembered a story I had heard about Michelangelo. When asked how he carved the statue of David, he told the inquirer, "I created a vision of David in my mind and simply carved away everything that was not David." I could see that Alea was outlining a similar process: Know who you are—love—and carve away everything that is not love.

Alea nodded as she heard my thoughts. *"Well, it is getting late, and you have another day of the seminar ahead of you. Remember this process; it will help you to help others."* She smiled and laid her hand lovingly on my cheek. Shivers rushed up and down my spine.

She then added, *"Matt, about your relationship with Sarah, consider that often our difficulty is in losing our vision of what we wanted the relationship to be, rather than losing the relationship itself. Often, losing what you had is not nearly as difficult as losing what you wanted. If you find this to be true, you will see that what you miss didn't exist; it was an illusion, and so is the basis for your pain. You have not been in pain over what you lost, as what you lost was a relationship in which neither person was happy. Rather, your pain is over your need for acceptance regarding the steps you took to make the changes that needed to happen. Now that you are letting go of your need for acceptance, you will see that others accept you more than you ever thought. We are all linked together. When one lets go, the others feel it and respond—even if they live in another state. In fact, the whole world responds, and you will find that miracles happen. Trust me. Try it; you will experience what I am talking about."*

In the time it took me to blink, she was gone. I gathered up my things and went across the street to eat dinner. I sat down in a booth and read the menu, my mind still going over all that had just happened. I thought about Alea's insights. She was right; my previous relationship was not what I was missing. I realized that instead I was missing a healthy, loving relationship, in which both people felt supported and happy. I decided, in that moment, that I was ready for such a relationship to come into my life. I didn't want to be alone, and I didn't want to just keep dating anymore.

I couldn't help but wonder about Alea. She was everything I wanted. I felt such a sense of familiarity with her and I was beginning to expect to see her show up, hardly even questioning her presence anymore. I fantasized about spending my life with *her. How could she be the woman for me, if I don't even know if she is real?* My rational mind dismissed the thought as quickly as I had conjured it up.

I looked across the restaurant to see a redheaded woman who was attending the seminar looking at me. She stood up and walked over to my table, saying, "Hi, I'm Betty. I really enjoyed your seminar today. Do you mind if I join you for a few minutes?"

I replied, "Go right ahead," welcoming the distraction from my thoughts.

She waited while I ordered dinner, then began telling me her story, how she and her mother weren't speaking to each other and how upset she was about it. Betty explained, "Every time I make an effort to get in touch or call her, she either doesn't return my call or hangs up on me. I just don't know what to do. I heard what you said about love today in the seminar. I want to clear this up with my mother so I can feel loved and loving again. This is getting in the way of my other relationships."

"How long has it been since you and your mother spoke?"

The woman looked forlorn as she answered, "Twenty years!"

The questioning look I had on my face must have made her feel that an explanation was in order.

"You know, it was the usual: 'Mother doesn't approve of daughter's choices in men.'" She laughed slightly at how common her problem was. "I went off and married a man my mother didn't like and worse yet, moved to another state. She told me then that she would never speak to me again if I left with him." Exasperated, she added, "So far, she's kept her word."

I was again shocked at how people hold onto issues and upsets for such a long, long time without healing them. I imagined how painful it would be to spend so many years in turmoil. The process Alea had led me through was fresh in my mind, so I decided to try it, hoping I could remember the steps. I asked, "What do you feel in your body right now, as you think about this?"

She answered, "I feel sick to my stomach and pressure around my heart."

"Do you like feeling that way?"

Betty looked as surprised as I did when Alea asked me the same thing, but humoring me, she answered, "No, I don't like it at all."

"I have discovered that all conflicts can be traced back to either a need for acceptance or a need to be in control, or both. Which do you think this is for you—a need for acceptance or a need for control?"

She had obviously never been asked that before, much less thought about it. She considered, then replied, "I think I have a need to be accepted. I want my mother to speak to me again. I want her to like me, if not love me."

I wondered whether there wasn't a little need to be in control mixed in—wanting to control how her mother felt. I could see how closely related the two needs actually were, as both led back to a need to love and be loved.

I said, "Well, I don't know exactly what this will do for your mother, but I do think it will help you to feel better, whether or not you ever get to speak to her again."

Ultimately, I figured that it was more important for the individual to feel healed and loving than for a relationship to continue. Some relationships are just plain toxic. As I saw it, getting the individual out of the non-loving feelings was more productive. So I asked, "Do you want to let the feeling go?"

She again looked at me oddly but answered, "Yes, I do."

"Are you willing to let it go?"

She sighed heavily and said with conviction, "Yes, I am ready and willing!"

"When?"

She thought it over for a moment, then answered, "Well, now, I guess—yes, now!"

I told her to close her eyes and focus on the discomfort in her stomach and heart, then to take a deep breath and let it go, allowing the trapped energy she was feeling to dissipate. After a few deep breaths, she said the feeling was gone. "There is no trace of it left!" She sighed contentedly and thanked me for my time. Just then the waitress brought my dinner. Betty said she would leave me in peace to eat and would see me at the seminar the next morning.

As she left, she said, "Thank you again. I truly do feel better!"

She sounded surprised, still not sure of what we had done that could make her feel better. I wasn't totally sure myself, as the process was new to me too, but I was glad it had at least helped for the moment. I felt a little skeptical that it had worked so well so quickly and wondered if it were always as simple. The only tangible evidence that anything had happened was that her face looked much more relaxed.

After dinner, I returned to my hotel room to make a couple of calls and take notes on all I had learned. I felt the time nearing to begin writing my new book. I wasn't sure yet what to call it, but knew that the principles I was learning, the ones on the golden rings, would be included. I turned to my journal and wrote until my eyelids would no longer stay open.

The next morning, I showered, dressed and grabbed some breakfast in the hotel restaurant before heading off to the seminar. I wanted to get there early to set up a couple of things before the people arrived. When I pulled up in front of the hall, Betty was waiting for me. She looked excited, yet I couldn't imagine why she had come an hour early to class. She greeted me enthusiastically with a hug. "Good morning! You will never believe what happened!"

I smiled a little tentatively and asked, "What?"

"Before I tell you, what time do you think it was when we spoke last night?"

"Well, the seminar was over at six o'clock, and I stayed for at least an hour before going to the restaurant. I would guess 7:30. Why?"

Smiling, she said, "That's the exact time I came up with, too. Listen to this! I got home around 8:15, and there was a message on my machine from my mother! She said she thought it was about time we spoke and healed the problems between us! The best part, Matt, is that the call came in at 7:40, just minutes after you helped me to let go!"

I stood there in shock. We hugged again, as I wondered if this is what Alea had meant when she said that miracles would happen. I thanked Betty for sharing her story with me and went in to set up for the day. As I arranged things, I wondered if this had to do with us all being connected. Alea had said that others would feel it when we let go. This certainly appeared to be evidence of that! It was hard to imagine as "just a coincidence," though part of me wanted to think so.

I greeted folks as they came in, and before I had a chance to start with my agenda, Betty stood up and said she had to share with everyone what had happened. As she told her story, I looked around. Some people were crying, others shifting uncomfortably in their chairs and still others looking at me as if I had just performed magic. I noticed a woman was crying just a few rows back. She sat slumped in her chair as if she carried the weight of the world. As I looked over at her she hesitantly raised her hand and quietly, almost pleadingly, asked, "Can you help me, too?"

I was suddenly aware that I was being pulled into processing these people's emotions in front of the room instead of one on one. I felt nervous, which I immediately recognized as my need to be accepted—my need to do it "right." I took a deep breath and let it go, choosing to trust the process.

I answered, "I'm not sure, but I will try. First, tell me your name and what seems to be the problem."

After introducing herself as "Sue," she started telling a story that soon had almost everyone in tears. As she spoke, I realized that she had a black eye concealed by makeup. The more she spoke, the more

I saw the bruises on her arms and the finger marks on her neck. She told us about her life: "I have been in six abusive relationships, three of which were marriages. The guy I am with now keeps beating me up, and for some reason I keep taking him back. I have been in this relationship for two years now, and I can't seem to get him out of my life. I don't know what to do. He won't leave. Every time I ask him to go, he beats me up." She stopped talking and just sat there crying, gripping her chair with one hand; the other trembled as it partially covered her face. Everyone turned and looked at me expectantly.

I asked her, "What are you feeling?"

She answered, "I feel scared. I'm all shaky."

"Do you feel anything else?"

"I feel pain in my neck."

I was very aware of the expectant eyes directed towards me from all over the room. I explained about the need to be in control and the need for acceptance, then asked her, "Do you think this is about your need to control or to be accepted?" I saw it as a severe need for acceptance but knew she must identify it for herself.

She wept again before replying, "I guess it's a need to be accepted. I keep taking him back because I want the love."

Alea's words of the previous night ran through my mind. Sue was mourning the potential loss of her vision of what she wanted, rather than the actual relationship. She, too, was protecting the illusion of a loving relationship rather than the reality of what she had.

I asked, "Do you want to let go of the feelings that are getting in your way?"

Her voice was nearly inaudible through her soft sobs. "Yes."

"Are you willing to let them go?"

She hesitated and then answered, "Yes, I think so."

Not convinced, I asked again, "Are you willing to let them go?"

A sigh shook her, as air forced its way into her lungs. "Yes."

"When are you willing to let it go?"

"As soon as I can."

I asked again, "When?"

"When he leaves."

The audience must have known where I was going, as they all looked anxious for her to see her own procrastination.

I asked again, "When are you willing to let it go?"

This time Sue realized what she was doing and answered, "Now."

I saw her body straighten, and the hand shielding her face dropped to her side. Audible sighs of relief could be heard around the room.

I led her through the process of breathing and releasing the energy, then had her check back in on how she was feeling. She answered, "I still feel shaky, but better."

I then asked her, "Which do you honor more—your fear or your peace of mind?" I wasn't sure where the question came from, but decided to trust myself and just ask what felt right at the moment.

She answered, "My peace of mind."

I led her again through the process of letting go. Then she said, "I don't feel it anymore. The pain in my neck is gone!"

Everyone laughed at the correlation of her boyfriend and her "pain in the neck." I was surprised at the change in the appearance of her face. She looked ten years younger than when she first spoke up. Her whole posture had changed: she was more erect, less hunched and definitely more relaxed.

I explained what I could to the group. "Trapped feelings are what get in the way of our knowing who we really are; they keep us from feeling love. If we observe ourselves, identify how we are feeling and let it go, we return to a positive state."

An older man in the back row raised his hand and asked, "I am afraid that if I let go, there will be a void. If I let go of my anger and hurt, what will be left?"

This had not occurred to me before. In light of all I knew and all I had been learning, I explained, "When you let go of the non-loving feelings, you aren't left with a void; you uncover your true nature. Love fills the 'void.'"

I managed to get back to my agenda from this point on and gave them the pearls of my knowledge about marketing and business. I wanted to continue exploring this "letting go" process, but didn't want to spend the whole day on it. After all, that wasn't what they had paid for, and I wanted to think it all through a little more before I taught it at greater length. I released them all for an hour-and-a-half lunch and went alone to a small restaurant to give myself some time to prepare before the afternoon session.

When we all filed back into the room, I thought I was experiencing déjà vu as Sue came bounding into the room, full of enthusiasm. She was a few minutes late, so most of the participants were back in their seats when she came to the front of the room and said, "You'll never believe what happened!"

I stood there anticipating her next remarks, wondering what could make this woman, so broken earlier, look so happy. She announced to us all, "I went home for lunch because I live near here—and he's gone! He packed up all his things during our morning session and left! All I found was a note saying he would never be back!"

I had never seen anyone so happy about breaking up before. She declared, "I can't believe it! All I had to do was let go of my need to be accepted, and he no longer had someone to control!" She turned and looked at me, and said, "Thank you so much!" Then she turned to the audience and said, "Thank you all so much, too!"

We gave her a standing ovation. As I clapped, I felt in awe of the power of this process. I had seen two "miracles" in twenty-four hours! I could hardly believe that it worked so well. I finished out the afternoon agenda with ease, and we adjourned feeling closer to each other than any other group to which I had ever spoken.

As I walked to the car, I felt Alea behind me. I turned to face her, smiling. She laughed, knowing that I knew she was there. With a hug, she said, *"I am so proud of you, Matt. Not only have you let go of your own feelings; you immediately used what you learned to help others."*

"I couldn't believe it, Alea. It was like magic. Thank you for helping me with this," I said sincerely.

"You are welcome. You should know that people won't always want to let go. You will come across some who simply aren't ready yet and would rather hold on. When that happens, you will need to let go of your need for control and move on." She smiled, then said, *"Don't become attached to the outcome of what you do. Just as love gets blocked by ego, your ability to do this work can be blocked by your ego, if you are not careful. Simply do what you feel is right, and*

be willing to stop if someone is not ready. When they are ready, they will find a way to let go, or rather, it will find them."

With a little lingering disbelief, even though I had witnessed it myself, I asked, "How does this work so fast? It almost seems like those miracle healings. It is hard to believe, Alea. How can one person let go, and the other shifts too? It doesn't make sense to me."

She explained, *"When you are angry, it affects other people's attitudes, right? When you are happy, it affects other people, too, yes?"*

I nodded in agreement.

She continued, *"The same thing happens when you experience a need to be in control or a need for acceptance. It affects and influences the people around you. They respond to you based on your attitude."*

"I can understand how, when you are in the presence of another person, they can be affected by your needs, but how does it work when people aren't even in touch with each other?" I asked with interest. I felt that once again I was coming close to an important piece of whatever puzzle it was that Alea and I were putting together.

"We are all connected, Matt. This is hard for one in a body to truly comprehend, but our physical connection is not the only way we are connected. Have you ever had the experience of thinking of people only moments before they call you?"

She went on while I nodded. *"We feel each other on much more subtle levels than just physical energy. When those women you worked with let go of their need to be accepted, the people from whom they needed the acceptance felt the shift on a more subtle level of connection, and it allowed them to make new choices in response to the new circumstances. We can't change people directly, but when we make changes within ourselves—energy changes—other people change in relationship to us."*

What she told me made sense; it was, barring unlikely coincidences, the only explanation that could account for the experiences of both women. I could see that the power of letting go was immense.

With that, Alea disappeared. I opened the car door, and there on the seat lay the next golden ring, beautifully engraved with the words *Let Go.* I picked it up and held it for a moment, feeling again so honored with each one of these gifts. Every time I received one, it marked some sort of milestone. I thought about what she had told me before: *"All together there are twenty-one, but the first seven form the seed."*

I counted in my mind. The first one had been *Surrender*, the second was *Live Each Moment*, the third was *Observe Yourself*, the fourth was *Be Courageous*, the fifth was *Remember You Are God and I Am You*, and this one, the sixth, *Let Go*. My heart skipped a beat as I realized that the next one would be the seventh, completing the "seed." I had no idea what that meant, but it seemed to me like a milestone among the milestones. I felt sure that once the first seven were understood, the seed would be planted and true growth would begin. Continuing with this gardening theme, I laughed at the thought that what I had been going through was only "ground cover."

Feeling that I had just counted my blessings, I wondered what was in store for me next. I could not get Alea off my mind and drove back to Sedona consumed with thoughts of her.

Alea was happy for Matt and delighted in watching his unfolding. Reflecting on all he had learned this weekend, she knew that letting go was one of the most important lessons to date. She was quite satisfied with the increasing level of his understanding. He had surprised even her with his willingness to share the process in front of a group so quickly after learning it. She could see that letting go of his need to be accepted would serve him in many ways.

Regarding the two women he had worked with, she marveled at what people endured in a lifetime—and how long they held onto their painful feelings. She considered what else Matt should know to help people with problems such as these; she wanted to be sure he deeply understood this process and she reviewed various elements of it for herself.

Matt had been right, when it comes to conflicts between two people, it is more important that the individuals heal than the relationship stay together. What we often fail to recognize is that we attract to us the exact people who will shine a light on what we need to work on. People with a need to be accepted attract people who need to be in control, and people with a need to be in control attract people who need to be accepted. The woman with the abusive relationships kept attracting abusive men because of her need to be accepted. The people who were attracted to her had a need to be in control. They were a perfect match—perfect in that each partner would allow the other to see, if they were self-observant, what they needed to let go of.

If we are attracting controlling people into our lives, it is a sign for us to let go of our need for acceptance. If we attract people who need to be accepted, it is a sign for us to let go of our need for control. The people in our lives serve perfectly as mirrors for us and point the way to the next steps in our growth.

In any event, the two needs are closely related, often intermingled, as they are actually just opposite sides of the same coin—in essence, the need to love and be loved.

This concept is really so simple. She knew that Matt would soon begin to understand that feelings are trapped energy created by repetition or an event that causes a significant impact. Words carry power, and when uttered with repetition or impact, they create feelings. Pure feelings are based on events taking place within a particular moment. However, over time, feelings are no longer pure but become mixed up with old, trapped feelings. Buried feelings get triggered when similar events take place or similar words are said, propelling the trapped energy into motion. When trapped feelings are triggered into motion, they create emotions—energy in motion.

Alea contemplated how we overreact to certain events or react more strongly than a situation seems to merit, due to this triggering effect of old feelings mixed up with present feelings, causing an emotional reaction. These emotions, in turn, support our beliefs. Often people try to change their beliefs by changing their thoughts, which isn't effective. Beliefs can be changed through releasing the feelings; once feelings are released, the beliefs go away. People can then return to experiencing true feelings in the moment, rather than the emotions that were created due to the triggering of old feelings.

The best way to explain it to Matt, should she need to, would be to compare beliefs and thoughts to bricks in a wall and feelings to the mortar holding the bricks in place. If you dissolve the mortar, the bricks will fall out of the wall.

Thus, when a painful issue comes up, one simply needs to ask: What am I hanging onto that causes me to feel this way? The steps are to first feel the feeling, then become aware of the feeling, observe the feeling, let go of the feeling, and finally, respond—from being present and aware—instead of react. This is quite different from what most people do, which is simply feel the feeling and then react—with no awareness or perspective, while still stuck in the feeling. By letting go of the painful feelings, they gain the opportunity to truly respond to the present moment.

Matt was becoming more and more aware of his inner wisdom. Soon she wouldn't have to explain these things to him at all; rather, he would begin to trust his intuition, which would allow him to simply know.

He had made it through the sixth gift. One more, and he would attain the seed, which would allow him to teach the concepts with true depth. He had awakened quickly!

Alea watched him as he drove back to Sedona, holding the sixth golden ring in his hand. She shared the warmth he felt and gave thanks for their closeness.

7

The Visitation

After arriving home, I lay in bed thinking about Alea and all that was unfolding. *Who was she? When would she come again?* I chuckled, realizing that I was almost completely comfortable with this woman materializing and disappearing in my life. It was becoming normal to me, expected rather than questioned. The why and how were no longer as important to me as the continued experience of her appearing. Though I still wondered about her, the joy she brought into my life and the wisdom she brought out of me far surpassed my curiosity. I drifted into sleep feeling content and excited about life.

The next morning, I sat at the computer to begin formulating all the notes and thoughts I had recorded into an outline for my book. I wanted to send Cindy something before she gave up on me completely. After considering the title for several minutes, I decided it could wait until I had a clearer picture of the book's contents. I knew it would be a self-help book that explained how to implement the concepts I was learning, but I wasn't sure how long it would take me to master and understand them well enough to fully share them with others.

Writing, preparing presentations and wondering when Alea might appear again filled my time for the whole week. Just as I finished a rough outline for the sixth chapter, the phone rang, delivering a pleasant surprise.

"Hello?"

The voice on the other end cheerfully said, "Matt? This is Nan."

It took me a minute to put the name and voice in context with Nan from Kauai and Santa Barbara, as it had been a while since we had spoken. I expressed my joy in hearing from her. "What a pleasure! How are you?!"

"I'm doing really well. I finally got my pictures back from the trip along the Na Pali, and I have some of you. I decided it was high time to connect with you and find out how things are going."

"I'm really glad you did. I feel like I've been going through a wonderful time of accelerated growth, which began just before you and I met and hasn't let up since!"

She was silent for a moment, then said, "Yes, yes, I see," in such a way that I felt as if she truly did see—and I recalled her psychic abilities.

Curious, I asked her how she had discovered that she had a psychic gift. She told me a story that disclosed the uniqueness of her early childhood. "Well, when I was little, I used to have dreams of things that really happened—like plane crashes and other disasters. It used to scare me a lot, but fortunately for me, I was born to a mother who honored intuition and the sense of knowing. She told me not to be afraid. She said that one day I would see this as a great gift that would give deeper meaning to my life. She was right! What I found out when I grew up is that often people receive disaster dreams because those have a 'louder volume' than more subtle psychic information. If one takes these dreams as a sign and develops the gift, a whole world of information can open up, information that can be useful for helping people on their journey here."

We were both silent for a moment, then she said, "Matt, I sense that you have a clear channel to your intuition, but you don't trust it. Let me ask this, if you don't mind: Have you spent a lot of time looking for answers outside yourself instead of inside?"

Once again I felt totally exposed, which ordinarily might cause me discomfort; however, lately, when exposed by the truth, I had felt invigorated and refreshed. I answered honestly, "Yes. I have searched for truth in thousands of books and many churches. I have even consulted a few psychics, but the answers just weren't in any of those places."

My thoughts turned to Alea, and I wondered whether the whole experience with her was another attempt to look outside myself for answers. Rarely, however, did Alea give me answers; more often than not, she simply asked the right questions. I was suddenly torn between wanting to tell Nan all about Alea to see what she thought, and wanting to change my thoughts before she could read them.

She went on, despite my considerations, "You have access to a lot of guidance, Matt. We all do, but I sense yours is very near, very close to you. It seems like you are beginning to trust in the guidance, but that you are not so convinced that it is your clarity, your intuition, your strength and power that are bringing that guidance to you. Everyone has guidance available to them; everyone can develop their intuition, but not everyone is ready. If your ability to perceive subtle information is working, Matt, know that you have achieved a readiness, and focus on developing it!"

I had to contain my laughter at the thought of Alea being "subtle." There wasn't much subtlety about a beautiful woman appearing before me and peppering me with profound questions that changed my life!

Nan interrupted my thoughts by adding, "I don't mean to be doing this spontaneous reading on you. It is just that my intuition told me to call you, and now I am feeling strongly that you need to look deeper at who you are. There is so much more to you than meets the eye."

I took in what she said, then asked, "Nan, if information comes to you in a, well, kind of mystical way—from an apparent outside source—is that the same as looking outside of yourself for answers?" I knew I wasn't being very specific, but I just wasn't ready to reveal my interactions with Alea.

Nan read between the lines and answered, "You must always look at the outside source, whether mystical or physical, and ask yourself a few questions. First, does the source of information empower you, or does it try to create dependence on itself? Second, how do you feel after receiving the information? Pay attention to how you feel in your body. Does the information ring of truth? If you feel an inner strengthening and peace of mind, listen. If you feel like you are dependent on the other for information on what to do next and how to do it—then be watchful. Plenty of souls are 'out there' who might love to pop in on us and be listened to, but they may be no wiser than the guy next to you on the bus. When true guidance comes to you, you will feel loved unconditionally—whether you accept the guidance or not.

"Third, ask yourself if the message delivered is one of love or of control. Does it help you to love yourself and others more, or just to love the source of information more? If the guidance passes these three tests, then know that even though it appears to be from an outside source, the inside work necessary in order to be ready to receive it must be honored as the force behind the experience. Guidance would not come to you if you were not able to receive it."

What she said made perfect sense. Even putting Nan herself to "the test," I could see that the information she offered turned the power back over to me. She was telling me to trust myself, that the answers were within me. I replied, "Isn't it the same in any relationship, Nan? I mean, if you get involved romantically with someone and give your power to them or create dependence in them—it will be unhealthy. The idea is to love unconditionally, not to create addictions and feed needs."

She replied, "Good point. I hadn't really considered applying the same 'test' to my romantic relationships!" She laughed out loud, then continued, "I hope this represents my readiness to do relationships differently! You may have shown me just what I needed to see!"

It made me happy to think that we were both benefiting from this conversation. The thought crossed my mind how funny it was that we were both single, able to communicate well, and we enjoyed each other's company, but neither of us were drawn to the other romantically. It felt good to have a friend like this, with no expectations.

We swapped stories for quite a while longer, when she announced, "My gosh, Matt! Look what time it is! We've been on the phone for over an hour already. I'd better get going or we'll be on all night."

Looking at my watch, I answered, "That sure went by fast! It's great to talk with you, Nan. Any chance you'll be heading to Sedona soon? Have you ever been here?"

"I have passed through once. It was beautiful! I'd love to come and spend a little time exploring there. I hear it's a pretty spiritually charged place!"

"There are few places like it on the planet. I would love to see you. You're welcome here any time," I said honestly.

I could tell she was looking at her calendar as she spoke. "Let me look at my schedule and see what I can do. I'll call you back in the next couple of weeks and set a time to visit, okay?"

"Great. I'll be looking forward to it."

After we hung up, I wondered what she would think if I told her about Alea and the golden rings. I couldn't imagine keeping it a secret if she were right here in my home. I felt so comfortable with her, so trusting. She definitely passed "the test." I felt loved, empowered and peaceful. I headed off to the kitchen to fill the only void detectable in my being.

From the refrigerator, evidence that I was a bachelor stared back at me as I shuffled through condiments and inedible remnants of take-out meals. Nothing of substance presented itself, so I got my coat and keys and went in search of dinner. I decided to treat myself to a nice sit-down meal, since I had worked hard all week, rather than just hit the deli at the health food store, as was my normal routine. I sat at the bar, not wanting to take up a whole table for just one person, silently wishing that Alea could join me.

Shortly after I ordered dinner, a couple came in and sat down next to me. I welcomed the company, and we got into a conversation. After about ten minutes, they asked, "What do you do?"

I answered spontaneously, surprising myself with my own answer, "I help people to let go of their ego-driven needs and have more love in their lives."

Just then, someone grabbed me by the arm and tugged on my shirt. I turned to find at my elbow an older man dressed in faded overalls, a red plaid shirt and an old felt hat. The stubble on his face looked as if he hadn't shaved in a couple of days.

He said, "Hey, buddy, you want to talk about ego?"

I replied, "No, I'm busy," and wondered what he was doing in this place, especially dressed that way, since it was a fairly expensive restaurant.

I turned back around to continue my dinner and conversation with the couple.

He tugged again. "Hey buddy, let's talk about ego."

Trying not to be rude, but a little annoyed at the interruption, I said, "No, thanks. I'm talking with these other people."

He persisted, and I finally said, "Okay, what do you want to say about ego?" I was reluctant to talk to him but figured that maybe if I humored him, he'd go away. He didn't look dangerous or anything, just a little odd. He was more the type you might meet on a street corner or a park bench feeding pigeons. Encountering him in the luxury of a well-appointed restaurant was a bit strange, but then, given the present circumstances of my life, this was a minor weirdness. At least he hadn't asked me to buy him a drink.

He returned my question with another. "What do you think ego is?"

I thought for a moment, wondering why he had wanted to talk to me so urgently. "I think ego is past programming that we hold onto and allow to control us."

He looked thoughtful and said, "You're close. Our ego is the *collector* of our past programming, rather than the past programming itself."

Curious in spite of myself, I asked, "Would you explain that?"

"You see, in order to be born into a physical, human form, the being must have some sense of self, of 'I,' in order to function in the world, to safely interact with that which is outside its body. The ego has the very important job of protecting us, including storing information that may prove useful later in protecting us from harm or pain."

I was intrigued. Here was this strange man in funny clothes, pulling on my arm asking to speak, and once the dam was opened, a deluge of ideas, *interesting ideas,* came pouring forth, catching me off guard and sweeping me downstream with them. Another strange and welcome occurrence in my newly eventful life.

The flow kept coming. "What has happened is that the ego, this aspect of the mind fed by the senses, has gotten out of control. Instead of serving our true Self, the soul, and allowing us to see all the issues that come up around us as opportunities to love, or to wake up our souls and realize our true nature, the ego has come to believe that we are only the body and the mind. The ego has taken this sense of 'I' in the wrong direction, thinking now that to be human means the physical 'I' rather than the spiritual 'I.' This has created a separation, a duality. Now, instead of protecting the soul while it's housed in a physical body, the ego protects itself. The ego has become ignorant of its own true nature, and in its ignorance, it fights to hold onto its position, this mistaken belief. It believes it is a physical being that may or may not be seeking a spiritual life, when it is, in actuality, a spiritual being experiencing a physical life."

He went on as I attempted to catch my breath, awash in the torrent of words. "Since the world around us is also veiled in this ignorance, the ego-sense constantly collects data and evidence that validates its existence and its sense of self-protection, and it stores this data as past programming. Our society provides constant feedback for the ego to store. Each event that separates us from others becomes the past programming that the ego refers to when making its case. When we suffer an emotionally impacting experience or are bombarded through repetition with experiences or words that identify us with our physical being or our small self, the ego gets confirmed in its stance. Every event in which we have felt powerless, hurt or wronged is food for the ego's ignorant belief that we are small instead of powerful beyond measure. Each of these stored events separates us further from the truth, further from our true Selves.

"The ego with its past programming is like a stomach that must be fed, and emotional distress is the food. It feeds on anything that makes people believe they are the ego, rather than their true Self. The ego has taken its job so literally that it has simply forgotten its own true nature. For example, suppose you ask a man who he is, and he tells you he is a janitor or a doctor. He identifies himself in this way with his job, rather than his true nature. The ego, in ignorance, has done the same thing."

I sat there, absorbing everything he said, by now floating with the current of the flood waters and enjoying the ride.

He continued, "Self-observation and awareness awaken the soul and activate it. The inner stirring that an awakened soul creates is hard to ignore. The problem is, having spent such an extended amount of time believing that we are separate from others, separate from God, we tend to search everywhere outside ourselves for happiness and bliss. The ego has a hard time letting go of its illusion and clings to its position of control. It fears extinction, it fears being wrong, it fears the unknown. The soul is so powerful, so unlimited, that it frightens the ego, what with the ego's strong identity with limitation and physical form."

Every time I thought of a question, he answered it before I could open my mouth. Everything he said made perfect sense. His physical appearance and old clothes were misleading. I made a mental note to observe how often I prejudged people without giving them a chance. I saw how my own ego and judgment got in my way.

As I listened intently, he continued. "The unobserved ego, in its ignorance, makes people think that they are the ego; it keeps them from knowing their true Selves."

I understood. "So the key here is knowing that we are not our ego?"

He smiled, his teeth startlingly white against his skin and his eyes mirroring his smile. Suddenly this somewhat seedy-looking man seemed beautiful, full of light. "This is true—and one of the main things people are here to remember."

He explained, "People easily remember everything that was ever said to them about what they did wrong or how they somehow weren't enough. These memories are the evidence collected by the ego, which feeds on these negative beliefs, holding onto and remembering them forever, unless we consciously let go of the feelings that hold these beliefs in place. When we remember the truth, we begin to view all events from the perspective of our divine nature, which is unlimited, rather than through the filter of the ego, which is limited.

"What people don't often realize is that the 'positive' events in life are also taken on and stored as ego-beliefs. Even the 'nice' things that are said to us are stored by the ego, if they feed the idea that we are separate from others. It blinds us from knowing that we are all one, just as much as the 'negative' data does. If someone calls you 'good'—

well, good compared to what? Compared to whom? The very notion of being good or bad separates us from others. The ego keeps us from knowing our true nature, knowing that we are all of one absolute source—which is God, Love. The point isn't whether we are *good* or *bad.* The only true question at hand is whether or not we are loving, or living according to the God–current within us.

"Also, what if someone tells you that you are good when you aren't doing your best? Will you stop at that level of performance, rather than stretch your abilities? World records are broken only because someone didn't allow the belief that 'the best' was truly the best. Even our 'positive' beliefs can limit us when we believe them and close ourselves to other possibilities."

I thought a bit, then asked, "In saying we are all one source, would an example be, oh say, ice cubes; they come in all shapes and sizes but are all made up of water, all the same substance?"

"Yes, precisely. God is love, and we are all love. Anything that separates us from ourselves and each other—and therefore from love—is ego-based. Even religion can do this, which of course is hard for the religious to believe."

I clearly saw the truth of what he said—religion has become so ego-based that we fight wars over it, killing other people in the name of God. I suddenly saw the *ignorance* of ego as the evil that religions refer to, for that ignorance causes us to do unloving things, hate ourselves, and be jealous and destructive. The ego causes us to be driven to attain more, be anxious, live out dramas and be constantly in pursuit, never believing that we have enough or are enough.

In contrast, it is the nature of our true Self never to be disappointed and always to know that we are in the right place at the right time—to be sensitive, calm, certain of our power and direction, confident, trusting and centered. Well, there is no choice. I far prefer the idea of living in awareness of and alignment with the true Self.

I could also see how our ego holds onto our "positive beliefs" and limits what we consider possible. Even beliefs like those found in many religions could narrow our minds and keep us from being open to new thoughts, new information—and thus hold us back from our own spiritual growth.

He then continued, "Did you know there are only six ego dramas in the world? People think their drama is unique to them, but there are really only six, and we keep rerunning them in endless variations. They are: relationship dramas, health dramas, money dramas, career dramas, family dramas and spiritual dramas. That's about it; everyone's issues fit into one of those.

"Ego stores these subconscious programs as energy trapped in our bodies, which we then project onto the outside world. We see only what we project. We see only through the filters we have created and we continue to experience what we project, until we let the stuck energy go. We think the world is out to get us because it keeps presenting us with the same dramas over and over. What we don't realize is that we are projecting those dramas, seeing the world through ego-colored glasses; we create our experiences. If we don't observe our egos and let go of the beliefs and feelings that we are holding onto, then we end up experiencing what I call *'Internal Bodily Turmoil,'* which just gets worse and worse. We get more deeply entrapped in blame and pain.

"When we don't observe and recognize the ignorance of the ego, we try to change our beliefs by changing our minds, our thinking, which is not where the problem lies. The mind is the direction-chooser, whereas the feelings are the energy stored in the physical body. What we need to do is observe what we are *doing and feeling* and let the energy go, instead of suppressing our feelings. This frees up the physical body, releasing pain from it at the same time. When we do this, it leads to what I call *'Universal Energy Flow,'* or the continuous, uninterrupted flow of love."

My mind was racing to keep up with him. I felt my heart pounding and knew that my ego was reacting powerfully to this information. I had the passing thought that this might mean his words had sneaked past the ego's barriers and reached the real me. "So, you are saying that through observation of the ego, one can actually see ego as an ally; it is really one of our greatest gifts, because it reveals to us that which we need to let go of. Without the observation, though, we get stuck, and the ego simply continues in its ignorance, keeping us separate, unhappy or in pain."

He nodded as I spoke. We then sat in silence for a moment. I observed this old man in his red plaid and overalls, thinking he was one of the most enlightened people with whom I had ever spoken. We both sat quietly in thought, and then he looked right into my eyes. The whites of his eyes were like snow, the blue of his irises clear and vivid. My heart was touched by his look as he said, "You don't know who I am, do you?"

"No, I don't," I stated honestly.

He touched my hand, and a tingling energy raced up and down my spine as he said, "Yes, you do. You remember."

I responded, "No, I don't."

He said quietly, yet powerfully, "I want you to keep one thing in mind: the Archangel Michael is watching over you." He touched my shoulder, and again I felt the jolt from his touch. I was stunned.

Just as I was about to ask him who the Archangel Michael was and why he was watching over *me*, the couple next to me tapped me on the shoulder and said good-bye. I turned to them briefly and when I turned around again, he was gone. I looked around the room; he was nowhere to be seen. I sighed deeply. All these disappearing people in my life were more than challenging to my rational mind. I had just been getting accustomed to Alea's comings and goings, and now this. Could this strange, wise man be the Archangel Michael in disguise? I searched my mind for any information I could have stored on the Archangel, but drew a blank. I decided to go home and search my personal library to find out more about him. I wondered whether anyone else had seen this man, or if in some odd way I had been hallucinating. Considering Alea's way, which I now accepted so nonchalantly, I worried that this might be a new psychological pattern developing in me. While fascinating, I just couldn't realistically call it very healthy. On the other hand, it seemed to be doing me so much good, for I certainly *felt* a lot healthier—or was that just part of the pattern? I needed a major reality check, but how could I define "reality"?

Just then the bartender walked by, so I asked him, "Excuse me, did you notice whether anyone was sitting next to me?"

He just gave me a funny look and said, "Yeah, I guess so," and then went on with his business, leaving me to draw my own conclusions. Well, that was sure helpful. I wondered if my ego was so into this mystical stuff that I was now projecting it everywhere. It didn't seem like an act of the ego, though, because I felt closer to my true Self than I ever had before.

I drove home, mentally replaying the incredible visit with Michael, wondering what life had in store for me next. I planned the next few days' activities, placing researching Michael and the ego at the top of my list. This topic fascinated me, and I wanted to know more.

I checked my messages as soon as I got in. There was one from someone named Daryl who had founded a nutritional supplement company. A mutual friend had given him one of my videotapes on marketing. He was interested in meeting to discuss contracting me to do training for his company. I wrote down his name and number and made a note to call him the next morning.

Before going to bed, I searched a few of my bookshelves for possible sources of information on Michael. I had a library of nearly four thousand books, so I resolved to continue looking through the rest of them the next day. I found a couple of books I thought might have what I was looking for and took them to bed with me. I read until I fell asleep, finding nothing on Michael.

I woke to the sight of the sunlight bouncing off the beautiful red rock walls surrounding my home. I lay there for a few minutes giving thanks for my life and all that was happening in it. Feeling joyful, I headed toward my bookshelves to resume the search for information about Michael. I read for hours in book after book, but none of them contained anything about him. I then got on the phone and called all the people I could think of who might know something, but none of them knew about Michael either. He seemed to be a well-kept secret. After a few more attempts, I gave up.

As part of my weekly ritual, I called my boys to see how they were doing. I loved them but didn't enjoy talking to them by phone, because it seemed to make the distance between us seem bigger. Not being able to see their faces made reading their short, one-word answers to my many questions difficult. Our displeasure at being apart rarely seemed to be eased by phone calls. I was sure that having their mother standing in the room listening, and then having to undergo a barrage of questions when they hung up, didn't help either. We made some plans for their next visit before saying good-bye. I hung up the phone, wishing I knew a way to heal the time and distance between us.

Returning Daryl's call from the day before, but reaching only his secretary, I left a message and went to work on my book. I wanted to be sure to record all of the ideas discussed with the man from last night. I wondered whether he was actually Michael himself. The more I replayed the situation in my mind, the more that seemed to be what he had implied. In any event, I began to think of the mysterious man as Michael, for want of an actual name.

My thoughts were interrupted by a return phone call from Daryl. He started the conversation by telling me he had only a couple minutes but he had wanted to return my call. We then proceeded to talk for two hours about our philosophies on marketing and business, the needs of his company, and how my consultation could help him. We held complementary viewpoints, and our conversation stirred both our creative minds. I shared my background and experience consulting with different companies, after which he asked if I would be willing to fly halfway and meet him in San Francisco. We made plans to do so the next day.

After hanging up, I returned to my bookshelves, thinking that if I couldn't find information on Michael, I could at least do some research on ego. I was curious about what different religions had to say about it, considering what Michael had said about ego and religion. I picked out several books and skimmed them, searching for definitions of ego.

I started with the dictionary, which described ego as, "the self as separate from others and reality." This struck me as fascinating; even *Webster's* knew about the illusion created by the ego. I continued my search, summarizing each definition in my notes.

I discovered how one spiritual master had defined ego: "Ego is the cause of separation between man and his true nature. By letting go, one awakens to his true power and true identity." This perfectly confirmed what Michael had said. I read on.

A book of love and spirituality stated, "Ego is fearful thoughts that create a parallel universe that doesn't actually exist. It has a life of its own and it will fight to survive."

One book on Zen Buddhism declared, "The ego is nothing more than a set of ideas, trapped within consciousness, that supposedly helps us occupy socially-defined roles. The memories are our false identity that create a gravitational pull against our true nature."

Each confirmed the other. They all said the same thing when you distilled the messages down. I wondered why so many people didn't see the obvious similarities among their religious faiths.

I then turned to a Bible translation, which aligned nicely with the others. "By dying to what once bound us, we have been released from the law . . . of attraction. . . . This law is always at work. . . . When you want to be good, evil is right there with you." It referred to the ego as "the sin living within."

Suddenly, I was struck with an understanding of what was meant by the idea that we are all sinners. It hadn't made sense to me before, because I saw people as good, as made in God's image. But now, in light of this new perspective on the ego, I could see how the ego in its ignorance, which is common to all people, could be seen as a "sinner." It seemed to me ironic that people who believed in this concept were close, but just slightly off track, because they still identified themselves and all humanity with the ego. If we are not our egos, we are not sinners. We are love. *The sin is the ignorance of the ego, separating us from that love.* The ignorant, unobserved ego is the evil about which we are always warned. This is what causes self-hate and hatred of others, and *this* is the "sin," because hate is in exact opposition to our true Self, our true nature of love. The unobserved ego is the very thing that causes self-hate. This reinforced my previous understanding of self-hate and the hatred of others as hell.

Yet another source defined ego as "edging God out." All these concepts were suddenly connecting for me. Again, I felt as though I was receiving pieces of a jigsaw puzzle one at a time, with no idea of what the finished picture would be. With each piece, the complete image grew clearer, but it was still in a process of emerging.

I continued my search, fascinated by what I found. A book on

Shamanism noted, "Whenever one experiences emotional distress, it stems from the ego or past memories. When you let go of emotional distress, you harmonize with the energy around you." I saw the recurrent theme of *letting go* in the different passages I read. It appeared that all of the different religions, at least those that I had looked up, were in agreement with Michael's theories. Again, I wondered who Michael was—and what he had to do with me.

By 10 o'clock the next morning, I was flying to California to meet with Daryl at a restaurant near the San Francisco airport. We spent hours getting to know each other and strategizing for his business. He explained his specific needs, and I outlined what I could help him with, how to avoid certain pitfalls and how I might assist in turning around certain attitudes that were sabotaging the success of his company. He told me his beliefs about his products and what they could do for the world. It was far more vital than mere nutrition. He had a vision of being instrumental in feeding the world. He told me that the expansion of his company was more than business; it was humanitarian. His products were designed to be totally balanced nutritionally. He claimed that wherever the body needs this superior nutrition, it goes. He professed that some people even had spiritual breakthroughs when they took it. I was a little skeptical, but in light of the last several months of my life, I opted to stay open-minded.

I felt drawn to something in this man; he had a sincerity about him and a gentle, calm wisdom that seemed authentic. The meeting was not only effective, but also very satisfying. Before we parted ways, he asked me to write a proposal and get it to him right away, so we could begin working together.

Just as we were about to depart, he turned to me and said, "If I sent you a book, would you read it?"

I said, "Sure, thanks."

He smiled and said, "Great, I'll send it as soon as I get home." With that he said good-bye.

As I flew back to Phoenix, my soul yearned to see Alea. So much had happened since I had seen her last. I wanted to share with her all that I had discovered. I wanted to share *everything* with her. How could I bring her to me?

The drive home passed quickly as I watched the full moonlight dance upon the rock sculptures, making them come alive and rendering my surroundings holy. I wondered when I would see Alea again, what the seventh gift would be and when I would attain it. Would Michael be a part of the seventh concept? Perhaps I had already realized the next truth! As I drove down the highway, I recounted Michael's conversation with me to see if I could concisely state what I had learned, so that when Alea appeared, I would be prepared. I determined, as I walked to my front door, that if I were to distill the entire conversation the message would simply be, *"I am not my ego."*

I went to bed and immediately fell asleep. Deep into the night, I dreamt that someone knocked on my door. When I looked out through the peephole to see who it was, all I saw was an eye, magnified, looking back at me. I was frightened at first and wanted to look away, but I kept on looking. The eye held my interest, even though it scared me. The deeper I looked, the less scary it became, and the more fascinating and intricate. I saw the beauty of the soul of this unknown being, who only moments ago had frightened me. The depth held me mesmerized. As my eye blinked, so did the one staring back at me, until I finally realized that the eye looking at me was merely a reflection of my own. I was looking into my own eye—into my own soul!

The dream was so symbolic of all I was going through. What a perfect example of how our egos project what we experience! I diligently wrote the dream down, along with the connections that I saw between it and all I was discovering. The more I wrote and reflected on it, the more meaning the dream took on. My own eye, looking at me, symbolized self-observation, which was certainly frightening at first, before it became fascinating. The illusions and dramas we conjure up are comical, once we are able to see what is really going on.

I felt that the eye also symbolized the realization that judgment comes from ourselves, not God. We think that God reviews our lives and looks at us with his scrutinizing, all-seeing eye, but in the end we discover that it is our own eye that judges us, while God simply loves us. The dream and its multiple meanings stayed with me into the day, long after I had written about it in my journal.

At midday, an overnight express package arrived from Daryl. Opening the package, I pulled out two bottles of his supplements. I immediately took a few from each bottle, eager to see what would happen.

At the bottom of the box was the book Daryl had promised to send. I wondered what was so important in this book that he wanted me to read it so badly, but for the moment I placed it on my nightstand to read later. I got busy working on the proposal for him. I wanted the contract to do training for his company, both because I knew I could help him and because I wanted to get to know him better.

After working into the evening, I went for a walk. The moon was still large and made the whole world appear magical under its light. Noticing that I felt more energetic than I normally did at this time of night, I wondered if it could be a result of eating the supplements. It felt good to walk after so much sitting, reading and writing, not to mention the sedentary time in the car and the plane.

As I strolled, I enjoyed the interface between my body and the world around me. My skin tingled as it touched the cool evening air. My feet felt as if they were playing a drum as I walked. As I took a deep breath, my lungs rejoiced in the expansion and release, while my nostrils flared as they inhaled the heavenly scents of juniper and sage. Every part of my body seemed to call to me and in listening I realized how long it had been since I had worked out. The message to me was clear: my recent resolve to have more balance in my life must include taking care of my body. The decision was made; tomorrow I would join the gym and start working out regularly.

As I walked back to the house with my new resolution, I wondered why Alea had not returned. Her absence was beginning to make me doubt that she had ever been real. Why would she come and then leave and not come back?

When I went to bed, the book Daryl had sent beckoned me from the nightstand, but I decided to read it in the morning and fell asleep. In the middle of the night, I sat straight up in bed as if I had been awakened. I looked around, but no one was there. I tried to go back to sleep, but I couldn't. The strongest urge to read Daryl's book nagged at me. After several minutes of lying there sleepless, trying to ignore the urge, I gave in to the calling, turned on my light and picked up the book. Opening it to the first chapter, I couldn't believe my eyes.

The whole chapter was about Archangels and described Michael and his mission on the planet! I hadn't mentioned anything about Michael to Daryl. Why had he sent me this book?

I read, absolutely fascinated. *Archangel* meant *Radiant One Who Has Achieved Great Responsibility.* The chapter explained that Michael is the Archangel in charge of watching over the soul volunteers who have come to Earth. He is here on the planet now to wake up the volunteers he has sent, to set them on their paths so they can fulfill their missions. The volunteers are here to bring God's seeds of life, beauty, peace and compassion—and sow them. Michael is here to help them with their training and protect them as necessary. The urgent situation on the planet right now, the book explained, is due to billions of people being out of emotional control. Our pattern has become unstable due to the misuse of free will. The Archangels are coming in to help us return to a peaceful, harmonious state. Michael is especially focused on strengthening people, helping them get involved in personal and planetary transformation. My heart sped up as I read about him. I remembered the words, "The Archangel Michael is watching over you," and wondered why. What did it have to do with me? Was I one of Michael's volunteers?

"What do you think? Or, more important, what do you feel?" she asked quietly.

I recognized Alea's voice but couldn't see her anywhere. I said out loud, "Where are you and where have you been?" Smiling, I added, "And don't stay away so long next time! I have a lot to talk to you about!"

She laughed at the scolding. *"Matt, don't you know by now that you don't have to see me to talk to me?"* She then appeared at the foot of my bed. I still wanted to know how she did that.

I didn't answer her question, but instead launched into telling her all about Michael and meeting Daryl. I felt like a kid coming home from school to tell my mother about everything I had learned and all the new kids I had met. She listened politely, even though she looked as though she already knew everything I was telling her. She shared my excitement, anyway.

"So, tell me about what you discovered with Michael."

This part I had rehearsed: "I am not my ego."

"Wonderful," she said, *"now tell me what that means to you."*

She always had a way of pulling me out of my head, which was where I had rehearsed, and into my heart, which was where I knew what I was saying.

"I see now that the ego thinks we are our small, weak self, when actually we are our true Self, our strong, calm, powerful Self. When we don't stop and observe our egos and what we are doing, we spend our lives believing and identifying with the ego, instead of aligning ourselves with our true nature. The unobserved ego cannot be trusted, because of its ignorance. The ego holds onto our mistakes as proof that we are not divine or holy, but rather, 'only human' and in need of the ego's help. This ignorance of the ego leads a person into desperation and hopelessness and away from the realization that we need not feel that way, that it is not our nature. If we observe ourselves and our ego-driven needs—the need to be accepted and the need to be in control—our ego has nothing to hold onto, and we are left with the truth—the source of who we are—love."

She nodded and asked again, *"What does that mean to you?"*

Asking me this for the second time jogged me abruptly. I suddenly saw how I allowed the "teacher in me" to distance what I knew and taught, by generalizing things and stating them as if they were true for other people—that is, "people" in the abstract—as opposed to really, actually, physically for me. I took a moment to search my heart for what this all meant to *me,* and I simply said again, this time from a place of knowing rather than thinking, "I am not my ego."

Smiling, she asked, *"And what do you feel Michael's mission here has to do with you?"*

I wanted to believe I was one of his volunteers, but I couldn't bring myself to say so. I wondered if this, too, were a trick of the ego. I answered, "All I know is that I want to help him with his mission. I want to help bring peace, harmony and love to the planet." As I heard my own words, I realized that it didn't really matter if I was a self-appointed volunteer or a "Michael-appointed" volunteer—as long as I was committed to doing the work.

She ceremoniously gave me the next golden circlet, which was engraved with the words *Know You Are Not Your Ego.* She then said, *"Just as the Archangels have achieved great responsibility, Matt, you too, with the acceptance of this, the seventh piece of the Master's Key, have a great responsibility. You have earned the seed of life, and with this knowing, you must take what you know and share it with others, not from a place of ego, but from your heart. You must plant this seed. If you do so, the seed will grow and your wisdom, love and sense of peace will grow along with it. As you share what you know, helping others to do the same, the vibration of the planet will raise from one of fear and hatred to one of love and harmony. Your mission will be fulfilled."*

With the earning of the seventh gift, I thought about how Michael's job was to bring the seed of life to the planet. As I held this precious gift in my hands, I felt honored and willing to accept my responsibility. As we sat in silent contemplation, I heard Alea's inner prayer. I recognized it as Saint Francis' prayer but had never heard it recited so sweetly, and never before had it meant so much to me. Tears flowed as I heard the prayer's meaning as one of letting go of ego and identifying with our true loving nature. I knew Alea prayed it as much for me as for herself:

"Lord, make me an instrument of Thy peace. Where there is hatred, let me sow love. Where there is injury, pardon. Where there is doubt, faith. Where there is despair, hope. Where there is darkness, light, and where there is sadness, joy. O Divine Master, grant that I may not so much seek to be consoled, as to console; to be understood, as to understand; to be loved, as to love. For it is in giving that we receive, it is in pardoning that we are pardoned, and it is in dying that we are born to eternal life."

This discovery was so important that she had to be sure he knew it in his heart, not just his head, before she released to him this piece of the key: Know you are not your ego. She shared his enthusiasm with delight, knowing that enthusiasm comes from the root words, "En Theo" meaning "In God." The

joy of his discoveries represented a further thinning of the veil between him and his true Self.

The ego is a difficult thing to teach someone about, as the ego itself blocks the incoming information. Consequently, the information often has to be repeated over and over again before it gets through, if it ever does. So often we resist hearing about it, letting the ego get in the way. The ego keeps us believing that everything small and trivial is important, keeping us angry and holding onto issues, possibly for lifetimes, rather than letting these shadows and shackles go and returning them to Source, to Love. This is the ego's misdirected attempt to protect us, to keep us from experiencing the same hurts and pains again. Unfortunately, the very act of holding onto these feelings and beliefs causes us to experience the pain again. The ego, in its ignorance, will build people up, only to leave them flattened. By thinking that our beings are bound by the limits of the ego, we are robbed of hope and confused about who we are and what we are here to do. This is the only evil we have to contend with; it is all internal, not some outside force. It is a trick of our own psyche. Alea wondered if Matt would see the similarity in the words "veil" and "evil."

Without an understanding of the nature of ego, it is easy to get trapped. The ego, in protecting us, convinces us that someone or something else is responsible for our actions and our situations. When we lay blame outside of ourselves for our problems, we look outside of ourselves for solutions. Thus we are convinced that we are powerless, limited. We often look to the wrong sources for help. However, each of us is responsible for our own energies and thought creations. When we accept our responsibility, we can achieve true solutions. With an understanding of the ego, we have choice. With an understanding of choice, we are truly powerful. We can choose not to participate in drama. We can choose to be loving and loved. We can choose to make a difference, to help others through our example. We can identify our sense of "I" with our true essence. We can see truth.

Once the ego is observed, we can help it to redefine its role as protector of the physical being, which embodies the spiritual being. The ego can be trained to record and store the evidence that surrounds us everywhere, that we are Divine Beings, spiritual in nature. The "electric current" of God-ness, of Love, runs through all beings. Matt had accepted these truths with the honor of the seventh gift and the completion of the seed of life.

Alea was happy to see Matt make a commitment to his physical being, as this magnificent system allows us to experience the totality of creation that surrounds us. This is certainly not something to take for granted. She knew, all too clearly from her perspective, what a treasured and honored gift a body is! It is the tool through which we are able to dance through life, mingling with the world around us, and of course, entwine joyfully with each other. It is the manner through which we deliver our love and experience our greatness. Certainly, this is a blessing to respect. She sighed deeply with the thought that many people take better care of their cars than their physical bodies. To one who knew her well, a twinge of longing might have been detected in Alea at that moment, as if a memory had awakened, a taste for which she yearned.

She wondered whether she should reveal more about who she was and the purpose of her visits. She didn't want Matt to get so caught up in his "past" existences that he pulled attention away from the present. Yet she knew that the lifetime they had shared and the pain experienced then had been instrumental in closing his heart. As his heart was now opening again, the possibility of remembering the pain also opened up. If those memories were revealed, would he close back down in the face of the pain? This was a risk she could not afford just yet. She sought guidance within. The answer came almost immediately: "Free will—let him discover it of his own free will."

8

Simplicity

I awoke after basking in a night of feeling Alea's presence. I was disappointed, though not surprised, to see no trace of her in the room. I mused, *If this is her version of playing hard to get, then I need to let her know she should "let it go!"* Something about Alea I couldn't quite put my finger on. She felt so familiar, as if I had a memory of her but couldn't remember the details, as though she were someone I knew but couldn't place where or how I had connected with her. The boundary was fuzzy between knowing her from long ago and knowing her in the present moment. When I saw her now, the familiarity I felt could have been centuries old or merely the several months that I could pinpoint on a calendar.

I thought about the night I woke knowing Alea's name. How did I know her name? Why was she in my dreams? I laid the seven golden rings out before me and wondered what they were for—besides being a gift of honor. Alea had said that they were more than symbols, that there were twenty-one of them, but these, the first seven, formed the "seed." I could not begin to imagine just what would be planted with this seed, but I had the feeling it was me who was going to continue growing. *Oddly,* I thought, *I do kind of feel different.* The only way to describe this difference was a sort of peace of mind or strength that I hadn't ever felt so deeply before. I picked up each ring and read its message. Uttering each out loud magically transported me in my mind to the moment in which Alea had presented each one to me. *"Surrender, Live Each Moment, Observe Yourself, Be Courageous, Remember You Are God and I Am You, Let Go, Know You Are Not Your Ego."* It felt good to read them, to *know* them at my deepest level, at least my *currently* deepest level! I seemed to be discovering depths beyond depths these days.

What had Alea said? I must master these steps in order to fulfill my purpose here? I reread each again and considered myself with each. I couldn't say that I had mastered the truths, but I had definitely found ways to apply the discoveries in my day-to-day existence. The more consciously I worked with these concepts, the more naturally they came to me. Especially "letting go;" that had seemed so complicated at first, but now it was as simple as observing my need for control or acceptance and releasing it with a breath.

An overwhelming wave of gratitude for Alea came over me, and I found myself wishing that I could do something for her. She seemed so selfless, so without needs, as if she were simply in service to—me? No, her service was bigger than just me. To God? To sharing these gifts? I suddenly wondered whether, when she left me, she appeared in other people's lives. Perhaps she was the "Johnny Appleseed" of personal growth! I laughed at the thought while picturing her out scattering the "seeds" all over, knowing that not everyone who received them would actually embrace the opportunity to sprout, to endure the growing pains. I wondered whether, if I were to wear the rings like bracelets, I would run into others who had received the same gifts.

At first I didn't like the idea of Alea sharing her love or this "seed" with others. I wanted her just to love me and for all her gifts to be mine. On second thought, however, I took a deep breath and let that notion go too, as love does not grow when the seed is held tightly in one's hand—away from the light. Still wanting to do something for

Alea, I sensed that all she really wanted was for me to understand and embrace my own growth—to ensure a good crop and to eventually become the farmer, helping her to spread the seeds. Satisfied for now, I carefully gathered up the treasures, placed them in a special wooden box on my dresser and turned my attention to more immediate tasks.

As I ran errands around town, I found myself looking at everyone, wondering if any of them were Michael's volunteers or Alea's "little sprouts," as I affectionately named them. The image made me chuckle. I wondered how I could tell them apart—as if they were members of two separate gangs. I searched people's faces, looking for signs. Did volunteers look different? Did they have some kind of identifying mark? Perhaps they all wore felt hats, like Michael wore in the restaurant, as a sign. I observed the heads bobbing past me. Did the "sprouts" wear Alea's golden rings as bracelets? I cast covert glances at the arms of passersby. I felt like a third-rate, B-movie detective and laughed at my own thoughts, trying to imagine the gang warfare between two groups such as these, outdoing each other in spreading messages of love. I saw visions of Cupid's arrows being shot from Michael's troops and love light beaming out of the eyes of Alea's forces, zapping people into wakefulness. The silliness overwhelmed me. People turned and looked at me as I laughed out loud, only to find me smiling as I stared back in search of their allegiance.

The irony was that we were probably all Michael's volunteers or Alea's sprouts, but perhaps we weren't all ready to wake up to the task. I couldn't help but think about myself, wondering where on the continuum I fit in. Which was I? Were they fighting for my "membership"? The thought amused me. I thought about what Michael stood for and all that the man in the restaurant had said. I believed in his mission and felt ready for the task, but couldn't quite imagine that this Michael thing was for real. Perhaps, I decided, it doesn't matter whether it was real or not. The mission was a good one to be committed to, no matter who the guy in the restaurant was or what he said. But then there was Alea and she, of course, had my allegiance, after all she had done for me!

As I pondered Michael's message and the things that had transpired in my life with Alea, I tried to sort out the difference between them.

Their messages were so similar. What had the book said?—that Michael was *"here to wake up the volunteers . . . who were here to bring God's seeds of life, beauty, peace and compassion, and sow them!"* Suddenly, I saw the "volunteers" and "sprouts" as one and the same! Alea and Michael were in cahoots!

The next thought hit me heavily. "Why were they both interested in *me*?" I wasn't sure I was ready to go where this question was taking me, so I drove home, trying not to see myself as a pawn in some divine chess game.

I walked into the house to the sound of the phone ringing.

"Hello?" I answered.

"Hi, Matt, this is Cindy. Remember me, your agent?" she said sarcastically. "I just thought I ought to check in with you to see how you are doing."

"Hi, Cindy. Things are going great. I've been working on the book outline and proposal. I will be getting it to you soon."

"Great, tell me about it," she said bluntly.

Letting go of my need for acceptance with a deep breath, I paused only for a moment as I put my thoughts together. "Well, as I told you before, I am writing a 'how-to' self-help book similar to the other, but this one will start with my story and share how I realized that what I was teaching wasn't complete. I am going to tell the reader about the day I woke up feeling empty, surrendered to realizing the truth and threw away my original manuscript." I took a deep breath, thankful that I felt strong in the knowledge of what I was saying.

Her silence was like the calm before the storm. I waited while she prepared her tactless speech. Matt, you don't seem to understand. Don't you see that by displaying your emptiness, you are doing a disservice to your adoring public? I know that motivational speakers are just people like everyone else, with perhaps more experience or at least speaking talent. I think the public knows this, too; however, they don't want to see into the glass houses of the people they believe in. They don't want to be reminded that their faith in these people is built on a fantasy, any more than they want pictures of Marilyn Monroe in curlers without makeup. I mean, really, don't you see that coming out and saying that you woke up one morning and threw away everything you had been teaching is going to make people question everything they have learned from speakers—not just you, but everyone? Don't you think this could cause more harm than good? After all, all things considered, it's better for them to have *something* to believe in. I would hate for your book to cause people to look at all speakers as unstable or to question their reliability."

I listened in amazement as she sang this all-too-familiar refrain. She reminded me of an ostrich hiding its head in the sand, while the rest of its body stood above ground in plain view. I shuddered to think that anyone would advocate keeping people oblivious or believing in fairy tales. The thought flashed through me that many of our world's leaders based their actions on that exact premise, and this idea abruptly saddened me as a personal revelation of the world's pain.

Choosing my words carefully, I responded, "First of all, by sharing what happened to me, I am not making any kind of statement about the validity of other speakers' material. In fact, I believe that what they teach is very important. The only problem is that in order for people to take the material and apply it in a meaningful way, they have to get rid of the old belief system, before they can add a new one. I am going to show them how to let go of the old stuff so they can better receive and apply the teachings, making them even more valuable.

"Secondly, people can grow from other people's experiences. I consider what happened to me to be a great blessing, and if sharing it with others causes them to wake up too, then I feel like my blessing has been multiplied. What you are suggesting is that we be a part of feeding people's ignorance and keeping them in their illusions, rather than educating them with the truth. I know that what I have discovered will help people know their true essence and will bring greater joy into their lives. If I don't tell them my story, they too may get caught in the same misunderstanding that I did. I don't want to contribute to their ignorance; I want to contribute to their enlightenment."

Cindy responded, sounding a little disgusted or perhaps embarrassed. "Oh, Matt, you are so idealistic. I think maybe your ego is greater than your wisdom. You really think you are going to change the world, don't you?"

I had to laugh out loud, comparing this conversation on ego to the one I had had with Michael. All I could say was, "Cindy, I don't know if I am going to change the world or not, but what I do know is that I must share the truth of my experience. I plan to help people learn how to let go of their illusions and dramas, rather than support them in maintaining them. This, my friend, includes you. If you and I are going to work together, I need to know that you are in support of waking people up to the truth and helping them to attain their highest and best good. If you simply want my book for the money and want to feed people's sense of being victimized and helpless, then we need to rethink whether we should be working together."

The silence on the phone was louder than before. I added, "I think you are a very talented agent, Cindy; I appreciate the support you've given me throughout the time we have worked together. I need you to know that I do take this work very seriously, and I would like you to as well, if you are going to sell it. Perhaps the best plan is for you to read the proposal and see if it makes sense to you. If you like what you read, then we will continue. If you don't, well, we will remain friends, but not work together. What do you think?"

She sighed heavily and then answered, "Okay. I will read what you send, and we'll treat it like a new manuscript requiring a new contract. I will let you know whether or not I will represent your work, or whether you should seek representation elsewhere."

"Thanks. I will let you know, too."

Taking another deep breath, I sent a silent prayer for her heart. I said in closing, "Cindy, I really do appreciate your help and your concern. Thank you."

She didn't sound convinced when she said, "Thanks, I'll be looking for your proposal. Bye."

"Bye." I held the phone in my hand, wondering how this would turn out. I could see how Cindy had to hold her position in one sense; she was an ambitious agent with a lot of talent, pushed on by the quest for money and happiness and rising rapidly in her profession. What I was saying would cause her to reevaluate her own personal mission and purpose, something she didn't appear ready to do right now.

I suddenly saw the complexity of presenting my work to the world. Just as Alea had told me that I wouldn't understand the lessons until I was ready, I could see that those who weren't ready simply would not understand what I was teaching, either. Cindy couldn't allow herself to embrace this subject, because right now her whole life was built on the very issues I was challenging.

This new awareness brought into focus the necessity of creating a process so simple that virtually everyone would be able to embrace at least some aspect of it. I could see how letting go was a huge part of that simple process, yet I sensed that a piece was still missing. I planted a seed in my mind that I wanted to develop a way of explaining all this in a simple, clear way that would help people to get around their egos, get out of their own way and wake up to who they truly were. I offered the task to my higher Self, knowing that in the back of my mind I would continue working on it until the solution was found.

Turning my attention to more immediate tasks, I sat down to plan out the next week.

The phone rang again.

"Hello?" I answered, not yet totally present.

"Matt? This is Daryl."

"Hi! How are you? Did you receive the proposal I sent?"

"Yes, that's why I'm calling. I'm putting a contract in the mail for you today. I was wondering though, are you available next week? I'm taking a trip to one of our stronger regions and would like to have you join me, if you can. I'd like to get started with you right away."

I asked for the exact dates and looked at my planner, replying, "I'm available, and I'd like to get started right away, too."

Daryl continued, "Great! Along with the contract I will include some details I want you to focus on. We'll be flying out together, so we can discuss the work in greater depth then. If you have any questions in the meantime, call me."

He remembered something and added, "Oh, Matt?"

"Yes?"

"Have you been taking the nutritional supplements I sent you?"

I was glad to be able to say, "Yes, since the day I received them!"

He asked, "Well, how are you feeling?"

"I seem to have a lot more energy, and my thoughts have been really clear. I'm not sure that it's due to the supplements, but I'll keep taking them and let you know over time."

Daryl laughed and said, "If you don't think your increased energy is due to the products, taking it longer won't convince you. I know what will convince you, though."

I could hear the smile in his voice, as though he had dealt with skeptics on this issue for years. I inquired, "Okay, what will convince me?"

He confidently answered, "Stop taking them! Then you will know what it has been doing for you!"

He had a point. If I wasn't willing to credit the ways I felt better to his products, I would probably be willing to blame the ways I felt worse on not taking them. This logic suddenly seemed absurd to me, that I should have to go through feeling worse in order to give credit where it was due.

Laughing, I said, "Thanks for the suggestion Daryl, but I think I'll just keep letting the nutrients do their thing. I like the way I'm feeling now."

He laughed too and said, "Good, you catch on quick. Have a good weekend, and I'll see you next week."

I said good-bye, thinking how much I looked forward to spending more time with this man. I sensed he and I had work to do together that stretched beyond this present business. As I hung up, I took a moment to give thanks for my life and the way it was unfolding. I wondered exactly where it was all heading.

The rest of the day passed quickly as I washed laundry, folded it and cleaned my already orderly home. I sat down at sunset and looked around me as the golden light streamed in the windows, spotlighting different works of art. I felt thankful, not for anything specific, just a general feeling of gratitude.

After dinner, I went to the computer to work on the outline and proposal for my book, determined to send something to Cindy within the week. Writing throughout the evening, I got lost in my work. Finally, when my eyelids started getting heavy, I stopped for the night.

The misty air hung around me. I was in the same place I had dreamt about before, with the staircase leading upward. It seemed to be Egypt or some equally exotic place, but nowhere I recognized as a place I had actually been. I found it strange that I was dreaming, yet I knew I was dreaming and was analyzing the dream at the same time. This dream had a unique quality, as though it were more of a memory—and yet I was asleep. As I wandered through this dream world, before me was a labyrinth laid out in beautiful stonework. It looked like a circular maze, but no walls obstructed my view to the center. Following the pathway with my eyes, I could see that there were no tricks or dead ends, just one spiraling path that led to the center, to the heart of the circle. I hesitated at the entrance, as if knowing that once I entered, I must continue on until I reached that midpoint; there would be no turning back. I took a deep breath, then stepped onto what I knew to be a very sacred path. It wound in and around, leading me to all the edges of its confined space. My mind was clearing in preparation for reaching the center, as if something very special waited there for me. As I approached the center, I saw a figure standing in meditation, cloaked in white, with a hood softly shielding its identity from view. As I neared, the person turned toward me, then pulled the hood away from her face, revealing her angelic beauty. Some part of me had known it was Alea, and indeed now she stood before me in the center, overwhelming me with love. I reached out to embrace her, when suddenly a constricting pain gripped my heart and immediately I woke up, losing the dream.

I whispered Alea's name into the darkness of my room. Tears began to flow from my eyes. I wasn't even sure why. I missed her, but this sadness seemed much deeper than the moment should merit. I whispered her name again, with an intonation that said, "Please, please come to me."

Immediately she appeared. No words were exchanged. I reached out to embrace her and, unlike the dream, she reached out for me, too. We sat quietly in my room, holding each other.

The love I felt as I held Alea was stronger than any I had ever known before. I took several deep breaths in order to pull myself into the present moment, letting go of the pain and sadness that I had no apparent reason to feel. I didn't want to break the magical spell of the moment, but fearing she wouldn't stay long, I asked, "Alea, what happened in that dream? It was so real, so painful! Please tell me who you are to me. Why do I feel like I know you and yet know nothing about you?"

She thought for a moment, looking torn as to how much to tell me. *"The dream, Matt, represents your journey toward the center of yourself. The labyrinth is an ancient spiritual tool used for taking a pilgrimage within. In your dream it was a metaphor for you and your life's journey. The walk into the center was a time for self-observation and letting go, to allow you to release whatever came up, in order to quiet your mind so that you could receive what awaited you in the center."*

I hadn't told her the dream, but she obviously knew all about it. She continued, *"The center, in this case, represents your heart. You were journeying there to receive and give love—to open your heart and receive guidance and strength for your journey ahead."*

"Why did I have so much pain when I saw you? I was so joyful that you were there! Why couldn't I receive you?"

She hesitated, then said, *"It wasn't me, Matt, that you were to receive. People and objects in dreams are usually symbols that represent an aspect of yourself. In your dream, I represented love and an open heart, which is what you were after. That is what you were to receive. Unfortunately, I was not the perfect symbol for love, as you also associate me with pain, pain from a very deep wound from your past. The love and the pain you feel are as deep and as vast as the sea, going back centuries."*

I looked at her quizzically, not sure whether I really believed in past lives, then responded, "Are you saying this is from a past life? Were we together? I want to remember! Why can't I remember it?" I had the same sensation that I sometimes get when I wake up in the morning, knowing I've been dreaming but not being able to remember the details.

"It will not serve you now to know the details of your past lives. It is hard enough to let go of the challenges from your present one! You do, however, want to carry forward the love and wisdom gained along the way. That is all you really need."

She smiled in a way that always made my heart give a little hop, then added, *"What I do wish to explain is that your pain from the past has been held far too long. Our love left your heart with a wound, and the scars left you impaired in your ability to love and be loved. I am here now to help you heal the wound and to open your heart so you can step into authentic power and fulfill your purpose, which is of great importance to many."*

I looked at her and whispered, "I think you've already healed me." Then, smiling, I added as proof, "I love you, Alea." On one hand, it was odd to tell her this, as I still wasn't sure if she was a guide, an angel, a ghost or a magician, any one of which was not a normal object of my attention. On the other hand, telling her that I loved her was as natural to me as loving the sunshine. Either way, it had to be done; the feeling was not negotiable.

She looked at me with such intensity that I almost turned away. I had never encountered anyone who was so fully present with me. I met and held her gaze.

"I love you too, Matt."

I felt her sincerity and at the same time waited for the "but . . ." statement that I could sense was coming.

She smiled, knowing my thoughts, and said, *"Matt, we have always loved each other, and we always will love each other. I am always with you."*

We smiled into each other's eyes, enjoying the moment.

In the few minutes of silence that followed, I reviewed my life, or rather my love life, in light of what she had said. As I watched myself in my mind's eye, I again saw how closed my heart had been. I watched myself go through all the motions, but without the depth of passion that makes life so grand. Just as I had gathered cotton as a small boy, putting it in my sack and lugging it behind me, adding to it as I went, I had done the same thing with my pain. In this case, the bag had started half full, and I had just kept filling it up and carrying it with me, which made it impossible to run, jump and skip with the enthusiasm of a child. I was far too weighted down. I could easily see that it didn't matter which life the pain came from, this one or one past; if I kept gathering it up without letting it go, it was my burden now, just the same. It hurt just to watch, and I could see that I wasn't healed completely after all.

With tears welling in my eyes, I asked, "What do I need to do, Alea, to heal my heart, to release this pain?"

She put her hand on my heart and quietly said, *"Close your eyes. See yourself standing at the entrance to the labyrinth once again. This time as you walk in, every time a feeling emerges, stop, breathe and release the feeling that you are holding onto. Observe yourself and let go. Observe yourself and let go."*

Following her directions, I walked the winding path toward my heart. I felt as if Alea were walking the labyrinth right behind me. I observed that, too, and let it go. Soon we were on opposite sides of the labyrinth within my mind. Then, only moments later, we were walking side by side. With the next turn on the twisting path, we were once again on opposite sides of the labyrinth. I observed how the path pulled us apart and brought us together again and began to see the metaphor that mirrored our lives outside of the labyrinth as well. I then breathed and let that go, too, trusting the process, the ebb and flow. With every few steps a thought or memory popped into my mind, allowing me another opportunity to observe and let go. It was as if I were emptying the bag of cotton as I went, with each step reaching in, pulling out a handful, and letting it fly away with the wind.

Alea's instructions continued, *"As you approach the center, Matt, know that this is where you will receive God's love and wisdom—your love and wisdom. Breathe deeply. Sit down in the center and allow yourself to be filled. If any feelings of doubt, pain or fear emerge, observe, breathe and let go. Return to the center, to your heart. Breathe."* I sensed that she was sitting with me in the center—always with me, just as she had said.

Her words alone were soothing, but wrapped together with the sweet tone of her voice and the love I was feeling, I felt more at peace than I ever had. It was as if I had just come home after a long, long journey. No thoughts came, just a sense of quiet. I reveled in the absence of pain!

As I meditated, I heard Alea's voice guiding me. *"Envision a speck of light in your heart; a bright pinpoint of light."*

I did as she asked and "looked" into my heart. Just as she suggested, I saw a small speck of light twinkling there.

She continued, knowing that I was seeing it, *"Now, breathe in deeply and allow that light to grow, little by little, until it has filled your entire heart."*

Again following her instructions, I saw my heart turn golden with the brilliant, vibrant light.

"Just as your heart's job is to pump blood throughout your body, allow it now to pump this healing light throughout your being."

What followed reminded me a little of the magnificence of flying over a city at night, watching all the lights below connected by the streams of light flowing down the freeways. I saw the light journeying outward from my heart through my arteries, spreading to my veins and out to the capillaries. Once the network of pathways was "enlightened," I fused them all together, filling the spaces between. My body felt warm and tingly as I envisioned being filled with the healing light and saw it cleansing me, consuming all impurities, burning up my pain. It felt good to just sit quietly, enjoying the sensation of breathing the light in and out, like a rising and falling tide within me.

"Now, Matt, imagine that light to be love. Imagine the light to be God's love. Let it continue to be your life support, your true power, coursing through your veins, strengthening you, healing you."

I felt the shift within me as my experience of the light turned into love flowing through me. Ecstatic and calm at the same time, I reveled in the feeling and never wanted to feel any other way again.

I had no idea of how much time had passed when Alea's words again permeated my being. *"Now it is time to gather up all that you have received and take it out into the world with you. It is time to leave the center, united with God, for the journey outward. With each step, instead of gathering pain, now gather strength and empower others, gather love and give love, a free-flowing exchange rather than a one-sided collection. Breathe. Feel the freedom. Dance the pathway when you feel it. Be yourself!"*

As instructed, I walked the winding pathway back out of the labyrinth, feeling more centered and balanced. Near the exit, I felt a sudden lightness, the likes of which I had not felt since early childhood. A giggle of pure delight bubbled up, and I half-skipped, half-ran the last few dozen steps, the way I had when I was only three or four years old. Within this magic circle, all the self-consciousness and embarrassment that I would have felt doing this in "real" life was banished, and I once again experienced that most fleeting of all things—childhood in its pristine innocence. Then, as I paused, ready to leave the labyrinth, I remembered the words of a Zen master: "The innocence of a child is beautiful, but ignorant. When we return to innocence as adults, we bring all of our experience with us and release it, choosing to let go of what our egos believe they have learned, and fully experiencing each moment as fresh and newly-created. This is, of course, the truth that is to be rediscovered in innocence."

I heard Alea's voice as I stepped off the pathway, *"Whenever you feel off-balance or out of sorts, return to center, return to your heart. You have the ability to do this any time, anywhere. All you need to do is observe, let go and return to love, then take any necessary action from there."* She added softly, *"You may now open your eyes."*

I looked around me, relieved to see that Alea hadn't disappeared. "Thank you, Alea, that was really, really wonderful." I couldn't imagine what else to say. Everything seemed insignificant after the power of what I had just experienced.

"It is now time for you to go back to sleep, Matt. As you sleep, the meaning of all you have been through will assimilate and settle more deeply into your soul."

"Alea, can I really return to that peaceful, loving place any time I want to?"

"Yes, you can. Any time!" She looked as if she were about to leave.

"One more question, Alea. Will you always be there with me?"

Alea's face suddenly seemed sad. Not sure whether I was seeing emotions on her face or merely projecting mine onto her, I waited while she searched for the proper words. *"Matt, as I told you before, I am always with you, whether in the center or wandering on the pathway. Always, no matter what. However, there will be times when you are not at all aware of my presence. You will think you are alone. At those times, return to center, return to your inner knowing. You will feel me there beside you."*

She thought a moment longer and added, *"More important, you will find yourself there. I am not the source of the feeling of love you found there, Matt. God is. You are. All I did was help to lead you to it. You do not need me to feel it. You do not need me to find it again."*

I experienced the same feeling that I had right before my girlfriend, Bonnie, broke up with me in the eighth grade. A knot tied in my stomach. I mustered up the courage to ask, "Alea, are you leaving soon? I mean, am I going to see you again?"

"Again? Yes, and soon. However, the time may be coming for you to branch out on your own for a while, a time to practice your skills. Know this, Matt, I will be back. After all, we have work to do!"

I must not have looked relieved, because she added, *"I will only get in your way if I stay. You have a lot of loving to catch up on, and I, well, I am not the only one who should be enjoying the pleasure of being loved by you."* She smiled in her special way, which made it seem as if everything would be all right, even though I was teetering on the edge of sobbing out to her not to leave. I could not understand the depth of my reaction.

She touched my heart and said, *"It is not happening to you now, Matt. Right now we are together, and soon we will be again. It is time for you to get some sleep. Don't worry, I will be back soon. I promise."* She kissed my forehead and motioned for me to lie down.

Following her orders, I laid back on the bed, suddenly aware of how tired I was. She smiled one more time before I drifted off to a deep, needed sleep, while she disappeared into that other world from whence she came.

When I awoke the next morning, I felt refreshed. I reviewed the events of the previous night as I took my morning shower. The imagery Alea had guided me through was like being awake during a dream and having the ability to change it as I went. I thought about the love I had felt at the center of the labyrinth and became aware that while I wanted to be in a loving relationship again, I could create that feeling of love without a partner. I did not need to search outside myself for love; I didn't need someone else to feel love! Love was something to share, not something to find. I wondered about Alea's words, *"I am not the only one who should enjoy the pleasure of being loved by you."* Exactly what did she mean by that?

After breakfast, I looked at my calendar, realizing that my trip with Daryl was quickly approaching, and set my sights on preparing for the journey ahead.

I joined Daryl when his flight stopped over in Phoenix, heading toward Montreal. I sat next to him and, after the usual "catching up" on how things were going, we began to discuss the situation with his company and the issues with which he wanted help.

He explained, "Many of our people got involved with selling our product from more of a spiritual and nutritional choice rather than a business one. The good news about that is, they are in support of the humanitarian vision; the bad news is that they aren't very business-minded. In fact, sometimes they are downright anti-business-minded. It seems that somewhere along the line, a huge portion of our population has come to believe that 'spiritual' and 'poor' are synonymous. The challenge we have is how to show them that they can be spiritual, share the products as a tool of their spiritualism and still make money doing it. What I want you to do is to give them the business tools they need to be successful, while at the same time keep them involved in the bigger picture of spreading harmony, balance and nutrition around the planet."

"That shouldn't be too hard," I commented, then asked, "How did you get involved in this business, Daryl?"

"I used to be a Montessori school teacher, and I was watching the productivity of the children. I saw swings in their ability to focus and learn, and came to recognize over time that their daily nutrition had a direct influence on whether they were able to learn or not. Their social interaction was also directly affected. When they weren't well nourished, they weren't nourishing to others—simple as that. When their bodies weren't well fed, their brains weren't well fed. I became curious as to what the most nutritional foods were and started doing research. I wanted to be able to offer specific suggestions to the parents, so they could more easily help their children to learn and to get along with others. Now, after much more research, my nutritional products are spreading to hundreds of thousands."

"If they're spreading so well, what is the actual problem in the business?" I asked.

"Turnover in our sales staff. If the people who believed in the product were to be financially successful and stay in the business, we would grow so much faster and be able to spread its use at a much greater rate. I want them to see that making a lot of money will only strengthen their ability to share the products. If they can't pay their phone bills, how can they sell anything? As it is, people love the product, take it, attempt to sell it, then stop selling it because they are not business people—although they do generally continue to take the supplements. I want you to teach the people who love the product how to sell it and be successful selling it, for their benefit, our benefit and the benefit of the people with whom they will be sharing it."

"It sounds like they need to master the art of networking, which is really just the art of connecting people. I'll give them some tips along with the practical steps they can take to truly be successful in this business."

"Great. That is just what we need."

We sat thinking quietly for a few minutes when it occurred to me to ask Daryl, "What do you think the most important thing is? I mean, the most important quality in a person?"

Without hesitation he answered, "Being resourceful."

I must have looked surprised, because he went on to explain, "When people are resourceful, they see their options instead of their obstacles. They are solution-focused, instead of problem-focused, and they are better able to be productive."

"I see what you mean. I like that word, as opposed to being positive or negative. It has a proactive nature to it, as if a person who is resourceful is empowered to take action."

At this point both Daryl and I returned to our own thoughts. This word *resourceful* was intriguing to me. As my passion for words often leads me to do, I broke up the word into its parts, looking for its deeper meaning. *Re-source-ful*: once again full of source!

I turned to Daryl and said, "Have you ever thought about what the word *resourceful* means, literally?"

"Not really, why?"

"Re-source-ful: *once again full of source!* The 'source' being where all things originate! If we can help your people to be *resourceful* in their business, we can help them be full of source, of God, of love, while they do their work!"

Daryl nodded as he thought about what I had said. Not waiting for his response, I added, thinking out loud to myself as much as to him, "Being resourceful is about being in the moment, connected, aware, peaceful, clear. It is a space in which ideas flow, creativity is at its best and true happiness can be experienced."

"Yes! When someone is not resourceful, they get stuck, resistant to seeing solutions," Daryl elaborated.

Reflecting on the idea, and liking it more and more, I said, "Thank you for sharing this with me, Daryl. I've been looking for a word that more simply defines this resourceful state of being, instead of using the terms *positive* or *negative.* Those words are so relative; one does not exist without the other, and the boundary between the two is fluid, moving, dependent on one's perspective. *Resourceful* is a state of being that isn't relative. It just is."

As I spoke, everything clicked into focus, as if layers of transparencies on an overhead projector had just fallen on top of each other, illuminating the relationship between all the concepts I had been learning. I saw in that moment that letting go is the key that allows us to return to a resourceful state, where we are not controlled by our ego-driven needs. I remembered Michael's words about *Internal Bodily Turmoil* and *Universal Energy Flow,* and realized that a state of resourcefulness is where this energy flow exists. I recalled Alea saying something about "stepping into one's authentic power." Resourcefulness is being in touch with authentic power—the power of source. In resourcefulness, energy expands, and the person is like a satellite dish, able to receive ideas and tap into universal wisdom. This flow is where we are able to manifest all we have envisioned in our imaginations. The flow exists in the moment, by being present in the now. Internal Bodily Turmoil gets created when we are not resourceful, by holding onto energy that does not serve us, that is not based in love. In turmoil our energy is restricted, stuck, unmoving.

The simplicity I was searching for unfolded before me: *Let go of the feelings that get in the way of feeling resourceful, and thus allow universal energy—authentic power—to flow freely through you to manifest your visions. Resourcefulness!* This summed up the goal of all the other ideas with which Alea and I had been exploring.

Upon arriving at our hotel, Daryl and I checked in, made plans to meet for dinner in an hour, and went to our rooms to unpack and get settled. I immediately got out my journal and took notes on my most recent thoughts. The hour passed quickly.

We ate in a nearby restaurant, discussing the next day's events.

Daryl said, "I'll start the morning off, covering the things I want to share with my people, and then I'll introduce you."

"Sounds good." I was looking forward to working with them. We finished up, walked back to our rooms and, after minimal reorganization of my materials for the next day, I went to bed. With the time difference, it was still a couple of hours earlier by my body clock, but I knew that morning would come a couple of hours earlier also. I lay there for a half hour without sleeping, running thoughts through my mind. I kept seeing ways that resourcefulness fit in with my work and the concepts I wanted to teach. Finally, I sat up to meditate, figuring that perhaps I could clear my mind and calm down enough to sleep.

I sat cross-legged on the bed and took some deep breaths, wanting to see if I could recreate the feeling I had had in the center of the labyrinth, this time without Alea's guidance. Someone had told me once about meditation, "Imagine you are sitting on the edge of a river, watching the boats go by. The boats are your thoughts. It is okay to watch the boats, to observe them—just don't get on the boat and find yourself down the river. Stay on the bank." It made so much sense to me! How many times had I climbed onto the "boat" of a thought, only to come back to awareness several minutes later? Focusing one's mind definitely required practice. I climbed off the boat of thinking about meditation and sat quietly on the bank of my mind, breathing deeply, observing. After several minutes, I found the feeling of God within me, the quiet, peaceful, strong sensation hidden within, and held it as if holding a small child in my heart. Half an hour later, I felt completely reconnected, as if the small seed of quiet, peaceful strength had grown to fill my whole being once again. Rejoicing in my successful journey within, I lay down and went to sleep.

I awoke ready to start the day. When Daryl and I met for breakfast, he went over the plan one more time before we went to the hall where the day's events were to be held.

This audience didn't have the typical sales-staff look. No three-piece suits and ties, no mirror-polished Italian loafers were found here. Casual and colorful, the people entering the room had "individuality" stamped all over them.

Daryl started the morning by greeting everyone and giving them an update on new product development and the status of the company. He shared his vision of feeding the world and touched people's hearts with his genuine and deeply felt commitment to his mission. I watched as several people wiped tears from their eyes. After an hour, he introduced me.

I began with a story about my own experiences building a network, then began sharing with them the tips that had made my business shift from zero income to tens of thousands a month. Their response seemed flat, as if they were uninterested. During a break, I went outside to regroup. My need to be accepted was stirring within and getting in the way of my being able to be present and effective. Taking a deep breath, I released the air and the feeling, then went back in to the gathering group. I decided to bring the issues out into the open, instead of hoping they would just let them go.

I asked the group, "What are you in this business for?"

The answers I received were, "To spread harmony and balance on the planet," "To feed the world," and "To help people live more balanced, productive lives through properly nourishing their bodies." Just as Daryl had explained to me, one gentleman even said, "I don't care about making money; I just want to share the products." Many in the group nodded in agreement. I thought about how committed in one sense these people were to what they were doing, but they didn't seem to understand the cause-and-effect aspects of their choices. With their commitment to the cause, they could also be rejoicing in the benefit of the effect of their labors.

I addressed the man who had just spoken, asking his name and why he wanted to share the products. He appeared to be about thirty-five and was dressed simply in jeans and a T-shirt that had pictures of endangered animals on it. Answering my question, he said, "I'm John. I want to help people."

"So your objective is to share your products with as many people as possible?"

"Yes."

"If you shared your products with ten people who shared them with ten people, wouldn't you be responsible for sharing nutrition with a hundred people?"

"Yes, but I don't want to be money-oriented."

"You don't have to be money-oriented to build a business—you have to be people-oriented. A cause-and-effect relationship is at work here. If you have the cause of going out and helping people by sharing the product, and if you hold the mission of this high in your heart, then sharing it with as many people as you possibly can will bring at least two effects. One effect will be that you make a difference on the planet through your efforts, and the other will be that you make money for making that difference."

John rolled the whiskers of his neatly trimmed beard between his thumb and his index finger, then answered honestly, "I guess I feel that if I am really here to make a difference and help people, making money for doing it lessens the goodness."

I responded by asking the group, "Do you see that everything you do makes a difference on the planet one way or another, and that without getting paid for it, you wouldn't be able to do it?"

Without waiting for any answers, I asked, "If you didn't make any money sharing this product, what would you do for a living?"

I got a series of answers, everything from, "waiting tables" to "working at the recycling center" to "teaching school."

I then asked, "How much of your time would you be spending making enough money to live on?"

They again responded with everything from, "forty hours a week" to "eighty hours a week."

"If you were doing these other jobs full time, how much time would you have left over for sharing the products and making a difference?"

A few responded, "Not much!"

Feeling a little victorious, I said, "If you don't get paid to share the product, you won't be able to afford to share it. The money is just a measure of how well you are doing at sharing your mission and making a difference. Make your cause to be people-oriented, to talk to as many people as you possibly can, to share this with everyone, and to allow the money to simply be the effect of your efforts."

They were getting what I was saying, but I noticed that I was not feeling really resourceful. I was being successful in convincing them intellectually; they may have had new thoughts, but they undoubtedly still had the same feelings inside them. I had let go of my need for acceptance earlier, but now I was trying to control—second-guessing their answers—to convince them. I took a deep breath again, and let go of that need as well.

I explained how our need to be accepted and our need for control are the two ego-driven needs that get in our way and make us feel stuck. I told them about the state of resourcefulness, where we are once again full of source, able to see options clearly and to be creative.

"The goal is to be resourceful as much of the time as possible, and in order to do that, we need to be self-observant and to let go of these feelings when we become aware of them. Letting go allows us to return to resourcefulness. Once we have gotten into a state of resourcefulness, this is the place from which to take action. If we take action without being resourceful, the action will be driven by our egos, instead of our true Selves."

I then asked, "How much of the time do you think you spend in a resourceful state?"

The answers were called out, "10 percent," "15 percent," "5 percent," "40 percent."

"How would your lives be different if you were to be resourceful 80 percent of the time, or if you could instantly return to resourcefulness the minute you were aware that you weren't?" I could see the wheels turning in their heads, as they considered the possibilities.

I added, "We all want to make a difference on the planet; we have already established that. If we aren't happy, if we aren't resourceful, we can't make a difference. The most important thing on this planet is for you to be happy; if you are happy, you are resourceful, and you will make a difference, guaranteed. What happens is that we hold onto issues for years, sometimes lifetimes, that get in the way of our being resourceful. We honor our anger more than our resourcefulness, we honor our jealousy more than our resourcefulness, we honor our hurt more than our resourcefulness, and we honor our dramas more than our resourcefulness. Some of us are living a drama called 'Search for Tomorrow,' some are living 'General Hospital,' some are living 'The Young and the Restless,' or, many of you may relate to this one—'The Guiding Light.' You are the star in your own drama. If you don't like the way it is going, rewrite it, rescript it. It's your drama, you can change it."

I said, "Let's look at this concern about being money-oriented."

I turned my attention back to John. He had been listening attentively, trying to make sense of what I was saying. I was sure that the information I shared challenged the pattern of at least twenty years of his chosen lifestyle. He appeared to pride himself in living a simple, good life with few excess material goods. "What does being money-oriented feel like to you, John? What does it feel like in your body?"

He looked thoughtful for a minute, then said, "I feel a constriction around my heart. It feels really uncomfortable. I don't want people to think I am selling them something for my benefit, like I am making money off of them."

"If you could put a name to that feeling, what would that be?"

"I think it's fear."

"What are you afraid of?"

"That people won't like me. Hmmm—I think it even goes beyond people to God. I am afraid that God won't like me, either."

"Would you consider that a resourceful or a non-resourceful feeling?"

"Non-resourceful."

"Is it moving you closer to your objective or further away?"

"Further away."

"So tell me, is it a need to be accepted or a need to be in control?"

"I think it is a need to be accepted."

"Do you like feeling that way?"

He looked at me as if I was stupid. "No, I don't!"

"What you originally thought was a concern about being money-oriented isn't that at all; it is a need to be accepted, to be loved." I went on to explain to the group, "Originally, John thought that being money-oriented would keep him from making a difference on the planet, when in actuality, his need to be accepted is getting in the way of making a difference on the planet. The need to be accepted has just been mislabeled as a money issue. This feeling moves us away from our vision, and the need for approval is what is creating the feeling."

I went on, "It requires three things to let go of a feeling: intention, willingness and commitment. It also requires three things to hold onto an issue: intention, willingness and commitment. It requires the exact same things to let go as to hold on, except hanging on requires immense amounts of energy, while letting go requires no energy, only choice. Any time we are hanging on, we are not moving toward our vision. In fact, our vision has changed from helping other people to protecting our egos and gaining acceptance, which is keeping us from sharing the products."

I turned back to John and asked, "Which do you honor most, your need to be accepted or your vision?"

He answered right away, "My vision!"

"Do you want to let go of your need to be accepted?"

"Yes, I do."

"Are you willing to let it go?"

He answered hesitantly, "Hmmm. . . . Well, I think so. I'm not sure."

I asked again, "Which do you honor the most, your need to be accepted or your vision?"

"My vision."

Again I asked, "Are you willing to let go of your need to be accepted?"

He stated more easily, "Yes."

"When are you willing to let it go?"

"Right now."

I instructed him to take some deep breaths and release the energy that was constricting his heart. With each breath, I could see his face become more and more relaxed. I led him through three or four breaths, until he announced, "The constriction is gone!"

Addressing the whole group, I said, "If you each become self-observant and let go of any feelings that are getting in the way of being fully resourceful, before you set out to share your products or opportunities with others, you will be in a much better position to fulfill your vision of bringing more balance and harmony to the planet, because you yourselves will be balanced and harmonious."

Speaking to John directly, I said, "Anytime you start to feel the constriction coming back, stop, observe it, breathe and let it go. Then take appropriate action from the new state of resourcefulness."

Once again I returned to the whole group. "This is a people-oriented business. Remember that we are all looking for the same thing. Some look for it selling nutritional products, some look for it doing seminars, some look for it in things, some look for it in wars, murders, drugs or alcohol. We are all looking for more love, joy and happiness, and these exist only in a resourceful state. When you share these products—or anything else for that matter—from resourcefulness, you show others the possibilities and give them permission to do the same. In this way, with or without the product, you are truly doing what you set out to do, fulfilling your mission of making a difference, by spreading love throughout the world."

The seminar ended with everyone feeling joyful, renewed and better able to build their businesses and their lives. Daryl simply hugged me, and I knew that he was pleased. I was sure he and I would get into a long philosophical discussion later, and I looked forward to it. I felt strong, as if this material was just flowing through me, without my having to think so much about it. I could see that when I let go of my needs for acceptance and control, I got out of the way and the Universal Energy Flow could move right through me.

I liked the understanding that was unfolding before me of the many applications of letting go and becoming resourceful. They applied equally well in business and personal struggles. I couldn't help but wonder what my life would have been like if I had learned—and applied—all of this much sooner. I offered thanks for being able to use it now!

Alea was waiting for me when I got back to my room.

"I'm so glad to see you! I wasn't sure how long it would be until I saw you again," I blurted happily.

She responded empathetically with, *"I know. I'm happy to be with you too, although it is important that you remember I always am. There will come a day when you no longer see me at all. What is important is that you feel me with you; this is what truly matters. There will even come a day when you are no longer aware of feeling me; it will just be a natural state of being."*

During both this visit and the last she seemed to be preparing me for her absence. I didn't like the idea, but I didn't want to spend the time I had with her worrying about a future time when she wouldn't be with me. That didn't seem very, well, resourceful. I switched my attention back to how good I felt being with her.

Suddenly, spontaneously, out popped the question I had had ever since she first appeared to me. "Alea, are you an angel?"

She laughed out loud and said, *"Well, I guess that depends on what your definition of an angel is—but I don't have wings."* Sensing how serious the question was to me, she added, *"I am not of your dimension, Matt, as I'm sure you already know. I am able to visit here only to fulfill my purpose and mission. I appear to you in a physical form to help your rational mind accept me—and my guidance."*

She laughed again. *"I'm not so sure that has worked, though!"* She obviously knew how much my rational mind struggled with all the strange—and wonderful—experiences of late.

Seeing the concern and love in my face, she added, *"Matt, I am sure you know this already, but for clarity, I want to make it explicit. Our love for each other is very special and, as I said, goes back a long, long time. However, in this lifetime, romance is not why we have come together. We are here to support an even higher mission. We can love each other, as we do, and yet I am not of your world now. You have not hallucinated me, and yet others do not see me. While our love is appropriate—love is always appropriate—I am here to assist you in your very important purpose: Love in a much bigger sense."*

I knew in that instant that what she said was true. I blushed with embarrassment that she obviously was aware of *every* thought I had ever entertained about her. I took a deep breath, let go of any preconceived notions of happily-ever-after, and prepared to embrace whatever lay ahead.

She went on, *"The first part of my mission has been to set you firmly on your path. You have gained the seed of life, as you know, but merely having it is not enough. It must be planted deeply and watered so it can take root and bear fruit. You have now reached the point where you are ready to take this on."*

She smiled knowingly and said, *"So, tell me your latest discoveries—since it is there that you will find the tilled soil—or soul, if you will."* She laughed at her own pun.

I wanted to analyze everything she had just said, but she was looking at me expectantly, leaving me little room for analysis. I answered her question, telling her all about my life of late, even though I was aware she already knew about it. It felt good just to verbalize it.

"I like working with Daryl, at least so far. I feel as though he and I are going to be really good friends over time."

"What is so special about him?"

I wasn't sure exactly how to describe him to her. "Well, he just has a very peaceful way about him. He seems to be in the moment, calm, clear. . . ." I realized it then. "He seems to be very resourceful!"

She kept smiling as I went on, "I discovered, through talking with Daryl, the term *resourceful.* I love the simplicity of it; either we are being resourceful or we are not. Either we are full of love, or we are not. Either we have let go, or we have not. It makes it all seem so simple!"

"Tell me more."

"Well, I see the connection between this and what I have already discovered since you showed up. I have been putting all the pieces together in my mind. When people have the courage to be self-observant, they can see whether they are holding onto something that is getting in the way of their resourcefulness. Resourcefulness is our natural state, full of Source, full of God. It is here that we are able to experience the moment. By letting go of our ego-driven needs, we are able to return to who we truly are—resourceful, loving, creative beings. We need to observe, let go, become resourceful and then take action." I added, "If no action is required, we simply need to observe, let go and then become resourceful."

She nodded, as if there were something more I needed to add. I thought for a few minutes, then said, "It seems to me that resourcefulness wraps up all the other concepts and gives them deeper meaning. Is resourcefulness the soil you were referring to, Alea?"

She looked serious as she said, *"Without it, the seed could not grow."* She handed me another golden ring with *Resourcefulness* embedded in it. This one was larger than the others, as if it could encircle them all.

I cradled the circle in both hands, once again feeling the honor deeply. I still did not know what I was to do with all these rings, but I was keeping them safe, reviewing them from time to time, sensing that they held a deeper meaning than I could currently understand. I ran the message of each through my mind. My skin tingled as I felt each meaning.

I shared my thoughts with Alea. "They seem so simple to me now. Each one *is*, each one *has* such a clear ring of truth!"

Alea looked at me, as if she were searching for just the right words. *"Now Matt, you are ready. Go forth with these Rings of Truth, master them and teach them to others."*

She put her hand on my heart and said, *"Trust yourself. Be resourceful—full of Source—in all areas of your life, and know that you are loved. Now, go forth and love!"*

With that she was gone and I was left alone. I observed myself, took a deep breath and let go. Returning to resourcefulness, I prepared for my journey home, wondering if Alea would ever be back.

Alea watched Matt as he sat there alone. The more he mastered the Rings of Truth, the shorter the periods she was able to remain in physical form, as it became less necessary. She treasured these brief experiences of having physical senses again and considered how lucky human beings are, without even knowing it. They spend so much time judging their bodies and abusing them that many have forgotten that a body is a very wonderful gift! The ability to smell the scent of fresh flowers, listen to harmonious music, slip into the calming turquoise waters of the sea, taste the lips of the one you love, touch a kitten's soft fur, feeling it purr, or create and hold a newborn child in your arms—all these are precious gifts. She could have gone on and on, naming the advantages of having a body and living on this beautiful planet. Humans are indeed blessed. Of this, she was well aware.

Matt had to go forth more and more on his own, or he would misplace his strength, thinking it was coming from her instead of from the powerful Sourcewell within. Besides, she was never really very far away.

With each deep breath Matt took, Alea breathed light and love around him. She happily anticipated what was yet to unfold for him and admired his willingness to journey forward resourcefully. Change is not an instant process, and she knew he would have to consciously remind himself to let go and be resourceful over and over again.

After all, resourcefulness is our natural state of divinity, where our imaginations are most creative, and from whence we are able to take proper action toward the manifestation of our visions. Resourcefulness is the ultimate state of "response-ability," in which we respond with the most clarity to the events and circumstances that are presented to us. Letting go eliminates blame, dissolves anger and releases hurt. It puts us into a responsible state, where we are clearly the creators of our circumstances. We are receivers, satellite dishes of all possibilities. In resourcefulness, we can see the opportunities that surround us everywhere. When we let go, love fills the void that our ego-driven needs once filled.

Alea continued to observe as Matt began to meditate. Matt had gravitated more and more toward daily meditation, because that, in itself, was a process of letting go and becoming resourceful. She was pleased to see him choose this action, as she knew that it was in this quiet, connected state that his resourcefulness would quickly grow very strong and familiar. Then, in any given moment, when the state of resourcefulness slipped away, he would more easily and quickly be able to find his way back to it. The process of meditation was building a pathway to Source so solid that he would never lose his way.

The more resourceful and in-the-moment Matt became, the more joyful and peaceful Alea felt as well.

Knowing

After putting the finishing touches on the book proposal, I slipped it into a large envelope and addressed it to Cindy. The title *Authentic Power* had come to me as I awoke one morning, and I couldn't get it out of my head. It seemed to perfectly sum up the ideas the book would contain on *letting go, resourcefulness, love* and the other concepts symbolized by the golden rings. Pleased with this accomplishment, I mailed it on my way to Phoenix to pick up Nan.

As we greeted each other with a hug, I said, "It's great to see you! I'm so glad you decided to come—even if it is just a quick visit!"

Nan replied, "I'm really glad to be able to come, too, Matt. Thanks for being so gracious on such short notice."

We gathered up her things and began the two-hour drive back to Sedona. I was happy to have her company and looked forward to the wonderful discussions she and I seemed to have every time we spoke.

As we drove, we got the more day-to-day conversation out of the way. She filled me in on what she had been up to and shared about her new relationship.

She explained, "I would have brought Steve to meet you, but he's on a business trip this week. It was a good opportunity for me to get away, too. Our last conversation really helped me examine how I was looking to my partners to empower me instead of coming into relationships already empowered. As soon as I saw what I was doing and refocused my energies, a wonderful man showed up in my life! Part of why I came here was to thank you in person for helping me see what I had been doing in my relationships!"

I smiled and accepted her appreciation. "I'm glad our conversations are as useful to you as they are to me! I have been going through a very similar process lately, recognizing that I can create love without another person, and then share my love instead of looking for it." I added honestly, "I have to admit, though, I feel more ready than I have ever been to meet someone special to share it with." She nodded with understanding.

I really wanted to tell her about Alea and Michael, and all that had unfolded in my life over the last year, but decided to wait and see how the weekend progressed. I trusted her totally and knew she would understand all of this.

We laughed and chatted happily all the way back to Sedona. After lunch, we wandered around the shops and galleries, exploring the many beautiful Southwestern treasures they held.

"Tomorrow I'll take you out to the canyon, and we can enjoy the creek, if you'd like. Have you ever been there?"

She replied, "No, but I have heard it's a wonderful place!"

We stopped at the market and gathered enough goodies to get us through the weekend, then went home for the evening. Watching the sunset, we sat out on the deck nibbling on snacks, neither of us very hungry after our late lunch.

Nan went into another one of her spontaneous readings of my energy. I could tell she was doing this by the way she looked at me, as if listening to something or someone I couldn't hear.

I finally couldn't take it any longer. Laughing, I asked, "Okay, okay—what have you discovered about me now?"

She laughed too, saying, "Oh, sorry, I didn't realize I was being so obvious."

My curiosity growing, I asked again, "Well?"

"It's hard to say. I just keep getting the feeling that you want to talk to me about something very important. I have had this feeling for days, which is one of the reasons I made a point of coming to visit. I just can't quite get a reading on what it's about. The best way I can describe it is that it feels like you are pregnant and in labor, but trying to hold the baby in instead of letting it come out."

We both laughed at the image, but I was once again astounded at how accurate her assessment of me was. Even I hadn't completely realized how much I wanted to tell her everything, but had held back, waiting for the right moment. She looked at me expectantly, while I debated with myself over when—and what—to tell her. At least it was no longer *if* I should tell her. For now, I decided just to validate her suspicions but put off a full explanation for a little longer.

"You sure are good at that, Nan. You nail me right on the head every time! I do have some very important and rather strange things that I would like to share with you, but it isn't really a topic we can cover quickly. If you don't mind, I think I would rather wait until tomorrow to talk about it, when we have both had a good night's sleep—maybe by the creek."

She respected my request and didn't pressure me to say more. We enjoyed the rest of the evening together, and then I showed her to the guest room.

We both said, "Good night," but as I turned to go to my room, she added, "Oh, Matt—sweet dreams!"

Ordinarily, I would have thought nothing of a comment like that, but between the look on her face and my previous experiences of Nan's words, I found myself expectant.

I laughed and said, "I feel 'pregnant' again! Sweet dreams to you, too!" She smiled, and we both went to our rooms.

As I drifted off to sleep, I thought I smelled the sweet scent of incense burning, presuming in my half-awake state that Nan was burning it.

Again, I found myself aware that I was dreaming, yet enmeshed in the dream at the same time. I stood in the desert looking out over rolling hills and rock formations. I was completely alone. The land looked thirsty and in need of nurturing. Suddenly, all the rocks and grains of sand turned into thousands and thousands of people, spreading as far as I could see. Their skins were all the earth colors of the desert—red, brown, gold, black and tan. Every culture from around the world was represented in a glorious display of colorful costumes. My stomach and heart suddenly collided as I realized that all these people were looking at me, with copies of my published book in their hands. I jolted awake even more abruptly than I had fallen asleep and sat up in a cold sweat, heart pounding. It took me several minutes of breathing deeply, telling myself that it wasn't happening to me now, to get my heartbeat back to normal. I laid back down, keeping my eyes open, thinking about the dream.

The adrenaline pumping through my system must have been considerable, since it took me at least an hour to fall back to sleep. I used my time to analyze the dream and why I had felt so frightened. The symbolism emerged as I reviewed the scene. I recognized the fear to be anxiety about putting my work, my beliefs, my discoveries—and myself—out to the world. All in the same weekend, I had sent my book to the agent and was planning to tell Nan about the unexplainable experiences I'd been having. It was no wonder that this "pregnancy" analogy occurred to Nan; I was about to birth a book and share my "baby" with the world. This fear had to be my need for acceptance. I concentrated on letting it go and returning to resourcefulness. I envisioned the loving light flowing through my body and then easily fell into a peaceful sleep.

The dream recurred during the second half of the night; only this time I wasn't scared. I stood there watching all the people watching me. I was calm, loving—resourceful. Just before waking up, I noticed a stick of incense burning at my feet.

When I opened my eyes, morning had come. Feeling as though I had hardly slept at all, I rested for a few minutes longer before getting up and preparing for the day. I was glad to know Nan was there and that I could share my dream with her. A little wistfully, I realized again how much I enjoyed a woman's company. For only a moment, I wondered if I would ever have another relationship, beyond the casual dates I had had over the last few years. I let the thought go and embraced the new day.

Nan was drinking orange juice and looking through my book collection when I emerged from my room. We greeted each other, and she asked, "Did you sleep well?"

At first I thought she was mocking me—knowing full well that I had not—but upon seeing her expression, I realized she was sincere. "Well, I don't know if that is the way I would describe it."

I continued, "I had a vivid dream last night about sharing my work with the world."

I described the desert and the people, telling Nan about my book and my fear of seeing all those people holding it, looking at me. She listened thoughtfully as I spoke. I explained, "After I let go of my need to be accepted, I dreamed the same dream, only the second time I was able to stand there and accept the fact that all those people were looking to me, knowing me, reading my work."

She said, "That is a very powerful dream, Matt." Then she asked, "What is your biggest fear about sharing your work—or telling me whatever it is you've been holding back, for that matter?"

"I guess I don't think people will believe me. I mean, some of it is sort of hard to believe," I answered honestly.

"Do you believe it, Matt?" she asked intently.

My answer was reluctant and unconvincing. "I think so. I mean, yes, I do."

She smiled and asked again in a new way, "Do you *know* it?"

I must have looked at her quizzically, because she continued, "There is a huge difference between thinking something, believing it and knowing it."

I thought for a minute about her words and could see the truth of them. While I pondered, she asked again, "Do you know the truth of your work and your experiences, Matt?"

My doubting mind wanted to dispute everything that had happened to me, but I recognized that reaction as part of my need to be accepted. Logically, if I disputed it first, then no one else could hurt me by disputing it. If I acted unsure of what I meant, then I could easily regain their acceptance by simply changing my mind. Yet again, I let go of my need to be accepted and returned to resourcefulness. From there—the calm, peaceful and strong place within—I could feel my true knowing of what I had to share and the importance it held in the world. From resourcefulness, I could see that the state of "thinking it was true" originated from my need to control, "believing it was true" came from my need to be accepted and "knowing its truth" came from true resourcefulness.

I answered from a place of strength. "Yes, Nan. I know the truth of my work and the value of my experiences."

"Good," she said simply, nodding as she heard the resolution in my voice.

As we drove the short distance to the canyon, I began telling her my discoveries about the importance of letting go of the needs for acceptance and control. I defined resourcefulness to her and recounted how I had recently applied it in my life.

She listened intently, soaking up all the concepts, interrupting only to comment on the beauty of the area. As we started hiking along the creek, she said, "Matt, I am impressed by the growth you've gone through just since I first met you. You have gained so much clarity and wisdom! Tell me, how is it that you discovered all of this?"

We sat down on a huge boulder next to a swirling pool and spread out towels to sit on. The sun was shining brightly and the warmth felt wonderful against our skin.

I considered how to answer her question and, resting in my inner knowing, reached into my backpack and pulled out the eight golden rings with their powerful inscribed messages. I arranged them on the towel between us, in the order in which I had received them, not saying anything more.

Delighted with their beauty, she picked up each one and held it, read its literal message, and then appeared to read it through psychometry, as well. I had heard about psychics who used a piece of jewelry or an object to get information. We sat in silence for a long time, as she went through the same process with each one. Apparently satiated, she looked up to me with her eyes dancing in mystery and said, "Please tell me your story, Matt!"

I smiled, feeling as if I had Alea's blessing in what I was about to do, and began to tell the wonderful story of the Rings of Truth that lay between us. I started with Alea, explaining the love and the pain between us to the best of my ability, and the wonderful way she guided me toward understanding. I told her about meeting Michael and how the book with information about him arrived coincidentally, right after I met him. I described the labyrinth and the love in the center. I shared my new understanding of letting go and returning to resourcefulness and showed her how all this wove together. I explained why the ring of resourcefulness was larger than the others, as it encompassed them all.

Once I got started, it was hard to stop. Everything seemed to fit together like pieces of a puzzle. My enthusiasm was contagious, and Nan and I laughed and cried, completely engaged in recounting the magical experiences of my spiritual journey. Hours passed without either of us realizing it, until the sun disappeared behind the canyon wall.

As we gathered up our things she said, "So Michael is out there waking up his volunteers, huh? I wonder if Alea is just here for you, or if she is working with Michael on lots of people."

I replied, "My sense is that she was sent to me because of our past. It had something to do with healing my pain from our previous time together."

"I have had a couple of different friends tell me about Michael recently, or some kind of visit from him. He seems to get around in a quiet kind of way. It's almost like an underground club." She laughed and said, "Maybe everybody is just afraid to come right out and admit they have had an encounter with Michael! I mean, I can see why it wasn't an easy thing to tell me—about him or Alea."

I asked, "Has it occurred to you yet that *you* may be one of Michael's volunteers? After all, how many friends have found reason to tell you about him now?"

She looked surprised at the question; obviously it had not occurred to her. "Well, that is an interesting thought. So, what you are suggesting is that the reason I'm hearing about this over and over again in different ways is because it is one of the subtle ways Michael starts to stir things up?"

"Honestly, Nan, I am no expert on the ways of Michael. It just seems to me there might be a reason you are 'coincidentally' being told about it. You might just want to stay open to the possibility and see what else happens."

She smiled and nodded. "Yes, I suppose I should! I guess that being a volunteer for spreading the light of love isn't such a bad mission to be a part of. In fact, I like the idea!"

By now we had worked our way back to the car.

"Matt? Thank you for sharing all this with me. I can certainly see now why I felt so drawn to visiting you. I feel excited, as if I'm in onto something really big! I do feel 'woken up' in a sense!"

We hugged before we got into the car, and I sent a prayer of thanks that sharing this had been easier than I had anticipated; it was actually invigorating. I, too, felt more awake, just from the sharing. It seemed as though the ideas had sifted to a deeper level of understanding while I put them together out loud.

Over dinner we promised to stay in touch and support each other through our growth. Nan said, "It helps a lot to have a spiritual support system—even if it is only one other person. I would really like to continue sharing and exploring the different things that we both encounter! Oh, and by the way, I *do* want to read your book as soon as it's done!"

I smiled, still a little uncomfortable about putting all of this into writing and out into the world, and said, "Thank you—I'll give you the first signed copy!"

"Thanks! Matt, all this must be what I was picking up on when I did that reading on you when we first met. I think the time is now for you to teach this material. I mean *really* teach it, not just as part of a business seminar, but as a personal growth seminar in its own right."

Just as in my dream, I saw myself once again speaking before thousands of people, teaching them about letting go and returning to resourcefulness. Without even realizing what I was saying, I answered, "I think so, too. That is exactly what I plan to do."

We returned home and slept the night peacefully. Right after breakfast, we packed our things and headed back to Phoenix. I put an overnight bag in the car, as I planned to do some business while in the city that might take longer than just the afternoon.

As she gazed out the window at the intensely beautiful surroundings, she said, "A weekend is hardly long enough to come to a place as wonderful as this!"

I replied, "This is so true, Nan. We didn't even scratch the surface of what this area has to offer."

"Well, I guess I will just have to come again!" she announced happily.

I walked Nan to her gate. As I watched her disappear down the hallway to the plane, I went over my "to do" list in my mind. I decided to grab a quick bite to eat in the airport restaurant and then go on to my business meeting.

Sitting down at the counter, I ordered a sandwich and then looked around me. A woman who sat one seat away looked extremely sad. The more I watched her, the more concerned I became. After fifteen minutes of sitting in such close proximity without any connection, I wondered what had happened to her. Finally, when the waitress brought her bill, she glanced my way and nodded.

Looking for some way to start a conversation, I said, "You have a great tan. Are you just getting back from somewhere tropical?"

She looked up again, a little surprised, and said, "Oh, thank you. Yes, I spent the last month in Hawaii."

I replied, "Hawaii is one of my favorite places. Which island did you go to?"

"Kauai."

"Kauai is my favorite island!" To lighten things up a little, I added, "Did you know that's where Puff the Magic Dragon lives?" She laughed slightly, and I asked, "Were you there for business or pleasure?"

She was hesitant to tell me at first, but opened up after a moment. She looked as though she appreciated having someone to talk to. "Both, actually. I went there to get my head together."

I could relate to that! Interested, I asked, "Well, how did it go?"

She sighed and made a half-smile. "I brought the same head back home that I went with. I think I need some therapy." Somewhat sarcastically she added, "Do you know of a good therapist?"

"Why do you need a therapist?"

She shook her head and said, "I don't know why I'm telling you all of this. I guess it's okay because you are a total stranger. I need to see a therapist because I don't know what I want to do with my life."

I asked, "What do you do now?"

Sighing again, she answered, "I'm an 'Earth mom.' We live out in the boonies without electricity and amenities."

"Do you like it?" I prodded.

"It was okay, for a while."

I went further. "Do you have an 'Earth husband'?"

"Yes. He loves it. It was his idea," she answered with another heavy sigh.

Nodding, I asked, "So, you have 'Earth kids'?"

Smiling, she said, "Yes, two. They love it out there, too."

"Do you mind if I ask you another question?" Not waiting for her permission, I went on, "If you could do anything you wanted to do, what would it be?"

She hesitated. "I couldn't do that, because . . ."

I interrupted her, saying, "Don't think about why you can't—what would it be?"

"I don't know . . . uh, I'm a really good computer programmer." Then she blurted out: "I would write software for children that would make a difference on the planet."

A light went on in her head. "Oh, my God! That's it! I went away for a month to figure this out, and in the last few minutes before I go home—I get it! Thank you so much!"

I smiled. "I didn't do anything but ask you the right question, but you're welcome!"

Her whole demeanor had changed. She looked at her watch and said, "I really have to go! Thank you, again. Thank you so much!" She gave me an impish grin. "Looks like we're going to have to get some solar panels to run my computer!"

With that she was up and running through the airport. I sat there laughing to myself. I really liked helping people to be happier; it made me happier, too! As I thought about her transition, I became aware of how important it is to be clear and how uncomfortable a lack of clarity feels. She was probably unable to see the picture clearly because she was focusing on why her ideas wouldn't work instead of what she really wanted. She was also trying too hard. After all, "to try" simply means "to struggle," and she had certainly been doing her share of that!

The conversation with Nan about the difference between thinking, believing and knowing popped into my mind. I considered the definitions of each, in order to make their differences clearer. "To think" is to contemplate. Thoughts are not definite, as we change our minds all the time. "To believe" is to hold an opinion—which of course can be changed. "To know" is to be certain. To *know* is true clarity.

In a daydream state, I smiled at the image that appeared to me. I saw in my mind's eye Jesus standing at the edge of the water before stepping onto it, saying, "I am going to *try* to do this. No, I *think* I can do this. No, I *believe* I can do this. No, I *know* I can do this!" Of course, trying, thinking and believing weren't even part of the picture for him. He knew what he could do. I suspected that doubt was never part of the picture when he went forth to do the miraculous things he did.

A twinge of missing Alea ran through my body. I would really have liked to share some of these thoughts with her. I wondered when she would show up again and instinctively searched the faces scurrying through the airport. Coming back to present time, I glanced at my watch, realizing it was time for me to leave the airport and go visit some clients for whom I was consulting.

I spent the afternoon helping them develop their instructor training program. As the afternoon wore on, it became obvious that I would need to stay another day. I took a break to reserve a room and called my friend, Joe, to make plans to meet for dinner at five o'clock to celebrate his recent promotion. I had two hours before dinner so, keeping an eye on the time, I returned to the task of finding the perfect person to train the other instructors for this business. Mary, a past acquaintance from Southern California, popped into my mind. I saw her clearly, standing in front of a room teaching the course. I let the thought go, not knowing how to track her down, and continued working on developing the course. Two more hours passed slowly as I entrenched myself in details of the training program. When we stopped for the evening, I went to meet Joe at a restaurant.

He was waiting for me when I walked in, so I joined him at the table. We talked superficially about what was happening in each of our lives and I found that my tolerance for unimportant matters had plummeted over the last several months. As we ate, he drank a whole bottle of champagne and ordered another. With each drink, he became louder and louder, bordering on obnoxious. Sitting there with Joe, who was obviously gearing up to order yet another bottle, was such a strange contrast to the time spent with Nan, Daryl and Alea. It was actually a strange contrast to the events of my whole life of late. I had observed a lot of transitions toward resourcefulness recently, and now watching such a dramatic and intentional shift away from resourcefulness made me uncomfortable. All I wanted to do was get away from him so, after dinner, I congratulated him again on his promotion and said good-bye.

As I walked across the restaurant, a woman at one of the tables grabbed my arm and literally pulled me into the booth, saying, "Here is the woman you wanted to meet." I didn't for the life of me remember ever talking to this woman, but one look at the woman sitting beside her convinced me I did indeed want to meet her. Blond hair framed her face, and the light from the room bounced off her hazel eyes. I noticed that she was petite and thought she looked like a bride in her white dress.

The first woman said, "This is Jessie. Now you two go on, get acquainted!" and she got up and left us alone.

I thought I should tell "Jessie" that there must be some mistake, as I didn't know her friend, but I couldn't bring myself to say it. As I looked at the beautiful woman sitting across from me, I thought perhaps it wasn't a mistake at all and introduced myself. We smiled at each other as I said, "Hi, I'm Matt. Nice to meet you." I couldn't believe how nervous I was all of a sudden. I had been on plenty of dates since my divorce and hadn't ever felt like this. She smiled and nodded, as we both leaned in closer to talk over the noise and music. Maybe coming here wasn't such a bad thing after all!

I learned that she was divorced and a corporate executive for a large company. She was also very nice. We explored each other's interests, values and life desires—at least as best we could in a loud and crowded restaurant. We talked and asked each other questions for another hour or two, completely losing track of time.

Not wanting to lose the opportunity to get to know her better, I said, "I'll be in town until tomorrow night. Would you like to have dinner tomorrow? I'd love to get to know you better—in a quieter setting."

She responded without hesitation, "That would be great!"

We exchanged phone numbers and made plans to get together. Just before we separated, I admitted, "Jessie, I have a confession to make."

Realizing that she probably thought I was going to tell her I was married or something equally uncomfortable, I added quickly, "That woman who introduced us, your friend? Well, I have never seen her before in my life. I don't know why she introduced us, but I am glad she did."

Laughing at the irony, Jessie said, "Well, I believe in happy accidents! I'll ask her about it the next time I see her, but I am glad she did it too. See you tomorrow!"

I went to offer Joe a ride home, but he declined. It seemed funny that I had been so irritated by him earlier, and now I was thankful, because in an odd way, his intoxication brought Jessie into my life. Something in my heart told me it was no accident that we had met, and that she indeed was, "The woman I wanted to meet!" What a strange coincidence.

I went to the hotel and tried to sleep, but all I could do was toss and turn. I wanted to share my excitement with Alea and hoped she would show up, but when it became obvious she wasn't coming, I finally rolled over and went to sleep.

I arrived at my client's office the next morning and turned my attention, as much as possible, away from my anticipation of the evening and to the task of finding the right instructor for their program. The secretary handed me a fax that was waiting upon my arrival. I couldn't believe my eyes! It was from Mary, the woman whom I had envisioned only the day before. She was inquiring about employment as a trainer for the company so I called her immediately.

"I was so surprised to get your fax! I had just been wondering how to get hold of you!" She explained that she had gone through the program a year ago and had recently gotten the idea that she would like to be an instructor, which motivated her to inquire. Out of curiosity, I asked, "How long have you wanted to be an instructor?"

She thought for a moment and said, "Not long. I guess the idea occurred to me about three o'clock yesterday afternoon. Why?"

"Oh, nothing, just wondering." I saw no reason to explain to her what a "coincidence" it was that at that exact same time, I had envisioned her in front of the class. Still, it was quite a surprise. Perhaps I would share it with her some day; for now I was content pondering the connection between my clarity and the manifestation of such immediate results. It seemed more and more obvious to me that being clear about what you want is the most crucial ingredient in being able to attract it.

At midday, I called Jessie at work and confirmed our plans for the evening. As I hung up, I felt the wave of nervousness I had experienced when we met wash over me again. I observed how I was feeling and knew I needed to let go of my need to be accepted. I was amused with myself as I observed my hesitation in letting it go. I kind of liked the feeling, as I hadn't cared about someone *in this way* for a very long time. I enjoyed the flustered feeling for a minute or two, then took a deep breath and let it go. I knew that eventually my need for acceptance would interfere with the relationship if I didn't. If nothing else, I needed to let it go so that I could function at work for the rest of the afternoon! Again, time passed slowly, but I wrapped up the day feeling content that I had accomplished what needed to be done.

Excited about seeing Jessie, I pulled up to her house holding the bouquet of flowers I had brought for her. I took a deep breath and opened the car door, feeling like a teenager.

She was beautiful. My nervousness dissolved almost immediately with her easy style. She thanked me for the flowers and put them in a vase, asking if I wanted a glass of wine or a beer. I declined, explaining that we had reservations for dinner in twenty minutes, so she gathered up her things and we left. I took her to a nice, romantic restaurant. It was a perfect date; we got to know each other over fine wine and peaceful music provided by a harpist who sat in a pool of soft light. The harpist's graceful movements at the strings added another level of art to the sounds of the instrument.

I learned that Jessie had grown up on a small island in the Florida

Keys and that her parents divorced when she was young. Her childhood had been filled with turmoil.

I listened intently as she told me about it. "My father kept me during one of my visitations with him when I was eight. He took me away from my mother and brother. It wasn't really scary, because he was my father, not a stranger. I just didn't understand why I couldn't see my mom anymore."

I asked, "What happened?"

"Well, my dad had taken me to another state and put me in school. A distant relative who knew I was missing happened to be working in the cafeteria at the school and recognized me. It was really one of those miraculous coincidences. After they took me back home, my dad stopped paying child support, and we never saw him again—we haven't yet, anyway."

I tried to imagine how hard that would have been, as she went on, "I got out of school by the time I was seventeen and moved to Arizona when I was eighteen. I had always thought I was going to go to college, but an uninspiring teacher convinced me I wasn't smart enough. That, along with a few other distractions, put an end to that idea. Instead, I got a job as an administrative assistant in the corporate office of a national drugstore chain, and have worked my way into my current position with the same firm. It isn't the job of my dreams, but it's been a good experience." She smiled. "Well, there you have it, that's my story."

Laughing, she added, "Oh, by the way, I don't think I'm not smart enough anymore."

I marveled at how many difficulties she had overcome and how many obstacles she had managed to navigate around, making something out of her life despite her family challenges. Her perseverance and determination were admirable. As I listened to her story, I felt my heart swell with appreciation. I knew I could fall in love with her, given the opportunity. I shivered at the thought, not sure whether the idea scared or delighted me. I dismissed it, telling myself that it was too soon.

I asked, "If that isn't the job of your dreams, what would be?"

Jessie replied instantly, as if it was something she had thought about a lot. "Someday I would like to open a small school and work with children as I see a real need for alternatives to regular education. I think it would be a lot of fun. I want to inspire children to be their best and to follow their dreams—and not to let anyone convince them that they can't."

I could tell that visions of the future were dancing in her mind as she told me a few of her ideas for making the school special. It was impressive to see how she had managed to take a bad experience from her own life and turn it into motivation to help others.

She then asked me, "So, now that you know all about me, what is your story?"

I wondered how much to tell her, but since she had shared her childhood with me, I thought that would be a good place to start. "Well, believe it or not, I was born in a train depot in the small, and now nonexistent, town of Headrick, Oklahoma."

"A train depot?"

I went on with the story of my childhood, which seemed far away and unreal as I told it, even though it was true. "After my father got out of the army he did several odd jobs for a living, from picking cotton to fixing up old cars. He wasn't particularly trained to do any one thing, but he took pride in whatever he did, always striving to do it well. He was a pool hustler when I was born. He used to go out drinking and playing pool every night, and we lived off of what he earned—in part, anyway.

"My grandfather worked for the railroad and was responsible for maintaining a section of the railway. My grandparents lived in a section house, which was a three-story, old, ugly, gray house by the tracks. I remember being so scared whenever we went there. The bedroom windows were all painted over, so no light could come in and you couldn't see out. For a child, it was a really spooky place. I always expected something to jump out and eat me up when we were there."

We both laughed at the fears so many children have in common. She asked, "How did you come to be born in the train depot?"

"Well, we lived in a boxcar right next to the station. I guess my grandfather made arrangements for us to live there. Anyhow, my mom went into heavy labor one day in the train station. They called the doctor, and he rushed over and delivered me right then and there. I guess I was in a hurry and there wasn't time to move her to a hospital."

Jessie sat there looking fascinated and, I guessed, a little surprised. She asked, "Did your father play pool for a living through your entire childhood?'

I answered, as if I watched a movie of my memories, "No. He was really good but wouldn't play his best at the beginning of the evening. He would get better and better as the evening progressed. People would win when they first played against him, but as the games went on, he would start winning and keep on winning until the end. One night, some guys got mad and beat him up badly. He came home with the whole side of his face ripped up and bloody, with pieces of gravel embedded in the cuts. I can still remember how upset my mother was. My father quit playing pool that night. He got a job in the fields for a while, until he fell and hurt his back. After that he did whatever he could for money, taking different odd jobs here and there."

As I told Jessie about myself, I wondered what it was like for her to date someone like me. Whenever I stopped to recount my history, I surprised myself at how far I'd come. This was something she and I had in common, although the details were different.

We swapped stories for a couple of hours. By the end of the date, I was completely enthralled; my best guess was that she was, too.

Looking at my watch, I said, "I still have to drive back to Sedona tonight, so I'd better get going. Will I see you again?" This was the moment of truth; her answer would let me know whether she was enjoying the evening as much as I was—or not. I took a deep breath and let go of both hopes and fears.

She smiled and took my hand, saying, "I sure hope so! When will you be back in town?"

"I'm planning to come back next week for some consulting, but I'm not sure of the exact day yet." Although it seemed too far away, I asked, "Can I take you out to dinner when I come? I know of another really nice restaurant in town I would love to take you to."

"Any chance you want to stay another day and come over to my house for dinner tomorrow night?" she asked directly.

I sighed in relief, impressed that not only did she want to see me again, but she wanted to see me soon. Considering the possibilities, I said, "Well, I could stay, I suppose." I wanted to ask her what she was doing all day, since I really didn't have plans, but again, I didn't want to be too pushy. Besides, I already knew she was working. We decided to meet at six o'clock at her place.

As I walked her to her door, she asked, "What are you doing tomorrow? I mean, until dinner?"

"I don't have any plans." Laughing, I added, "Technically, I'm waiting for dinner."

"Why don't you call me in the morning, and we can plan something for the day? That is, if you'd like to." She smiled, then added, "The way I figure it, if you are willing to stay in town another day, I can at least take a day off. We could go for a hike, or to a museum, or catch a movie. . . ."

Smiling back, I said, "I would love to spend the day with you. I'll call you in the morning." We paused at that slightly awkward moment when you aren't sure whether you should kiss or hug, or how you should end the evening. In some ways, I felt as if I had known Jessie forever and would know her forever from this moment forward, yet rationally I knew this was still our first date. I decided on the hug and the kiss. Apparently I made the right decision, as she returned them both before we said good night.

I went to the hotel and checked myself back in, joyful at the way the evening had gone. I slept soundly, waking the next morning feeling well rested. I wondered how early to call Jessie. I decided to wait until nine, which seemed like a torturous amount of time to wait. I showered, dressed and watched the time as patiently as I could.

She answered on the first ring, "Hello?"

"Hi, it's Matt. I wasn't sure how early to call. I hope I didn't wake you up."

In her straightforward way, she said, "Are you kidding? I've been up for a couple of hours. I'm ready for the day. What sounds like fun to you?"

"Well, there are some nice places to hike not too far from here, if you want to get outside."

Decisively, she said, "Let's go to Clear Water! There are some beautiful waterfalls there, and some great places to hike."

"Sounds great. I'll come get you."

She answered happily, "I'm ready, whenever you get here."

We filled the day with hiking, cloud watching, rock hunting and holding hands. It was so easy to be with her. I could already tell that I was going to have a hard time living a couple of hours away.

We stopped at the market to pick up a few things and went to her place. She declined my offer to help her with dinner, so I poured us both a glass of wine and looked at the books on her shelves and at her music collection while she prepared the meal. Nothing was out of place in her home; it was very well-ordered, with lots of small touches that gave it a comfortable feeling of being lived in and cared for. Like me, she had chosen a simple but colorful Southwestern decor that perfectly matched her environment.

Talking late into the evening, we explored our feelings about getting married again and found that both of us were interested in the idea, if the other person was the right one. It was funny that I could even think about remarrying, much less talk about it with a woman. Even though my marriage had been over for several years, it wasn't until recently that I had been able to let go of my negative feelings about it and declare my readiness for an ongoing relationship.

She then asked me, "How do you feel about having kids?"

I explained, "I hadn't really thought about having more kids; I already have two. I guess I wouldn't be opposed if the circumstances were right. What about you?"

I could see right away by the look in her eyes that kids were part of her future. Somehow, the thought of having a child with Jessie felt okay with me.

She answered positively, "Yes, I want to have children."

As two adults who had both been previously married, neither of us was anxious to go through another divorce. We asked a number of pertinent questions in an attempt to get to know each other more fully and then, apparently satisfied with our discoveries, turned our conversation to making plans for the weekend, which was now only a few days away. Jessie was working the rest of the week, and I had quite a bit on my agenda as well. I wanted to spend as much time with her as I could, so we decided that the next weekend we would begin on Friday night instead of Saturday.

She asked, "Do you want to come back to Phoenix, or do you want me to come to Sedona? You can stay here if you want, instead of getting a hotel. I mean, I have the space, if you want to save the money." She blushed a little at the potential implication of her invitation.

I answered her with another question, "Would you rather get away to Sedona? I'd love to show you my home, too."

She gracefully accepted, saying that she loved going to Sedona. I couldn't believe this was happening. In some ways finding a woman who was making me even think about a committed relationship again was almost more miraculous than the mysterious comings and goings of Alea. Jessie was energetic, enthusiastic, intelligent, and with every moment we spent together, becoming more precious to me. I looked forward to the weekend and the opportunity to see her again.

"I'd better get going, or I may never leave. I do need to get home," I said, hugging her good-bye.

Jessie said suddenly, "Oh, I almost forgot to tell you. I spoke with my friend from the restaurant the other night. She said that she left so quickly because as soon as you sat down, she realized that you weren't who she thought you were! She was really embarrassed and apologetic—that is, until I thanked her repeatedly!"

Laughing again at the cosmic "coincidence" that brought us together, we finally kissed good night.

Driving back to Sedona, I wondered what she would think if I told her about Alea and the golden rings. I didn't want to tell her about something that might make her change her mind about me. On the other hand, I didn't want to conceal the things that were most important to me, either. I decided I would wait and see how things developed between us before I told her, and then only if the timing was right.

I knew I was teetering on the edge of falling in love. My head argued with my heart regarding the rationality of such a thing, but my heart was winning, because my head couldn't come up with any convincing contrary reasons.

It was late when I finally made it home. Just before I fell asleep, I thought of Alea. I wanted to share my excitement with her. It seemed strange to me to be falling in love with one woman and wanting to share my feelings with another whom I also loved, but my love for Alea was different. I couldn't quite explain it, but it wasn't the same. I was beginning to understand why Alea kept telling me that ours was a unique relationship. I fell asleep smiling.

The next day, I put in a phone call to Jessie and caught her at her office.

"Sorry to bother you at work; I just wanted to thank you again for the last two days we spent together."

She replied, "It's okay, I'm glad you called. Thank you, too! I'm going to leave work a little early tomorrow, so I should be there by 6:30 or so."

"Great. I'm really looking forward to seeing you."

"Me too. Should I bring anything in particular?" she inquired.

"Well, you may want to bring some shoes for hiking, and I thought maybe we'd go out for dinner at least once. Everything is pretty casual here, though. You don't need to bring anything in particular—just you!"

We spoke for a few more minutes, then I let her get back to work. I was having a hard time containing my desire to have her with me and wished that she could just appear, like Alea did; I didn't want to wait. Thankfully, it was already Thursday, and she was due tomorrow. Somehow I kept myself busy until the anticipated moment arrived.

At 6:30 on the nose, the doorbell rang. My heart beat loudly as I went to the door. She stood there, smiling in her easy, natural way. We hugged, and then I helped her with her bags. She laughed as we carried in her things, saying, "I wasn't sure what to bring, so I'm afraid I brought enough for a week rather than a weekend."

I held back my impulse to say, "Bring enough to stay forever!" but instead said, "No problem, there is plenty of room." With that, I led her to a guest bedroom, as I didn't want to make any assumptions about how the weekend would go. I felt a little awkward as I tried to balance showing her respect with a lack of expectations, and letting her know how much I liked her and wanted to be with her.

I chose my words carefully, saying, "You can put your things in here," instead of, "This is your room." I blushed a little, as I felt that was a good compromise, leaving all possibilities open.

After I showed her around and made dinner, we went for a walk. I told her about Cindy and the book. She listened carefully, commenting here and there, and we continued on in silence. Starlight surrounded the rock formations, making the evening feel magical. I reached for her hand and then pulled her around so we were facing each other. Looking straight into her eyes, I said, "Thanks for coming up here, Jessie. I am really happy you are here." I leaned down and kissed her gently, and we just stood there, holding each other, for what seemed like several minutes. A light breeze wrapped around us in a swirling motion so noticeable that we both commented on it. It felt like a blessing from the universe. Indeed, I did feel so blessed to have her in my life. It was odd to feel so strongly about someone I had known such a short time, but in this moment, I didn't want to ever be without her. A shooting star streaked across the sky; we both watched as it disappeared. We then turned and walked back home.

Sitting out on the patio, we watched the sky and talked. Then the time came to go to bed. I showed Jessie where the towels were and gave her an extra blanket so she wouldn't get cold. Fighting the desire to lead her into my room, I kissed her good night. We both hesitated and then parted ways for the night. I did not want to rush the relationship, and at the same time was already thinking that she was going to be my life partner. I went to my room and lay in bed thinking about the wonderful woman on the other side of the wall, finally falling asleep after what seemed to be hours.

In the morning, the light streamed in my windows. It took me a few minutes to get the sleep out of my head, remembering what day it was and that Jessie was in the other room. I took a shower to wake me up, made some tea and went out on the patio to wait for her. The sun was rising quickly over the landscape that unfolded before me. I would never tire of this view and its magnificence. She joined me on the patio. We embraced each other and the morning and, sipping tea, watched the day begin in silence. I had met few people who could enjoy silence with another person, particularly one met so recently. Often people felt that they needed to fill the space with words, or know what the other was thinking, or worry about what they were going to say next. With Jessie, everything was easy. Silence was comfortable and honored, yet communicating was easy, too. Even during the quiet spells in our conversation, I felt as though we shared everything we were observing.

I pierced the silence, asking, "Are you up for a hike and a picnic?"

"Sure, where do you want to go?"

"I was thinking about heading out to one of the energy vortexes; a river runs right by it, and there are some wonderful rock formations we can climb. Do you know about the vortexes, Jessie?"

"I've heard of them. They are areas of measurably greater energy, or something like that, right? I've never paid that much attention, but it sounds like fun to me. Let's go!"

We packed some food for a picnic and headed out. On the drive I pointed out places of interest, showing her my favorite spots as we drove through town and telling her the names of the different rock formations as we passed them. We parked, put the day packs on and began our leisurely hike.

I wanted to tell Jessie more about me and what I had been going through lately. Although I had been sharing bits and pieces with her, I hadn't told her the whole story and had said nothing about Alea and Michael. It was such a major part of my life that leaving it out seemed misleading. At the same time, I wasn't sure exactly how to approach the subject. It had been easier with Nan, because so many of our previous conversations had involved similar topics. I chose not to bring it up yet; instead, I asked questions about her religious beliefs. I figured, that way, I would at least know what kind of reaction to expect and could build a base upon which to lead into the topic.

She explained her perspective to me. "I believe in God, without a doubt; I'm just not sure what I believe about him. I know that sounds funny, but I feel more than I know intellectually. I have a deep sense of spirituality, but I haven't found a church or one set of beliefs that I could say I believe in completely. I love Christ and his teachings, and I also enjoy the teachings of other prophets and teachers as well. I guess I'm fairly open to a lot of possibilities and pick and choose what feels right to me."

It seemed to me that I had said almost the exact same thing to my boys when they asked me about religion.

I stated, "I don't believe in God." She gave me such a surprised look that I hurried to explain before her surprise turned into disdain. "I don't *believe* in God; I *know* God. There is no doubt in my mind, therefore no need for mere beliefs." We both laughed, and her obvious relief showed.

I then asked, "What about personal growth? Do you read self-help books or go to workshops?"

She paused, then answered, "I have read a few books. Seems like they all say the same old thing. I don't really have any interest in going to workshops either. I do believe in personal growth, if that is what you're asking. I just don't have one prescribed method or any one teaching—or teacher—that I follow. Basically, I am happy with my life and I like who I am."

"I like who you are, too!" I blurted. She turned and smiled at me.

The canyon was opening up in front of us. The smell of juniper and sage reached into my soul and pulled up memories from my past. Jessie and I paused for a moment and listened. The silence here was like nowhere else in the world. The air held a sweetness that made me want to breathe in forever without stopping to breathe out. I just wanted to be full of its scent. We stood there, holding hands, looking out across the canyon, listening to the breeze blow through the rocks. A feeling of ancient times blew through me with the wind, as if I were suddenly standing here a hundred or even a thousand years in the past. I imagined that it looked exactly the same, with the exception of an occasional airplane breaking into the scene, drawing us back to reality.

I wrapped my arms around Jessie and said, "I have the feeling that living two hours away from you is going to become totally unacceptable soon."

She responded to my touch and my words. "I know what you mean. What do you suppose we ought to do about it?"

Our eyes met briefly as I said, "Well, I'm not sure. What do you think?"

She laughed and said, "I'm not sure either." Neither of us was ready to say all that we were both thinking; we hadn't known each other "long enough," at least by conventional measures.

"Well," I added, "I'm sure the solution will become obvious with a little more time. I just know already that I want to see you more."

She smiled and leaned against me. "I want to see you more, too. I suppose you are right, the options will become obvious before long." As if an afterthought, she added, "Just for the record, though, if one of us is going to have to move, I would rather live in Sedona than Phoenix." She smiled as she offered her willingness to make the changes necessary for us to be together.

I smiled back and said, "Well, in the meantime, since I work out of my home, I can arrange to work from Phoenix, at least some of the time."

As if we both realized at the exact same time what we were actually talking about, we both blushed a little and held each other in silence again, content with our mutual feelings.

Meanwhile, the clouds had begun to gather at the head of the canyon. They had been white and puffy all day as they passed overhead; now they were dark and menacing—with a different, more intense beauty. We could smell rain in the near distance.

I asked, "Do you want to leave before we get rained on?"

"I suppose we should, but look how dramatic this weather is! I love watching storms."

"Me too. There's an overhang over here, if you want to watch from a slightly dryer place. Although we'll undoubtedly get drenched if we stay."

"Let's just watch for a little longer." We worked our way toward the overhang.

I held Jessie close, feeling her heartbeat against my chest as we watched the clouds move swiftly, swirling and igniting in flashes of lightning when they collided. The thunder that followed vibrated through us. We were held spellbound by the unleashed power and splendor.

I asked, "Can you smell that—the smell of earth and water mixed together? I love the smell of rain when it first starts to fall."

She added, "Yes, it seems like it releases all the hidden scents of the plants and rocks. I love how clean and vivid everything looks after the rain, too."

It was a good thing we both loved the rain so much, because before long the wind blew it right into our overhang, soaking us both. We giggled as we wiped the rain out of our eyes and kissed the drops from each other's lips. Mother Nature provided an unparalleled show for us, and we watched for hours before I said, "What do you say we go home, climb in the hot tub or build a fire to warm up?"

She agreed, and before long we were making our way back down the road, holding hands all the while, the rain following us home.

I turned on the bubbles, checked the temperature, and climbed into the hot tub. Jessie joined me only moments later with two glasses of wine. We listened to the rain falling on the patio roof while we soaked our sore muscles and cold bones.

I inquired, "What is it that you want out of life?"

She answered thoughtfully, "I want to share life with someone I love, raise children and enjoy the beauty that surrounds us—like today."

She then asked me the same, "What do you want?"

"I want to share my life with someone I love and share moments like today, too. I want to constantly grow and learn, and then share what I discover with others, so that they can live more joyful, loving lives. I also want to make a difference on the planet through my speaking and by writing books that will be useful tools for people."

She nodded as she listened.

I felt compelled to add, "Jessie, I need to let you know that sometimes I worry about whether I am a good father."

She looked a little concerned when she asked, "What do you mean?"

"I love my boys, but I don't feel like I'm doing them justice as a father. When I lived with my boys, I wasn't the kind of guy who went out and threw the ball around with them, you know? Now that we are apart, I don't get much practice. I'm just a little uncomfortable around kids and noise and activity, even though I love children," I attempted to explain.

"Does that mean you don't want to have any more kids?" she asked with obvious disappointment.

I thought for a moment and then answered honestly, "No, I'm willing to have kids—if our relationship goes in that direction. I just want you to know that this is an area that I think I need to work on. It doesn't come naturally to me. Maybe I'm just afraid because it is such an awesome responsibility. I feel like my boys got ripped off when I got divorced and I just haven't been able to make it up to them." After a moment of self-observation, I added, "I don't know, it sounds like maybe this is my guilt talking."

It seemed so strange, on the one hand, to talk about topics like this with her after so brief an acquaintance, and at the same time, it couldn't have felt more natural.

"I'll love the kids and help as much as I can; it just isn't my area of natural ability or expertise. I may need help with learning how to be a really good father. I want you to know the truth; I don't want to mislead you." It was hard to be so honest, knowing that I could be scaring away the woman of my dreams.

She looked thoughtful for a moment and then must have decided that it was okay with her, because she kissed me in a manner that made me think our relationship was progressing, rather than ending.

After I caught my breath, I said, "What do you say we get out of the hot tub and put some dinner together? I'll cook, while you get cleaned up, unless you'd rather go out?"

"Let's stay here. I'm not all that hungry. I would be fine with just something light, like a salad. How about you?"

"I'm happy staying here. I'll put something together." With that, we climbed out of the tub and went to our independent bathrooms to shower and dry off.

After a light dinner of fish and salad, we cleaned the kitchen and then went into the living room. She asked me about different pieces of art that I had collected and wanted to know the story behind each. We laughed, shared stories and kissed intermittently for another hour. I went into the kitchen to get us something to drink and when I came out, Jessie had disappeared. My first thought was that I had another Alea on my hands, but upon second thought, I began to look around for her. I heard something on the other side of the house and, following the sounds, I found her building a fire in the fireplace—in my bedroom. I set the drinks down, pulled her toward me and pushed the door shut.

We woke the next morning rejoicing in the expression of our love. I delighted in looking across the pillow and seeing her face framed sweetly by her hair. She looked just as beautiful to me when she first woke up as she did the rest of the day. We plotted and planned how we could spend as much time as possible together from this point forward. I told her about the work I was doing with Daryl, which would bring me through Phoenix to the airport, but with some irregularity. I would also be spending a few days in Phoenix in the upcoming week for consulting, which could possibly include the weekend. We decided to play it by ear. Since it was still raining, we spent the day snuggled up, enjoying the fireplace and each other.

As we hugged good-bye, I looked directly into her eyes and whispered, "Jessie, I love you."

She smiled and whispered back, "I love you too, Matt."

Letting her leave that afternoon was one of the hardest things I had done in a long time. My heart and soul just did not feel indulged enough, and I didn't want to wait three more days to see her. I figured I could get away by Wednesday.

I watched as she drove away, taking a piece of my heart with her.

I walked around the house for a few minutes, not sure how I wanted to fill my time. I distracted myself by calling my boys to see how they were doing. They filled me in on the details of their lives and left me missing them as well as Jessie. Not exactly an improvement in my emotional landscape! At the same time, though, I felt joyous to the core of my being.

I reflected on my life and the many changes that had occurred since Alea had made herself known. I wondered where she had been lately, as I reviewed the ways I was now different. I was more open, more able and willing to love, better able to experience the moment and happier. I even felt more artistic and creative, which found expression in my writing. Another change was that my thoughts were far more focused on spirituality than ever before and I was more willing to explore "mystical" ideas. I wondered whether Alea had induced these changes or whether the changes had induced her.

As I formulated the question in my mind, I heard her voice answer, *"Both, Matt. You opened the door for me to come to you by surrendering to new possibilities. The more open and loving you were, the more willing to feel, the more aware of me you became. The more aware of me you became, the more open, loving and able to feel you became."* I looked around, but she did not materialize. Nonetheless, it was comforting to just hear her voice.

"Alea, I miss you. Where are you?" I felt funny talking to an empty room, but thought it was worth a shot.

"I'm here, Matt." She appeared on the other side of the room. She went on to explain, *"I cannot stay long in this form. It takes a lot of energy to maintain a body. There will be times when just talking—without seeing—may have to suffice."*

Concerned, I asked, "Is something wrong, Alea? Are you okay?"

She smiled and said, *"Everything is perfect and as it should be. It's just that I now have limited time to spend in a body. I came specifically to guide you on your path, and you are now well on your way. My physical form is no longer as necessary. I want to use my remaining time wisely."*

I thought for a moment and asked, "Why was it ever necessary, Alea? Couldn't you just have told me what you wanted me to know?"

She laughed out loud. *"I needed my body because part of my mission here was to jump-start your heart and get you to feel love again. Maybe I am underestimating myself, but that would have been pretty hard to do with just words. Now, you tell me—how receptive would you have been to just a voice with no body?"*

She continued laughing at the thought, and I had to concur, "I suppose you're right. It was hard enough to accept your presence in physical form. I suppose I would have really thought I was going nuts if I had just heard voices. Alea, if you want to conserve your energy, I suppose I can handle just hearing your voice for now." I didn't want to be responsible for wasting any of her precious time.

Suddenly, her voice emanated through the room, though her body no longer stood before me. *"Thank you, Matt. There are still occasions when I will need a body, and I want to be sure that I can still create it when I do."*

I spoke in the direction where I had last seen her standing and just pretended she was still in front of me. This made it easier to talk to her. I felt a lot like Major Nelson in the old TV sitcom, *I Dream of Jeannie,* the only difference being that Alea did not call me "Master." I laughed at the analogy. "I'm feeling a little bit manipulated on the love thing, but thank you for doing it, Alea. You were irresistible."

"Thanks. It was the least I could do. Now, enough about me! Tell me all about this new love of yours!"

"Her name is Jessie, and she is wonderful. The more time I spend with her, the more I think she's the one I want to spend my life with. Have you seen her, Alea? Do you know her? Were you there?" I was sure my enthusiasm carried in my voice.

"Yes, I know her well, and I agree. Jessie is a wonderful woman, and I am very happy to see that you found her. I am even more pleased to know that you were open enough to let her into your life—and your heart."

I asked Alea sincerely, "Is Jessie one of the miracles you referred to—the kind that can happen when I let go and become resourceful?"

"Indeed, Matt, she is. So what do you suppose will happen between the two of you now?"

"Well, I know it is probably too soon to say this, but I am honestly thinking of trying marriage again." I could hardly believe I was hearing myself say these words. I hadn't ever thought I'd remarry.

"Listen to me carefully, Matt. Clarity of language is as important as clarity of heart and mind. Remember how powerful intention, willingness and commitment are? These three qualities are put forth into the world, in part through your choice of words. Words are extremely powerful. Consider this: When you put a series of letters together properly to create a word, what do we call that?"

"Spelling," I answered.

"Yes, and when words are strung together properly to create a certain magical result, what is that called?"

I suddenly saw the connection she was making. "Casting a spell—or spelling!"

She continued, *"The words you choose to use have power, Matt. Part of being clear is choosing to use the words that most clearly express the truth of how you are feeling, but also those that will work with you powerfully to create the results that you wish to create."*

I understood the value of what she was saying, but didn't understand what she was referring to until she said, *"Now, listen to this sentence: 'I am thinking of trying marriage again.' What does this choice of words reflect to you, and what result do you suppose will be created?"*

While I felt a little like I was being admonished, I knew Alea and her love well enough to know that this wasn't the case. It was just harder to receive her guidance without the visual assistance of seeing the love that poured forth from her eyes while she spoke to me. I answered, "What I'm really saying with those words is that I'm not convinced, and that I'm going 'to struggle' in marriage again. It feels awful to say it that way."

"It feels awful to hear it that way, too. Consider for a moment that the words you have strung together into a sentence are so powerful that they actually 'sentence' you to experience what you have said! If what you are saying is not what you want to live out—it would be worth your time to restate your feelings and sentence yourself to a life of joy! Now, return to resourcefulness and tell me from there, what you really want to say."

My mouth dropped open slightly in awe. I never thought of spelling a word as casting a spell for a certain result, nor had I ever considered a sentence to be sentencing myself—or someone else—to living out whatever I said! Now, listening to this beautiful voice explain it to me, it made perfect sense. I made a silent vow to be much more conscious of the words I chose to use, then closed my eyes and followed Alea's instructions. Taking a few deep breaths, I let go and moved into my heart. I stayed in that place for a few minutes, then answered, "I am in love with Jessie, Alea, and I know that I am going to marry her and spend my life with her—happily."

"Now then, how does that feel to say?" she asked lovingly.

"Really different!" I had let go of the drama of being afraid, and I liked this feeling much better!

"Alea, I need to tell Jessie about you and all that has happened since you showed up. I am a little concerned it will scare her away."

"The process is the same in all situations, Matt. Self-observe, let go, get resourceful and take action from there. When you take action from resourcefulness, it is steeped in clarity. If you follow those steps, you cannot go wrong."

I thought about my conversation about clarity and knowing with Nan, and then about how later my clarity of vision seemed instrumental in causing Mary to contact me from Southern California at just the right moment. I realized that I had stated clearly my readiness to have love come into my life—from resourcefulness, not a need for acceptance, and *poof*—Jessie had showed up, Now my clarity of words had just created a more powerful message.

I reiterated, "The recurring theme here seems to be clarity. It's as if clarity is the magnet that attracts the results."

Jokingly she asked, *"Are you sure about that?"*

I stated clearly, "Yes, Alea, I know it!"

Alea's voice laughed with mine, at which point I noticed a jeweler's box on the table before me. Her voice rang out, *"Go ahead, open it!"*

Symbolic of an engagement ring but large enough for my wrist, I found the next golden circlet inside the plush box, inscribed beautifully with the word *Clarity*.

Going along with the engagement theme, I said, "Why, thank you, Alea. I accept your proposal."

Her delighted laughter faded but her presence remained vibrantly close. Of this, I was completely clear.

Alea basked in the love she felt for Matt and her joy over the new love opening up in his life. Even though she knew the value of clarity well, she enjoyed watching the results of it every time. It always seemed like magic, when in reality it was simply a universal law at work, somewhat like cause and effect, or in folk terms, "You reap what you sow." Now that Matt had gained an understanding of the importance of clarity, as he continued to master it, he would help others to be clearer as well—much as he had done with the woman at the airport.

Miracles can happen when, from resourcefulness, people set their intention, willingness and commitment in alignment with their thoughts, words, feelings and actions. She knew what the world would be like if people were to gain a true sense of how powerful they are with words. There is no stronger weapon, nor any greater tool. Words can injure someone for many years, cause a riot, move thousands of people to inspired action or soothe a breaking heart. She reflected on all the things said to children in frustrated moments, which were then carried with them, influencing them, for the rest of their lives. There was no doubt in her being that if people would realize that their words indeed sentenced a child to a lifetime of feeling stupid, or a lifetime of feeling unloved, they would be more watchful of the words that they use in their sentences. It saddened her to think of the things people say to themselves.

She thought of people who waste their words, using so many, so often, that others stop listening to them, or those who use streams of monotone words that hypnotize the listener. Yes, people are more powerful than they know. What if schoolteachers were taught how to use their words effectively, so as to uplift their students, and what if they taught the kids to do the same? She was sure that the use of a simple tape recorder, which would allow teachers and parents to hear themselves in self-observation, would move many of them to refine their art.

Her thoughts turned to the great world leaders through time who, with command of words and clarity of vision, had inspired entire nations and spread their messages throughout the world, touching people's hearts. She paused for a moment and felt the awesome potential of such a great thing—clarity. She liked the way it sounded when uttered, as it reminded her of the ringing of temple bells, a sound she dearly loved.

She now reflected upon the ways in which Matt had grown. She saw him becoming more balanced, utilizing all aspects of his being rather than just his linear, logical side. He was now accessing the parts of his brain which allowed him to be more creative, more sensitive, more aware and more fun. Most important, he was now listening to his heart and had gained the insight to share what he found there with clarity. She smiled at the thought. Jessie was lucky to be finding him now!

Alea knew that Jessie was meant to come into Matt's life. Of course, Jessie had no idea how big a step marrying one with a mission such as Matt's was going to be. However, Alea was confident that she was fully capable of the task. The irony is that everyone has the same mission of opening hearts and spreading love, but not everyone embraces it to the extent that Matt has—and will. It takes an equally rare being to support this kind of magnitude. It would not always be easy for either of them, but the rewards would justify the effort, ten-fold.

From a state of resourcefulness, Alea created a clear vision of the future, and as a gift to Jessie and Matt, blew her vision out into the universe, as if blowing a kiss to God.

10

The Vows

"There is something I need to tell you, Jessie." I took a deep breath, let go and practiced again, thankful that she wasn't really in front of me listening as I spoke out loud. The drive to Phoenix was affording me plenty of time to get it right. "This is kind of hard to believe, but I really want you to know. . . ." Shaking my head at how I sounded, I caught sight of my own reflection in the rearview mirror. The quick glance into my eyes was long enough to capture a glimmer of my own soul, just enough to remind me that if I told Jessie from a place of doubt and disbelief, she would receive doubt and disbelief. I had to share from my clarity, wonder and excitement, if I wanted her to hear those things. I rolled down my window and let the passing wind blow away any doubts, and I continued the drive in trust that just the right words would show up at just the right moment to tell Jessie about Alea and the magical world that I had grown to love.

Glancing at my watch, I figured I would roll into Phoenix around one o'clock. I had a full afternoon of consulting ahead and a dinner date with Jessie at six. I hoped the day would go quickly, as all I really wanted was to be in Jessie's arms, looking into her beautiful, playful eyes. A glimmer of mischievousness sparkled in them, as if she was in on a little joke or secret that the rest of the world didn't know. The secret gave her permission to be happy, no matter what was going on in her life. I found myself accepting the same authorization for happiness whenever I was around her.

I spent the afternoon consulting with the training company, which had claimed to value my advice. Today, however, we reached a bit of an impasse that left me feeling a knot in my stomach. From where I stood, outside the company looking in, I could easily see what they needed to adjust in order to solve their current problem with their trainers. From where they stood, inside the company looking at each other, they didn't understand what I was saying at all. I tried repeatedly to show them that the material they were asking their trainers to teach was out of balance; it was all head-to-head information, with no connection to the heart. Even when they were working with emotions, their methods kept people thinking and talking instead of feeling and letting go. They needed a balance between material presented in an academic style and heart-opening experiences. True growth requires an understanding of information, along with the related experience of feeling it.

I explained to them the importance of the balance. "You are not just teaching *material*, you are teaching *human beings*. The value for the participant has to be your number one priority, both for ethical reasons and because they will be your strongest sales force if they have gained enough benefit."

We went round and round while they tried to convince me that my suggestions wouldn't work, and I tried to convince them they would. The solution seemed so obvious to me in the beginning, but by the end of the day, I had begun to wonder whether I was missing something and whether they were right, as they had been relentless in holding their position. I knew that the doubts popping in were my old beliefs and old patterns, and that I needed to let go in order to move forward. Even my own internal process was a combined approach of head and heart; I knew I needed to let go, but if I didn't take action, didn't feel it, nothing would change. We parted ways, planning to continue in the morning where we had left off, after letting everyone sleep on it overnight.

I went to the restaurant early to wait for Jessie and to clear my head. Sitting down, still a little confused, I ordered something to drink. The events of the afternoon had so involved me that they had even managed to take my mind off my excitement about seeing Jessie. As I sipped my drink, I felt a tap on my shoulder. Turning, thinking Jessie had also arrived early, I was surprised to see the man from the restaurant in Sedona, wearing the same overalls and felt hat—Michael!

Before I could even greet him, he said, "Tough day, huh? I have a message for you. You are a really nice guy. You have a tendency to listen to others and let them pull you off track, but I have to tell you that you're right on with what you're doing, and there is no time for you to be off track. Follow your heart!"

Just then, Jessie walked in. Michael simply said, "I'll see you later."

I stood to welcome Jessie, then turned around to introduce her to Michael, but he was walking out the door.

Jessie sat down and asked, "Who was that man?"

Relieved that she had seen him too, I took it as a sign to go ahead and answer her question honestly. Taking Michael's advice, I checked in with my heart and followed it right through the telling moments. "Have you ever heard of the Archangel Michael?"

"Sure, I've heard of him, but I don't know anything about him. Why?"

"Well, I'm not sure if this guy is him or is a messenger of his, but this is the second time I have bumped into him in a restaurant, in two different cities, and each time he has come up and given me guidance. He is a very wise old man."

Jessie looked quizzical, and then she started laughing. "Him? He doesn't look like much of an angel to me, not to mention an Archangel!"

I understood her doubt. "I know—that's what I thought, too, when I first saw him, but after I spoke with him for a while, well, he is one of the wisest people I have ever met."

I paused for a moment, then continued, "Actually, Jessie, some things have been happening in my life lately that are rather, well, mystical and unexplainable, although wonderful. I really need to tell you about it all, before our relationship goes any further, because it has come to be a very important part of my life—and so have you. Are you up for an evening of hearing an amazing and wonderful tale? It may take several hours."

She sat back in her chair, smiling, and said, "I'm not going anywhere until you are done!"

Punctuated only by dinner, I began telling Jessie all about Michael and his mission to wake up his army of volunteers. Seeing that her response to that was going well, I moved on to Alea and the golden rings, the meaning of each gift, and the series of events that led up to our "accidental" meeting in the restaurant. I even told Jessie my fears about losing her if she thought I was crazy and how I had practiced in the car on the way here. She reached out and held my hand, reassuring me of her place in my life.

When I finally stopped for breath, she asked, "Do you think I will be able to meet Alea some day?"

"I don't know, Jessie. I have no idea if she is visible to anyone else. So far, I would say that she hasn't been. However, I could ask her and see. My best guess is that she is some sort of spirit guide who has come to help me. She had to come in a physical form rather than an ethereal one to wake me up. Let's just say I was sound asleep!"

It felt good to laugh with Jessie. Then she looked at me seriously for a moment and said, "I bet you couldn't have attracted her into your life if that were the case. There had to be some kind of awakening going on before she showed up." I felt a surge of pure joy. She believed me! The relief I felt was a measure of how much this meant to me.

The restaurant was almost empty, and the employees were busy cleaning up for the night. Several hours must have passed without our noticing.

As I paid the bill, Jessie asked, "So, Matt, what do you suppose this big mission of yours entails? I mean, when you look toward the future, what do you see?"

I closed my eyes for a moment and saw the image of the dream I had had when Nan was visiting. Even now, it took my breath away. I answered as we walked out to the car, "When I look to the future, the image I have is of thousands of people being helped through my book, and of teaching the concepts that each of the Rings of Truth holds. I honestly am not sure of it all, Jessie, but the picture I get is that people are starving for nourishment and especially love. They are starving for lives based on the spiritual truths which have been taught throughout the ages. They want connections with others that touch their hearts, rather than just words they can quote that don't change the quality of their lives. They want to apply their spirituality in their daily lives, but they don't know how."

As I spoke, I saw again the importance of both understanding intellectually *and* experiencing the feelings, in order to have true growth and transformation.

I continued, "I have seen the power of letting go and becoming resourceful; after all, it brought you into my life! I want to share these skills with people, so they can let go of the stuff that is blocking their connection to Source, blocking their connection with each other, and stopping them from giving and receiving true love. I want people to know God's love, not just believe in it. I want to be instrumental in turning us into a 'God-loving' people instead of a 'God-fearing' one. Our relationships with each other, ourselves and God would be so much healthier if they were based in love, rather than fear. Love is a far stronger motivation for goodness."

I went on speaking to Jessie, thinking out loud. "The image that just came into my mind was how prehistoric people constantly feared God, believing that thunder, lightning and other natural phenomena were actually the wrath of God for something they had done wrong. Then, as our knowledge of science improved, we realized the causes and no longer interpreted these events in the same way, but the old belief system that God punishes us didn't go away. That eliminated personal responsibility, putting the blame on God instead of the responsibility on us! When we place blame outside ourselves for our problems, we look outside ourselves for the solutions—as opposed to letting go, getting resourceful, listening to God's guidance and taking inspired action.

"I see it all so clearly. God does not punish us, Jessie, nor does God judge us. God simply loves us, while we punish and judge ourselves.

Our lives contain cause-and-effect responses, consequences—some of which are experienced immediately, some after a delay. We are responsible for what we experience! We create the pain. We create the pleasure. All the while, God loves us and guides us, allowing us to paint the picture. Just as parents allow their children to learn from the natural consequences of their actions whenever possible, they also set up guidelines to protect the child. Take the Ten Commandments, for instance. I now see them as guidelines God set up for our happiness and protection, rather than the threats of punishment I was raised imagining them to be."

Jessie and I drove around talking a little longer, before going back to her place. As we walked in the door, she said, "Matt, I'm so glad you shared all this with me. You are right, some of it is a little 'out there' and hard to believe, but the funny thing is, I do believe it—and you. I see the importance of your mission and will support you, however I can."

Without even thinking about it, I pulled her toward me and said, "Jessie, I love you, and I want to spend my life with you. Will you marry me?"

I must have looked as surprised as she did, because as we looked at each other, we both started laughing. When we quieted down, she answered softly and seriously, "Yes, Matt, I will marry you."

Nothing more needed to be said. We walked into her room and spent the night weaving our love and our lives together.

Not having slept much, we both went into work a little bit late. Neither of us wanted to go; we would far rather have spent the whole day enjoying our new engagement. Not having thought about the situation at work for a single moment since I had spoken with Michael, I walked in resolved to do as he had suggested. My heart was telling me to hold onto my position, but I felt no need to push. I just waited to see what everyone else had concluded overnight.

No one at the company had changed their minds; in fact, they all seemed to be even stronger in holding to their positions. Their need for control was getting in the way of their ability to see other options. We spent the morning rehashing the same perspectives as the day before. I repeated my point of view. "Your company offers a money-back guarantee on seminars and has a 50 to 60 percent refund request rate. This is not an acceptable percentage. Do you see that this indicates that something needs to change? What I see is that you are trying to help people with their emotions by teaching them how to analyze everything and change their thoughts, which keeps them entirely in their heads. We need to give them a balance between the intellectual—so they know what we are talking about—and related experiences, so they feel what we are talking about and can then choose to do something different. We need a balance of both if we want people to gain value. Either one, without the proper balance of the other, isn't going to be very successful. Bottom line, folks, you have been doing this for a while and you are losing money. If you keep doing the exact same thing and expect different results, you are going to go out of business."

They still refused to see what I was sharing with them so, taking a deep breath, returning to resourcefulness and taking action from there, I simply said, "As I see it, I have four choices. I can either continue trying to change your minds, which is obviously not working, nor is it going to work. I can keep consulting with you as best I can and continue resisting the way you are doing this part, because I know it will not work. All this will do is make you blame me when the business fails. Another option is that I can accept your decision, continue taking your money to consult, and try to help you as the chips fall where they may. This would ultimately be taking advantage of you and compromising what I know to be true.

"This leaves me with only one option—to follow my heart, stick with what I know to be true and wish you luck as you go on without me. I cannot continue consulting for you if you are not going to allow any changes. If you like the business just as it is, you do not need a consultant, and I do not need to waste either our time or money." Then I added with sincerity, "I wish you well with your venture here." I gathered up my things and walked out, leaving behind a group of faces that reminded me of the school kids the day I left high school for good.

Once outside, I expected to feel disappointed, but I didn't. If I had left from a place of ego or anger I would have felt bad, but instead, before taking any action, I had let go and returned to resourcefulness. I knew the truth of what I was telling them and had followed my heart, as Michael suggested. Now, I felt strong and ready to move forward.

I went back to Jessie's to take care of some other business until she got off work. I called my home for messages and returned a call from Daryl.

"Hi, Daryl. This is Matt, returning your call."

"It's good to talk to you. Are you in Sedona?"

"No, I'm calling from Phoenix. I was just wrapping up some consulting here. How are things going with your business? Did you get any response from the last group we spoke with?"

"As a matter of fact, I did! I have gotten numerous phone calls from people thanking us for the seminar, and in addition to that, sales in that area are on the rise! I wanted to set up the next training with you."

He shared the dates he needed me, and we made the necessary arrangements. I then said, "I really enjoyed our time together, Daryl. I have the feeling that you and I have a lot of things in common. Our philosophies are similar, and I suspect that our life missions are similar, as well." I wondered whether he, too, was one of Michael's volunteers, since he had given me the book that had provided my first information about Michael.

Daryl agreed. "I bet you are right about that. In fact, I have been working on putting my vision on paper recently. Have you ever done that, Matt? I mean, commit your vision and mission to paper? It's a different experience than just saying or thinking it."

I imagined that he was right. "No, I haven't, but now that you mention it, I think I will."

He responded enthusiastically, "Well, when you do, send it to me, and we can compare notes. Better yet, why don't you bring it on our trip next week, and we can look at them on the airplane."

We finalized the plans for our trip, and just before we hung up the phone, I said, "Oh, Daryl, by the way, I got engaged last night!"

"Congratulations! I don't recall hearing you mention that you were seriously dating anyone. Who is she?"

"Her name is Jessie, and she is wonderful. I'll tell you all about her when we get together. Thanks for the congrats! Talk to you soon."

I tried to take care of some other business, but all I could think about was putting my vision down on paper. I still wasn't completely comfortable hanging out in Jessie's home when she wasn't there, but I found some paper and a pen and chose a spot to meditate and write. I sat quietly for a little while and then, when I felt ready, put pen to paper and started writing.

After scratching out a few sentences, reordering some of the words and refining the statement, I realized that this was even more powerful than I had imagined. I was not only putting the letters and words in the proper order to create the most precise results, but I was writing them down in black and white. It felt binding to do so, as if I were completing the steps of the "spelling," or as if I truly were sentencing myself to living out this mission. I liked what I was writing, so it felt good to commit it to actualization. My vision, once I had it down, filled me with awe. I felt a bubble of joy moving up through my body, expanding my heart as I looked at the words.

I read it out loud to see how it sounded. *"My vision is: To reopen the hearts and minds of people all over the world to a new awareness that is based in the essence of resourcefulness. To 'wake people up' by exposing them to the Letting Go principles as a process of self-improvement, creating a society of empowered individuals working together in cooperation for the good of all."*

Resonating deeply in my soul, the words gave me the shivers as I read them. I rewrote the statement neatly on a card so I could set it where I would look at it often. I made a mental note to thank Daryl for suggesting that I commit my vision to paper, as this definitely added to my clarity and solidified my commitment to the mission.

After I shared my vision statement with Jessie, we spent the evening together talking, laughing and making plans, the most immediate of which had to do with the distance between our homes.

"Were you serious when you said you would be willing to move to Sedona, Jessie?" I asked, still in a state of wonder at my good fortune.

"Are you kidding? I love Sedona! I'd move in a heartbeat, but I probably ought to find a job first. I'm not sure whether I'd want to sell my house or rent it out for a while. We'll have to think about that a little."

"Well, how soon do you want to get married, and when do you want to move?" I was trying to be rational, but I didn't want to be apart anymore, at all. My head was screaming to slow down, but my heart felt very ready. I added another question, "What kind of wedding do you want?"

She smiled at the barrage of inquiries. "I haven't thought about all these questions yet. Part of me just wants to sneak away and get married in a private ceremony. Since we've both been married before, I don't feel the need for a big wedding. I don't know, what do you want?"

What I wanted was to run out and find somebody to marry us that very moment, but I said, "I don't want a big ceremony either; I want to have just a few folks there who are really important to both of us."

We held each other for a few moments, excited about the direction in which we were going.

I broke the silence by saying, "Why don't you start dinner. I want to arrange my next visit with the boys; I want you to meet them as soon as possible."

She smiled and headed for the kitchen, saying, "I can't wait to see them. Going from no kids to two sons is going to be quite a step; I want to get started!"

I spoke with the boys and their mom, making plans for them to visit right after I got back from my trip with Daryl. Sarah was reluctant to let them come during the school year, but since I saw them so seldom, she relented. They were happy to be coming, and I couldn't wait to see them.

Throughout the evening, Jessie and I explored each other's feelings and made plans for our immediate future. She decided to give notice the next day and begin the process of moving.

As we sat in bed talking, I asked, "Are you scared? I mean about getting married again?"

"I think I should be, but I'm not. I can't really explain it. I know we haven't known each other very long, but it just feels right. What about you? Do you think we are moving too fast?"

I pulled her closer to me. "I think the rest of the world will think we are moving too fast, but I don't. I want to be with you, Jessie—always. Starting now!"

She put her head on my shoulder and after several minutes of silence asked, "Do you think I could meet Alea?"

At the mention of her name, shivers went up and down my spine.

The only other person who had ever said her name out loud was Nan, and that had been different. Nan had never asked to meet my mystery woman. I suddenly felt the rightness of introducing Alea and Jessie, both of whom I loved so much.

I replied honestly, "I don't know Jessie, but we can try." It seemed like ages since I had spoken with Alea myself.

She waited, looking at me expectantly, while I sat there.

I explained, "She usually just shows up when she wants to; I'm not used to asking. I have to admit that I'm a little uncomfortable talking out loud to the room, asking her to come. What if she doesn't? I'm going to feel pretty foolish."

Before Jessie could respond, I heard Alea's voice saying, *"The only foolish thing, Matt, is thinking that I wouldn't come."* The pure sweetness of her tone soothed my heart.

I looked to Jessie to see if she had heard Alea, too, but she was still nodding in understanding of my previous confession, apparently unaware of Alea's communication.

"I just heard her, Jessie; did you hear that?" I asked hopefully.

"No, I didn't hear anything," she said, disappointed.

"She can't hear me, Matt. I'm sorry. She can't see me right now either. Tell her to simply feel. If she listens with her heart, she will be able to feel my presence." Alea's words came through clearly to me, but again, nothing registered in Jessie's expression.

"Um, Jessie, she just told me that you can't hear her or see her right now, but that you can feel her if you listen with your heart. I don't know how to tell you to do that, though. Just see what you feel, I guess," I explained with some difficulty.

I could see Jessie trying. She closed her eyes and relaxed. Suddenly, the hair raised on her arms and she said excitedly, "Oh Matt, I just felt something, almost like a breeze! It felt so loving, like a wave of calm washing over me."

Joyously, I exclaimed, "That's Alea! She is simply love itself!"

Jessie's eyes welled up with tears, she was so obviously moved. "I have never felt anything like this before. Will you thank her for me?"

Feeling great reverence for the moment, I whispered, "I don't think I have to. I'm pretty sure she can hear and see you just fine." Feeling funny talking out loud to Alea, I tried just talking to her via telepathy, wondering if she could hear me and why I was able to hear her when Jessie couldn't.

Alea's voice resounded back, *"Yes, Matt. I can hear you. I am sorry that I cannot appear before Jessie just yet. You must trust that it's better that she believe by feeling the truth first. It's important that she trust and believe in you and feel the truth with her own heart, before we give her more tangible evidence. Do you see that her believing, without hearing or seeing me, means more to both of you than it would if I were to appear?"*

Instantly, I saw Alea's point. If Jessie and I were going to get married and spend our lives together, it was essential that we build trust in each other without having to "prove" ourselves. If Alea had shown up, then I could not have known with certainty the depth of Jessie's trust and faith in me. Now, Jessie was following her own heart, as well as mine, to build the trust between us. I thanked Alea and sent her a mental hug. I heard her laugh softly in the distance and then fade away.

Jessie asked, "Did she just leave, Matt? I felt something change."

"Yes. Yes, she did." I was still basking in Alea's love as I answered. "I'm so glad you could feel her, Jessie; I wasn't sure you would be able to. Thank you for believing in me, for trusting me."

"My pleasure!" she said, smiling. "Alea is a wonderful gift for you to give, Matt. Thank you for wanting to share her with me."

We fell into a deep sleep, wrapped in each other's arms.

The following week was filled with planning for the upcoming changes. I had already been to Sedona and back and was now heading to the airport to work with Daryl. As Jessie dropped me off, I promised to call her every day. Even though I was only going away for four days, it was hard to leave. I was to meet with Daryl in Dallas, and we were flying on together from there.

Greeting each other at the gate, we settled into our seats before entering into any meaningful conversations. Shortly after we took off, Daryl asked, "So, did you write out your vision statement?"

"Yes, I did. You were right; it is a completely different experience to commit it to paper! I brought it with me—did you bring yours?" I asked, as I started digging into my briefcase to get it out.

"I've got it right here!" Daryl answered. "Here, let me read it to you."

He unfolded a piece of paper that he had carefully stored in his shirt pocket, cleared his throat and began to read. "I see a transformation where tens of millions of people participate in the creation of a peaceful world by sharing products, ideas, opportunities and feelings that nurture ourselves and our planet. Acts of conscious kindness are our natural way of being; no one harms another, people nourish each other in such a way that healing of body, mind and spirit spreads from person to person. We are an enlightened, peaceful people."

He smiled when he finished, at which I concluded that a powerful vision statement is one that makes you feel good when you read it, and his obviously did. I, in turn, read mine to him.

Daryl said, smiling, "Different words, same meaning!"

I agreed. "Yep, now that we have created the vision, all we have to do is play with whoever shows up!"

We both laughed at the thought, as I reviewed how many people had "shown up to play," as my vision had become clearer, including Daryl!

I explained to him, "Part of my personal vision recently was the clarity that I wanted to meet the right woman. Shortly thereafter, a friend of mine, Joe, asked me to meet him at a restaurant for dinner, and then he proceeded to drink himself into oblivion."

Daryl laughed, nodding as I continued, "Ordinarily, I'd have thought that he was the wrong person to 'show up and play with' for helping me create my vision, but as it turned out, he detained me long enough at the restaurant for me to meet Jessie! Sometimes the people who don't seem to be a contributing part of the vision are really keeping us still long enough for the other players to show up. It goes to show that we just have to hold a clear vision, stay open and then see what happens!"

Daryl added, "What do you say we make a vow of commitment to our missions here on the planet."

"What do you mean? What kind of vow?" I asked, curious.

"Let's commit to staying here until everyone is enlightened!" he answered, looking as serious as I had ever seen him.

"Do you mean in this body? Could be an awfully long time!" I wasn't sure I knew exactly what he meant.

"Doesn't really matter if it's this body and this lifetime or not. I just mean that our souls are committed to this mission, and we won't give up until we are done—no matter what. I personally like having a partner of sorts in the effort. Let's take a vow of commitment to the cause and support each other in manifesting a more loving and peaceful planet!"

We each made a vow, which raised the level of commitment significantly, as if putting it on paper had not been enough! We sat there, hurtling through the atmosphere at five hundred miles an hour, committing ourselves to an eternity of turning the world around. After we shook on it, we both started laughing, as if our souls were deeply satisfied. We were quite pleased with ourselves. I had a strange feeling that I had taken this vow before.

I asked Daryl, "Do you know much about the Archangel Michael?"

He looked thoughtful, then answered, "Not much, why?"

"I had been searching for information on him and wasn't able to find it. Just as I was about to give up, you sent me that book. The whole first chapter had the information on him that I had been looking for."

He smiled and said, "What a coincidence!"

He had that look that said, "*If* you believe in coincidences"—but he didn't say so.

I added, "Michael apparently has the mission of waking up his volunteers—people who are here to help others reach enlightenment."

Daryl nodded, adding, "Now that you mention it, I remember reading about him."

Throwing caution to the wind, I said, "I think we are his volunteers, Daryl. I think that is one of the reasons we have met each other and why we are taking this vow. It says in the Book of Daniel that when the world is in real trouble, Michael will reappear. I think the time is now, and that he is calling on us to help."

Daryl looked thoughtful, then replied, grinning, "That works for me! I'd like to find out more about him, but of what I recall, you're right. Our missions are right in alignment with his."

Once checked into our hotel rooms, I called Jessie to let her know I had arrived safely. We finalized plans for my return and caught up on each other's news. Arrangements were in place for me to fly in, pick up the boys and bring them back with me to Phoenix, where Jessie would pick us up. From there, we'd all go to Sedona, so they could get acquainted. I was looking forward to sharing them with Jessie, and vice versa.

After we hung up, I decided to call Nan and update her on what had happened in my life since she had come to visit.

Telling her about Jessie and how she and I had met, I said, "I'm not sure when or where we are going to get married, but I'd really like you to be there if you can."

Nan exclaimed, "I'd love to! Just let me know when, as much in advance as possible, so I can make plans. You know, Matt, ordinarily I would launch into a 'don't you think this is kind of quick' lecture, but when I 'check in' on this, the reading I get is really positive. I am so happy for you!"

I asked, "How's your relationship going with Steve?"

"It's going great. Each new day brings new discoveries. We are really being conscious about this relationship. Recently we each wrote down our personal guiding values, prioritized them and then compared our lists. Fortunately for us, in many important areas we were in agreement, and the areas where we weren't were at least complementary."

I shared with her, "I just went through a similar process with a friend of mine, only instead of comparing our values, we were comparing our vision statements. It was really powerful to write them down. Have you ever done that?"

"No, but it sounds great. It seems like a natural next step. I'd like to do it."

With enthusiasm, I added, "We discovered that our visions, while worded differently, held the same meaning. We took a vow of commitment to them."

"What do you mean? What kind of a vow?" she asked.

I answered seriously, "We committed ourselves to staying here until everyone wakes up."

Nan laughed out loud. "I guess you two are going to get pretty old! You do realize that that could take quite a while, don't you?"

Her laugh was contagious. "Oh, I figure only a couple more centuries. No, really, we figure we may have to come back a few times to see it through, but we're committed for the duration—however long that may be."

She was silent for a moment, then said, "Hmm. I wouldn't mind being in on a vow like that—that is, of course, if you guys figure you might need some help with this little goal of yours."

I welcomed the thought of assistance with the mission. "The more the merrier!" I swore her in as best I could on the telephone and sealed the eternal camaraderie between us.

"Welcome aboard, Nan!"

She sounded deeply sincere as she replied, "Thank you, it's my honor to be here!"

After agreeing to stay in touch regarding the wedding, I hung up, pleased beyond words to know that we were bound together in this seemingly casual but hugely significant way.

The seminar went well and the days went by quickly. While I thoroughly enjoyed my time with Daryl and the work we were doing together, I also looked forward to the following week.

Daryl and I parted ways after confirming our next trip. I flew into Oklahoma, where my boys were waiting at the airport. The flight provided a perfect transitional time to get reacquainted, and by the time we arrived in Phoenix, we were once again a family. When I spoke with them on the phone, I had told them I had someone special I wanted them to meet, so while we were on the plane I told them a little more about Jessie. I knew they would like each other, but I was a little nervous about the introduction, nonetheless.

Jessie was there when we arrived. The boys shook her hand politely as I introduced them, and then I greeted her with a hug. I was immediately impressed with her way with children—or in this case, young men. She asked them questions and shared ideas, not seeming at all unnerved by the many one-word answers so typical of their age. I could easily imagine her in the school of her future vision.

As we drove back to Sedona, we filled our time sharing jokes that we'd heard. I wondered how the boys would handle it when it became obvious that Jessie and I were staying in the same room. While I had introduced them to women before, I had never had anyone stay with me while they were visiting. I took a deep breath and surrendered in trust that it would all work out. Their visit here would only be for four days, so any relationship building between us all would have to happen fast.

We filled the weekend with movies, hikes, games and storytelling. Surprised at how easily the boys and Jessie got along, as if they were old friends, I counted my blessings once again. The feeling between us all was as if we were already bonded and familiar—and no uncomfortable moments arose about Jessie's and my close physical relationship. If the boys had any questions or misgivings, nothing in their words or behavior indicated it. I felt relieved and grateful. I imagined that the ease we all experienced must have been one of the miracles gained with letting go and trusting.

On the night before they were to leave, we sat down to dinner and "the talk." After everyone had finished dessert, I said, "Jessie and I have something we'd like to get your opinion on."

They looked at me with anticipation. Jessie's and my eyes met for a fleeting moment. I had no idea what I would do if the boys didn't like the idea of us getting married. I hadn't thought through what I would do if it wasn't okay with them.

Continuing, I said, "I would like to marry Jessie, and I want to have your approval." I almost laughed out loud when I heard my need for acceptance stated so bluntly. I took a deep breath and let it go as best I could at this moment, feeling the importance of my sons' approval fluttering in my solar plexus for a second or two before I settled into "let go" mode.

Jessie added, "I'd like your approval, too. We wanted to have all of us get together so we could get to know each other. I've really enjoyed our time together the last few days, and I look forward to more!"

I imagined that the boys were going through all kinds of concerns, as this made it absolutely obvious that their mother and I would not ever be getting back together. The more I imagined, the more uncomfortable I became.

In the meantime, they simply looked at each other for a minute, and then Jerry shrugged and said, "It's okay with me. When are you getting married?"

Before I could answer, Tim said, "Yeah, it's okay with me, too." He then got up and hugged Jessie, which nearly brought us both to tears.

I cleared my throat and said, "Thanks, guys. That means a lot to me. I don't like making major decisions without having you be a part of them. As for when we're getting married, we aren't sure, but we would like to do it soon."

Tim suggested innocently, "Why don't you keep us here for the rest of the week and do it next weekend, so we can be here!"

We all started laughing, and then Jessie said, "Well, that *is* soon!"

She and I looked at each other, and I said, "That's not a bad idea. What do you think, Jessie? Can we pull this off in less than a week?"

Smiling, she said, "Well, I suppose we could, as long as we keep it really small. I want to have my family come. What about you?"

"Well, other than the boys, I need to see if Nan can come, and I'll let my family know, though I suspect they won't be able to make it on such short notice."

Turning to the boys, I said, "Of course, I need to call your mother and get her blessings—or at least her permission to keep you longer."

Jerry said, "Mom won't like it, but she'll let us stay. We're both doing okay in school." He got up and went to the phone. "I'll call her, and then you can talk to her."

As he dialed, I took a deep breath and released any anxiety I was harboring about telling my former spouse I was getting remarried. I was sure she wasn't going to be happy about it, not because she had any hopes of us ever being together again, but rather because it added an exclamation point to the concept of our divorce.

I listened while Jerry explained to his mother that he and Tim were both doing well in school and that they wanted to stay another week. He then said, "I'm going to put Dad on, so you two can work it out."

He then held the phone out to me. Signaling that I would take the other line, I went into the bedroom to talk to her, so that the boys wouldn't be listening, in case it got unpleasant.

After greeting her, I explained, "I was hoping it would be okay with you if I kept the boys through next weekend. It was unexpected, or I would have asked sooner, but I'm, uh, getting married next weekend, and I'd like to have the boys here."

The silence on the other end of the line indicated that she wasn't exactly okay with what I had just said. I imagined all kinds of things she might be thinking about why I was getting married so unexpectedly. I switched my concerns for myself to concerns for her and tried to soften the news by saying, "I'm sorry, Sarah. I know this isn't an easy thing to hear. It isn't easy to tell you."

She very quietly replied, "Let me know when they'll be back, and I will pick them up at the airport."

"Thank you, Sarah." I really meant the appreciation that I expressed, recognizing how easily she could have made this difficult and how uncomfortable it was to have this conversation.

I heard her voice break as she said, "Bye, Matt," and before I even got to say good-bye myself, the line went dead.

I sat sadly for a moment and said a prayer for her. I wished that she would be able to get through this easily and that she would find happiness in her life. With another deep breath, I moved from my past to my future and went into the other room to let them know that we could proceed with our plans.

It was as if the whole family suddenly switched into high gear, and a festive atmosphere sprang up among us. Tim settled into making decorations, cutting out bells and making paper chains for the house. Jessie and I made a quick list of people to call and started discussing where we wanted to get married.

Jerry pitched in, "I know where! You know that place where we went camping in the canyon, Dad? The spot by the big tree and that huge boulder we like to sit on, right where the stream is? I think you should get married there!"

I agreed, "He's right, Jessie; that is a beautiful spot. It feels magical there."

"Well, it's settled then! Thanks, Jerry!" she said appreciatively.

We made the necessary phone calls, and before we all went to bed, the wedding plans had been set in place. We even had written our own vows; the words flowed naturally onto the paper as we each expressed what it was we wanted to say to the other. The only unfortunate part was that Jessie had to go back to Phoenix to work for the rest of the week; she would have to leave in the morning.

Lying in bed, we talked over a few of the immediate logistics. "We'll drive you back down early tomorrow, since we all came up in one car. Maybe we can go get the license and shop for rings on your lunch break; then I'll bring the boys back up here until you can join us on Friday."

Snuggling, she said, "It's a good thing I gave notice when I did! Matt, are you really okay with this happening as fast as it is?"

Pulling her even closer to me, I confirmed, "I love you, Jessie. I would marry you right now if I could."

Early the next morning, all four of us piled into the car to take Jessie back to Phoenix. We plotted out the rest of the details as to who was going to do what during the week and dropped her off at work, agreeing to pick her up for lunch. The boys and I ran around town looking at rings that we could show Jessie when she was free. Then, during lunch, we took her to a jewelry store where we had found some rings the boys and I liked. When we showed them to her, she got tears in her eyes and confirmed our choices immediately. We ordered the inscriptions, simple statements of our names and the date, and Jessie arranged to pick them up on Thursday. We then got the marriage license. Everything proceeded with such ease; we were obviously doing something right! We took her back to work and made plans to talk that evening.

Holding her close, I whispered, "I am going to miss you every minute until next weekend."

"I am going to miss you, too! I'll talk to you tonight. Have fun with the boys!" All three of us hugged her and left, waving good-bye.

"So, you guys like Jessie?" I asked, knowing the answer, but wanting to hear it anyway.

"Yeah! She's great, Dad," Jerry said.

Tim piped in, "Yeah! I like her, too!"

"Yeah, me, too!" I mimicked, causing us all to laugh, which helped to relieve the pangs of saying good-bye to her.

The week overflowed with preparations. After the ceremony, we would have a reception at our house. We had invited several friends and relatives to join the party. Unfortunately, my family couldn't make it. Just as I had suspected, the notice was too short. Plus, my father was under the weather. I promised I would bring Jessie out to meet them all one of these days.

Jessie arrived Friday afternoon, having left work early. By the time we went to bed, all the details were in place, and we were ready for a celebration!

I awoke early, just before the sun came up. Kissing Jessie's forehead, I whispered, "Jessie, wake up!"

She whispered back sleepily, after looking at the clock, "Why?"

"Because I want to share a special moment with you on our wedding day. This is the only time we can do it!"

Opening her eyes a little wider, she asked, "Are you serious? You want me to get up? Where are we going?"

"Out on the deck. Come on, trust me!" I pulled her outside by the hand.

It was still completely dark, and the stars were glimmering all around us. The crisp morning air smelled clean and refreshing. The moon was nearing the horizon in the west, and the sky was just starting to lighten in the east, changing the black to a royal blue near the horizon.

Jessie got into the spirit of the moment, saying, "It is really beautiful out here! Forgive me for asking, but what are we doing?"

I laughed quietly and said with poetic dramatization, "We are watching the transition from darkness to light on this, our wedding day!"

She smiled, and I added, "This moment in time is symbolic of what this day in time represents. Transition. Change. Moments of transition are some of the most beautiful we ever experience. I don't want to miss a second of it." I pulled the still-sleepy woman toward me, and we watched in silence as the first rays of sunshine spread their light over the horizon.

She quietly exclaimed in a voice fitting the moment, "Oh, Matt, that is the most magnificent sunrise I have ever seen! Look at all the colors! It feels magical, like a blessing just for us! Thank you for bringing me out here."

The light swirled across the land, alternately spotlighting various clouds and rock formations, one at a time, as if personally greeting each. Then it was our turn. We seemed to be encircled in glowing light, as the sun danced its way into day. We stood there on the deck, sharing our private wedding day ritual, until we heard rumblings in the house, signaling that the morning had officially begun.

Pulling all the last-minute pieces into place, we drove out to Oak Creek Canyon and into a small parking area where we met everyone else. Jessie's brother, his wife and kids, her mother and grandmother were already there when we arrived. Nan, Steve and the minister pulled in only moments later. Together, after proper introductions, we began the short hike to the special spot Jerry had picked out.

The minister made the sacredness of the moment explicit. "We are gathered here today in Holy Matrimony to witness and to celebrate the coming together of two separate lives. *Holy* means 'Whole' and 'Beautiful.' *Matrimony* comes from the root word meaning 'Mother.' Thus, it is fitting that we are outside, surrounded by the beauty of our Mother Earth. The image of Mother at the time of marriage represents creativity, the birth of something new and wonderful—a miracle. Today we are here to witness the exchange of promises to love, honor and grow together between Matt and Jessie—the birth of their lives together."

She continued, "Commitment is not a thing to take lightly, nor merely words to be said. Commitment must be an act of the whole being, a trinity of the body, mind and spirit. Nor is commitment a one-time event, but rather an ongoing, conscious process, requiring maintenance and renewal daily. As the sun rises each morning, let that magnificent event remind you each day to commit anew to that which you hold sacred: love, harmony, intimacy, laughter. Make this vow, not only to each other, but also to each of the values that you hold dear, for in living these values, your love for each other will also thrive.

"Marriage symbolizes the intimate sharing of two lives, yet this sharing must not diminish but rather enhance the individuality of each partner. A marriage that lasts is one that is continually developing, while it grows in understanding of the other. Deep knowledge of another is not something that can be achieved in a short time, and real understanding of the other's feelings can develop fully only with years of intimacy.

"We must give ourselves in love, but we must not give ourselves away. A good and balanced relationship is one in which neither person is overpowered or absorbed by the other.

"We are here today to celebrate the love that Matt and Jessie have for each other and to give recognition to their decision to accept each other totally and permanently. In this exchange, you also make a commitment to life, to fulfilling your life purpose and to supporting each other in doing so."

Jessie and I looked at each other. Tears welled up in both our eyes as we listened to the words that were uniting us. I wished that I could capture the moment and save it to relive it again and again.

We turned and faced each other, and I felt as if my heart were going to burst open with love as I said, "Jessie, I take you as my wife. I pledge to share my life openly with you, to speak the truth to you in love. I promise to honor and tenderly care for you, to cherish and encourage your own fulfillment as an individual, through all the changes of our lives."

Jessie looked more beautiful than I had ever seen her as she said, "Matt, I take you as my husband. I pledge to share my life openly with you, to speak the truth to you in love. I promise to honor and tenderly care for you, to cherish and encourage your own fulfillment as an individual, through all the changes of our lives."

Continuing, the minister explained, "The ring has no beginning and no end; it is eternal and everlasting. These rings are symbols of the unbroken unity of love, now to be manifested in your married life. As they are made in the form of a circle, they represent the truth of the law of life: 'As we give to each other, we receive from each other.'"

I couldn't help but think of the golden rings that Alea had given me as the minister spoke of the symbology. She brought me back to the present by saying, "With the acceptance of these rings, let them be a symbol to remind you of your acceptance of each other, just as you are now, unchanged, yet ever changing."

The minister took up a ring and said, "Bless this ring, O God; bless Matt who gives it and Jessie who receives it."

As I placed the ring on Jessie's finger, I pledged, "With this ring, I thee wed. Let it ever be to us a symbol of our love."

After the second ring blessing, Jessie also vowed, "With this ring, I thee wed. Let it ever be to us a symbol of our love."

Turning to the group, the minister said, "May each one here say his or her own vow of commitment to assist Matt and Jessie in remaining true to this winding path, no matter which way it turns, knowing that they have chosen to walk it together. May they always come back to the center of the circle where they stand now together in love. May we all pause in prayer and bless this marriage."

The silence was tangible. I felt as if we were in the center of the labyrinth, with love surrounding Jessie and me, filling us. I saw the similarity of the winding path we had walked to get to this sacred spot, the ritual of commitment, and the return walk out, strengthened in union to continue on our missions. As we stood in silence, I felt the presence of Alea blessing us and knew that God indeed had received this commitment from us. We were one. As I looked at the woman to whom I had just pledged my love and my life, I was overwhelmed with joy from the deepest part of my being.

After several minutes without any sound other than the creek water tumbling by, the minister turned again to the family and friends gathered and said, "Does anyone want to offer a blessing out loud?"

Nan stepped forward and offered a song, inviting us all to sing with her, after we caught the words, *"May the long-time sun shine upon you, all love surround you; may the pure light within you guide you all the way home."*

After several rounds of harmony, we once again returned to silence. The minister looked back to us and said, "At this moment, each one of us gathered here blesses Matt and Jessie. May their pathway of happiness be recognized through the light of love, causing their lives to unfold in harmony, abundance, health and self-satisfaction. May their home always radiate an environment of love, well-being, happiness and unity. And whoever enters their home, may they be blessed and inspired by the harmony and love that dwells there. May they realize that true marriage is a symbol of infinite oneness, and not of possession—causing each to reveal their faith, their talents and their love to the other. It is the recognition of this oneness that will enable them to live faithfully together, and to perform and keep the covenant and vows made now so sincerely between them. We, here now, believe they live in the midst of love, peace, health and security, and shall abide accordingly. Amen.

"Inasmuch as you, Matt, and you, Jessie, have consented together in the bonds of wedlock and have witnessed the same before God, your chosen witness, your families, and these friends present, and have pledged your faith and your love, each to the other, I now pronounce you husband and wife. Go forth in love!"

Cheering swelled from the group as I kissed my beautiful bride.

After taking pictures, we turned to begin the short walk out to the cars and then home for the party. Most of the people had already started out ahead of us when Tim said, "Look, Dad, someone left a wedding present for you on the big rock!"

He ran over to get it as we looked on in wonder. He handed us a small box without a second thought and then darted down the trail after his older brother. Jessie and I stood there alone, looking surprised.

"Well, I guess we won't know until we open it. Go ahead!" she suggested.

The sunlight filtered down through the trees, lighting up the box as I pulled off the wrapping and opened it up. There, placed neatly inside by Alea, were two beautiful golden Rings of Truth. One was engraved with the words *Follow Your Heart* and the other simply with *Commitment.*

Jessie took them out and held them for a moment. Feeling honored with the gift, I was looking at the rings and hadn't noticed that Jessie had looked back toward the large boulder by the creek. I turned my gaze in the same direction when I heard the gasp that Jessie let out. There, standing on the rock, was Alea, looking angelic as ever with sunlight streaming down behind her.

As quickly as I caught a glimpse of her, she once again disappeared. Jessie announced excitedly, "I saw her, Matt! I saw Alea!"

Alea, too, felt the magic of the moment. As tears of joy ran down both Matt and Jessie's faces, she offered her own prayer for their union and knew the depth of its rightness.

Watching as they examined the golden rings, she felt the warmth of the appreciation Matt sent to her. She knew that he felt her presence, and she loved watching his growth. He had opened his heart so much over the last year.

Through his intention, willingness and commitment, he had let go of so much that was in his way. At the same time, he had reached out and embraced aspects of his being to which he had long ago lost his connection. He was journeying the distance from his head to his heart, which is a pathway many never even find, much less undertake.

Now that he had discovered his heart and opened it, he was following it more and more, trusting the messages it sent him. She knew he would discover that whenever there was a conflict or a struggle, any non-resourceful feelings, there was likely to also be a heart that was not being heard. It was all a matter of trust. He was learning to use his intuition to listen, then trust the guidance from within. With Matt, as with most people, it was easier to trust a perfect stranger than to trust himself—easier, but not always wiser. The more the heart is followed, the more one will want to follow the heart. He was well on his way.

She turned her blessings toward Jessie. She was beautiful and kind. Alea was happy to see her again, as their love had deep roots as well. Alea surrounded Jessie with a prayer of strength, knowing that the path she had chosen would not always be easy, although the rewards would be great.

She was glad that Matt had taken his involvements to this degree of commitment; she knew that great success required this level of dedication. First his vow with Daryl and Nan, and now his vow to Jessie—each was a vow to love. A vow, an oath made to God, was obviously not one to take lightly, and she felt confident that Matt was prepared for the journey that lay ahead.

Alea considered the life-path before them and the ones from whence they came. Now that Matt had the seed, from it all the rest would grow. As he mastered each of the concepts, growth could now accelerate. He had planted the seed in the soil of resourcefulness, then nourished it with clarity and commitment by following his heart. Now he would discover the many different aspects of what it meant to live resourcefully. The roots of resourcefulness would grow deeply into the soil, developing the different attributes that together make up this part of the key. She was eager to see the results. With a little smile, she reminded herself to let go of any desire to see results before their time to appear.

The time was now for Matt to discover and depend upon his own strength. The infinite well of wisdom and power within was his for the asking, as it is within each person. He had to become a master of his responses to circumstances in order to fulfill his commitments. While she didn't relish leaving him on his own, she knew that she must. No one is asked to handle more than they are capable of, and Matt was no exception. He had attained the necessary skills, and now he needed to apply them in all situations to verify their practical application, along with the real results they would bring. She hoped he would discover along the way that feelings of being "alone" could be remedied by a remembrance that we are "all-one." In connecting with others, his heart would open even more, and his healing would be even greater.

As Jessie and Matt turned to walk back along the trail, neither of them heard her as she whispered with tender love, "Good-bye." They merely felt a gentle breeze brush across their cheeks, as soft as a kiss.

11

Into Me See

As I packed for the next workshop with Daryl, I wished I didn't have to leave so soon after our wedding. It had only been a couple of weeks, and I just wasn't ready to be away from Jessie. We were still in the process of rearranging the house, combining our things and turning "my space" into "our space." The phone interrupted my thoughts.

"Matt? This is Cindy." Her voice sent chills up and down my spine, even though the room was at normal temperature. Something in her tone told me that this was not going to be good news.

"Hi, Cindy! Did you get a chance to look at the proposal I sent you?"

"Yes, I looked it over and think you have some interesting points. I also think that what you have put together is well written, but I honestly don't think I am the agent who should represent you. I have to admit, your stunt of throwing away your previous manuscript has left me a little apprehensive. I don't want to put all the required energy into getting this into the right hands, only to have you discover something new and throw this one away, too. I hope you understand."

I felt like a boy being punished with a lack of trust based on previous actions, rather than an understanding for my present situation. I knew the value of this work and couldn't imagine throwing it away. I also knew that people were hungry for this kind of information. A wave of disappointment washed over me.

All I could bring myself to say was, "I understand, Cindy. Thanks for the time you've put in already."

I didn't think that telling her she needed to let go of the past and move into the present was advice she was ready to receive.

She tried to ease the situation by adding, "That's not to say that when you are completely finished and ready to go, I wouldn't be willing to reconsider. I mean, when you are sure you are ready to publish."

I replied, "Thanks, Cindy. We'll see. I'll be in touch. Bye." I had a hard time concealing the emotions in my voice, so I hung up quickly. I was taken off guard, not recognizing how much I had assumed and hoped she would like what I had written.

Sitting on the edge of the bed, I tried to sort out my conflicting feelings. They ranged from disappointment to a sense of relief, as working with Cindy was seldom a pleasant experience, despite her skill at doing her job. Being rejected didn't bother me nearly as much as the sense that this would delay the publishing of my book. I rationalized, knowing a greater opportunity must loom in the near future, but believing that didn't seem to help. I tried to "think positively" by focusing on the thought that there were plenty of other agents who would take my book, and that "every rejection is that much closer to an acceptance," but it just wasn't enough to turn my feelings around.

I felt a bubble of self-doubt boiling to the surface as I questioned for a moment the truth of my experience. Once again, my need for acceptance was causing me discomfort. I sat quietly, observing myself, focusing on the uncomfortable feeling in my stomach and taking deep breaths until the feeling dissipated. Once I felt that I had regained a place of resourcefulness, having let go of fear, I made a plan to proceed with the writing of my book. From this place, I held no doubt.

Jessie came into the room, expecting to see me packing, but instead finding me sitting quietly. She looked at me inquisitively but didn't ask questions, knowing that I would explain to her if she waited.

"That was my agent, Cindy. She has decided, for now, not to represent my book. It sounded like her issue was more of a trust issue with me than a dispute over the value of the material."

Jessie listened thoughtfully, then said, "Well, how do you feel about that?"

I appreciated her question rather than the lecture on how I "should" feel which so many others would have felt inclined to issue. I answered honestly, "At first, I was disappointed, but once I let go of that, I was able to see my next steps. Now I'm actually relieved not to be working with her anymore. Thanks for asking."

With that, I pulled her to me and gave her a kiss of appreciation. I once again counted my blessings and thanked the powers-that-be for bringing her into my life.

For a brief moment, the thought of Alea popped into my head. I had been so preoccupied with the wedding and blending Jessie's and my lives, that I hadn't even noticed that she hadn't been around at all lately. In fact, I hadn't actually spoken to Alea in what seemed to be ages. A twinge of sadness crept into my inner picture. I dismissed it, convinced that I just hadn't discovered anything important enough lately to merit her attention.

Before long, I was kissing Jessie good-bye and once again on the road, heading into a new adventure. While I didn't like leaving her, I enjoyed working with Daryl, and I was passionate about speaking. I liked the creativity of it. Sometimes I surprised myself with the things that came out of my mouth, which often emerged as if guided by an inner source of wisdom.

As was becoming our routine, I hooked up with Daryl en route to our destination, and we continued on together. We plotted and planned along the way, and I showed him pictures from the wedding. Daryl had a way of asking one or two questions that cut right to the core. Now was no exception.

He asked, "If you were to summarize into one word the most important aspect of a relationship, what would it be?"

I was completely stumped. My first thought was love, but that was too, well, predictable. A multitude of words passed through my mind:

caring, complete, fulfilling, but none of these seemed to be the one word I would use. I replied, "You've got me on that one, Daryl. I'm going to have to think about it. No one word seems to quite fit."

Daryl smiled in his simple way that seemed to indicate that he had just given me a clue to the next piece of my quest. He then said out loud, "Well, when you figure it out, let me know."

I assured him that I would, knowing that my mind would not rest until it had come to a conclusion.

We arrived, settled in and went to dinner, as was also our set routine. I tried to explain my feelings to him over sushi.

"This 'one-word' thing has had me thinking, Daryl." He smiled as I continued. "I feel so familiar with Jessie. I can be myself. I feel accepted, known. A word is right on the tip of my tongue for the feeling, but I can't put my finger on it."

"I am sure you will before our time is up!" He laughed quietly, offering no help at all.

Thinking two could play at this game, I asked, "What about you? What word would you use?"

This time he laughed right out loud and said, "I'll tell you after you remember your word; I wouldn't want to influence your experience with mine!"

We laughed and talked well into the evening, then retired to our rooms to prepare for the two-day seminar ahead.

I called Jessie and shared Daryl's question with her. She thought for a few moments and then said, "Hmmm, that is a good one! I think I would say love or maybe consideration."

I agreed that both were good words, and certainly important, but for me there seemed to be yet another word that was eluding me for the moment. It had something to do with having a sense of being heard, even when I hadn't said anything. We went on to other things, reviewing the events of the day.

The next day went fairly well, although I felt that my presentation was a little off. I went through all the same material I had before, and the people seemed to respond, but I noticed that I referred to my notes often, not sure of what I was going to say next. I felt almost lonely afterward. I talked with Daryl over dinner, to see if he could reflect to me something I hadn't been able to see.

He first went over what he thought was going well, which was basically all of the material I had shared. "The people are responding positively. I can tell this is getting in and making a difference to them. All I see that you need to do is simply be with the people when you speak."

He then went on to the material that we were going to cover the next day, leaving me to interpret *be with the people* any way I deemed fit.

Later that night, I lay in bed in my hotel room, drifting in and out of sleep with the words *be with the people* haunting me. I didn't know what Daryl meant. Since his style was to walk around the room, speaking from all sides, front and back, I imagined that perhaps I was making too much out of his words, when all he probably meant was to get out there and literally *be with* the people! Even after reaching this conclusion, the words continued to roll through my mind as I tried to fall asleep.

My dreams were active in the night, both strange and wonderful. I saw myself with children all around me, but instead of feeling alienated as I always had, I ran and played with them, as if I were one of the group. A small boy with reddish brown hair walked right up to me. I kneeled down and looked into his eyes, so innocent and pure. I felt a tremendous love for him. He put his hand on the top of my head and slowly drew a line downward with his finger, across my face, down my throat to my heart, and rested his hand there. Then he continued the imaginary line and drew an arch between my heart and his. Back and forth, he made the same motion, returning his hand to my head, then down to my heart, then to his own heart. He never said a word, just looked at me with an almost pleading look in his eyes, as if imploring me to journey the same route, from my head to my heart to his heart. Then he disappeared.

I woke up with tears welling up in my eyes. As I sat up, one escaped and chose the same path the boy had drawn, rolling down my cheek and dropping from my chin with a splat onto my heart.

In that moment, as if my consciousness was only now able to soften and see the subtlety that I had missed before, as if my life were passing before me, I viewed repeated opportunities that I had missed to truly connect with other people. I had walked down busy streets without really seeing the people who passed by. I had heard my boys talking, without listening to what they were truly saying—beyond their words and into their meaning. I had even made love without being fully present or connected to my partner. I had mastered being present *with myself* in the moment, but had I mastered being present *with another person* in the moment? Sadly, I didn't think so. As the boy in my dream appeared to be telling me, this was about journeying the distance from my head to my heart, and then crossing the bridge from my heart to someone else's!

Then I realized that when I taught I often spoke *to,* rather than *with* the people! I kept the same kind of distance from them. I had a sense of "me and them," rather than a sense of "us." I wondered, in the darkness of my room, how many people I had done that with throughout my life. The question frightened me a little. Feeling more alone in that moment than I had in a long, long time, I saw again how I had managed to isolate myself emotionally. I was sure that this was a form of protection I had developed as a boy, which had served me then but only kept me distant from people now.

Surely I hadn't done this with Jessie! Or had I? I wondered what her perception would be, whether in some way she sensed my distance even from her. I wished she were here, so that I could practice really sharing the moment with her. It was such a subtle shift, one hard to articulate, such that I wasn't exactly sure what I would do differently in the future. It seemed to be more of a *being different* than a *doing different.* It required self-observation *and* a focused awareness of connecting with the people around me. Perhaps it would come from looking into their eyes, meaning the *"hello"* when I greeted them, having genuine interest in how they were doing and authentically sharing how I was doing. It appeared to be a matter of being conscious of the other person's heart, in the moment, as well as my own. The thought crossed my mind that perhaps this was the quality I had been seeking to identify when Daryl asked me to name the most important thing in a relationship—*intimacy*!

Overwhelmed with a desire to talk with Alea, I wondered where she had been and why she hadn't come to comfort me with her wise presence. Where was she? I quietly called out to her, imploring her to come to me. No Alea. Waiting and watching, I called out to her again, a little louder, thinking she must not have heard me. Still, no Alea. My heart pulsed with a dull ache. The distance between myself and all others, in this moment, felt immense. I couldn't bear the thought that Alea was gone. Surely this wasn't true! I thought back to her words during our last few visits, and with a sinking feeling in my stomach, I remembered how she had seemed to be preparing me. She had told me this time would come.

What else had she said? I racked my brain, trying to remember, to find a clue to the way out of this abandoned feeling. She had said she was always with me and would always be back. I took a deep breath. It was obvious that I needed to let go. I resisted, as letting go of Alea was not something that I could ever want to do, now that she had entered my life and helped change it in such a profound way. I told myself that it wasn't Alea that I had to let go of; instead it was my need for control. I took another deep breath, then another. It took several breaths to even begin feeling a slight easing of the painful hold on my heart.

With each breath, releasing my discomfort, I felt more connected to Alea. After another and another, I remembered that it is in resourcefulness that love is strong. It is in resourcefulness, the center of the circle, that I could find Alea and all that she represented. Closing my eyes, I envisioned her as she had appeared in the labyrinth and imagined crossing the bridge between our hearts. Filled once again with calmness, strength and trust, I fell back to sleep, eager to cross the heart-bridge to everyone with whom I came into contact.

During the second day of the seminar, everything seemed different, as if I were seeing through a new pair of glasses. Everyone in the room seemed in clearer focus, and the material flowed from me without my having to refer to any of my notes. I truly *saw* the people—I felt connected, as if I knew what they were feeling. I experienced a heightened awareness of what was happening throughout the room; I knew who was crying, who was tired and who needed me to repeat what I had just said. Before the day was over, I had fallen in love with every one of them. This depth of connection left me feeling exuberant rather than lonely as I so often had after speaking.

The response from the audience confirmed the difference as well. In addition to the standing ovation, no one wanted to leave. They all stayed around, talking excitedly with each other, as if a sense of community had been created—all because of a shift in me. I became aware of the power we each have to change situations, not by trying to change the people around us, but rather by changing ourselves. When we change how we respond individually, people change in response to us. As I became more intimate with my audience, they too became more intimate. I realized it fully, now: the need to be connected is one of the strongest that humans possess, and tapping into it had given a new depth to my presentation.

Returning to my hotel room, I was eager to call Jessie and share with her my new discoveries. As I opened the door, the flashing red light on the telephone grabbed my attention as it blinked brightly in the otherwise dark room. I listened as Jessie's voice told me that she had an important message and to call her right away. It didn't sound good by the tone in her voice; I returned her call immediately.

The phone rang several times before she picked up, and with each ring I became increasingly more anxious for the news.

"Hello?" Her gentle voice comforted me immediately.

"Hi, Jessie? Is something wrong? I got your message."

"Matt, it's your father; his cancer is spreading. They don't think he is going to live more than a day or two. You need to go see him right away." She had never met my father, but the compassion in her voice was as strong as if she had known him personally.

I sat quietly for a moment, Jessie respecting my silence, her support flowing over the distance between us. My father was dying. A flood of emotion invaded me, as memories of my brother's death from cancer several years ago added to the feelings I now experienced. I did not want to go through this again.

In my numbness, I simply said, "I love you, Jessie. I'll call you from my parents' place. I am going to see how soon I can fly out."

She wished me well before we hung up. "I want to be with you, Matt. I'll look into flights right away. Be safe, and know that I love you, too!"

The room seemed suddenly darker and infinitely more lonely. First Alea had left me, now my father. My father! Fathers weren't supposed to die! They were supposed to live forever. I felt like a little boy as these unreasonable expectations forced themselves into my adult mind. I hadn't even been that close to my father in recent years, and yet I still suffered a sudden and tremendous sense of loss. He had never said much, but he was there, he was my father and I loved him—and he loved me.

After calling Daryl to explain, I managed to get a few hours of uneasy rest, then caught an early morning flight out. As I sat on the plane headed for Oklahoma, it occurred to me how self-absorbed I had been through all of this. I had given no thought as to how my father was feeling, and concern for my mother or sisters hadn't even crossed my mind. Once I was there, I would be more empathetic of their pain and their needs, but right now, in this moment, the whole world revolved around me. This was my loss, my sadness and my immense pain.

Movies of my father's life passed through my mind as I flew toward him. As I watched the scenes, I realized with a rising frustration that in every one of them he was smoking. Smoking was a part of him; I couldn't picture him without a cigarette. It was like watching an old black-and-white movie, made when smoking was the "in" thing to do, when Bogart was tough and cool. Now, my father had become a victim of being cool, of being one of the boys.

I wondered how many things we did to gain the acceptance of our peers that eventually ended up killing us. I looked at the people on the plane around me. They were definitely not commercials for good health. My eyesight suddenly seemed to shift; I could see subtleties that I had never noticed before. I felt as if I could tell if someone was sick just by looking at them. I could see broken hearts and feel sadness. I could feel the love between young sweethearts and the unexpressed enthusiasm of children confined to their seats. One after the other, I looked around at the people and connected with them, empathized with them—shared the moment with them.

As I became increasingly aware of the people around me, my eyes rested on a man who was fidgeting in his seat a few rows up. Surprised that I hadn't noticed him earlier, I saw that other passengers around him were watching him, too. Apparently, he was not "all there" mentally, as he passed everything to the flight attendant, including his dinner tray, behind his head to get it out to the aisle. Headphones, soda cans—it made no difference what it was—he passed them all behind his head, as if passing them in front of himself would violate some very important rule. Fascinated, I watched, appreciating the momentary relief from thoughts of my father.

The people around him established eye contact with each other, shrugging and rolling their eyes in a common bond of annoyance. A lady sitting behind him twirled her finger next to her ear and made a dismissive gesture with her open hand, as if to announce to anyone watching her that she had no kind of relationship with this abnormal person, even though she was seated close to him. I watched as fear and judgment were expressed without words. We'd all seen his type before walking down the street carrying on a conversation with himself. On a street it could be more easily ignored; being in a confined space with him evoked a whole different set of reactions. Here, the man did nothing to anyone else, kept completely to himself, but somehow people felt personally violated on account of this intrusion into their flight. I felt a sudden wave of compassion as I tried to imagine how a person like this would get through the world safely. How did he survive? While others made comments like, "How many Quaaludes do you think he's on?" and laughed together about him as if he had chosen to be crazy, I said a silent prayer for his well-being and safety. I felt the fear of the people around me and said a prayer for them as well, sad that our fear made us so angry and judgmental rather than caring.

The man continued his strange behavior throughout the flight, and once, as I made my way back from a trip to the restroom, met my eyes with his. I smiled at him as I passed his seat, feeling gratitude for the lesson he had provided me. A sudden thought occurred as I sat down: *Did Michael's volunteers include people like this—people who offer us daily opportunities to express compassion and love?* I mulled over this idea for the remainder of the trip and came to the conclusion that it was very possible. Even if this man was not such a volunteer, it sure wouldn't hurt to treat him and others like him as though they were!

As we began our descent, my attention returned to my father. I was thankful that the older of my two sisters, Judy, would pick me up at the airport. She was the only other member of my family who understood the importance of taking care of her body. In fact, she was likely responsible for my own awareness on the subject. It was always hard for me to spend time with the rest of my family because, while I loved them all dearly, their lack of attention to their health was hard for me to watch. And now, one by one, I was watching them die, first my brother, now my father. I knew that my mother would be next and then my youngest sister, Sharon. I wanted to shake them all and say, "Don't do this to yourselves!" *In reality,* I admitted, *I didn't want them to do "this" to me, either.* Death always seems hardest on the living.

My sister took me straight to my father's hospital bed. As I looked at him, my stomach and my heart sank together. While my father had always been thin, I had never thought of him as tiny. Now, as he lay before me, only a shrunken image remained of the man I had known. He looked as though he weighed only about sixty-five pounds and was drifting in and out of sleep. Even in his unconsciousness, his hand moved back and forth to his mouth, as if he were trying to smoke a cigarette. The movement came so naturally to him that, although it saddened me under the circumstances, this signature gesture drove home the reality that this frail skeleton lying in front of me truly was my father. I supposed that this was no different to him than any other breath he'd taken. Every now and then, he opened his eyes and looked at me, making me believe that he knew I was there, and then he would drift back to sleep—or unconsciousness—I couldn't tell which.

Watching him intently as his chest rattled with each breath, I could see the effort that merely breathing was for him. I sat there for hours, holding his hand, wanting to know him, wanting him to know me. I wanted to talk to him, to tell him that I loved him. I wanted to thank him for everything he had done for me. I wanted him to know that I forgave him for being distant and for being poor and for all the other things that had made me so angry with him. I urgently wanted to hear him say that he forgave me too, and that he was proud to be my father.

We sat there in silence; those words would never be shared. Why hadn't I spent this kind of time with my father before? Why had we taken each other for granted and held onto past moments that kept us apart? Why did I wait until it was too late to come to his side just to be with him? I felt the grief rising, beginning to overtake me.

The pressure in my chest from holding in my tears became too much to withstand. One by one, the tears escaped, rolling down my face. My father opened his eyes and looked at me as I tried to wipe the tears away. Never before had he seen me cry as an adult, nor had I seen him give in to tears, either. Both of us had been controlled by the lifelong belief that men don't cry—at least not in front of each other—as passed down from one generation of stoic men to the next. Now, in our final moments together, we let down our male masks. I leaned over his bed, careful not to disturb the tubes that led into and out of his body, and hugged him. I felt a quiet, reserved, yet definite sob come from him, and I felt in this moment that we knew each other better than we ever had before.

With all the energy left in him, he reached up and wiped away a tear, as if to regain his masculine composure, and drifted back to sleep. Then, with one final breath, my father became a memory.

I had never actually watched someone at the moment of death before. It wasn't dramatic, as in the movies; it was—peaceful. One minute he was breathing laboriously, and the next he was simply quiet. Now, as I looked at the empty body in front of me, nothing remained about him that was my father—all traces of him had disappeared. I glanced around the room, having read about hovering spirits looking down on their own body at the moment of death. Somehow I wanted my father to know that I knew he was no longer in the body before me. I wanted him to know that I knew he was more than that—that I knew he still existed, even though his body was no longer alive. I looked around again, as if expecting him to materialize and say, "Here I am, Son!" but it was totally quiet in the room; no spirit appeared.

I tried to imagine what my father would say, what he would be feeling as he looked down at his own body, lifeless. Was he seeing his life pass before him? Was he now feeling the kind of unconditional love that I knew God bestowed upon us while we evaluate our own lives and experiences? I wondered whether he was happy with his life. I wondered if he felt a sense of completeness or if, as he reviewed all he had said and done, he was left wishful that he had done something different, something more, something of greater impact on humanity.

I whispered good-bye to my father and offered a prayer of thanks that I hoped was worthy of the man who had raised me. Although I still felt no hint of his lingering spirit, I trusted that he could not only hear my words, but was now capable of reading my heart as well.

Crossing the bridge from my heart to someone else's at a moment like this was almost unbearable. The loss suddenly became very real. My heart pounded in my chest, beating against my ribs, as though they were suddenly a kind of jail cell. Claustrophobia overwhelmed me and I felt an immediate and pressing need to escape.

I emerged from the room, knowing I needed to tell my family of his passing. They sat in the waiting room outside of his door, just as I had seen them years ago on fishing trips huddled around the campfire, only now they were huddled around an ashtray. The scene was complete with rising smoke. They all looked up expectantly, as if to ask whether I wanted a cigarette and offer me a chair as the rightful heir to this throne of death.

The mixture of love, disgust and grief was just too much for me. An uncontrollable surge of anger exploded through my body. In total frustration, sandwiched between what sat dying before me and what lay lifeless behind me, barely recognizing my own actions, I approached the ashtray altar and kicked it across the waiting room. Sand, ashes and butts spewed forth as shocked faces stared at me in disbelief. In this moment, resourcefulness was not within my grasp. In fact, I didn't even pause to look for it. I turned and stalked out, feeling powerless to stop the ignorance in the world.

I knew I needed to regain some semblance of a connection to Source, so I headed outdoors for a walk. Where was Alea? Why did I feel the farthest from her when I needed her the most? Finding a bench on the hospital grounds, I sat down and cried, more deeply than I had in years, releasing all the pent-up energy of my emotions.

After what seemed like forever, I took several deep breaths and focused on letting go of the pain I had stored in my body. Finally, I reached a point where I could begin to observe myself, to separate from my emotions. From this perspective I made more sense out of what was happening. I was in a state of resistance. I was angry at my father, not so much for dying as for not *avoiding* dying—or at least not putting it off by making healthy choices. How many times had I told him that smoking was bad for his health? The doctors had told him several years back that he wouldn't make it much longer if he didn't stop smoking, but he continued anyway. He ate poorly, too. Why didn't he take better care of himself? And my family! How could they watch each other die, one at a time, and not take more responsibility for their own health? I didn't understand. The anger I felt was directed at the doctors, too! They just kept prescribing antibiotics, one after the other, for every infection, until the medications no longer worked. Ironically, it wasn't even the cancer that killed my father; it was an infection upon which antibiotics were no longer effective. Why couldn't they see what was happening?

As I felt myself getting pulled into my anger instead of just observing it, I realized that this anguish was all about my need for control. *Listen to me! Why don't they . . . ? Why didn't he . . . ?* and *I knew this would happen!* This was all the language of someone needing control. With a huge sigh, I let go and released myself from the effort to control something that was not within my scope and range of ability. With another breath, I began the challenging shift of moving from resistance to acceptance.

As I let go of my anger, I moved into sadness. I was sad that I hadn't said what I wanted to say to my father before it was too late, and that I hadn't told him that I loved him. I wished I had thanked him explicitly for the times he took me fishing and worked on my car with me. I was sad that my family would never again go on a fishing trip or camping trip, although we hadn't for years anyway. I was sad that my father wasn't ever going to meet Jessie, and that he and I would never have the chance to really know each other. I saw this as my need for acceptance—my family's acceptance and my father's acceptance, but most of all for my own self-acceptance. I took another deep breath and let that go as well.

As I moved into a more resourceful state, my thoughts turned to Alea again. I wanted to talk to her, to share my most recent experiences and thoughts. I couldn't imagine why she would leave me at a time like this. In that instant, I felt as though I were taking a final exam at school. *Was Alea just testing me? Had she pulled back so she could simply watch how I handled all these events? Had she really abandoned me, or had she given me wings to fly with and then pushed me out of the nest?* I closed my eyes and imagined that Alea was standing in front of me. Her beauty shone brightly, even just in my mind's eye. A warm surge of love flowed through me as I focused on her, reminding me that God has a reason for everything and that nothing is unjust or happenstance.

If Alea had really been in front of me, she would have asked me what I had discovered. I felt compelled to answer, even though no one had really asked. At first, nothing came to my mind, but then I began talking out loud to myself, figuring that if anyone saw me, they would just figure that I was one of the hospital's mental patients. "What have I discovered? Well, I found that once again, when I let go of my need to be in control and my need for acceptance, even if the circumstances don't change, I feel better able to go forward, better able to make choices."

My thoughts turned to my conversations with Daryl and my experiences of *being with* the people in the seminar, and again with the people on the plane. When I was resourceful with other people, fully sharing the moment with them, I felt much more connected, less alone, less isolated. It seems as if this intimacy with others defines a deeper level of resourcefulness, a place where our guards and masks are dropped and where we simply *are with* each other. The word *authentic* popped into my mind, and out loud I said, "Authentic Intimacy."

I saw the boy from my dreams bridging the gap between our two hearts. I said, "Authentic Intimacy is when we are in the moment together and are ourselves with no ego needs, just acceptance and compassion." The face of the man on the plane drifted into my consciousness, and his troubled eyes responded to my smile as they had before.

I looked toward the hospital entrance and felt again the immediacy of my father's death; my family was undoubtedly wondering what had come over me and where I had gone. A pang of sadness struck me again. Try as my ego might to make me feel guilty, I warded off the "should haves" and the "why didn't I's." When I didn't entertain them,

I noticed that a huge amount of my pain disappeared, causing me to wonder, *How much of our grief is really guilt invading us?* I followed that thought to the next logical question, *What is guilt?* and answered my own query, *Guilt is merely a need for acceptance turned inward.* At the time of someone's death, we feel as though we haven't done enough and should be doing more. We wish we had done more to control, more to avoid our loved one's death, and more to forgive and be forgiven before they die. The irony is that when we feel guilty, we aren't resourceful, which means we aren't being authentically intimate in the moment. We miss spending the last possible chance to share an intimate moment with someone by allowing our ego-driven needs to create guilt and remorse.

I offered thanks to God that I had had one authentically intimate moment with my father before he died, and I carefully avoided any remorse over the lost moments, lest I step into a pile of guilt. I was sure it would stick to my shoes and follow me into the future, stinking up my life, if I weren't careful. It felt good to laugh at that image, as I sat there under a big tree on the lawn of the hospital, even though my father lay dead inside.

As I stood to go call Jessie, sure she would be concerned over what was going on, I looked to the tree that loomed over me. I hadn't really noticed it the entire time I sat there. Now, as I truly saw it, I felt its presence as a comforting force, as it had offered protection, beauty and shade throughout my grief and contemplation. I reached up and touched the bark, imagining how many people had sought out this nurturing spot while dealing with their pain at the hospital. It must have "seen" some pretty tender sights in its lifetime, yet still it stood strong, offering support to others. Strangely, I felt as if I were having an intimate communication with the tree, with no pretense, no control issues, no need for acceptance—just me, the tree, compassion and acceptance.

As if in a meditative state, I stood there, recharging my batteries. A gust of wind rustled the leaves of the tree, causing them to shimmer. Something sparkling on one of the low branches caught my attention. Feeling peaceful and connected to All That Is, I tried to see what was shimmering in the light. I jumped up, grabbed the branch and pulled it toward me, still unable to see exactly what had caught my eye. I pushed the leaves away, and there, encircling a slender, leafy twig on the lowest branch of the tree, hung a golden ring. My heart skipped a beat as I reached up and took it down, knowing it had been placed there just for me. If I had not paused to share that moment with the tree, I would have missed it altogether.

My whisper hung in the air. *"Alea!"* Still nowhere to be seen, I knew she was here. She hadn't really left me! I held the ring close to my heart, as tenderly as if it were Alea herself. Nodding with understanding, I read the engraving out loud to the tree, sharing with it the word, *"Intimacy."*

Somewhere in the back of my mind, I heard an echo bouncing back, *"Into me see."*

She wrapped her arms around him, though he didn't know it, and tenderly held him while he gathered himself together, preparing to go back and face his family. Times like these were hard for everyone, she knew from witnessing many such experiences. No matter how many skills we have, nothing quite prepares us for the loss of our loved ones. Guilt often intensifies our grief, but on top of that is the genuine loss of a friend and the realization that we now have to carry on without them.

Returning to resourcefulness can help, but even from a resourceful state, our choice might be to cry and allow ourselves the room to grieve, knowing all the while that we are more than our emotions, that there is a place within that is undisturbed by the turmoil. Knowing, also, that the person who has passed on is more than the body and is also undisturbed by the transition. The love continues, even when the body does not.

These resourceful thoughts usually come after the initial pain of loss. She was pleased that they had entered Matt's mind so quickly, comforting him even as the pain swept through him. She watched him make his way slowly back to the hospital.

Everyone dies, yet we are so resistant to it, afraid of it. It remains so unknown, so uncontrolled. Matt had begun to see that death is the ultimate control/acceptance drama. We want to control what happens to us, how we die, where we go after we die, and we want the acceptance of the "Judge," still incorrectly thinking that there is a judgmental entity outside ourselves. If people only knew that God is truly the essence of love, and that no judgment is possible in that essence! If they knew God, instead of just believing in God, they would know that they already have the ultimate acceptance. Not knowing this simple truth, they just get in their own way.

It was hard to stay hidden from Matt while he went through so much suffering, but she knew he had to understand and internalize the fact that his strength and wisdom were his own in order for him to truly be empowered to do what he was here to do. People have a tendency to rely on outside sources for their connection to God, for their connection to truth and for making all their decisions. She wanted to be sure Matt was self-reliant, knowing that in resourcefulness, infinite wisdom and ability lay within for handling, enduring and transforming any situation. It was not a test, as he thought it to be, but rather more like practice—though there was really no such thing as a practice run at life. She rephrased her own explanation, affirming that all circumstances were opportunities for growth.

Alea was pleased that Matt had discovered the value of intimacy. Without it, people go through life feeling very lonely, unknown and disconnected. Once they learn to let down their masks and become authentic, in the moment, with other beings, the results are delightful! While Matt had just begun to consciously experience intimate moments, she knew that the more he chose to be present with another, the more easily it would happen, without even trying. Eventually he would truly know that he is connected to everyone and everything. It is virtually impossible not to feel love for another entity, whether it is human, plant, animal or even simply material, when one takes the moment and authentically connects with it. Enjoying the image, she saw the process as a giant "connect the dots" game, only in this case it was "connect the hearts."

Alea pondered the many ways in which one could become intimate and share an authentic moment. Some of the most magical things are missed completely if the moment to be with them is not taken. Remembering the beautiful essences of flowers, she considered how one could be given flowers, hold them and put them in a vase without ever really receiving the flowers, without ever sharing the moment with the flowers.

Even something as simple as eating an ice cream cone could be appreciated as a vivid moment of intimacy. So often we eat without receiving the full experience of the taste and the texture—the gift of nourishment. Eating is so much more satisfying when we take a moment to enthusiastically honor the food with our full attention.

Sadly, Alea considered that enthusiasm was almost a lost art. She offered a prayer, wishing that everyone would have enthusiasm for every moment, for every breath, for every smile, for all one's senses, abilities, creativity, self-expression, humor—the more she listed, the more enthusiastic she became! If only we would "pretend" that each act, each moment, was an offering to God, while at the same time a gift from God—she smiled at the deep satisfaction of joy that would come of that game of "pretend!"

Intimacy is the gift that comes from enthusiasm, of being "in God" and truly alive to the miracle of the moment. It is an opening of oneself to receiving the blessing that the moment has to offer and sharing that appreciation with another—truly sharing the full experience of the moment. It is a matter of honor, of taking a moment to honor another with the presence of one's full attention, receiving each other.

Alea felt Matt's eagerness to return to Jessie so he could be more fully present with her, as well. People in relationships so often suffer from loneliness because they don't know how to be connected. When they let go of their ego needs and spend authentic time together, even if only for a few minutes each day, it changes their relationships forever. She smiled at the knowledge that there is nothing like making love when fully present and aware of the one you are with, going deep into the eternal, timeless moment of true intimacy together.

Matt had begun to discover the layers of resourcefulness: having clarity, following one's heart with commitment and being authentically intimate in each moment. She looked forward to what he had yet to find—each a treasure to behold; each ring of the key another way to deepen resourcefulness.

She watched as he disappeared into the building with his fingers wrapped around the Ring of Truth he had earned. She smiled when he stopped to smell the flowers on his way.

12

The Symphony

I looked around at my family; they, too, were in the midst of grieving. The mess I had made with the ashtray had been cleaned up, and no one brought up my unseemly display of frustration. Apparently the news of my father's death had minimized its impact.

One by one, my family began to leave the hospital. Mom wanted one more moment with my father before we took her home. She quietly went back into his room alone and said her final good-byes to the man with whom she had spent half a century of her life. While I waited, I thought of Jessie and how hard it would be to say good-bye to her, and we didn't even have a fraction of the history together credited to these two. I couldn't imagine what this must be like for my mother. I heard her muffled sobs through the door, but decided it best to trust her grieving process and save the comforting for her return.

Her face was streaked with tears as she stood in the doorway, hinged between the past and the future. She seemed stronger somehow, as if in saying good-bye to her "other half," she had once again restored herself to a whole. Taking a deep breath, she seemed to be gathering all the energy she could muster, in order to leave behind her what needed to be left and to face whatever came next. My mother's strength inspired me.

I crossed the bridge from my heart to hers and hugged her in a way that I never had before. As we stood there holding each other, the weight of recognizing that I was the only man left in the family settled over me. I felt myself stand up a little taller and hold her a little tighter, as if the responsibility implied by this fact required extra depth and volume. My mother had always been a pillar of strength, and now was no exception, and yet I could tell that she was in no hurry to break the embrace between us.

I didn't want to make the same mistakes with her that I had with my father. With her still in my arms, I took a deep breath and released the past. Years of stored up emotions, judgments, unfulfilled wishes and expectations dropped to the ground and slithered away—as if they were unable to remain in the midst of so much love. We turned together to face the future, one step at a time, and left the hospital behind us.

We drove my mother back to my parents' home on the edge of town. At the first opportunity after we arrived, I called Jessie, sure that she was anxious to hear from me. It had been a long twenty-four hours!

"Hello?" The sound of her voice was like cool water in the desert.

"Hi, Jessie, sorry I haven't called you sooner. It's been a hard day. Before I go into it, though, how are you?" I wanted to be sure she was okay before I launched into a monologue about myself and my father.

"I'm fine, Matt. Just a little worried about you. How is your father?"

A silence fell over me like a brief cloud settling on my shoulders, and then I answered, "He passed away this morning." For the moment, I could find no more words.

Jessie filled in the gap. "I'm so sorry, Honey. I wish I were there to comfort you. Are you okay? Is your family okay?"

"Everyone is all right, and everyone is pretty shaken up. I don't know what it's like for other people, but losing a parent is a strange experience. I mean, parents represent strength, wisdom, nurturing and support, even if they don't live out those qualities very well. When one of them dies, it feels like you are losing more than the person that you love. It feels as though an important piece of your support system has been removed, even though in my case, I haven't called on it in years."

The image of my life as a pyramid with a solid foundation came into my mind. I imagined one of the huge foundation stones upon which it had been built being removed, leaving the entire structure out of balance. I shared my picture with Jessie.

She replied, "Yes, I can see how it would feel that way. It is like losing your past—your history—in a way, too."

Her voice trailed off, and I knew that she was thinking about her own father, wondering where he was and what he was like. Even stranger than losing a parent to death would be having one who had chosen not to be around anymore. I shuddered at the thought of that pain, and hoped that one day Jessie would have the opportunity to be present with her father and forgive him for the things he had done—and not done.

"I love you, Jessie," just popped out of my mouth; nothing else seemed appropriate.

"I love you too, Matt. I called the airlines; the first flight I can get would arrive tomorrow afternoon. I thought I should wait to talk with you before I bought it. I have it on hold, though. Have you discussed plans yet?"

"We haven't talked about the details yet, but I'm going to help my mother settle things. I'm really glad you're coming; I don't like being away from you so much and after we get home, I'm going to have to leave again fairly soon because I have a seminar in Los Angeles in a few weeks."

"Let me make the arrangements and get back to you. I'll see if I can fly out any earlier."

"Just let me know; I'll pick you up at the airport. Thank you, Jessie, I can't wait to see you."

I hung up feeling as though some of my foundation was being restored. It concerned me for a moment that to merely replace the foundation stones with other stones that could also be removed was not such a good idea. As I looked with my mind's eye, I saw that there was an even greater foundation below these stones—Mother Earth, God, Goddess, Source—from which the true support, strength and nurturing comes. I saw that no matter what we did to our "structures," our true foundation was God. I found great relief in resting directly on the only permanent and true source of strength.

Letting go of any held emotions and tensions, I breathed in the precious air that fuels the fire of the soul. What a tremendous resource air is, and how instrumental in our being resourceful! Feeling reconnected to Source, I rejoined the family members in the dining room as we began to plan our next steps. The conversation often drifted into reminiscences about old times. Our memories were punctuated with tears as we relived the many experiences we had shared. As I practiced being really present with my mother and sisters, I felt closer to them than I ever had before. We all went to bed with a little extra love filling the gap where my father used to be.

A call from Jessie came in first thing the next morning. "Matt? My flight arrives at two o'clock this afternoon. Can you pick me up?"

I was so thankful that Jessie was coming; my only wish was that she could have been able to meet my father and to meet the rest of my family under happier circumstances. "I'll be there. Thanks, Jessie, for putting it all together."

Just as she was about to hang up, she said, "Oh, Matt? You know when you asked me what I thought was the most important ingredient in a relationship?"

"Yes?" I responded, curious as to what she had to say.

"Well, I've been thinking about that a lot and I finally settled on what I think is the most important thing."

"Me, too. What is yours?" I looked forward to telling her all about my discoveries and my newly acquired understanding of intimacy.

"At first I thought of things like love and kindness, but you can have love and kindness in a relationship and still feel lonely. The thing that I think is most important is intimacy. I don't just mean the physical kind, but rather being truly connected to each other—do you know what I mean?"

A waterfall of laughter poured from me and settled into a gentle pool. I said, reassuringly, "I'm only laughing, Jessie, because after virtually the exact same deliberations, I came up with the exact same word! I'm looking forward to your arrival, not just because I want to talk about it more with you, but also to practice being fully present in the moment with you."

"Hmm—I'm looking forward to that, too!" she said with a slight intonation that indicated she was now thinking of the physical form of intimacy. We shared our common understanding and appreciation of the sentiment and then parted ways, as if hanging up the phone would allow her to arrive more quickly.

The next call was to my boys. With the sudden nature of my arrival in Oklahoma, I hadn't even managed to call to let them know I was here or to tell them about their grandfather. I spoke with Sarah and she agreed to bring them over for the weekend. We had a better than usual conversation as she expressed her sorrow over my father's death and we shared some memories about him. I felt as if we were actually listening to each other and sharing on a personal level—something we hadn't done in a long, long time—if ever.

I surprised myself when I said, "Sarah, I'm looking forward to seeing you when you drop the boys off. Thank you for your support through this—and my wedding. You have been really great." I paused, then added, "I don't know if it would be too uncomfortable for you—with Jessie being there and all—but you are welcome to stay for the services if you want to. I know my dad was really fond of you and the rest of the family would love to see you." She had stayed in touch with my family since she moved back to Oklahoma and let the boys come visit their grandparents whenever they wanted to.

I could tell she was thinking about what I had said before she spoke. "Thank you, Matt. Your family has always been good to me over the years, but I'll have to think about whether or not I'll come. I want to pay my respects and all but, well, I'm sure you understand that it might be a little awkward."

"I'll understand whatever you decide, but at least be sure to come in and say hello to Mom. She would appreciate that, I'm sure."

After assuring me she would, I asked to speak to the boys. I knew they would be upset to hear about their grandfather and didn't want to leave the difficulty of telling them to Sarah. As she got off the phone, I felt like better friends with her than we had been in years. She put Tim on one line and Jerry on the other so I wouldn't have to repeat the news twice.

After a few minutes of checking in with the boys on how they were doing I said, "I have something really sad to tell you."

Tim said, "It's Grandpa, isn't it?"

I assumed he just guessed since he knew his grandpa had been so sick. "Yes, Son. He died yesterday. I was with him when he went; he was very peaceful."

Tim started to cry and said, "I dreamed about him last night. He came and gave me a hug. It was so real!"

Jerry was quiet, too quiet.

I had heard about spirits visiting loved ones in their dreams. "He was probably coming to say good-bye to you, Tim. Did you dream about him too, Jerry?"

"No, but I knew. I could feel him yesterday. I almost called, but I didn't want to wake him up if he was sleeping."

I was impressed with how sensitive they both were. "I'm sorry to have to deliver this kind of news to you guys. I wish I were here for happier reasons." Still hearing Tim's sniffling, I said, "Hey, Timmy, I know this is hard, but your grandpa was in a lot of pain. Fortunately, he's free now."

Between sniffles he said, "But it won't be the same without him."

I agreed, "No. No, it won't," remembering that our grief is more about the living than the dead.

Jerry asked, "How's Grandma?"

"She is pretty sad but she's trying to keep her spirits up for everyone else. I bet she could use some hugs from the two of you. I asked your mom to bring you out to the house for the weekend. I think she's planning to drop you off on Friday afternoon."

"Okay. See you then." Jerry hung up abruptly and I worried that he wasn't able to express his grief as easily as Timmy did.

I could still hear Tim crying. "Are you going to be okay, Son?" It seemed like a stupid thing to ask, but I didn't know what to say to make him feel better.

"Yeah, I guess."

"Well, I'm here at Grandma's if you are having a hard time or want to get a hold of me, just call. Jessie is coming in tomorrow and we're both looking forward to seeing you."

He said he would call if he needed me. I asked to speak to Sarah again.

When she got on the line, I said, "Sorry to leave you with two grieving boys. I'm a little concerned about Jerry. He got off the phone really quick."

"I'll check on him. I'm sure they'll both be okay. See you Friday." She hung up almost as quickly as Jerry had, leaving me concerned about them all.

As I joined my family in the living room, everything appeared normal, with the exception of the lack of my father's presence. I half expected to see him walk down the hall and pour himself a cup of coffee. Having heard stories of people who, after having limbs amputated, could still feel them itch after the accident or surgery, I imagined that the expectation of seeing my father was much like still experiencing the itch of a "phantom limb."

By all appearances, it was a day like any other. No one spoke of my father's death, or the funeral or future plans. I couldn't decide if this was healthy or a sign of serious denial, but decided to let go of my need for control and just experience what was happening. My mom and Sharon were making eggs, bacon and potatoes, filling the house with all-too-familiar scents of home, while Judy and I ate some fruit and caught up on the latest life events. I couldn't bear to tell my mom that I didn't eat red meat, lest she think I was judging her. I noticed no one had smoked around me since my confrontation with the ashtray. I skirted the issue by sharing the news and worked my way around the bacon during breakfast.

Everyone was happy to hear that they were going to be meeting Jessie, but they looked at me a little oddly when I told them of the possibility of Sarah coming as well. They all liked her so I knew she was welcome, but I could see they were already anticipating the discomfort of the two women being in the same place at the same time. I was deeply thankful that I had learned the art of letting go and could see many opportunities arising for practicing the skill. I hoped this wasn't going to be too uncomfortable for Jessie.

After breakfast, I went for a walk to clear my head. It was a beautiful day for wandering the roads that led through farm after farm.

I was suddenly filled with a boundless appreciation for all living things. I sat down on a boulder under a huge tree and just observed the world around me in awe. Alea came to mind, and rather than feeling her absence, I chose to feel her closeness instead. After all, she had said she was always with me, and if that were true, then the issue was one of whether or not I allowed myself to feel her presence. I chose to feel. Sitting in contemplation, I reviewed the steps through which I had passed and tried to imagine where it was all leading. I imagined that if I started studying the process for any underlying patterns, perhaps I would be able to see the picture "on the box lid" of this jigsaw puzzle. If so, perhaps I could start by at least putting the border pieces in the proper places.

I replayed the events: Alea and Michael had led me through the process of letting go, at which point I had earned the "seed," which once planted in practice, brought about resourcefulness. I quietly wished that they had introduced me to resourcefulness first, so I could have bypassed all the rest. I dismissed that thought quickly, however, knowing that I had to observe the other stuff and let it go first, or I might have mistaken some of my ego-dramas as characteristics of resourcefulness. I took a deep breath, feeling quite resourceful in this particular moment.

I watched a milkman drive his delivery truck down the old road; I hadn't seen one of those since I was young. I enjoyed the nostalgia of the jaunt back in time before returning to my analysis.

A phrase from my thoughts stood out: characteristics of resourcefulness. . . . I saw that each of the Rings of Truth I had harvested since planting the seed seemed to be fruits of the resourcefulness tree while up until then they were more like directions—the steps. I was amused with the unfolding gardening motif as I sat here among my "roots." Returning again to my quest for deeper understanding, I recited out loud the truths that had been revealed since I had learned about resourcefulness: *Clarity, Follow Your Heart, Commitment, Intimacy.* Each of these seemed to be a different facet of resourcefulness, as if it were a diamond which shimmered with new depth and dimension every way I turned it.

I held the imaginary diamond in my hand as if it were a crystal ball, and asked it what was to be revealed to me next. Instead of the answer I was wishing for, I heard, as clearly as if it were said out loud, "What is required of you now?"

The question threw me from my peaceful, contemplative state back into the throes of the immediate needs of my family. In the midst of our grief, we needed to prepare the rituals surrounding my father's death. The question haunted me, "What is required of you now?" The accent on "you" was not to be missed; after all, this was my quest.

I thought about how hard it was to be in my parents' home, or to clarify, how hard it was to be resourceful while in my parents' home. It was so easy to be in judgment of my relatives and their lifestyles. What was required of me in order to be in their home and be resourceful at the same time? Acceptance. I needed to be accepting of the way they were, without trying to change them. I could see that while this was just another way of looking at letting go of my control issues, it brought resourcefulness to a deeper level. In order to love and be loved, we need to accept each other.

I repeated my thoughts out loud, as if answering whoever had asked the question: "What is required of me now is acceptance of my family and Sarah—just as they are. I can see this includes not only my immediate family, but also my extended family of humankind. If I can accept even what I consider to be unacceptable, then perhaps I will truly understand the concept of resourcefulness." I realized in that moment that I considered death to be "unacceptable" and therefore something I must master accepting.

I closed my eyes in meditation, and after only a few moments saw myself once again standing at the edge of the spiraling labyrinth path. I quietly worked my way to the center, as I had previously done with Alea's guidance. I released any thoughts that arose as I went, while I prepared for the quiet opportunity to receive wisdom. This time, when I reached the heart of the labyrinth, Alea was nowhere to be seen. Instead, as I entered, I saw my father, my brother and many other people I had known when they were alive, all sitting there quietly. Very peacefully, one by one, people came and went from the center without disturbing each other. I wondered why I was in the labyrinth with all these others who had already died. I felt uncomfortable for a moment, as if I didn't belong. I then saw my mother and the rest of my family walking into the labyrinth and realized that we are all on the same path, just at different places on the journey. The recognition sank in that we all make it to the center, this illuminated place of love, in our own time, in our own way.

In my mind, I sat down and meditated, focusing on allowing others to be themselves. It was a matter of trusting the process, of truly believing that everyone is on the path to their own center, and of allowing them the honor of finding their own way. I looked at each of my "lost" loved ones and worked on accepting their deaths and—with even more difficulty—accepting the way they chose to live their lives. I held the vision of each until I felt an inner forgiveness, a subtle shift that allowed me to let go and move on. After gaining the clarity of the concept, I was determined to follow my heart with commitment toward acceptance. I readied myself for taking the next steps with an open, accepting heart.

It occurred to me that much of my mental focus concerned itself with where I was going, what my life meant and what next bit of wisdom I could glean out of my experiences. I wondered if I could free myself from even this subtle way of distancing myself from the present moment of resourcefulness. With that thought, I felt compelled to see how far I could get if I literally turned my back on looking ahead altogether. Within my own mind, I rose from my position of meditation, ready to journey back out of the labyrinth. I spontaneously turned around to walk out backwards. With no idea how I would get out without looking where I was going, I began, one step at a time. Within no time, I was easily negotiating the twisting, turning pathway—not by looking to see where I was going nor where I had been—but instead by simply seeing where I stood at each moment and readjusting if I stepped "out of line."

Once I reached the outside edge of the circular pathway, I felt complete with my meditation. I opened my eyes and took in the countryside around me. The question, "What is required of me now?" resounded like a minute-by-minute mantra, reminding me to constantly look at where I was in the moment and to readjust my direction, based on my current position.

Looking at my watch, I saw that at this exact moment, "where I was now," was running late for picking up Jessie if I didn't hurry! Thankful that I had long legs, I picked up the pace and walked quickly back the way I had come, returning home. I greeted my mother and sisters, borrowed the car and joyfully went to the airport.

I managed to make it on time and waited anxiously at the gate, anticipating holding Jessie in my arms again. It had only been a few days, but it felt like a lifetime had passed.

Jessie looked like a seasoned traveler when she arrived, and I realized then that we had not traveled anywhere together yet. With our quickly planned wedding, we had bypassed having a honeymoon. I made a mental note to remedy that oversight in the very near future, as I pulled her to me and hugged her like never before, fully present in the moment.

I took her out to a late lunch so we could catch up before entering a household full of people.

She asked thoughtfully, "How is your mother doing, Matt? I can only imagine how difficult this must be for her."

A picture of my mother operating "business as usual" came into my mind. "She seems to be holding up okay, at least on the outside. It's hard to tell what's going on with her. She's had so many difficult situations to deal with in her lifetime that she's gotten very good at concealing her emotions from us. If you had seen her this morning, you'd have thought we'd all come home for Christmas or some other cheery occasion. I can't decide whether my family is severely in denial of death, or if they are all just really good at letting go and moving on."

Jessie nodded and said, "Sounds like my grandmother, when my grandpa died. I think that generation of people were just taught to deal with their emotions privately."

"Yeah. Well, we are going to have to talk about it pretty soon, because we have to finalize the burial and funeral plans." I thought for a moment and then added, "It's so strange, Jessie. Funerals are like a rite of passage for the family, more than for the dead. Dealing with a death requires a perseverance and endurance that is unknown until needed."

I didn't need to say more. In the quietness of the moment, Jessie reached out and held my hand. She was already a master at crossing the bridge from one heart to another.

"How'd the boys handle the news?"

I sighed and said, "Tim was pretty shaken up and started crying. He had a dream about his grandpa right after he died and I think that may have allowed him the sense of saying good-bye. I'm not too worried about him because he's still pretty expressive about what he's feeling.

"I'm not really sure what is going on with Jerry. He's at that age where he doesn't voluntarily tell me how he's feeling and I'm afraid that he won't have a way to deal with his grief if he doesn't talk to somebody. I don't want him to just stuff his emotions about this and have his pain show up in other ways."

Jessie asked, "Won't Sarah help him deal with it?"

"I don't know. Honestly, it's been so long since I've observed them interact, I don't know what their relationship is like. Actually, I'm a little worried about how she's going to deal with her grief, too."

After a minute, I added, "Jess, Sarah is going to bring the boys out to the house Friday afternoon. I invited her to come to the service since she has known my family for so long. I probably should've talked with you first, but it just seemed like the right thing to do. She might not come, but if she does, I hope it doesn't make things too uncomfortable for you."

She shifted slightly in her chair. "I suppose it could be pretty awkward, but I understand why you invited her." She took a deep breath and I could see that she was trying to prepare herself for the onslaught of having to meet all of my family, deal with a funeral and my ex-wife.

"Just let me know if you are having a hard time and I'll do whatever I can to make all this go as comfortably as possible." I felt the sudden responsibility of my words and quickly decided that I needed to let go or I would go nuts trying to take care of everyone. I was confident Jessie would be able to take care of herself and that she would let me know if she were having a problem.

As we drove back to my mother's house, I showed Jessie some of my old stomping grounds. While we had moved around a lot when I was a child—even to California for a short while when I was eleven—we had stayed in this same general vicinity while in my teen years. A lot of my memories were captured in the scenery as we passed by. This part of Oklahoma was one of the few places in the country that hadn't changed much in the last fifty years.

When we arrived, my mother and sisters were in the midst of cooking a huge meal. My aunt and uncle were coming to meet Jessie, and everyone was relatively cheerful—or at least distracted from our original motive for gathering.

My mother shook Jessie's hand, welcoming her with the slight reserve that was typical of her. Jessie, however, just reached right up and hugged her saying how happy she was to meet her and how sorry she was that it was under these circumstances. Mother smiled, thanked her for coming and then returned to her business in the kitchen. Jessie offered to help, but they assured her they had it under control.

I took Jessie's bag into "my room" and then proceeded to show her around, sharing my past with her through each trinket, picture and painting. A bit later, my sisters finished in the kitchen and joined in the walk down memory lane by telling stories about what I was like when I was young. As they were all talking and laughing in the living room, I noticed my mother leave the kitchen and go out onto the back porch.

Following her out, I found her crying in the rocking chair. When she saw me coming, she tried to quickly wipe away the tears with her apron. My heart cried out to help this woman who had wiped away so many tears in her lifetime—both mine and hers.

"It's okay, Mom, you can cry. I understand." I did my best to reassure her.

"I'm sorry, Son. I don't want to spoil the party. Your Jessie is very nice."

"Thanks, Mom. I'm glad you're getting to meet her, but this isn't a party, and you are not required to entertain or take care of us. We're here to take care of you, not add more work to your load. I wish I could say something to make this easier. There just aren't words that make the pain go away any faster." I reached out and put my hand on hers. "I love you, Mom."

She wrapped her arms around me in a slightly slumped embrace—she in the rocking chair and I kneeling in front of her—and cried.

I added, as I rubbed her back gently, "It's okay. It helps to cry," knowing how difficult it was for her to allow herself to do so in front of me.

We held onto each other for several minutes and then, as quickly as her tears started, they went away. I felt her take a deep breath as the wave of pain passed. We both knew another wave would come, but until then, she felt ready to face the world again.

Not wanting to upset her more, but knowing we had to deal with some of the details of death, I said, "We do have some things to take care of, Mom."

She assured me, "Your uncle is seeing to the funeral arrangements for me. He's coming to dinner to go over them with us tonight."

I was relieved to know that things were being taken care of even without my realizing it. I helped her up and gave her another hug, during which we both took a deep breath, releasing some pent-up energy. Then we went back into the house to join the others.

The evening was relatively uneventful. Mom was right; my uncle had everything under control. The family was gathering Friday night here at the house, and the funeral was scheduled for the next afternoon, with the burial to follow. He had arranged the purchase of two cemetery sites, side-by-side at my mother's request, so that when she passed on too, they could be together.

It must be a strange experience to be getting older, watching your life mate die, and then purchasing your own burial site, acknowledging beyond a shadow of a doubt exactly where your life is leading. I shook my head, thinking that all my concerns about the future and what I was supposed to do, learn and be, were all leading to the exact same place. There was no avoiding it, at least as far as I knew.

The rest of the family continued talking, sharing stories and reminiscing, while my mind drifted toward thoughts of death and birth. Alea had certainly implied that she and I had been together in a previous lifetime. I had not been raised believing in reincarnation, but over the years had certainly been exposed to a lot of people who did. Now the notion was commonly accepted in conversations with a significant portion of the population. Where once you were looked at as odd for believing in reincarnation, now the same held true in many circles if you didn't. Part of me liked the idea, and part of me just couldn't imagine it. I liked thinking that if I didn't get it right in this lifetime, I would be allotted another to keep working on it. However, I didn't like the thought of going through all the struggle and drama again. Perhaps, I consoled myself, we get to take our wisdom with us into the next life and pick up more or less where we left off, so we don't have to go through the struggle to the same extent each time. Or maybe we have to struggle just as hard, but each time with a different aspect of ourselves and our growth. With each incarnation perhaps we add another piece to the puzzle, something more to take forward with us, until finally we do get the whole picture.

I remembered the conversation Alea and I had had about what a blessing it is to have a body and to be incarnated. If our souls don't die, I could see how one might wish to return to a body to experience the magnificence of the senses and to continue growing in the ways that only interaction with others can accomplish. In that instant, I saw the mastery of our relationships with others as the ultimate vehicle for growth. The interaction of egos and bodies bumping into each other is what gives us cause to remember who we really are and the opportunity to put that knowing into practice. We do a magnificent job of giving each other opportunities for practicing acceptance, if only we are aware enough to recognize the opportunities when they knock. Without self-observation though, we can't "see the forest through the trees," and get caught up in the drama instead of transforming it.

I looked across the room at Jessie listening intently to my uncle's stories. Had I known her before? My eyes scanned the rest of my family. Had I known them all before? Would I know them again?

My thoughts were interrupted by their laughter, and I realized they had been talking to me without getting any response.

Still laughing, my uncle said, "Where'd you go, Son? Looked like you just checked out!"

I laughed too and explained, "Sorry, I was getting all philosophical and lost in my head." I saw no reason to bring up my exact thoughts at a time like this.

After clearing the table, we moved into the living room to continue talking. Everyone seemed to be doing pretty well, but every now and then something would be said that would make them think of my father, and one or the other of us would start to cry, being comforted by the rest.

We went to bed relatively early, as we still had busy days ahead. In our room, Jessie and I talked about the dynamics of my family and the observations she had made about each person's personality. She had an uncanny way of being able to sum people up quickly.

"I like your family, Matt. They've been very kind to me. It must not be easy to welcome a new person to the family while dealing with a death at the same time, but I'm glad I came."

"I'm glad you came, too." She had her head on my shoulder as we talked about the multitude of things going through my head of late.

"Jessie?" I made sure she was still awake before I continued. "All of the thinking I have been doing about death in the last few days is making me kind of antsy to 'get on with it!' I don't want to put anything on hold anymore."

"What specifically do you feel like you want to 'get on with?'"

"I want to do more seminars that are geared toward personal growth. The information on letting go and being resourceful is what people are really interested in learning, and that is what I'm really interested in teaching. I know the power of this work, and I'm ready to do it."

"Sounds good. What needs to happen in order for you to do more of that?" she asked sleepily, but interested.

"Well, I need to start promoting myself and letting people know. Getting the book finished and out will help a lot, too. I have that seminar coming up in a couple of weeks with a Jewish group in Los Angeles. I'll start promoting my work while I'm out there." I thought for a moment, then added, "All it really requires is my getting focused, clear and committed; the rest will fall into place, I'm sure."

"Well, you sound clear and committed to me!"

In just moments, I could tell by the change in her breathing that she had fallen asleep. I kissed her forehead and lay there feeling blessed a little longer before I, too, slept.

Friday approached quickly. Sarah showed up with the boys just before the rest of the relatives arrived. When I saw the car pulling into the driveway, I went out to greet her hoping to get a "temperature check" before she came in and met Jessie. I hadn't seen Sarah for more than a minute in over a year—just long enough to pass on the boys. I paused on the front porch to take a moment for self-observation and letting go. I wanted to be resourceful and move toward healing the rift between us. She was just getting out of the car as I approached and didn't see me coming.

Startled she said, "Oh, uh, hi, Matt." She regained her composure quickly and added politely, "It's nice to see you."

I felt compelled to hug her and held my arms out to gauge her receptivity. She looked reluctant at first and then with a sigh of resignation, allowed herself to be hugged. Tim and Jerry were next in line and after getting hugs they went into the house to see the family and Jessie, leaving Sarah and me alone in the driveway.

I asked, "Are you going to join us tonight?"

"Matt, I've given this a lot of thought and I just don't think it is a good idea. I'll come in and give my respects to your family, but I'm going to go before everyone else gets here. I don't think it's fair to your new wife and, quite honestly, not something I want to put myself through either. I hope everyone understands."

I was actually quite relieved. Even though Sarah would have been welcome, I didn't really want to subject any of us to the extra tension—myself included. All I said was, "I understand. Come on, let's go inside."

By the time we got to the house, the boys were doing their best to cheer up their grandma. Everyone stopped and looked up from what they were doing when we walked in. It felt as if someone had hit a "freeze frame" button on the living room scene. The depth of my next breath broke the momentary tension and Judy and Sharon immediately came over to hug Sarah with my mom not far behind. Once all the greetings were out of the way, I introduced Sarah to Jessie. They shook hands and said, "Hello."

Jessie said, "I've really enjoyed getting to know your boys. You have raised two very special young men."

Sarah glanced over at them and smiled. "Yeah, they're pretty good boys. Thank you. They seemed to take a liking to you, too. I could hardly get them to stop talking about their last visit. It sounded like you had quite a full week."

I wasn't sure if that was a good thing or a bad thing in her mind, but decided not to worry about it. After a little more small talk, Sarah went into the kitchen to spend some time with my mom while I took advantage of the opportunity to see if Jessie was okay. I pulled her into "our room," gave her a kiss and said, "I'm just checking in. Are you okay?"

I could hear the tension in her voice. "Yeah, I'm all right. It was a little weird to see the four of you out by the car looking so much like a family. I'll be honest with you, Matt. This isn't easy. Your family has been nothing but nice and at the same time I find myself being so self-conscious. I don't want to say or do the wrong thing."

A tear escaped and rolled down her cheek. I wiped it away and kissed the trail it left. "Jess, you are perfect just the way you are. They won't be able to help but love you—they already do! It's just that this is really difficult timing. I wish you could have met everyone under different circumstances. As for Sarah, I know this is hard but believe me, it's probably even harder for her."

A hurt look flashed across her face and I quickly added, "I didn't mean to belittle the difficulty for you, Jess. I'm sorry. I just meant. . . . "

She held her finger up to my lips to silence me and said, "I understand. It's okay. We better get back out there or it is going to get even weirder when they have to come looking for us." She took just a minute to pull herself back together and then we headed back out into the living room.

Within half an hour Sarah left. Tim stood on the porch waving good-bye to her and before he even put his hand down, he began waving hello to other relatives arriving. I noticed Jessie duck back into our room and decided to let her have a few minutes alone to process her feelings and prepare for the arrival of new guests. She emerged looking fresh and rejuvenated. She was either a really good actress or she had been doing a little letting go of her own!

The evening was like a family reunion; all our cousins and relatives came to the house. With so many people, the potluck-style gathering created quite a feast. Jessie met just about everybody before the night was through. It felt like an odd combination of wedding reception and funeral mixed together. I thought it funny that the major life transitions were all celebrated in much the same manner—so much so that it was hard to tell them apart.

The guests left two or three at a time until only immediate family were left. Jessie excused herself and slipped off to bed, while my father's sister, Irene, and I somehow gravitated to the back porch. We hadn't seen each other in years, and it was nice to catch up.

I asked her how she was doing, and she replied with a twinkle in her eye, "Oh, I'm okay for an old gal. I ache a little here and there with my arthritis and all, but I'm okay. I have my church group and the girls I play cards with once a week. I'm happy enough."

We sat in silence for a few minutes, and then she said, "Your Jessie's a nice gal, Matt. You've done well for yourself. It's too bad we couldn't meet at a happier time."

Enthusiastically I responded, "Yes, she's wonderful. I'm glad you think so, too."

Then came the classic relative questions, "How come you two got married so quick? Are you fixing to have a little one?"

I couldn't help but laugh. "No, there's no 'little one' on the way—not yet anyhow. We got married quickly because, well, it just seemed like the right thing to do. We love each other."

"What church did you get married in?" she asked, somewhat concerned.

"No church. We got married outside in a beautiful spot next to a creek." I could see it in my mind's eye, as clearly as if I were standing there now.

"No church? I never heard of such a thing!" She was truly shocked.

I quickly reassured her, "There was a minister though!"

The relief on her face was visible for a moment; then she suddenly looked worried again and asked, "What religion are you? You aren't that same thing your sister is, are you?"

The intonation in her voice implied definite lack of appreciation for my sister's religion. I felt a surge of strength from my soul as I replied, "I belong to no religion and all religions."

"Hmpfff. What does that mean?" she asked, not sure if I was serious or joking.

"It means that I respect all religions, as long as they are food for the person's soul. Great truths are taught within each religion, and they all serve the people they touch. My perspective is that each has its place. I honor them all for the service they provide of bringing people closer to God."

"But what God? They don't all believe in the same God! You have to watch out for those false gods!" she said with deep concern.

"Aunt Irene, there is only one God, but people call him by many different names." I wanted to say "him or her" but figured I was already treading on thin ice.

I continued explaining, "It doesn't matter if you call God 'Jesus,' 'Buddha,' 'Allah,' 'Wakan Tanka,' 'Krishna,' 'Holy Spirit' or the many other names God answers to. It's all the same God. It's just like 'water,' which is also called 'agua,' 'H_2O,' 'wai,' 'wasser' and 'eau'—among its many other names around the world. Not only does water have many names, but it also comes in many forms—ponds, rivers, rain, ice, mist and oceans; yet, it's all water. It is the same with God."

I could see the wheels turning in her head. She answered softly, "I never thought of it that way."

I reached out and took her hand. "Many people don't, but it makes sense when you consider it. God has made himself known all over the world in different forms, with different names to meet the needs of the people in those areas at those particular times. If you study the teachings of the different religions you will find that they, like people, may look different on the outside, but the insides are made up of the same stuff. They all teach people to 'love thy neighbor' and 'do unto others as you would have them do unto you.' They all teach you to be the best you can be, to love God with all your heart, and that it is in giving that we receive. It is man, not God, who has created the differences."

I was on a roll, and since she looked truly interested, I went on. "That's why I honor all religions. The reason I belong to no one religion is because of what people have done to those religions—not because of disrespect toward God. Look what people have done in the name of religion: they fight and kill, pillage and plunder, steal land, condemn and judge! How much further can you get from God? After all, what are the characteristics of God? I mean, what do you think he is like?"

Her face lit up as she responded immediately, "Oh, he is the all-loving, all-forgiving one!"

I agreed, "Yes, he is, and if we were made in the likeness and image of God, shouldn't we be all-loving and all-forgiving, too?"

"Well, yes, I suppose. . . ."

"Shouldn't we also be all-accepting?" I continued, without waiting for an answer. "The bottom line is that everyone is searching for the same thing: for Source, for love, for themselves. The different religions are all just various avenues for getting to the same place."

The image I had had in my last meditation came to mind, so I said, "You like music, don't you? Can you imagine an orchestra without the string section? Or without the percussion? The whole world is like a symphony with each person taking a part in it. Without all the 'instruments'—the religions, races, cultures, personalities—the music would simply not be the same. Imagine if we all accepted each other with love! What beautiful music we would hear! We can't sit in judgment of each other and be spiritual; we have to be accepting, compassionate and loving—in the likeness of God! We don't need to just go to church on Sunday; we need to be in church all the time, no matter where we are. You see, it is not in the believing as much as it is in the being. We ought to leave the *lie* out of *believing*—oh, and the *v*, too!"

We both laughed, breaking up the intensity of the conversation. I looked over at Irene, who then said, "Well, Son, you have certainly given me plenty to think about for one night!"

She smiled and squeezed my hand appreciatively, then said, "We'd better get back inside. I feel like I've been at church tonight! Thank you!" She then added, "Matt? Who'd you learn all that from?"

"No one." No one she could relate to, anyway.

"No one? Surely you studied all this under someone!"

"If I had studied under someone, they would have studied under someone else, and they under someone else. It would have been passed down from generation to generation and finally to me and then on to you. Well—you know how rumors are!"

I could tell that she was remembering how all of us used to play "rumors," passing a whispered message along, laughing at how it had changed by the time it arrived at the last person. Just then, I winked at her, setting her off in a giggle, and she strolled back into the house, shaking her head.

I sat there alone watching the night sky, simply enjoying the moment, before I too went in and joined Jessie for the night.

The next morning Jessie and I went for a walk with Tim and Jerry.

Jessie asked, "How are you two doing?"

Jerry said, "Fine," leaving us with no more information than we started with.

This time Timmy was the quiet one.

Jessie asked, "What about you, Tim?"

He looked up at her and answered, "I can't stop thinking about Grandpa. It is so weird to be around everyone and not have him there. I keep expecting to see him or think of something I want to show him and then I remember that I can't."

Jessie was empathetic. "Yeah, I remember feeling that way when my grandfather died, too. Believe me, guys, it's hard to handle the death of someone you love no matter what age you are. What's important is that you allow yourselves the time you need to grieve. It's normal to be angry and it's okay to be sad. Everyone handles their feelings in their own way. It's even okay to be happy." She looked at Jerry when she added, "And if you feel like crying, whether it's in the privacy of your room or in front of your family, please don't hold it in. It's important that you release your emotions instead of bottling them up. Be gentle with yourselves and with each other because you both may be a little sensitive on account of your grandpa's death. Remember that your mom is grieving too, and will likely need your extra understanding for a while."

Jerry looked back at her in a way that made it appear that he had taken in what she had said, but it was hard to tell. We walked in silence for a little way, each of us lost in our own thoughts when Jerry finally spoke.

He asked no one in particular, "What do you think happens to someone when they die?"

Timmy immediately replied, "They go to Heaven. At least I'm sure Grandpa did."

Jerry didn't look satisfied and looked to Jessie and me for more clarification. I wasn't sure I wanted to tell them that I was beginning to seriously believe in reincarnation, but I didn't want to be dishonest with them either. "I've been thinking a lot about this myself and I can't tell you that I know for sure, but lately reincarnation has been making a lot of sense to me—meaning that when we die we are reborn in another body to continue our evolution. The idea is that we are all here to grow, learn and master certain spiritual concepts and until we do, we come back again and again to continue our journey."

Jerry looked thoughtful, as if he might be able to buy into the idea while Timmy looked horrified. I imagined I heard his youthful voice saying, "I'm going to tell Mom on you!" but I didn't really.

Jessie added, "I've read quite a few books on life after death and there's actually a lot of evidence that verifies what you're talking about." I squeezed her hand in appreciation of her support.

Tim asked, "But what about Heaven?!"

"I'm beginning to think Heaven and Hell are the way we live our lives, rather than a place we go to. Haven't you seen some people who are constantly unhappy no matter what life brings them? Their lives are hell, while other people seem to be happy no matter what, even with the same set of circumstances. I really think we visit Heaven or Hell right here in each lifetime."

Jerry changed the subject slightly, "What about ghosts, Dad? Do you believe in ghosts?"

Alea immediately came to mind, but I dismissed the thought of her quickly. "Yes, I do, but what do you think?" I was relieved that he was talking about some of his concerns.

"I think Grandpa has been hanging around for the last few days. It's kind of creepy. Shouldn't he be moving on—going wherever spirits go? Even though I love him, I don't really want his spirit hanging around me."

Tim looked frightened and said, "Me, neither!"

Jessie said, "When I was a little girl and my grandpa died, I was convinced he came back to check on me. Every year on the anniversary of his death I would get especially scared, but I never told anyone. I was afraid of the dark and of being alone. I think that sometimes it takes spirits a while to figure out that they are really dead, before they move on."

Wide-eyed Timmy asked, "What did you do?"

She put her hand on his shoulder. "I finally figured out that my grandpa loved me and that he didn't mean to scare me. In fact, I decided he didn't even know he was scaring me so I just told him out loud that it was time to move on and that I loved him, but didn't want him to hang out around me anymore."

Jerry asked, "Did it work?"

"Apparently, because I never felt him again. I really don't think spirits can bother us without our permission. Anytime you are scared, or even just uncomfortable, you can ask them to leave. Remember to ask your guardian angels for protection, too."

By now we were almost back to the house. I told the boys that I enjoyed hearing their thoughts and that we could continue the discussion anytime they wanted to. Both of them looked a bit relieved as they headed into the house to get ready for the service.

The entire family attended the funeral. This and the burial were the hardest parts of the whole death experience. Seeing my father in an open casket, no longer looking like my father, was so eerie—like mourning a stranger. It was not the last picture of him that I wanted to have in my head. This body was no longer him. The essence that was my father was no longer there. Perhaps that is why they have open-casket funerals—to assist you in letting go of the bodily form of your loved one. Either way, it wasn't my preference to hold this particular image of my father. Instead, I turned my attention to the large crucifix hanging on the wall above the casket. Ironically, this wasn't the image of Jesus that I wanted to hold in my vision, either. I closed my eyes and meditated through the service, holding an image of both my father and Jesus, alive and well—together.

After the service, we all proceeded to the cemetery for the burial. This last step added a finality that was hard to accept. In some strange way, it seemed almost cruel; burying someone is what you threaten to do to your little brother to scare him, not what you actually do to someone you love. That, accented by the space earmarked for my mother right next door, made it almost unbearable. Without conferring over what we were each feeling, none of us had a dry eye. Even Jessie was crying, without ever having met my father. The feeling at a burial is universal; it doesn't need to be personal to be impacting. We quietly said good-bye one last time to the man who had contributed all he knew how, the best that he could, to our lives and our family.

Jessie and I stood there in silence for several minutes after the others began returning to their cars; Tim and Jerry had gone on with my mother. I spontaneously said aloud to my dad, "Father, I accept your death and appreciate your life. Thank you for all that you have done for me." Taking a deep breath to release my anguish, I looked up toward the sky and spoke directly to God. "Dear Father, thank you for all that you have done for me. I accept your grace, in whatever form it comes. Amen."

Reaching into the pile of dirt with my right hand, as if offering flowers to a shrine, I dug my fingers into the dirt and then scattered it inside my father's open grave. As I released the dirt from my grasp, I quietly repeated my prayer of appreciation and acceptance. I then reached down with both hands and picked up a final scoop. Holding my hands out over the grave, I let the dirt sift through my fingers like sand through an hourglass, each falling clump marking a lifetime of memories, showering my father with love.

I gasped as Jessie and I gazed at my outstretched hands. Once hidden in the dirt, now revealed more brightly with each passing second, was a golden ring of truth. We just stood there looking at the mystical circle of life that lay in my hands. Shaking the remaining dirt away, I then read the inscribed message out loud: *Acceptance.*

A wave of peacefulness washed over me. Jessie must have felt it, too, because I could see the goose bumps that covered her skin, as so often happens at magical moments. All she whispered reverently was, "Alea must still be here!"

This I knew to be true. With no more doubt in my heart as to her continued presence, I carefully placed the golden circle in my pocket, so as not to draw attention to our quiet miracle. With Jessie's hand in mine and love in our hearts, we left to join the others.

The next day, Jessie and I prepared to fly home, after multiple hugs and reassurances to my family that we would be in touch. I pulled my mother aside and said, "I want you to call me if you need anything. Don't be shy about it."

"Oh, I will, Matt. Thank you."

I knew my mother well enough not to let her off that easily. "Mom, I know you. I know you won't want to be 'a bother.'" We both laughed, knowing full well that she would say exactly that.

"I don't want you to go without, just because you are concerned about bothering me. You are my mother and I love you. You are not a bother!" I pulled her to me, and we hugged as I whispered, "Promise me you'll call if you need anything. ANYTHING!"

"I will, Son, I promise."

Not wanting to miss the opportunity, I said, "Mom, I love you."

She blushed a little and said, "I love you, too, Son." She then turned back to where Jessie, the boys and my sisters were saying their good-byes and said to Jessie, "I don't know how my son got so lucky as to find you, but I'm sure glad he did. You're a welcome addition to our family, Jessie."

They hugged, too, as Judy looked at her watch and said, "We better get going; I don't want you to miss your flight." The boys climbed in the car so they could see us off at the airport before their mother came to pick them up.

We waved good-bye, leaving my mother and younger sister dodging the cloud of dust left by the car.

Alea enjoyed Matt's discovery of the treasure—not only the golden ring, but also the understanding. As long as one holds onto resistance instead of acceptance—of anything—it is not possible to continue on from a state of resourcefulness.

Now Alea knew how right she had been to set Matt on his own. She felt as if she were watching a seed grow into a tree—strong and steady. These concepts were becoming his own; he was owning his power and wisdom and sharing it with others. Achieving acceptance is of vital importance. No one can awaken others with judgment; only with resourcefulness can resourcefulness be ignited.

She was pleased that Matt had sought out the labyrinth as a place of retreat. The metaphors that one can find while walking it are often the keys for opening the next door for personal growth. His discovery that he could monitor his own progress by simply accessing his present position was a good reminder for him. And the question: "What is required of me now?" was an excellent way to approach self-observation, evaluation and the redirecting of one's path.

She especially appreciated Matt's analogy of all the different people representing different notes in a musical scale or the different instruments in an orchestra. She envisioned what the world would be like if people only knew how beautiful they could be together if they accepted each other's "sounds" and worked with one another instead of against; accepting rather than resisting their differences. If each would take responsibility for his or her own instruments and play them well, the result would be music to everyone's ears.

Matt was understanding the value of acceptance and taking on the task of mastering it. True acceptance doesn't mean one has to agree with another's behavior nor like the circumstance. It only means moving into a state of acceptance and resourcefulness before taking the necessary action steps to make changes. If, as in the case of death, no action can change the circumstances, one still needs to move into resourcefulness in order to heal. Acceptance is the first step on that path.

Acceptance can be hard at first, but when we truly accept—that is, accept ourselves, our conditions, our bodies, our circumstances, other people, and most important, all we deem unacceptable—then we are in a position to make a difference. When we are resistant to 'what is,' it is virtually impossible to respond appropriately. Alea considered the subtle change necessary in order to master this: as it is now, people look for what is unacceptable in order to hate it, to resist it. If they would merely switch to looking for what is unacceptable, let go of their need for control and accept what they discover, then they would be empowered. Acceptance leads inevitably to growth.

Asking the question, "Am I part of the solution or part of the problem?" is a key to any issue that arouses feelings of judgment or dislike. The mere act of hating something is non-resourceful and a contribution to the problem. From resourcefulness and acceptance, people can make healthy, conscious choices toward resolution.

The irony, of course, is that in order to be resourceful, one must let go of the need to be accepted and at the same time master the art of acceptance. When one lets go of the need to be accepted, and focuses instead on accepting others, one gains acceptance—no longer "needing" it, because one "has" it.

Knowing that Matt was well on his way to deeply understanding this warmed Alea's soul. If an observer were to see her now, she might be taken for a proud mother—or the conductor of a fine symphony.

She watched as Matt and Jessie boarded the plane to return to Arizona. She blew them a prayer of safety, disguised as a tailwind, upon which they were carried home.

13

Breaking the Chain of Pain

It was good to be back home. Even though it had not been that long since we had left, a lot had happened. Jessie and I took a few days to regroup from the emotions of the trip. She took pleasure in showing me some of the changes and additions she had made to our home. Our merging was becoming more and more complete each day.

I prepared for the upcoming seminar in Los Angeles and worked on the book, pleased that in the midst of everything else it was coming along well. I made arrangements for a second seminar to be given while I was in L.A., feeling that now was the time to take active steps toward sharing with others what I knew.

Jessie and I savored our time together. It was an odd combination of feeling totally comfortable with each other, as if we had known each other for years, and discovering new things to delight in on a daily basis. I loved to watch the way she crinkled her eyes and nose when she laughed; it was as if her whole face smiled instead of just her mouth.

It wasn't long before I discovered how much she loved animals, which was a trait she got from her mother—a definite carry-over from her childhood. While some people collected figurines, Jessie's mom collected exotic animals as a hobby. She had a petting zoo of sorts that boasted a camel, a panther, a tiger, some snakes and monkeys, among other miscellaneous critters that they received from other zoos or from private citizens who hadn't realized how much work exotic animals could be. People would stop by her family's little menagerie on their way through town, and schoolchildren would come on field trips. Now, as an adult, she still had a childlike enthusiasm and sensitivity around animals. We had already begun a miniature petting zoo of our very own, including a couple of lizards from the local desert and a golden retriever puppy that looked at Jessie just the right way to get adopted as she walked past a pet store window.

Within the week, I bade farewell to her and the critters and headed to Los Angeles for four days. I looked forward to these seminars and hoped they would be the first of many personal-growth-oriented—rather than business-focused—workshops.

I settled into my hotel room, unpacked and prepared for my presentation. As I had done many times before, I pulled out my *This Date in History* trivia book to find a fact to share as a point of interest in my workshop. Much to my surprise, I discovered that on the same date as the seminar, over fifty years before, Hitler had been elected Chancellor of Germany. Not sure whether or how I might use that fact, I jotted it down and put it with my notes.

After calling Jessie, I went to sleep. All through the night I felt as if I were in an exotic place, wandering through the earthen streets, watching craftspeople hawking their wares. As I turned down a side street, children gathered in groups to beg for money, calling out, "No mama, no papa," holding out their dirt-covered hands. The pleading look in their eyes was painful to see. My first instinct was to run, hiding myself from the reality of their existence. My second inclination was to give them everything I had in an effort to rescue them. With this choice, I would run out of money quickly, leaving many of them and myself in the same boat. Within my dream-state, I forced myself to take a deep breath, walk with an even pace through the crowd of outstretched hands and begging eyes and simply accept their presence, allowing them to be in my dream, trusting their process. I whispered a prayer of safety and love over each one I passed, and as I did, one by one, they disappeared.

I woke early the next morning, reviewed my notes, and got ready to go.

I arrived before anyone else, set up the hall, then sat inconspicuously in the back of the room to meditate before the people arrived. I took several deep breaths, releasing any expectations for the day, and then imagined a beam of light running from the sky, down through my spine and deep into the ground. As I did so, I visualized myself as a tool through which Heaven and Earth connected. I felt myself to be an instrument of peace. Reveling in the sensation, I could have stayed there all day, but the door opened, pulling me back into my purpose for the moment. One by one the people appeared.

Once all had gathered, I began by welcoming them and introducing myself. "A gentleman recently asked me if I considered myself to be a motivational speaker. I thought about it for a moment and said, 'No, I consider myself to be a wake-up call.'"

Several people in the audience laughed as I went on to explain, "Many people are wandering around on automatic pilot, and their plane isn't going where they want it to go. I see my role as someone who helps to wake them up so that they can see not only where they want to go, but where they are right now. Let's start today by finding out what you hope to get out of the class."

I looked at them expectantly. One called out, "To get rid of blocks." Another added, "To be less judgmental."

One after another they answered, "To feel good," "To heal," "To raise self-esteem," "Reduce stress," "Clarity of vision," "Attract abundance and wealth," "To be more connected, surrounded by like-minded people," "To overcome anger and resentment." The list went on and on.

I was impressed with the wide range of hopes for the day—everything from getting more money to healing relationships to healing bodies. It reminded me of my first conversation with 'Michael,' when he said that there were only six human dramas: relationship dramas, health dramas, money dramas, career dramas, family dramas and spiritual dramas. I could clearly see that all people really wanted was to be free of these.

I said, "We are all looking for the same thing. Some look for it doing seminars, some by selling products, others by reading books; some look for it in war, drugs, alcohol, even murder. We are all looking for more love, joy and happiness in our lives.

"What is happiness? Is happiness being healthy? Is happiness having money? A nice car? A nice home? A good relationship?"

The audience answered "No," after I paused to let them think.

I continued. "Let's look at what else happiness is not. Is happiness being sick? Having no money? Having a broken car? No home? A bad relationship?"

Of course they again answered, "No."

I went on, "If *having* these things is not happiness and *not having* these things is not happiness, then what *is* happiness?" Giving them a moment to think, I then added, "*Happiness* is whatever *is happening* in the moment. It is a state of being fully present in the moment and accepting of whatever is. It is a matter of being *resourceful*."

I went on to guide them through an experience of resourcefulness and of letting go, teaching them the process of breathing away pains and stuck emotions, once they had set their intentions, willingness and commitment to let these go.

Then I recapped, "Happiness is letting go of *who we think we are* and getting resourceful—back into Source—*who we really are*."

I called on someone with a question. She asked, "If we are happy now, regardless of our circumstances, why do we have dreams and goals?"

I responded, "Would you rather be happy or unhappy on your way to your dreams and goals?" I laughed and added, "I once had a friend who explained to me that being rich doesn't eliminate your problems; it just lets you arrive at them in a limousine!"

After the laughter subsided, I continued, "Our objective is to get rid of our karma, our dramas, and get back to Source. Since we don't realize that we can be happy *right now*, we set goals for when we think we will deserve happiness. *When* I accomplish this or that, *when* I earn this much money, *when* I lose ten pounds—*then* I will be happy. If we achieved a state of happiness now and worked on purposeful goals, think how much more joyful life would be! Consider also how much more value we would have to offer to others!

"Problems are our greatest gifts, because they are the mirrors that allow us to let go and grow. Problems point us right to the energy that is stuck in us. Let's say we have a great idea. The idea passes through the conscious mind, where we house our visions and goals. Here the great idea can look even greater. From there it passes through our unconscious mind, and this is where the 'problem' crops up, because this is where we house all our programming—our built-up feelings and belief systems—all those inner voices or feelings that judge, criticize, limit, negate or otherwise derail our great idea. Actually, our beliefs and feelings can work for us or against us at this point, but if we have a large buildup of uncleared emotions from past experiences, our programmed beliefs feed on those emotions as fuel, resulting in a state known as Internal Bodily Turmoil. This alone can stop us in our tracks from continuing on toward our goals. Our storehouse of beliefs and old feelings is capable of keeping us in our dramas.

"The good news is, in order to get out of being blocked by this brick wall of past feelings and beliefs, we have a choice. Our choices are either to let go of the beliefs and old feelings and move toward Universal Energy Flow, or to stay in Internal Bodily Turmoil. If we allow ourselves to stay stuck in our dramas, we generally don't accomplish our dreams and goals, and we create unhappiness. On the other hand, if we choose to experience Universal Energy Flow—whether or not we accomplish our immediate goals—we create *resourcefulness,* and we are then much more likely to achieve our dreams, because we are operating from within the flow of universal creativity.

"In order to get into this state of being, this Universal Energy Flow, we must participate in a two-step process consisting of first, self-observation and second, letting go."

I went on to demonstrate how, when we are stuck, it originates from either a need to be accepted or a need to be in control. Always, when we are unhappy—lacking resourcefulness—it is a sign that we need to let go of one or the other or both of these needs.

As I spoke, I felt the Universal Energy Flow moving through me. It was a tingly sensation, like a power surge. I felt a strength, a knowing of the truth of this material. The people listened intently, hanging on every word as if it were food for their souls.

I explained, "Self-observation is the first step. This is slightly different than self-awareness. With self-awareness you may be aware that you are angry, yet at the same time you still identify with yourself as being angry. On the other hand, when you move into a state of self-observation and can *observe* yourself being angry, you separate yourself from the emotion. From this perspective you can recognize that there is more to you than your emotions. It is impossible to truly *observe* an emotion and to be in the emotion at the same time.

"Just by observing yourself, you've already begun the process of letting go. Then all you need to do is set your intention, willingness and commitment, take a few deep breaths to release the energy stored in the form of feelings, and let them go. Once you return to resourcefulness, you open yourself for the Universal Energy Flow to assist you in creating your dreams and vision."

Looking around the room, I saw people taking notes, soaking up the information like sponges in water. I loved how the information I had gathered, learned and internalized had become such a part of me that it was readily accessible, there for my taking, for my offering.

I moved through the different aspects of resourcefulness as I understood them, and began to share about my most recent discovery of one of its facets—acceptance—and the importance acceptance plays in being able to move forward resourcefully.

"When we are resistant to someone or something, we get stuck. We aren't resourceful. When we aren't resourceful, any action we take will likely contribute to the problem rather than the solution. If we find that the appropriate action is 'no action,' at the very least, if we let go and remain resourceful, we are happy."

I glanced at my watch and sent everyone to lunch, planning to resume our discussion of acceptance when they returned. After the room emptied, aloud I said, "Alea, I don't know if you can hear me, but if you can—*thank you.*"

I didn't hear any response but felt a tingly wave wash over me that convinced me that she was aware of all that was taking place.

As the seminar participants returned from lunch, I quickly looked over my agenda and began the second session. "What do you consider to be *good*? What is *bad*? What is *right*? What is *wrong*? *Positive*? *Negative*? What is *acceptable* to you? What is totally *unacceptable* to you?"

I paused to let them share their answers, then continued. "What is the difference between a child who steals a candy bar and Hitler, who killed millions?" I answered my own question. "The difference is a matter of degree. Can you accept that the child stole the candy bar? What if the child who stole the candy bar used a gun to steal it? Can you accept that? That is a few degrees worse, right? What if the child killed someone on the way out of the store? That is a considerable degree worse, right? What is good and bad is relative. What is acceptable to us is not a matter of good and bad, or right or wrong; it is a matter of degree and our judgment of the degree. When we accept that which we deem *unacceptable*, we return to a resourceful state. It is only in resourcefulness that we can be truly happy. It is only from resourcefulness that we can make decisions and take actions that will make a difference toward solving the problem—if a solution is possible."

My research from the night before suddenly popped into my head, and without any thought as to the fact that this entire group was Jewish, I said, "Do you know what happened on this day in history? Today is the anniversary of Hitler's election as Chancellor of Germany."

The word "anniversary" immediately made a young woman in the group think I was suggesting that this was worthy of celebration, rather than just a historical fact. She indignantly yelled out from the middle of the room, "That son-of-a-bitch killed my grandparents. He shouldn't be recognized for anything! I hate him, and I'll hate him until the day I die."

The passion with which she felt her words was apparent to us all. Her comments triggered an avalanche of similar sentiment; the reactions spewed vehemently into the air, one after the other. Surprised by the intensity of feeling, I stood still and observed. For a moment I felt panic as I had unknowingly rubbed salt in an open wound that soon festered and became contagious. I took a deep breath and let go of my fear. Then, I simply said, "Wow, you feel pretty strongly about that, don't you?!"

Affirmations shot back at me from all corners of the room. I could feel their anger, which had now transferred from Hitler to me. Many of them shouted out justifications for their feelings. The tension in the room had grown thick, and I watched as each person's comments ignited the next, like some sort of candle ceremony. Before long, virtually everyone in the room was "lit up," and their forthcoming actions hinged on my next words. I knew that if I didn't handle this well, they would get up and walk out.

Not sure what to do, I took another deep breath, at which point all I said was, "Where is Hitler now?"

The first young woman who had spoken so vehemently once again shouted with the same magnitude of passion, "That son-of-a-bitch is dead, and good riddance!"

Before the rest of the crowd followed her lead, I said calmly and clearly, "It sure doesn't sound like it to me."

The whole room fell into a silence. Not even a whisper could be heard, and while it was really only seconds, it was uncomfortably long. The stillness was broken moments later by the same young woman, who had now just woken up. "Oh my God! We're the ones keeping him alive!"

Audible gasps filled the room, mine among them. A quiet murmur followed, as one by one people woke up their awareness through self-observation. I gave them several moments to think it all through and then explained, "In your resistance of him, you are stuck with him. Your resistance is taking you out of resourcefulness—even into hatred. You are allowing him to keep you unhappy, to continue hurting you, even fifty years later. In actuality, he isn't the one hurting you now, you are.

"The idea here is to accept him and what happened. That doesn't mean you should approve of it or be passive about it. It only means that if you do not accept it, you cannot be resourceful, and if you are not resourceful, you are unhappy. If you are unhappy, you are contributing to the problem instead of the solution. If you are going to take an action, you always want to take it from a resourceful point of decision. In the case of Hitler, no outer action is possible. He is dead. What he did is now in the past. That being the case, again, you want to let go and be resourceful—in which case the action to take is internal instead of external.

"The most important thing on the planet is for *you* to be happy and resourceful, because if you're not, the people around you can't be either. Accepting what you consider to be unacceptable will free you."

Scenes from my dream the night before popped into my head. I thought about the begging children and how I had wanted to help them, but didn't have the resources to truly do so. I could now see that rather than reacting to the situation in the moment—as was my first inclination—I had observed the situation and myself in it, become resourceful and then responded. With the resources I had had available to me in the dream, my only option had been to pray for the children, which had seemed to help. Since I then woke up, it's not clear if I would have chosen to take further action later. All I knew for sure was that within my dream state, I had felt a lot of compassion for the children and had wanted to help solve the problem rather than contribute to it. Clearly, a resourceful state of being was the necessary first step, whether in my dream or in waking reality.

I closed my presentation for the day with some thoughts I had been toying with concerning compassion. "When we move into a state of *acceptance*, we are better equipped to be compassionate toward others and their situation. When we are compassionate, we are compelled to take some sort of action to assist—even if that action is merely an internal prayer for another being.

"Sometimes being compassionate means not taking any action at all, because it would interrupt what the other person is about to discover for themselves. Sometimes compassion means taking the approach of 'tough love,' with a withdrawal of assistance, which causes others to take action for themselves rather than to continue to exist in a codependent situation. Sometimes compassion means giving your all—everything—to help another being. All of these may be compassionate responses, so how do you know which action to take? The action we choose to take must be based in resourcefulness, or it runs the risk of being inappropriate.

"I am going to leave you with some questions. In order to answer them, you must be self-observant. The questions are: *What actions are you taking? What are the results? Are you taking them from a resourceful state or a reactive state?*"

I paused to allow them time to think, then said, "If you don't like what you see, let go, return to resourcefulness and re-choose. Every moment of every day, you have a new opportunity to re-choose your actions, thoughts and feelings. It is in your power to accept, it is in your power to be compassionate and it is in the now moment that you will discover happiness. The secret is to align all your actions with your resourceful Self."

I briefly reviewed the main points of the day and ended to a standing ovation. A flood of people gathered around to tell me their personal stories or to ask questions based on what they had heard. The woman who had spoken so vehemently against Hitler came up and thanked me sincerely. She hadn't realized how much hatred she had been carrying around and was joyful over the prospects for her life, now that she had let that burden go. As I spoke to the people gathered around me, a woman still sitting in the audience caught my eye. Distracted for a moment, I looked up to see that it was Alea! My heart started pounding, and I wanted nothing more than to race over to her, but the group of people around me made that impossible. As my eyes locked onto hers, it was as if time stopped for just a moment. It felt as though everyone around me had frozen, and the only thing that mattered was Alea.

As she held my gaze, I could feel the love radiating from her, even across the room. She smiled her brilliant smile, winked at me and then disappeared right before my eyes. As I stood there in shock, the people around me kept asking questions and talking to me, oblivious to the fact that I had fully disengaged my attention for the moment. I returned my focus to them, happy to know that Alea was nearby. Every now and then I would look around the room to see if she was still lingering, but she was nowhere to be seen. One by one the people left, until I stood there alone, my heart full.

I happily took myself out to dinner. While I was waiting for the food, I thought some more about compassion and taking action. As I tossed some ideas around in my head, I heard a voice behind me and felt a tug on my shirt. "Hey, you want to talk about *compassion*?"

I spun around on my stool to see Michael standing there, still in his funny felt hat and again wearing overalls. I greeted him excitedly and inquisitively. "Hi! What are you doing here in L.A.?"

I wanted to hug him, feeling as though we were very old friends reuniting, but I wasn't sure that he was the hugging type.

He smiled, and his eyes twinkled as he said, "Shouldn't surprise you so much; after all, this *is* the *City of Angels.*"

We both chuckled, and then he asked, "So you've been thinking about compassion? That is my favorite subject. If everyone held just a bit more compassion in their hearts, well, indeed this world would be a different place."

He had a faraway look in his eye, as if he could see what the world would be like—what the world *could* be like. He sighed loudly as he brought himself back into the here and now. "So tell me, what are your thoughts on compassion?"

I answered carefully, as I hadn't really formulated a complete perspective yet. "Well, as I see it, compassion is a necessary ingredient to taking any steps toward helping someone else, or changing a situation. Without compassion, you end up helping either out of judgment—a need for control—or a need for the acceptance you will get from others. When we act out of these needs, rather than from true compassion, we may not make the right choice, since we are busy serving ourselves rather than the others."

Michael listened intently, nodding. He then added, "You know why people avoid compassion, Matt?"

I didn't recall ever telling him my name, but I wanted to hear what he had to say, so I didn't ask him how he knew it.

He continued, "People don't want to feel compassion for a number of reasons. One is that they are so caught up in their own pain and drama they are afraid that if they allow themselves to care about others, it will be just plain too much. System overload! Another reason is that many of them don't even care about themselves and their own lives, so how could they care about someone else? They don't yet know that we are all made up of the same divine stuff, and when we help another, we help ourselves. When we help ourselves from a centered place, we help all the beings of the planet."

He barely stopped for air before going on. "Speaking of the planet, do you know what surrounds this planet?"

I thought he was going to launch into a lecture on our depleting ozone, but he didn't wait for me to answer. "This planet is completely encircled with a chain of pain."

Immediately, I saw the planet in my mind's eye, but this time instead of the peaceful blue-and-green orb that filled me with awe, I saw it wrapped up by chains with padlocks, constricting it, hiding its beauty. I felt a stab of pain in my chest as I envisioned this.

He continued, "People are in tremendous pain, and they think it is because of their spouse or parents or children or lover or boss—when it is really because they are stuck in judgment rather than compassion, drama rather than resourcefulness. They have not yet woken up to the magnificence of who they are. They are not seeing beyond the veil of ignorance."

The way he spoke held no judgment. It sounded matter-of-fact, like a mere observation. I asked quickly, before he could speak again, "How do we wake them up, Michael?"

I startled myself by calling him by name, still not sure that he *was* Michael, but he didn't even miss a beat. He responded immediately, as if he had anticipated my question, "We can't! They must *choose* to wake up. What we can do is begin with ourselves and model happiness, so they will *want* to wake up. We must first start with acceptance of others and compassion in our hearts. We cannot be in judgment of those not yet awake, or we remain a link in the chain of pain. As we work on perfecting ourselves, letting go of our own pain, we become way-showers to others, lights in their darkness. Even beyond what we *do*, it is *who we are* that shines the brightest."

He paused for a moment with a look on his face that was loving and compassionate. He then added, "Our responsibility is to not remain a link in the chain of pain. With every link that lets go of its hold, the chain weakens. We must break the cycle. Every being who is dedicated to this path as a light-bearer can personally be credited with touching thousands—some even millions. The presence of the light nudges others, stirring up the inner knowing, waking up the Being within, reminding their very essence of who they really are."

He looked almost mischievous as he said, "It's a noble cause, don't you think?"

I had to agree, but I wanted to know more. "So if we can only help others by waking up ourselves and living in alignment with our true essence, how do we stay awake? How do we keep focused on taking the right actions?"

He looked at me with a near-nod and said, "Imagine that when you die, you review your life in the presence of the Holy Spirit—with total unconditional love surrounding you, keeping you safe. . . ."

"Yes?" I'm sure it sounded as if I were pleading for him to continue, which was pretty much the truth of the matter. Man or angel, he held me fascinated.

He ignored the interruption. "Imagine that, at that time, you don't experience your life from *your* viewpoint, as you did when you first went through it, but rather you *relive the experience that others had as a result of knowing you or resulting from your actions. In other words, you feel what they felt on account of you.*"

Images of several people I had known flashed through my head. Not only seeing my encounters with them from *their* side, but *feeling* what they had felt, almost made me nauseous in some cases. Others came to mind with whom, as I felt their experience, a wave of appreciation and respect washed over me. After I had worked through the people I knew well, like flashcards flipping by, my mind turned to the strangers who had encountered me. In the case of a few, my actions left me with a distasteful sensation—the drivers I had become angry with, or the homeless people whom I had judged, then walked right past, pretending that they didn't exist. Yet, the vast majority were people for whom I had done something kind, such as allow them into my lane of traffic or open a door for them. The feeling generated by acts that had no other purpose than to be kind filled me with warm and loving appreciation.

I tried to imagine experiencing the ultimate effects of all my actions, but the ripple effect became too great. I could see the immediate results in the first layer or two of people who were directly affected, but when I tried to imagine the people they affected and the people that those in turn affected, all because of what I had done, it was overwhelming. I gasped at the thought of just my schoolteachers alone! I was sure there were days when what I did—or even just the expression on my face or my body language—caused them to be less patient with someone else—perhaps even their own families. I could not bring myself to think about how it had spread from there.

I shared with Michael, "That's a heavy dose of wake-up medicine! What a lesson in compassion! If everyone could feel that, they would shift in a hurry."

"Actually, they already do feel it—when others treat them the same way, but that doesn't appear to be enough," Michael answered with a sadness in his voice. "You see, it is a slight twist on the Golden Rule, *Do unto others as you would have them do unto you.* It is actually *Do unto others as you do unto you.* The problem is that many people have such low self-esteem. They do very cruel things to themselves and, therefore, very cruel things to others. You have to love yourself enough to feel worthy and deserving enough to have *others do unto you* things that are respectful and kind. Unfortunately, many people are in abusive relationships and somehow manage to convince themselves that they deserve that kind of treatment—then they often treat others the same way. Their code seems to be, *do unto others as others have done unto you.*

"This is the chain of pain, Matt. The way to stop it is to recognize that the first link is the pain within you, within each individual. Through self-observation, letting go of judgment and blame, embracing acceptance and compassion—with a truly great and generous heart—the chain of pain can be broken."

I was deeply contemplating all that he said, when he added with a sparkle in his eyes, "Many people, when they walk through the world, make it a game to size people up, judging their bodies, their behaviors, their efforts and their beliefs. What if instead we made it a game to accept people just as they are and rather than curse them, send them a prayer of blessing?! With each prayer sent with compassion, a link is broken. This not only breaks the chain of pain, but spreads compassion ripples around the planet!"

With that he looked at his watch and said, "Oops, gotta go! See ya!"

He smiled, got up and walked out of the restaurant, leaving me to ponder all that he had said.

I wondered where a guy like him had to go in such a hurry but could come up with no clues. Why would an archangel be wearing a watch, anyway? I finished my dinner, which was now getting cold, and went outside for a walk. As I strolled through the city, in a relatively rough area, I practiced accepting everything I saw through compassionate eyes. I sent a blessing to the little boy who looked too young to be on the street at night alone. Instead of judging his parents for allowing it, I sent them a prayer of safety and understanding. I blessed the guys hanging around smoking. I prayed for the hookers standing on the corners. I prayed for the ministers and congregations of the churches I walked past. I prayed for the police officers who were making their presence known. As I walked past a large building, I caught a glimpse of my own reflection in the window, and without thinking, I blessed myself as well. When my walk was finished, rather than feeling despair and hopelessness as I normally would have from the same experience, I felt invigorated, hopeful and content. I was breaking my link in the chain.

As I headed back to my hotel room to prepare for the next day, Alea came to mind. I had hardly had time to even think about her since she had appeared during the seminar. I did not understand why she hadn't come to speak with me. My heart ached for just a moment. I observed myself, took a deep breath, and sent Alea a prayer full of love, understanding and thanks, recognizing that I didn't have to understand to be compassionate and accepting.

I reached into my pocket for the key to my room; my hand gripped something smooth and circular instead. Knowing that I had left all the Rings of Truth at home in a very safe place, I worried that I had inadvertently missed one. As I pulled it out, much to my surprise, it was a ring I hadn't seen before. My heart swelled with love as I heard Alea's voice say, *"Compassion."*

It was difficult for Alea to endure distancing herself from Matt. She so enjoyed hearing him share his discoveries with childlike enthusiasm. She was confident that he was gaining enough trust in himself that soon he would be aware of her presence again.

After listening to his seminar, Alea was pleased with the depth of mastery with which Matt shared the concepts. They were becoming part of him, no longer something he was seeking. She knew they would serve him well.

She paused to consider the meaning of compassion. Its essence is that of genuine caring for another. It does not mean getting hooked into someone else's problems or taking on their problems as one's own; it merely means honoring another with one's love and prayers—and when appropriate, action.

The phrase is apt, "There, but for the Grace of God, go I." If we would view each other, not from judgment, but from appreciation and understanding, compassion would spread like wildfire. If we would stop for only a moment to observe ourselves and the results of our actions before we did and said things, how differently we would behave.

It isn't just what we say and do that affects those around us, but even how we feel as we approach different situations. When we are angry, even without speaking, others can feel the energy. When we are happy, others can feel that as well. The ripple effect takes place not just from what we do, but who we are and how we are internally.

Alea visualized the whole world surrounded with love and compassion. She saw each person like an antenna sending out radio waves of energy that others can pick up; each energetic pulse radiating enough of a charge to wake up another's heart. She smiled at the possibilities. What if people were to look around and see each other as God in a costume?! The game's challenge would be to discover the God within—to treat each being as if the God within them matters, to have compassion for even the best disguises, especially the ones that trigger judgment and that masterfully camouflage the real, hidden divinity.

What if everyone sought to make the lives of the people they encounter better—even if only with a silent look of knowing? She filled her vision with resourceful energy, as if it were a helium balloon, and let it go, trusting that it would safely journey the distance around the globe.

She turned her sights back to Matt, who was now sitting on the bed in his hotel room, meditating with the ring of compassion in his hands. Alea knew that between him and the other volunteers here on Earth, her vision—and Michael's—was more than possible; it was alive and growing.

14

Authentic Power

I woke the next morning with the ring of compassion still on the nightstand where I had left it. I glanced at the empty pillow beside me and missed Jessie. Wishing she were traveling with me, I called her quickly to tell her I loved her, even though I had spoken with her just the night before.

This day, I had another seminar to do. This one was open to the general public and was a market test, since most of the other workshops I led were for already-formed groups who came to my seminars as a group decision. I wanted to see if there were substantial numbers of people out there in the general public who would come to my presentation on an individual basis, simply out of their own interest in the topic, as advertised and promoted in the media.

As the people entered the hall, I thought about what Michael had said regarding the worldwide chain of pain. Observing them, I noticed how much pain was evident on various faces. It showed up in several forms—a few looked angry, some skeptical, some looked just plain hurt. My first impulse was to feel their pain in my own body which, upon second thought, didn't seem too resourceful. Instead, I let that go and turned my energy toward providing a class that would help them. I said a silent prayer for everyone's healing.

Before I began, I looked up just in time to see Nan walk through the door! Quickly, I made my way to the back of the room to welcome her.

I exclaimed, "What are you doing here? What a wonderful surprise!"

After we hugged, she answered, "I saw your ad in the paper and decided to see my dear friend and learn some new things! I have been really looking forward to this."

"I have been meaning to call you, but timing has been challenging. Are you free for dinner this evening? I'd love to fill you in on some things and hear what's new with you."

Nan replied, "I was hoping you'd be available! Maybe lunch, too—that is, if you have the time. It looks like you have a good turnout! There must be three hundred people here!"

Pleased, I looked around to see that she was right. "I had gotten a good response with reservations, but this is an even better turnout than I expected. I'm so happy that you're here, Nan. Thank you so much!" I gave her another hug and returned to the front of the room to begin the class.

After a couple of hours of introducing people to letting go, resourcefulness and Universal Energy Flow, I thought I'd add a little about what Michael and I had shared the night before.

I asked, "Have you ever noticed how much pain people are in?" After pausing to give them time to think, I went on. "The planet is encircled in a chain of pain, and our own pain creates a link in that chain. Every time we let go of our fears, every time we let go of our anger, every time we let go of blame and judgment, every time we return to resourcefulness, we break a link in the chain."

During a guided imagery to experience letting go, a woman in the front row started crying. Once I started the presentation again, she looked as if she were going to explode with something she wanted to say. I observed her for a minute and noticed that her whole body appeared to be in pain. Finally, I asked her name and if she had something she wanted to share. She told us her name was Kate, at which point she burst into tears.

I waited for her to take a few breaths, then asked, "What are you feeling?"

She said between sniffles, "I don't know what I feel." She then added after a moment, "I feel like there is a battleship trapped in an iceberg inside my chest."

Impressed with her colorful description, I inquired further, "What does that feel like?"

She answered without hesitation, "Tight and restrictive. Like I can't breathe."

"How long have you felt this way?"

Her reply surprised us all. "Well, uh, let's see . . . forty years."

I could hear the entire audience gasp at how long this woman had held onto such pain. They had such empathetic looks on their faces, as if her healing would relieve them, too.

I asked, "What else do you feel?"

Kate thought for a moment, then answered, "My legs are in pain." She pointed to her inner thighs.

"How long have you had that pain?"

Still crying a little, she said again, "Forty years."

I then asked, "What caused the pain?"

"I don't know."

"How old were you forty years ago?"

"Thirteen."

I trusted myself and the questions that naturally popped into my head, one after another. "What memory do you have prior to thirteen?"

She looked as if she were searching her brain, every nook and cranny, and then responded, shaking her head, "I have no memory prior to thirteen."

She started crying a little harder with that new awareness. I said gently, "Let's not worry about that. Let's see if we can get rid of that battleship. Do you like the feeling? Are you using it for protection?"

She paused and said, "No, I don't like the feeling, but, I . . . I do think it has been protection."

I prodded her further. "Which do you honor most, your protection or your freedom?"

She replied, "Um, well, my freedom." She sounded hesitant, as though not quite convinced.

I continued, "Do you want to let the feeling go?"

She looked as if I had hit her with the question and stammered, "Um, I think so."

I asked again, "Do you want to let the feeling go?"

"I am pretty sure."

As I asked again, I could see the audience struggling right along with her. They wanted her to express her intention, sensing that if she didn't make the decision, she would be stuck with the pain for another forty years. "Do you want to let it go?"

Each time I asked, she came up with another half-yes, half-no kind of answer. Finally, after the fourth or fifth time, she said, "Yes, I want to let it go, but I'm afraid."

The audience simultaneously let out the breath that they had all been holding.

I changed to a new question with the intent of now exploring her willingness. "Are you willing to let it go?"

She answered a little hesitantly, "Yes."

Wanting to be sure that she was positive, I checked, "Are you sure?"

Kate's tears were renewed as she blurted out, "No, I am not sure. I'm afraid."

I asked her in a new way, "Do you want to stay with the feeling, or are you willing to let it go?"

There was no reply, so I narrowed the options back down. "Are you willing to let it go?"

We could see the internal battle she was going through. She then clearly announced, "Yes," bursting into racking sobs that shook her entire body.

I didn't let up. "When are you willing to let it go?"

She didn't answer, but just kept crying. Her breathing got very heavy, and the tension in the air was thick. By now, several people were crying, in touch with their own feelings. Everyone wanted her to let go of the pain, as much for themselves as for her.

I calmly asked again, "When would you like to let it go?"

Between sobs, she said, "I . . . I don't know." Her voice was muffled, her face buried in her hands.

Suddenly, she raised her head, eyes wide in shock. "Oh my God! I remember, I remember!"

Between sniffles and tears and attempts to breathe, she whispered loud enough for us all to hear, "He raped me. My own father raped me!"

A hush fell over the room as we all listened to her story. There was barely a dry eye as we relived with her the abuse she had endured for years as a child.

I felt tremendous compassion for her and great relief at the same time. I trusted this process enough to know that even though she was in a vulnerable position at the moment, she was actually at one of the most powerful points of her life—the point of decision to hold on or let go.

When she finished telling us what had happened to her, I asked in a calm, nonjudgmental voice, "Kate, when do you want to let this go?"

She looked up and said, "I don't know if I can."

I nodded to show her that I had heard her and then asked again, "When do you want to let this go?"

She took a deep breath, looking as if just the process of remembering and telling the story had relieved some of her pain. She answered, "I want to say, now."

The group was leaning forward on their chairs, full attention on Kate. I could see how much they all wanted her to let go, to break this incredibly strong link in the chain of pain.

I asked her one more time, "When do you want to let this go?"

She took a deep breath and announced, for the first time with a strength of commitment, "Now!"

The entire room full of people jumped up in a standing ovation. Kate looked around and started laughing and crying at the same time. She got up and hugged me and then turned and started hugging all the other people who had supported her through this process, people she didn't even know. The next twenty minutes were spent with people hugging and sharing about what had just happened. As I watched from the stage, I marveled at how right Michael had been—the joy found in the release of one person's pain was felt by everyone in the room. The chain had weakened.

After everyone settled down, I said, "Let's check your feeling again. How do you feel now?"

She smiled and said, "Open, free, loving—wonderful!"

I then replied, "Stand up a minute. How do your legs feel?"

She looked down at her legs for a minute, as if to see the pain, moved around a little and then exclaimed, "The pain is gone! Oh, my gosh! It's the first time in forty years!"

I then inquired, "And the battleship?"

She laughed and said, "The battle is over."

Everyone laughed with her; they indeed had been witness to the battle she had gone through and won. The feeling in the room was one of shared valor; she had done it herself, and we had given her our total support.

I explained to the group, "While this looks like one of those miracle healings you may see on TV, I assure you that it isn't like that—although it is miraculous. It seems too simple, because it is simple! However, it isn't necessarily easy—as you can see. Every one of us has the power to release our bottled-up feelings and pain. It requires intention, willingness and commitment, but it can be instantaneous. I've seen it happen many times. The challenge is that we develop unconscious methods of protecting ourselves from others, such as weight, pain, illness, even anger, and we seldom stop to observe ourselves long enough to see that our very protection is the thing that keeps us from getting what we want—happiness and love. When we observe and get clearly committed, we can let it go. We can find resourceful ways to protect ourselves and still be happy and loving. For instance, we can implement boundaries and clarity of communication—options that were not necessarily available to us as children.

"Once you've learned this process, the object is to let go as soon as a new pain is introduced, so that you don't even bother storing the energy anymore. By observing what you are feeling and letting go, you can remain in the resourceful state."

Someone asked, "Will her pain stay gone? It's kind of hard to imagine, even though I went through the process with her, that it is over—

after forty years. I know people who have been through similar traumas and who have spent years in therapy but are still in pain."

I answered, "In this case, her pain was clearly caused by stored-up feelings from an emotionally-impacting—and repeated—experience. That is different than a physically caused pain. It's possible that she will feel the pain again, but if she does, all she needs to do is repeat the process with intention, willingness and commitment and let it go again! It will be considerably easier next time, if it is even necessary. Eventually, letting go becomes habitual, and you barely have to think about it. Breathing deeply and releasing the energy consciously, through your breath, is the key.

"I don't mean to put down therapy, because it certainly has its place and excellent therapists abound; however, most of them are not trained in the process of letting go, and consequently, they take the long route to healing. Letting go seems too simple, because we are not taught to do it. Nor are we used to recognizing and utilizing our own power to release.

"I often hear people justify their pain by saying it is their karma or fate, but the way I see it, karma or fate is the event or circumstance that you have been given to handle. How you handle it is entirely up to you; it is your choice. In this case, the rape and abuse were her karma, but how she chose to deal with them was a matter of free will. Fortunately, she has made the choice to let go. Once you've done that, you are freed from the karma! It is only in holding onto it that it continues. The whole point is to let go and return to resourcefulness.

"Many of you are thinking about people you love who are in pain and how they could benefit from letting go. Instead of going out and immediately trying to process everyone you know who is in pain, your true, authentic power is in breaking your own link in the chain.

"Look at how we all feel right now. Can you see how Kate's release has made all of us freer? Didn't you feel wonderful when she decided to let her pain go?" The nods stirred around the room as people looked at each other, smiled and acknowledged the woman who had given us this gift.

"We each affect each other. When you let go, those around you are also freed." I wanted to make one more point. "Sometimes our circumstances serve as the wake-up call to put us on our path toward growth, toward realizing who we really are. I know of a woman who attended workshop after workshop seeking answers, but sat in the audience glowering at all the men in hatred, including the instructor. When he asked her why she kept coming back if she hated him so much, she explained to him that she hated all men because she had been raped when she was seventeen. He asked her when she had started her search for healing and spirituality, and she said, 'Eighteen.' He then asked the million-dollar question, 'Do you think you would have begun your search for growth without the event of the rape?' She thought for a moment and said, 'No, I don't think I would have.' In that moment, she woke up and began her return to resourcefulness and authentic power—which led her to forgiveness, healing and even appreciation for her life circumstances.

"I bring this up only to point out that karma or fate is not a state of being, it is a set of circumstances that you encounter or are born into. How you respond—either holding on and creating a link in the chain of pain, or letting go and breaking the bonds—is up to you."

A woman asked, "Are you suggesting that rape is a good thing?"

Understanding her concern, I answered, "Of course not! I am suggesting that what you create out of it can be a good thing. If you reframe the event and look at it from another angle, you will see that—even though the event may be horrible—what keeps it horrible eternally is how you handle it. You have the power to turn your circumstances into gifts by what you create out of them. Sometimes people take an awful event like that, then turn around, change the course of their lives and end up helping thousands of others because of their experience. Remember, good and bad are relative. The key is to be resourceful."

Someone else asked, "How can you tell if it is just a memory, or something you need to let go of?"

I explained, "If it is not happening to you now but is interfering with your happiness, you need to let go."

With that, I looked at my watch and released everyone for lunch. They walked out, talking noisily and happily.

Nan walked up and said, "Wow! That was awesome. You know, Matt,

I watched you and your aura the entire time you worked with that woman, and you didn't even flicker. You stayed right there with her, present in the moment, the whole time. That is hard to do under that kind of pressure!"

I appreciated her feedback, as the funniest dialogue goes on in my head when I am in front of the room. I told her, "I'm glad to hear that! If you could hear the voices in my head the whole time, you would laugh. Part of me is totally comfortable and confident, trusting the process completely, while another part of me is saying, *Look what you've done now! How are you going to get out of this one! What a hornet's nest you've stirred up now!* and other doubting things like that. It's pretty funny."

Nan said, "I think everyone has doubts when they start something new or get a little out of their comfort zone. It's nothing to be concerned about. Care to join me for lunch?"

I smiled and said, "I'd love to, but we'd better watch the clock, because knowing the two of us, we could talk through the whole afternoon."

During lunch, we caught up on all the events since the wedding. I told her about my father and Jessie's visit with my family. She told me that she and Steve were still together—and happily so. The time flew by quickly, so we opted to do dinner as well, to give ourselves a chance to catch up in greater depth. I still wanted to tell her about the latest with Michael and Alea, thinking perhaps she would be able to "read" into Alea's absence.

The afternoon session went well. In the midst of it, a man in the back asked me, "I understand that happiness is a state of mind and that if I am resourceful, I'll be happy, but I work in a job that I hate. In fact, I get up in the morning and dread going to work. How do I stay happy in that situation?"

The answer came easily. "First of all, you need to remember that you always have choices, and you want to get resourceful before you make any changes, so you are making the right choices. The next thing that you want to do is, if you are going to do something, be the best at it that you can possibly be. Let me share a story with you to illustrate what I mean.

"When I was just a teenager, I got a job at the local gas station. I worked for minimum wage providing service to the community, pumping gas, checking under the hood and washing windows. Now, some may say that this is the kind of job to hate, but I was determined to be the best gas station attendant this world had ever seen. Every day I would greet people, take care of them and thank them for coming in, and I loved my job—because I did it with love.

"Now, Bill worked with me. Bill hated his job. Every day he would come in and say, 'Some day I'm going to get out of this place.' When a customer came in, he would saunter over to their car and say, 'Yep?' and then grudgingly do whatever they asked for.

"Then one day, one of my customers asked me, 'Son, what are you doing in a place like this?'

"I said, 'It's my job, and I do it well.'

"He agreed, 'I can see that, but you're meant for even greater things; you ought to be working in the factory!'

"He told me he could get me a job there, so I said good-bye to Bill and the station and moved up to the assembly line. Now, some of you may think this is the kind of job to hate, but not me. I set out to be the best factory worker this world had ever seen. I worked so hard that I did the job of four people. They even did a study on me to see what I was doing that the others weren't. I loved my job, because I did my best.

"Then one day, a friend of mine asked, 'What are you doing in a place like this?'

"I looked at him, surprised, and said, 'This is my job, and I'm good at what I do.'

"He said, 'I can see that, but you're meant for even greater things; you ought to be in business!'

"He set me up with my own business distributing soap. Now, the point of this story is that it doesn't matter what you do—*if you do what you do with love, you'll eventually have only what you love in your life.* That is not to say you have to keep doing your job; you don't. You have choices, but until you make the necessary changes, do what you do with love! You have to admit, it beats the heck out of doing what you do with hate!

"Take Bill, for instance. Last month, I was back in my hometown showing my wife my old stomping grounds, so I cruised into the station just for fun. This old guy saunters up as I roll down my window and says, 'Yep?'

"I got out of my car and said, 'Bill, is that you?'

"He looked at me kind of funny and said, 'Yeah, I'm Bill, who are you?'

"I told him, 'Matt. Remember me? I used to work here with you twenty-some years ago.'

"Vaguely remembering he said, 'Matt?! Oh yeah . . .'

"So I said to him, 'What happened, Bill? I thought you were planning to get out of here.'

"He answered, 'Oh, I still am, one of these days.'

"You see, he hated his job, didn't do it well and spent twenty or thirty years doing it unhappily. Our resistance takes us out of resourcefulness, and we often get stuck in the very thing that we were resisting."

A new thought occurred to me, so I added, "The ultimate in integrity is to do whatever you do the best you can, to be the best you can be and to be happy while you do it. Then, from a state of happiness, if you choose to do something else, you are free to make that choice.

"I've always thought of integrity as being along the lines of doing what you say you'll do, being honest and aligning what you believe with what you say. If you are hating anything, there is no alignment in what you are doing. Most of us look to change what is outside ourselves instead of shifting ourselves into integrity—no matter what we are doing.

"Integrity, therefore, is doing whatever you do with love and honesty, being the best you can be at everything you do. When you have integrity, you will be happy, no matter what line of work you are in."

I closed for the day to an enthusiastic applause. A woman came up to me after I finished and asked, with disarming simplicity, "Would you be interested in speaking to the United Nations?"

Not sure at first if she was serious, I studied her face for clues. She must have sensed my hesitancy, so she explained, "I'm sorry. I should have introduced myself. My name is Jane."

She shook my hand, gave me her card and then continued. "I have some close associates who work with the U.N. to bring in people who have something of value to say. I was very impressed with your presentation today; in fact, you touched me very deeply. I think the U.N. would benefit from hearing you speak. If you are interested, I'll see what I can do to make it happen."

I smiled at her and said, "Well, thank you! I'd love to. If you can make it happen, that would be great." I handed her my card as well.

With that, she shook my hand again and assured me I'd be hearing from her.

After talking with the other people who came up to me afterwards, Nan and I left for dinner.

She asked, "Did you learn all of that stuff from Alea?"

I answered a bit wistfully, "Not all of it, but of course she inspired it. Michael, too. Actually, Alea has kind of disappeared."

"Kind of disappeared? I thought disappearing was her specialty," she replied with a giggle.

I acknowledged her humor with a smile and then explained, "Well, actually, appearing has been just as much her M.O. as disappearing, but she hasn't been around for a while. She does still leave me rings, and I saw her briefly once—in fact, that was just yesterday. Compared to before, though, she's all but gone. I was actually wondering if you had a perspective on why that's happening."

She closed her eyes for a minute, then said, "I'm getting two reasons. One is that she wants you to develop into the mastery that you were born to have—she wants you to trust yourself."

Agreeing, I replied, "I think she told me something like that herself. What is the second reason?"

She looked thoughtful, as if not sure she should tell me, then said, "The second reason, Matt, is that Alea loves you, and she has been the source of your pain before—and she doesn't want to contribute to any part of your pain now. She wants to help heal you, not hurt you."

Nan looked reverent, as if she had been allowed to see something sacred and beautiful. She added, "You two go back a long, long way. I am not getting all the details, more of a feeling of tremendous depth. You share a precious relationship."

She hadn't told me anything I didn't already know, or anything Alea hadn't already told me, but somehow hearing it again from another source was reassuring. I asked, "Who is she, Nan? Is she an angel? Is she a ghost? A hallucination? I just can't figure it out."

Sensing my anguish, Nan replied, "I've been trying to figure that out, too, and I honestly don't know, Matt. All I do know is that you are mastering what she has helped you to see, and I'm sure she is proud—whoever she is."

I dismissed her compliment with another inquiry. "The other thing I am having a hard time figuring out are these rings. I understand that each one symbolizes a new concept I have stumbled upon, but what am I supposed to do with the rings themselves? I can't imagine they are just mementos of my life. I keep feeling as though I'm supposed to do something more with them."

She nodded as she listened. "I can't help you there, either; they are as much a mystery to me. I am sure that you will discover the answers to your questions, Matt. You've been doing a great job so far. Remember, the idea is to trust yourself."

We spent the rest of the evening reviewing the details of our lives.

After a while, she asked, "The last time we had a good long talk you told me about your friend—uh, was Daryl his name? Anyhow, the three of us made a pact to stick around until everyone on the planet woke up, right? What happened to him? Do you still see him?"

I smiled and answered, "Yes, I still see him; about once a month he and I do a workshop together for his sales force. I was with him when I found out my father was dying. In fact, I'm overdue to call him, as I kind of had to rush off after our last presentation. I'm looking forward to the day when the two of you can meet."

I then added, "Jessie is going to wish she'd been here when I tell her that I saw you. She really enjoyed the little time she was able to spend with you when you were out for the wedding. You should come out and visit us again when you have a chance."

She replied, "I'd love to. I really liked Jessie, too. What does she think about all this business with Alea—and Michael?"

I answered, "Well, she was very supportive when I told her about it. She has felt Alea's presence, and even saw her once. That helped a lot, because she experienced for herself some of what I was talking about. Honestly though, we've been so distracted with other things lately.

That, and Alea not being around, has made it kind of a rare subject for conversation."

"I think that's another reason Alea has been lying low—to give you some time alone with Jessie. I sense, though, that you will be hearing from her soon."

We talked for hours and then parted ways. I thanked her again for coming and wished her good night.

She returned the sentiment with a hug, then said, "Give my love to Jessie, and let's keep in touch."

As we started to go our separate ways, she added, "Matt, are you feeling okay?"

I quickly scanned my body from top to bottom and replied, "I feel fine, why?"

She shook her head and said, "Oh, nothing. Just take care of yourself. See you later!"

I returned to my hotel room to find the message light flashing on my phone. Jessie had called while I was out and said she was going to bed, but to feel free to call anyway. So I did, immediately.

When she answered, I said, "Hi, Jessie, are you sleeping?"

She replied, "Actually, I was lying in bed reading. I miss you." Then she asked, "How is everything going?"

"It is going really, really well. Sorry I didn't call earlier, but Nan came to my workshop today! We went out to dinner afterwards and talked forever. She said to send her love."

She responded exactly as I expected. "Oh, I wish I'd been there! I really like Nan. How is she?"

"She's doing fine! What I want to know is, how are you doing?"

She sounded a little sad. "I can't wait until you come home. It seems like it's been a long time, even though it's only been a couple of days. For some reason, this time has been even harder than last time you left."

I felt a pang in my heart and responded, "Yeah, I know what you mean. I miss you lots, too. I'm going to do some promotional work tomorrow, and I'll be home the day after that. Maybe we can go camping this weekend, or something to get away together! We haven't even gone on a honeymoon yet—think about where you want to go, and we'll plan it when I get home."

"Okay, that would be fun! Is everything else going well? Did you get a good turnout today?"

"Yeah, it was great—nearly three hundred people. I didn't expect so many. When I get home, I'll tell you all about it. A woman did some letting-go work in class today that was incredible. She let go of stuff she had been hanging onto for forty years!"

"Wow, that's wonderful, Matt!"

I shared my growing confidence with her. "I feel as if this material is just flowing through me now, without my having to think about it. I'm so thankful."

"Next time, maybe I will come with you and see what you do!"

Warmed by her interest, I said, "I'd love that, Jessie."

Before we hung up I asked, "So, how are your critters?"

She laughed and said, "Well, the babies are all snuggled in for the night. They're a lot of fun. Oh gosh! I almost forgot to tell you! I went to several of the private schools and the alternative school here just to find out what they were doing and to learn what is going on in this area and one of them offered me a job! I'm going to start next week. I'll be helping with the administrative tasks and will also be able to work with the kids. It'll give me some experience with children and a reality check to see whether I really want to pursue this school idea. I've been reading all kinds of information on education."

"That's great! Congratulations!" I was impressed that she had taken such a big step toward creating her vision and looked forward to watching it develop.

"Thanks. It's quite a pay cut, but I have to start somewhere if I really want to work with kids. I'm really looking forward to getting started. Until then my favorite thing is waking up to the view outside our bedroom window. The rock cliffs around here are so magical. I don't think I'll ever get tired of looking at them. They seem different every time—with different cloud shadows and lighting. It's just breathtaking—the full moon seems to make everything come alive around here!"

I was so happy to hear her taking pleasure in the same things that I so appreciate when I am home. I said sincerely, "I love you, Jessie. I can't wait to see you and the rock garden when I get back."

We said good night to each other, and then I laid in bed thinking about how blessed I have been. My words from the day about integrity started rolling through my mind, so I decided to explore the thoughts a bit more before I fell asleep.

I wanted to talk with Alea. I always felt such clarity when she and I discussed these things. "Pretending" she was there, I decided to talk to her anyhow—besides, who could tell, maybe she would hear me!

"Alea? I don't know if you can hear me or not, but I'm going to talk to you anyway. I really miss you. I know you are 'always with me,' and all that, but it just isn't the same. Nan told me some of the reasons she thinks you have been staying away, and I just want you to know how much I appreciate your looking after me. But I trust myself now, so you don't have to stay away anymore. And as for this hurt issue—as you would say, *It's not happening to me now!* Whatever it was, whenever it was—you're the one who remembers it, not me; so let it go and come back!"

I laughed at hearing myself telling Alea to let go of the past. For a moment, I thought I heard her laughing, too. I got really quiet to listen, but by then the room was silent. I went on. "So, Alea, I want to talk with you about integrity. I've been thinking about it. Here are my thoughts: I think integrity is doing what is right, doing the best you can do and doing it with love in your heart. This is important because it builds trust. If you have integrity, people know they can count on you, they can trust you. Trust builds openness, because people will share things with you when they trust you. Openness builds bonds, because when people take a risk and share themselves with someone else, they have a common bond holding them together. Hmmm—and bonds build relationships! As I see it, relationships are the ultimate tool for realizing who we really are, because they bring all of our issues up to the surface so we can observe them, let them go and, ideally, make resourceful decisions."

It felt a little funny talking to the room by myself, but it made me feel closer to Alea, and I liked the thoughts that were coming through. I took a few notes in my journal so I could add the information to my book, then continued the conversation that sounded like a monologue. "Alea? I'm back. Integrity issues come up a lot around money, and I was just thinking—one should never let money influence a decision. I mean, of course money is a factor, but we should never let money influence us away from doing what is right. I don't mean what is legal; I mean what is right. A lot of things can be legal that aren't right."

Still imagining that she was listening, I added, "When I do what is right, I feel the Universal Energy Flow going through me—and I love what I am doing, whatever it is—such as doing unsolicited kind things to help other people. Alea? Thank you for waking me up."

Without audible words, I clearly felt her correcting me, and I replied, "Okay, okay. Thank you for mirroring to me the fact that I was waking up. Is that better? I know—you can't do anything for me that I am not already discovering for myself. Well, anyhow, I love you—whoever you are—and thank you for your influence in my life. Good night."

I thought for sure I saw something across the room, but when I looked again, no one was there. I felt our connection, though, and fell asleep after saying a silent prayer of love and protection for all I held dear—and that was a very long list!

The next morning, I took myself out to breakfast. While writing notes in my journal for the next chapter in my book, something landing on the floor caught my eye. The gentleman sitting at a booth across the aisle had just gotten up to pay his bill, and as he pulled out money for his tip, something fell from his pocket. I ignored it for a minute, busy writing and unable to see what it was from where I was sitting. But something gnawed at me to get up and look, so finally I did.

There on the floor, under the table, lay a crumpled hundred-dollar bill. I picked it up, looked for the man whom I hadn't really gotten a good look at and saw that he had already gone. A moment of discussion took place within my head, as thoughts fired back and forth.

One voice said, "Well, he doesn't even know he lost it," and then added for emphasis, "Finders keepers."

Then another, more rational voice said, "No, if that was you, wouldn't you want someone to at least try to give it back? It's not right to keep it."

Without further hesitation, I quickly went out the door and looked up and down the street, just in time to see the back of the man rounding the next corner. I must have scared him a little with the sound of running footsteps behind him, because he looked quite startled as he turned to face me in response to my touch on his arm.

I held out the hundred-dollar bill and said a little breathlessly, "Sorry, I didn't mean to scare you. I was just eating in the same restaurant as you, and this fell out of your pocket when you got out of the booth."

With one hand, he reached out hesitantly, not sure if I was for real. With the other hand, he checked his pockets to discover that indeed his money had fallen out.

Then, looking as if he wasn't sure if I were totally stupid or a saint, he said, "Thank you, thank you so much."

I loved the feeling of doing the right thing. As I walked back to the restaurant, someone tapped me on the shoulder. I turned to see a young woman standing there.

"Excuse me," she said, "but did you drop this? I think it belongs to you."

There, shimmering in her hand, was a golden Ring of Truth. I looked at her closely to see if she was Alea in disguise and said, "Thank you, yes, it does belong to me. Thank you so much!"

"You're welcome. It's so pretty. I know that if I had lost it, I would want it back!" With that, she turned and walked away.

I looked at the ring as it glistened in the sunlight. The inscription read, *Integrity.*

I slipped it in my pocket, shaking my head at the wonder of it all, and made my way back to the restaurant.

It was painful for her not to appear when Matt was talking to her, but she felt guided in her heart to wait just a little bit longer. She was glad she had waited, even though it took some restraint.

Matt was easily and quickly discovering—or rather, remembering—each new facet of resourcefulness and putting them all to work in his own life. Once he gathered and mastered these, he would have the Master's Key. With that, he could be instrumental in changing the world, breaking the chain of pain and restoring love in the hearts of all—if that's what he chose to do.

His recent discoveries were wonderful: Integrity is our true source of power. When we choose to be in integrity, we choose to be in love. When we choose to be in integrity, it feels good, right to the core of our being. Down deep, we all know what the right thing to do is, because anything else feels uncomfortable. That's why so many of us choose lives of discomfort: we have not yet learned how to listen to our feelings—or to trust them.

Integrity becomes easy when we recognize that we are all one. What you do to another affects you. When you hurt another, you are hurt as well. When you do a kind thing for another, you are blessed as well. When you do what you do with love, you will eventually only have what you love in your life.

Alea needed to complete her business with Matt, as she could not continue in the same manner much longer. The world was ready for this work; he was ready to do the work. She reviewed the changes she had observed him make: He was now more aware, more insightful, clearer, more intuitive, more loving, more creative, more open-hearted, more open-minded, more accepting and more honoring of others. He was softer now. Yes, that was a good way to put it. Softer. When someone is hard, they are not flexible. When we shift into being softer, we become open to growth and change. We operate from love. We are resourceful.

She giggled a little, thinking that having all these women around him had been good for Matt. Alea then sighed deeply. With all that done, all that was left was the final healing. This would be a time when she and Matt both would have to put their intention, willingness and commitment to the test—and let go. Just as some use their pain as protection, others use it to tie themselves to another through a bond of attachment that, while healthy in some ways, can also be addictive. Now would be the time for them both to let go of their magnificent past and make room for their magnificent futures.

She watched Matt as he went about his business and whispered, "Soon, my dear friend, soon."

Matt looked around as if he had just heard something, gave a little shrug, looked at his watch and then continued on his way.

15

The Dance of Life

My day had been successful. I had lined up several potential speaking engagements and met some key individuals in the corporate world of Southern California. Having worked my way into Orange County, I decided to stop for dinner before heading back up to Los Angeles for the night. All the running around had made me very hungry. I found a little place that looked good and set my sights on a healthy meal. I sat at the counter and started chatting with the man next to me. We exchanged the common courtesy of inquiring what the other did, where we were from and other friendly but superficial details.

After ordering, I felt as if the temperature in the room had gone up ten degrees. I asked the man next to me, "Is it hot in here?"

He looked around as if the answer could be seen, and then shrugged and said, "I don't think so." He then took another bite of his hamburger.

I wiped the sweat from my brow, took off my coat and loosened my tie. The waitress brought the sandwich I had ordered and gave me a glass of water before rushing off to her next task. I looked down at the food, for which only a little while ago I had been starving. Now, for some reason, I no longer felt hungry. I took a bite of the sandwich and could barely get it down. Still the temperature seemed to continue to climb. I took a sip of water and felt as if I was about to overflow.

The guy next to me said, "Hey, are you okay?"

I answered, unsure, "Yeah, I think I just need some fresh air. I'll be back in a minute."

I went out the front door and made my way toward a small brick wall under the front window where I was planning to sit and breathe. A mixture of heat, nausea and dizziness overwhelmed me. Suddenly everything went black and my world grew perfectly silent.

The next thing I knew, I still couldn't see anything, but I could hear some faraway voices talking. They sounded like an echo in a canyon, barely audible.

I heard one voice say, "I can't get a pulse. We're losing him! You have to get that I.V. in!"

The other responded anxiously, "The veins have collapsed. I can't get it in."

The first voice repeated, "We're going to lose him if you don't get it in! Still no pulse."

I felt Alea there. I couldn't see her—I couldn't see anything. I could only feel her presence and hear her voice.

"Matt, Matt!" There was concern in her voice, and yet there was a gentle calmness at the same time.

I responded without moving my lips, "Oh Alea, I'm so happy you're here. What's happening? Who are those voices talking about?"

"They are talking about you, Matt. Something is wrong. You passed out on the sidewalk in front of the restaurant."

I recognized the truth of what she had said. A sudden awareness of my body jolted me into total discomfort. I pulled back from my body and asked, a bit surprised, but not upset, "Am I dying, Alea?"

She answered clearly, *"That is up to you. It's your choice. Do you want to live, or do you want to die?"*

I heard one of the voices ask nervously, "How are you doing with that I.V.?"

I answered Alea, "I feel so peaceful here. I'm not sure I want to go back there—into that drama. What should I do?"

I knew she was giving me her sweet smile as she said, *"You must decide what you want. It is your choice, and you must make it now."*

With a wave of love, Jessie and my boys flashed into my mind, and then I became aware of the vow I had made with Daryl and Nan, to stick around until every human being had awakened.

"Still no pulse," echoed the voice in the far distance.

None too soon, I said, "Alea . . . I want to live!"

The voice sounded closer and relieved as it said, "I got the I.V. in!"

"I've got a pulse! He's coming around!"

My body hurt. My arm felt jabbed, and whatever I was lying on was very hard. My head was pounding; I must have bumped it when I fell. I opened my eyes to an up-close view of the cement. Still a little disoriented, half-conscious, I tried to move.

People were everywhere. I recognized one as the man who had been sitting next to me. He was telling a paramedic what had happened before I came outside. I tried to move again and heard a voice tell me to lie still. I reached up to wipe water from my face and saw that it was blood. In fact, I was lying in a pool of it. Not sure whether it was the best healing option or the best method of avoidance, I chose to sleep through some of this life-and-death experience.

I woke up in the emergency room with a nurse checking my pulse. It took me a few minutes to figure out where I was. Looking around, I tried to orient myself, then remembered the scene in front of the restaurant.

She welcomed me, "How are you feeling?"

Still confused, I inquired, "Uh, I feel all right, I guess. What happened?"

Matter-of-factly, she said, "You had a bleeding ulcer that filled your stomach up with blood. Apparently, you went outside the restaurant and passed out while you vomited it all up. You've lost a lot of blood."

That explained the pool of blood I had found myself in earlier. In an attempt to lighten things up, I responded, "Oh, how pleasant!" Then I stated, "I'd like to talk with the doctor."

She said, "He'll be back later. I'll tell him you want to see him. In the meantime I need you to sign this form giving us permission to give you a blood transfusion."

"I don't want one."

Visibly flustered she said, "But the doctor . . . "

"I'll talk to the doctor about it when he comes, but right now I just want to sleep. Can you also call my wife? She's expecting my call, and I don't want her to worry."

She took the number and assured me she would call. She signaled to another nurse to join her, whispered something to her about the blood transfusion and explained that they were moving me to intensive care. "There are no phones in intensive care, so we'll have to relay a message to your wife."

I saw them shaking their heads disapprovingly and closed my eyes, wanting to return to peacefulness, and said, "Thank you. Please don't scare her—I'll be fine."

Once again, I drifted back to sleep.

Several hours later, I was awakened again by the nurse checking on me. I asked, "Did you get hold of my wife?"

"Yes, we reached her. She'll be coming as soon as she can get a flight. She told me to tell you that, and I quote, 'Dying is against the rules. . . .' She said you would know what that meant, and she asked me to tell you she loves you."

I laughed, "That's sounds like Jessie! Thank you."

She then got more serious. "How are you feeling?"

I focused my attention up and down my body and said, "Well, I've had better days. I feel weak, tired. I think I bumped my head when I fell, so I've got a headache, too. I'll make it, though."

"The doctor came by while you were sleeping. You really need that blood transfusion."

I responded politely, "Thanks, but I'd prefer not to."

"You are really weak; you could use the blood," she said, concerned that I was still turning down their solution to my problem.

I asked, "Will I live without it?"

"Well, yes, I suppose, but you would get well a lot faster with it."

I tried to reassure her, "If I don't have to have it, I don't want it. I don't mean to be difficult, but I'm going to go home and let my own doctor work with me. I am a strong believer in holistic medicine and prefer to see what I can do through alternative means to heal myself, first."

She looked confused and asked, "Heal yourself?"

Too tired to go into great detail with her now, I simply said, "I believe we are all responsible for our health. I will work with the doctors—both traditional and alternative—but if I am going to heal, I have to be the responsible one."

Partly teasing, I told her, "I was thinking once about writing a book called, *From Medication to Meditation: Today's Health Practices.* It's sometimes confusing, the range of advice you get, even from regular medical doctors. The bottom line was going to be that in order to have a Healthy Self, you have to Heal Thy Self."

I could see her wheels turning until she realized the play on words. She smiled and said, "You've got something there. Great title, too, but if you don't get some rest, you won't be a credible source of information on health!"

I laughed gently and said, "Don't worry, I'm not about to expire now."

She laughed, too, and replied, "Good! That is a relief! I'll let the doctor know about your position on his recommendation."

After she left, I lay there thinking about the word "expire" and wondered why we referred to dying that way. I called the nurse back in and asked for a dictionary, which she brought in, only with the promise that right after we used it I would go back to sleep. She wouldn't let me do it myself, so I asked her to look up "expire."

She looked at me strangely, shook her head and then proceeded to do what I requested. She said, "Hmmm. This is interesting. It means 'to breathe out spirit.'"

She then took the dictionary and returned to making her rounds.

"To breathe out spirit," I repeated quietly. If dying is to expire or "breathe out spirit," then living must be to inspire or "breathe *in* spirit"! I suddenly saw the entire process of life to be one of giving and receiving spirit.

Just then, I remembered being with Alea when I had passed out. She had come to me! What had she said? As I tried to remember, it filtered in slowly and then became clearer. She had said the choice was mine to live or to die. Does that mean I have the choice of whether to expire or to inspire? If one chooses life, is the true meaning of "life" to inspire others?—or to live an inspired life? And if one does not, does that mean one isn't truly living? With all these thoughts and questions on my mind, I slipped deep into sleep.

In the middle of the night, I dreamt that Alea was standing over my bed. Jessie was there, and Nan and Daryl, too. I saw my mother and my kids, all looking deeply concerned. A number of other people who mattered to me were also there. They stood in a circle, forming a ring of love around me. No one said anything or did anything except stand there quietly, breathing. We just looked into each other's eyes with a giving and receiving of love and appreciation.

I woke the next morning feeling much stronger. From this strengthened perspective, the seriousness of yesterday's events became clear. Until now, it had all seemed unreal, but now the realization that I had almost died was sinking in. *What if I had chosen not to live? What then?* I seemed to have a lot more questions than answers.

Interrupting my thoughts, in walked Jessie. One look at me, and she started crying. She hugged me for a long time, then said, "Are you okay? You look so pale."

I tried to cheer her up by joking, "Oh, that's just because there isn't any blood left in me. My color will come back after I've manufactured some more."

She didn't even crack a smile, but instead asked me, "Are you in pain?"

Shaking my head, I answered, "No, just really tired. Sometimes my stomach hurts."

She wanted to know more, trying to understand what possibly could have happened. "Were there any warning signs? Were you feeling bad or having any pain?"

I assured her, "No, none. I had no idea there was anything wrong, until five minutes before I passed out. One minute I was starving, and the next I was totally full—of blood. It was one of the strangest things that has ever happened to me!"

I then added, "What's really important, Jessie, is that I came right up to the decision point, and I chose to live. I've been thinking a lot about life and death since I've been here, and I am so thankful to be alive—and sharing my life with you."

She smiled, wiping away her tears, and said, "I'm thankful, too." She squeezed my hand and added, "So, what happens now? What has the doctor said?"

"I don't know. I haven't seen him yet. The nurse said the doctor wants to give me a transfusion, but I refused it. I'm anxious to get out of here and go see my doctor at home. I'd like to see what can be done through holistic medicine to take care of this, before I get put on medication for the rest of my life. I want to do some research and avoid the side-effects that often accompany modern cures."

Jessie asked tentatively, "Are you out of the woods? Do we need to be worried about you in the immediate sense?"

I looked into her eyes and said, "Well, practically speaking, I am still in intensive care, so it must not be over. They did tell me that if everything continued on course, they would move me into my own room tonight. They check on me a lot, but they don't seem to be alarmed. I guess we won't know until I see a doctor. I'm expecting him this morning."

I then added, "I can tell you this, Jessie; right now I am seeing lots of things differently. Besides being extremely appreciative of life, I'm not afraid of death, but I don't want to die because I love living. I still have so much that I want to do!

"I had a wonderful dream last night; you were there, and the boys, and all the people that I care about the most. It was as if we were exchanging love and energy, and it wasn't just healing me, it was healing all of us. It was a give-and-receive exchange—with each of us independent yet interdependent at the same time."

She smiled at me and listened intently, then said, "It sounds like a wonderful dream. That's a pretty good analogy for life, isn't it?"

We both sat in silence, thinking for a few minutes, and then she changed the subject, saying, "My brother doesn't live too far from here. I'm going to stay with him until you get out of the hospital. Are your things at the hotel? I'd better go get them and check you out. Your eyelids are starting to look pretty heavy—you could probably use some more sleep."

I hadn't even thought about my stuff. I gave her directions to where I had been staying. Just as she was walking out the door, she said, "Let me know what the doctor says. I'll be back this afternoon. Matt, I love you."

She looked at me in a way that said, "Matt, don't leave me. Our time together is just beginning." But she didn't speak the words.

I answered her thought. "My time isn't up. I had my chance; I chose to stay! Don't worry, Jessie, and know that I love you, too!"

I'm sure I was asleep before she even got out the door.

That afternoon they moved me to a private room. Again, I asked to see the doctor.

Finally, he came to see me, explaining, "Sorry it took me so long to catch you awake. This thing has taken a lot of energy out of you! How are you feeling?"

"Tired, but okay."

He responded with a monologue, looking at the chart instead of me. "If you had taken the blood transfusion, you would have felt stronger faster. This is serious, and you have lost a lot of blood. The way I see it, you are going to be in here for about a week. Don't drink any coffee, no alcohol, no smoking. I'm prescribing a drug that will act as an antacid and help control the ulcer. Let the nurse know if you experience any changes."

He then turned and walked out. When Jessie returned, I told her what he had said, then explained, "Jessie, I want to go home to heal. It's a short flight back to Phoenix, and then we can catch a small shuttle flight from there. I don't like being here. Tomorrow, let's go."

She looked concerned. "Are you sure, Matt? I'd hate to move you too soon and have another problem."

Seeing the worry on her face, I took her hand and said, "I'll make you a deal. We won't decide until tomorrow, okay? I'll see how I am feeling and we'll take it from there."

She tentatively agreed, "Well, okay. Just make sure you are strong enough."

Assuring her, I said, "I will, I promise."

She stayed and read to me until I was out for the evening. Then she went to her brother's house for the night.

The next morning she came in with the sun, announcing cheerfully, "I couldn't stay away! I think they should have beds in these rooms for immediate family members, so we don't have to stay somewhere else. How are you doing, my love?"

I marveled at how cheerful she was. Still waking up, I said, "I don't know yet. I'll give you the first bulletin when I do, though!"

I looked at her more closely and underneath her smile I could see the signs of worry. It then occurred to me how much stress I'd put her through in the short time that we'd been married. She'd already had to meet all of my family and my former wife in the midst of family grief, endure a funeral and now this, not to mention handling the move, getting a job and befriending my children. I hoped she wasn't having second thoughts about the wisdom of marrying me.

The orderly brought breakfast, interrupting my thoughts before I said anything to Jessie. I committed myself to making it up to her—when I was able. I looked at the food with no interest, still a little hesitant to eat, not sure what my stomach would do. I looked at Jessie and whispered, "Today is the day! Let's make our getaway!"

She smiled and said, "Matt, I think you ought to stay one more day. You still look a little rough around the edges, and I want to be sure you are strong enough for the trip. Have you even tried walking yet?"

She had a point. I shook my head and pushed my tray to the side. "Let's see what happens."

I sat up, put my feet down and pushed myself into a standing position. It was harder than I had imagined it would be. A wave of nausea and dizziness hit me, and I immediately sat back down. "Okay, you win. I'll give it another day for recuperation's sake."

She wiped the concerned look off her face. "Thank you. I feel a lot better that way. I called Dr. Santos back at home. He said he would take a look at you and get you on some medicinal herbs right away. He told me to tell you that it's okay to take the medicine they give you while you are here, but that in the long run the traditional Western medicine for ulcers can give you liver cancer, so don't get hooked. He also said that he wants to run some bacterial tests on you."

I was overwhelmed with gratitude; her thoughtfulness continually surprised and delighted me. "Thanks. I feel more comfortable having his input. He's been my doctor for a long time. He knows what he's doing."

I spent the whole day reading, talking with Jessie and sleeping. She stayed nearby all day.

She had been right, of course. The next day I felt considerably stronger. I announced to the nurses that I was checking out, to their appalled disbelief. I assured them I would get adequate medical attention once I got home. They sent the doctor in to convince me otherwise, but it was no use; I was determined. He gave Jessie my prescription, with directions on how to use it, and suggested that I ought to expect to be on it for the rest of my life. We didn't discuss it with him, just took his input and thanked him.

The journey home was uneventful. Crawling into my own bed ranked right up there among my favorite things in the whole world.

Jessie tucked me in and said, "Tomorrow you have an appointment with Dr. Santos. I've arranged to start my job at the school next week instead of tomorrow. I want to be sure you are okay before I go in. They are being really nice and flexible."

I kissed her forehead and replied, "Thank you, Jessie. Thank you for taking such good care of me through this."

She looked curious. "The other day you said you *chose* to live over dying, and at the time I thought you meant that just because you were, obviously, still alive. Since then, though, I keep thinking about it, as if there was more to it than that. Was there?"

I smiled and explained, "Sorry I wasn't more specific at the time. Alea came to me when I passed out. I didn't actually see her, but I could feel her presence. I asked her if I was dying, and she said it was my choice and I had to decide right then. At that moment, it would have been easier to die, because I was somehow not connected with my body. Every time I thought about my body, I felt the pain it was in. It was more comfortable, even peaceful, to stay out of my body and avoid the pain."

She listened with fascination. "What changed your mind?"

I reached out and touched her hand. "You, and the boys, and my unfinished work here. Jessie, I have a sense that the preparation I have been going through with Alea's help is coming to a point where now what is left is spreading the work to help others. I feel passionate about this mission of waking people up—waking them up to joy, love and happiness. And I need to be alive to do that!"

We both teetered on the edge of tears prompted by the passion of what I was saying. Jessie whispered, "I am glad you chose life—for multiple reasons! I couldn't stand losing you so soon after finding you!"

We held each other with renewed appreciation.

The next day, Jessie took me to the doctor. He put me on some herbs and a strict, stomach-soothing diet. He explained that researchers had found new evidence that ulcers aren't simply caused by stress, as had been believed for decades, but rather by a bacteria that had only recently been discovered. He explained that antibiotics kill the bacteria, allowing the ulcers to heal. Testing me, he indeed found very high levels of the ulcer-producing bacteria, *H.pylori.*

Upon delivering the "good" news, he told me, "You are lucky that we found this so quickly. Many people walk around with extremely painful—and potentially fatal—ulcers, because of this bacteria, without ever knowing about it. It can even lead to cancer if left untreated. The unfortunate thing is that most doctors don't even know about it, so they prescribe, as your other doctor did, the best thing they know—an acid blocker, which relieves symptoms, but doesn't cure the problem. The drug itself can have deadly side effects in the long run."

It seemed so odd to me that some doctors would know this while others wouldn't. I wondered why they didn't have "doctor chain letters" that spread the word around, so they would all know the latest information.

Thanking the doctor, I said, "I will do my part to let the world know. Thanks so much for helping me heal this."

"My pleasure. Just watch what you eat, as certain foods may aggravate your system. Here's a list of some of the most common foods that cause problems; it'll probably help you with your grocery shopping. Remember to stay away from acid-forming foods like red meat."

On the way home, feeling a little impatient, I said, "It sounds like this is going to take several weeks to heal. When you think about everything having a reason, I have to wonder why this ulcer thing happened. You know what I mean? I don't understand what possible reason a time setback like this could have."

Jessie replied, "Maybe you should reframe the way you are looking at it. Maybe it isn't a 'time setback' at all. Maybe it's just a reminder to slow down and enjoy each moment along the way. Maybe it was a test of your commitment—and an opportunity to work on your book." She grinned at me. "Plus, I get to have you home for a while."

I could see that my need for control was interfering with my resourcefulness—also with my grasp of the obvious! Time with Jessie in our home, surrounded by the beauty of my beloved red rocks—things could be a lot worse! I took a deep breath and said, "Yeah, you're right. When I look at the results, I can see that what it has really done has been to renew my appreciation and gratitude. I really do feel blessed to be alive!"

Just then we came around the next bend to the sight of the most brilliant rainbow I had ever seen stretching out before us.

I pointed and exclaimed, "Look, Jessie! Look at that rainbow!"

She responded in awe, "It's so beautiful!"

Its colors were glistening in the morning light, getting brighter and more vivid as we drew closer. All the rainbows I had seen before kept moving as I got closer to them, thus never allowing me to reach the end. This one, however, seemed stationary, unmoving, undaunted by our threat of reaching its legendary pot of gold. As we kept driving, we got closer and closer to it. Around the next turn, cars were pulled over to the side of the road; people were taking pictures or just standing around watching this most unusual rainbow, as its majestic arc touched down right in the middle of the highway. It appeared we would drive right through it if we kept going. For some reason it never occurred to us to stop and join the onlookers. We just kept heading right toward the wall of color. I felt as though we were in a scene from *Star Trek*, about to boldly go where no one, to my knowledge, had gone before—into the color spectrum. As we passed through, the rainbow didn't dissipate as I expected, and it wasn't only a quick flash as I also might have thought. Instead, for several seconds, we were surrounded by the colors. Both of us were speechless as we saw the world through multi-colored radiance.

It all happened quickly, but once on the other side, everything looked even more beautiful than it had before. I noticed even the smallest things, the flowers blooming on the side of the road, a lizard scurrying from rock to rock. The thought of how close I had come to not ever seeing these things again, or holding Jessie's hand, or talking with my boys, choked me up. I reveled in appreciation for all that surrounded me. My eyes welled up with tears of gratitude, and I had to wonder if this was just a delayed reaction to the life-threatening experience I had so recently endured. I closed my eyes and said a prayer of thanks for my life and everything that it held.

As I wandered in my own world, Jessie pulled me out. "Wow, that was beautiful. Did you see that, Matt? We were actually *in* the rainbow!"

Still speechless with gratitude, all I could do was nod. As Jessie looked over to see if I was okay, a glimmer caught her eye. She exclaimed, "Look, Matt, look on the seat next to you!"

There, between us on the seat, was a golden ring. Our eyes met, both of us slightly in shock over the sequence of events.

She asked, "What does it say?"

I knew before I even looked that it was the ring of gratitude. Sure enough, I read to Jessie, "It says *Appreciation.*"

We both laughed out loud as she said, "So, there *is* gold at the end of the rainbow!"

Alea rejoiced because Matt had chosen life. She'd not been completely certain that he would, as the peacefulness of death is something that is usually quite unexpected to the dying. Somehow the living have created a vision of death as a horrible thing. When one actually comes face to face with it, it isn't always such a bad option. The hardest part is if a person is not complete with life. In this case, she knew that Matt wasn't ready to go, and she was happy to see that he had recognized that, too. He had renewed his commitment to his mission through the clarity of his choice.

Matt had come to a place of even greater appreciation for his life, the people in it and all that he encountered. Appreciation is the foundation for spirituality. It is part of seeing God in every thing and every action. It represents a trust in a higher purpose and greater force, a divine wisdom. When all is received with true gratitude, we realize that nothing but blessings surround us, that all we need to do is reframe our vision of the circumstance and, generally, the rhyme and reason will become clear. In certain situations, we may never know why something has happened, but by offering thanks to God for it, in trust of the divine plan, we move quickly into resourcefulness, reminding us once again of our Source.

Alea was convinced that Matt would heal quickly and resume his quest to wake the world, end the chain of pain and restore resourcefulness.

She watched as Jessie and Matt drove down the road, sharing the splendor of their magical moment together within the rainbow, and giggling about it like a couple of kids. She loved to see them happy, for it is only "in the moment" that true happiness exists. Her vision shifted from just the two of them as she pulled back her perspective into more of a bird's-eye view. Now she saw a car full of love and joy moving down the highway, surrounded by absolute beauty. When she pulled her focus even further back, she saw people getting back into their cars after observing a magnificent event. Some were talking excitedly, some were disappointed that the rainbow had left, and some were just anxious to get back to whatever they had been doing. But the children were all filled with delight, recognizing the simplest of blessings.

16

The Healing

Several weeks went by, during which I recuperated at home and worked on my book. That the manuscript was nearly finished pleased me. My strength was returning, and I was anxious to teach seminars again. Daryl and I had talked a few times; he'd called to see how I was doing and to check on how soon I'd be able to get back out on the road. We scheduled a workshop for the next month, sure that by then I would be close to 100 percent. We filled each other in on the different events in our lives and hung up looking forward to seeing each other again.

Being captive at home afforded Jessie and me some much-enjoyed time together. We went for daily walks, talking about our lives and what we each wanted out of them. She started her new job, but only worked half-days until I was fully recuperated. She absolutely loved working with the children and came home daily with funny stories to share on our walks. Being around all the kids amplified her maternal instincts. The yearning to be a mother was a strong force in her life. Given that perfectly reasonable—even exalted—excuse, we made love a lot.

One evening while we were reading out on the deck, I turned to Jessie and asked, "Remember when I suggested we go on our honeymoon? Have you been thinking about where you'd like to go?" I knew a vacation was well overdue.

She looked thoughtful as we watched the sun slowly sink on the horizon. "Oh, I don't know. I've always wanted to go to Egypt. What about you?"

I didn't want to take my eyes off her; the sunlight from this golden time of day was dancing off her hair, making her glow. "I'd like to go there, too, but it doesn't matter where, as long as we go together."

She smiled, "I'll do some research and see if I can find a spot that we'd both like."

The sun slipped behind a rock formation, sending rays of light toward the heavens. The clouds were instantly gilded, adding the final touch of magnificence. I uttered the only thought that went through my mind as I watched God's display. "This is miraculous. We are surrounded by miracles, Jessie."

The phone rang, interrupting my moment of awe. Reluctantly I answered it, "Hello?"

"Hi, Matt? Jane. Remember me? I'm the one who came up to you after your workshop in Los Angeles and asked if you would be available to speak at the United Nations."

Remembering, I said, "Oh yes! Hi, how are you?"

"Fine, fine. Thanks for asking. Hey, I've been working on getting you into the U. N., and I'm pretty sure I've got it sewn up. My friend who arranges it has taken my word about you so far, but before she finalizes anything, she'd like to speak with you and see a promo package. Would you mind giving her a call in the next few days?"

My mind was swirling as I wrote down the woman's name and number. The United Nations! I answered her, "No problem. I really appreciate the effort you've put in. Thank you, Jane."

She brushed off my expressions of gratitude by saying, "I'm not doing it for you, I'm doing it for the world—and it's my pleasure. Let me know how it comes out. Right now she said she has you penciled in for two months from now."

I could hardly believe my ears. "Well, that's exciting! I'll let you know what happens. Thank you again!"

I hung up the phone in a state of pleasant disbelief. Jessie called out, "What was that about, Honey?"

In a nonchalant manner, I teased, "Oh nothing, just the United Nations booking me as a speaker."

Her eyes opened wide and she threw her arms around me. "Oh, Matt, that's wonderful! Wow, what an impact you'll make there!"

I was touched by her confidence. She had no hesitation, no doubt of my ability; she accepted the fact of the invitation as an honor, one that was deserved.

We spent the evening celebrating, rejoicing in life and love, and giving thanks.

The next morning Nan called.

I was happy to hear from her; it seemed as if so much had happened since I had spoken with her last. "How's it going? It's good to hear from you!"

She said gingerly, "It's good to hear you! Every time I've thought about you in the last month, I've gotten this really uncomfortable feeling. Are you okay?"

I apologized for not calling her sooner and recounted the whole story, bringing her up to date.

She asked, "Are you okay now?"

"As far as I know, but of course I didn't know anything was wrong in the first place. It appears that I'm well on my way to restored health. I just have to watch what I eat; certain things aggravate my stomach."

"Well, you sound good. The other reason I'm calling is, I recently went through a business seminar in Los Angeles that was awesome. It's right up your alley; I think you would be a great speaker there."

Curious, I asked, "What is it about?"

Excitedly, she answered, "These folks teach about enlightened capitalism. Their focus is on how we can work together through a cooperative model, rather than a competitive one, to help each other achieve our dreams! The idea is that we all approach the class from a perspective of give and receive—if everyone goes there with the intent of giving their assistance to others, everyone will receive assistance as well. It's like a mixture of personal growth and business all in one."

I responded more to her enthusiasm than what she was saying. "I can tell that you really loved it, Nan. Are they asking the students to sell something?"

She quickly clarified, "No, the training is to help you do whatever you want to do. They don't have a hidden agenda. I promise."

Satisfied with her explanation, I asked, "When is the next one? What are the details?"

Sounding relieved that I didn't resist the idea, she answered, "I spoke with the founder, Sterling, and told him about you. He's interested in speaking with you. He is an amazing man, Matt. You can see it in his eyes—a true visionary, who has created this income-building forum as a place where our spiritual family can find each other. You wouldn't believe the people I've met there—it's like you and me, you know, lasting friendships. Real friendships. His wife, Linda, president of the company, is really special, too."

I had never heard Nan so excited about anything in the time I had known her. She wasn't the type to get caught up in hype and short-term enthusiasm. I trusted that she found true value there, or she wouldn't have called to tell me about it.

I asked her, "What do I need to do? Who do you want me to call?"

She answered, "The next class is in two weeks. If you call them today, they may still be able to put you in the schedule. Sterling and I got along really well. I told him about you, and he is expecting your call."

As soon as we hung up, I called him; we spoke for nearly an hour. While he did most of the talking, I found what he had to say to be of unusual depth. He had an interesting mixture of being intensely spiritual and a hard-core businessman at the same time, a combination I had rarely run into. I shared my background with him and arranged to speak at his next class. He offered me a trial opportunity to see how well I fit in with his organization. He requested that, even though I would only be speaking for an hour and a half on one day, I stay for the whole week to offer my consultations for free to the students for the duration of the week. He explained that the give and receive principle worked best that way, and that I would get the most out of it if

I were involved with the students and their projects. We hung up looking forward to meeting each other in person. I felt as though I had just encountered a whirlwind.

Confident that I was on a roll, I called the woman from the United Nations as well. I told her about myself and the kind of work I did and gave her additional references. After giving me her preferred dates and requesting a promo package, she said, "My friend Jane can't stop talking about your seminar, but that isn't what has me convinced. What I am impressed with is how different she is. Without getting into great detail, just let me say, 'Thank you.' Your work has really transformed her. Look, go ahead and put New York on your calendar. If there are any changes, I'll call and let you know."

I couldn't believe how well things were falling into place. I spent the following weeks writing and planning, as well as spending time with Jessie. We talked about the workshop Nan had gone to and my conversation with Sterling.

She asked, "So what do you get out of spending a week at this class?"

I wondered if she was unhappy that I was leaving so much or just curious. I sat in silence for a few minutes then answered, "I don't really know. I am mostly just following Nan's intuition—and my own. It just feels like something that I should do; I'm not really sure why." I added as an afterthought, "I guess I'll find out, once I get there. Are you sure you don't want to come?"

"No, thanks. I don't want to take the time off work. I really love what I'm doing and don't know why I would want to go to this."

My intent was to get up early the next morning, drive to Phoenix and catch a flight to Los Angeles.

Jessie came in to talk while I was packing and said, "I found this book about Egypt on your shelf. It looks pretty interesting. I'm going to read through it and see if it sounds like someplace we'd enjoy visiting."

Recognizing the book as one that I had had for years but never read, I smiled and replied, "Sounds good to me! Jessie?"

"Yes?"

I stopped what I was doing and came over and sat next to her on the bed. She looked a little concerned, as if whatever I was about to say was going to have some sort of major impact on her life. I put my arm around her and said, "May I have the pleasure of your company on a dinner date this evening?"

Between my father dying, my workshops and my sudden health problem, we hadn't been on an official date in a long time.

She laughed at the formal manner in which I had asked, and with a mock-Shakespearean flourish answered, "Why, Sir, truly honored would I be, at any hour to sup with thee!" It might not have been quite up to old Will's standards, but it made us both laugh, and of that I'm sure he would have approved.

We went to an early dinner at our favorite restaurant and then went to a movie as well. We held hands and acted like the newlyweds we were. By the end of the evening, I was convinced that my energy had been completely restored.

Early the next morning, I held her close to me and kissed her goodbye. She whispered, "The only way it's okay for you to leave for the week is if you promise to come back. Remember, dying is against the rules."

Kissing her again, I said, "I promise, Jessie, you're stuck with me for life."

Teasingly she corrected, "For a *long* life!"

We waved to each other until I rounded the corner. I missed her as soon as she was out of sight.

Not too many people were stirring at this hour of the morning, just the usual walkers and joggers enjoying the sunrise and cool air. I made my way out of town and hit the open highway, loving the solitude of driving in the desert. It provided me an opportunity for just letting my thoughts drift. The empty spaces were like a clean tablet for my ideas. I often found this kind of drive to be a most creative time.

This particular morning Alea came to mind, as she often did when I was driving. I wondered whether this was the way it was going to continue to be with her—leaving signs of her presence periodically, but never really coming around for a full conversation again. It saddened me to imagine. I thought of my youngest son—the imaginary friend he used to tell me about, and how sad he was the day he announced that his friend had left. I wondered now if he really had had a friend, and whether our assumptions about him making it up were all wrong.

I tried to imagine what Alea and I had shared in another life. It made me wonder whether I had done something wrong between that time and this, because I was still a human and she didn't appear to be. Of course, I didn't know what she was. Who's to say that a human is any less of an exalted being than those from the more ethereal realms, anyhow? Maybe it is merely choice. When we die, maybe we get to choose whether we want to come back and work things through on the physical plane or be part of the "support team."

I amused myself throughout the two-hour drive, trying to imagine different scenarios in which Alea and I might have been together. I also wondered what this "pain" was that she referred to. How had she hurt me? Not even able to imagine, I held the vision that we had loved each other very much and, as evidenced by our present relationship, that our love had endured through time.

Just before turning into the parking lot, I pulled up behind a car with a bumper sticker that read, *Expect a Miracle.* I laughed out loud, thinking, *What else is there?*

Simply the ability to fly from one place to another seemed miraculous to me. I proceeded to create a mental "miracle list" as I flew between Phoenix and L.A. which, if I'd written it, would have been several pages long. It included everything from babies being born to finding a parking spot in a crowded lot. I was not particularly choosy over what I deemed a miracle. It just had to be something that made me immensely appreciative, or something that boggled my mind—like rainbows, flowers, butterflies, space travel. . . . The list went on and on.

Once in L.A., I settled into the hotel and let the appropriate people know that I had arrived. An air of excitement filled the lobby. A number of people seemed to know each other and were hugging happily. I discovered later that they were previous graduates of the class returning for more. As yet, I didn't know what that "more" was. Since I was a participant as well as an instructor in this class, I wasn't exactly sure of my role or what I had come here for, and the initial discomfort of meeting a bunch of new people made me question my presence here. I entertained the idea of leaving, but regrouped and decided to throw myself into the process and experience it fully. After all, I was here.

Besides, Nan had said I would like it. From that decision-point forward, I embraced the opportunity.

Over two hundred students came, all dressed to impress, equipped with ideas and dreams that they wanted to develop. Some came to find funding for their projects, some came to learn more about business, others came to discover their purpose in life, and others still, like me, had no idea why they came. Perhaps someone they loved had just managed to convince them that they should.

As the week began to unfold, I could feel anxiety among the new participants. They had spent thousands of dollars to attend, which made the stakes seem high. In the beginning, they nervously searched for whatever they came here for. As the week wore on, they started to relax into the process and trust that they were getting what they needed, even if it wasn't exactly what they had thought they were coming to get.

The classroom where the instruction took place was a high-tech, multimedia room, and the instruction made use of three large video panels, laser lights and music to activate both hemispheres of the brain. Sterling had explained to me that the process was carefully researched and engineered to bring about accelerated learning and greater retention in the individual. All in all, the whole event was quite impressive. By the middle of the week I was beginning to understand why Nan had been so excited. This was more than a seminar, it was a world-class event.

Every minute of the day was filled. When we weren't in class, we were in networking breaks, talking to each other to discover our next steps and helping each other with contacts and ideas. Even the meals were organized networking sessions. As the week continued, people loosened up and danced in the aisles of the classroom while watching themselves on the big screens, as if they were in a music video.

I had never been to a workshop in which the people attending got so close to each other. The difference was the combination of spending a week together, sharing a phenomenal experience, and the vulnerability of speaking about our hopes and dreams. By the end of the week, it was as if people had known each other a lifetime, with bonds as strong as those of family.

When the time for my presentation approached, I went backstage to set up and found a quiet corner in which to meditate before going out. Within the time allowed me, I managed to communicate the simplicity and importance of letting go, as well as the value of resourcefulness. As I was speaking, I felt moved to talk about miracles.

"I saw a bumper sticker the other day that said, *Expect a Miracle,* and I had to laugh, because people could go through their entire lives *expecting* one without ever seeing and *receiving* one. We ought to change the concept to *Accept a Miracle!*"

Everyone laughed, and I went on to explain, "Miracles surround us everywhere; we have just gotten to a point of taking them for granted. Think about it. What qualifies as a miracle? If you ask a question in your mind and an answer comes to you, is that a miracle?"

I paused for a moment to let them think, then added, "I think so. What about a flower? Is that a miracle? How about a blade of grass that manages to work its way up through cement to reach for the light; is that a miracle? How about food that grows on plants? Water, that we can drink, that falls from the sky? What counts as a miracle for you?"

I stopped to let them think some more, then continued, "Consider this: not only are we given food to eat and water to drink, but every other thing we need to survive. And yet, it goes beyond survival. We are given everything we need to thrive. Look around—all the things that we need are delivered to us with absolute beauty and grace. It's not as if we were put in a cell in which our food is delivered and we are merely surviving in a bleak place. Rather, we are here in a place that, if we had just dropped in from some other place and time, we would consider to be Heaven, paradise. Beauty is everywhere we look, there is nothing else—unless we have created it.

"People think the Garden of Eden was a place that existed a long time ago and that the human species got thrown out for succumbing to temptation. In actuality, we are still in the Garden of Eden and we never got thrown out. We just gave in to temptations that pulled us from the mind-set of appreciation and thankfulness to one of want and greed and emptiness. It was a matter of an attitude shift rather than a change of locations. The same is still true today.

"How do you shift the attitude? By letting go, becoming resourceful—*once again full of Source*—and going forward from there.

"People spend so much time praying and asking for solutions to their problems that they forget to leave enough time to be open to receiving and for being thankful for what we already have. What we need to do is pray short and listen long—and take a look around with new fresh eyes.

"Instead of praying in desperation, pray in appreciation! Somewhere along the line we got the impression that giving is the ultimate act of spirituality and, of course, it is a wonderful thing to do. However, without the ability to receive, we have nothing to give, and we completely turn our backs on the gifts that God is offering us—not allowing God to give. A spiritual act is not complete if the giver gives, but the receiver doesn't receive.

"When you set out to create your projects, dreams and businesses, be sure that you are open to receiving the blessings along the way. Be open to receiving the perfect team members. Be open to receiving the capital that you are raising. Be open to developing and using the talents and skills that you have been blessed with to the best of your ability. Look around you for the grace and miracles that are everywhere. Become resourceful—accept miracles as part of the resources available to you! Take the miracles you've been given and share them with others. In this way, you honor God."

After I concluded, Sterling thanked me and invited me to speak again at the next class. I accepted his invitation, happy that the class was going so well.

By the end of the week, returning graduates began showing up; they were permitted to come back to the class on weekends for free, to network with the new students and other graduates. An air of festivity was mixed with a quiet sadness that this week-long experience was almost over.

Nan, now a graduate, returned for the weekend as well. She came up to me excitedly and asked, "So what do you think?"

We hugged and I said, "Awesome, Nan. This has been an incredible week. The magnitude of effort that goes into creating an event like this is overwhelming to think about. Oh, and you were so right about the wonderful people."

We walked into the lobby Friday evening, where a group of new and returning graduates were sitting around a woman I had never seen. From what I could gather from the conversation, she was an alchemist visiting for the weekend and was giving the people in the group some aromatic substance that was supposed to help them open up to their success, fulfilling whatever wish they might have. I watched as she anointed a woman with some sort of fragrant oil.

Almost as if on some invisible cue, the group seemed to dissipate suddenly, until Nan and I were the only ones left. The alchemist got up and stood in front of me. Something about her was intriguing, although I couldn't put my finger on it. She had a sparkle in her eye and a strength about her presence, but other than that and her taller-than-average height for a woman, I couldn't place what drew me to her.

She looked at me and announced, "I am Alexandria and I came here for you."

Surprised, I asked, "What do you mean?"

Ignoring my question, she pointed to the couch and said, "Sit down."

I looked for Nan's reaction to find she had already sat down to watch, intrigued by this woman. Alexandria had not attended the class and wasn't a past graduate, so it was unclear as to why she was even here.

She instructed me to unbutton the top buttons of my shirt and then held a small bottle up to my nose and asked, "Does that smell okay to you?"

The scent was heavenly, a mixture I couldn't identify but which sparked little memory synapses in my brain. She began rubbing it on my chest in a three-inch circle over my heart.

My brain struggled with whether or not to allow this, not at all clear about what was happening. Here I was at a business seminar, in the middle of a public lobby, and now I was being anointed by an alchemist? It was on the edge of being too weird, but on the other hand, my curiosity was piqued. I decided to proceed, but not without questions.

Sounding both skeptical and ignorant, I inquired, "What are you doing?"

She looked me in the eyes with a penetrating stare that had the intensity of some kind of bird of prey and answered simply, "I am protecting your heart."

Surprised, I probed some more, "From what?"

Now looking at my heart and the place she was rubbing, she answered humbly, "I don't know; I was just told to do this."

At which point she proceeded to anoint my head in various places, behind my ears, the base of my throat, the center of my forehead. If I hadn't had so many strange and wonderful things happen over the last year, I would have gotten up and walked away. At this point, though, not too much surprised me. I decided to relax and see what happened, resisting the urge to ask, "*Who* told you to do this?"

She then instructed me to close my eyes and open my mouth, saying she was going to put a drop of special clay in my mouth and as she did, she wanted me to hold a wish, as if in prayer. She told me to meditate on it.

Without taking the time to make a wish, my mind started thinking about putting clay in my mouth and why I would ever allow someone to do that. My heart must have been running the ship though, because the next thing I knew, a drop of a fragrant, almost rose-flavored, chalky substance was oozing across my tongue. Letting go of my thoughts, I felt very relaxed and spontaneously began to meditate. Within seconds I felt as if I left my body, and suddenly I was sitting among lotus flowers in the pitch black of night. Thousands of flowers surrounded me, as far as I could see in all directions. I looked up at the night sky and was treated to the sight of millions of brilliant stars. It was all so real, as if I were truly right there. I sat and enjoyed the peace and beauty for several minutes. It was so quiet, as if the silence had depth to it.

Someone in the lobby made a sound, which brought my attention back to the room. I opened my eyes to see Alexandria smiling at me. As I hugged her to thank her for the experience, I closed my eyes for another moment and was immediately transported right back among the lotuses again.

I pulled away from her and said sincerely, "Wow. Thank you. That was very relaxing."

Then after reviewing it all in my mind again, not sure what any of it meant, I added, "Well, I'm going to go up to bed."

She quietly informed me, "You aren't finished yet," and then turned away to pack up her things.

Nan walked with me down the hall, asking, "So, where'd you just go? I mean, within seconds your head dropped and you were gone."

"It was beautiful, Nan. It was a bed of lotus flowers and a pitch black night sky. The only light was from millions of twinkling bright stars." Even as I described it, I could see it in my mind as if I were there.

We passed her room on the way to mine and hugged good night. I then continued on, feeling ready for a good night's sleep.

I got ready for bed and, after propping up the pillows, leaned against them with my eyes closed, determined to think about what had transpired. Suddenly, I was again surrounded by lotuses. I sat there meditating in this heavenly, aromatic place, just as peacefully as I had done downstairs in the lobby. After some time, an arched window appeared off to the side, and then the next thing I knew, I was in some sort of a temple. People in white flowing gowns were moving about their business, ignoring my presence. It was very quiet; the only audible sounds were soft footsteps and the subtle rustling of their robes. As I looked around, I saw before me a bed draped with a sheer white curtain. The closer I got, the more obvious it became that a woman was lying on it. She wore a veil; I could see her eyes, but not the rest of her face. I knelt beside the bed and looked at her. I was suddenly struck with an inner knowing that the woman was dying and that she was someone that I loved and cared for very deeply.

As I knelt there I began to cry, torn with the anguish that I could do nothing to save her. I felt somehow responsible for her death, while at the same time powerless to change the inevitable. My heart ached as she looked at me with adoration.

I reached out and pulled the veil away. Seeing her face, I gasped and cried out, "Alea!"

Heart-wrenching sobs ripped through my body all the way to my soul, as I watched her take her last breaths.

I opened my eyes, still crying, to find myself back in my hotel room. My pillowcase was soaked with tears, and my body felt weak from exhaustion and despair. The clock indicated that somehow two hours had passed. Questions raced through my mind: *What had just happened? Was that Alea now? Is she dead, or was that a glimpse back in time to the life we had shared together?* Maybe I had just fallen asleep, and it was a dream—a very real dream.

I sat up on the edge of the bed, trying to recover from the vision I had endured. I closed my eyes for a moment and immediately I was once again right back among the lotus flowers. Staying there for only seconds, I was suddenly transported again to the temple, only this time I stood in front of it. Almost as if viewing a movie in reverse, Alea was still alive, and I was now viewing what my life with her had been like. I watched as she and I walked along a river's edge, laughing with joy in each other's companionship. The love we held for each other was so strong; I could feel it just watching.

Then there was a flash, like a scene change in a film, and I was suddenly in prison and being told that Alea was to be poisoned as my punishment. I sensed from the vision that somehow she and I had managed to communicate telepathically, which was against the law, and consequently we were both being punished.

Again I was ripped with anguish. I forced myself to open my eyes so as not to have to endure it again. After washing my face, I went back to bed, willing myself to sleep immediately.

The next morning, I woke up still exhausted. I lay in bed thinking about what had transpired the night before, trying to make sense out of the vision. *Had my love for Alea caused her to be killed as my punishment? Was this the pain Alea had referred to, that had not been healed?* I could see, if this were true, that I would never be able to forgive myself for doing something that would cause her to lose her life.

All of this seemed to create more questions than answers, and I desperately wanted to talk with Alea. The phone rang, pulling me back to the reason I was here in the hotel at all. "Hello?"

"Matt, it's Nan. Are you up?"

I answered quietly, "Hi, Nan. Yeah, I'm up, just moving slowly. Where are you?"

She said cheerfully, "I'm in the lobby. I was wondering if you wanted to have breakfast together. You sound tired. Are you all right?"

"Yeah, I'm all right. I'll tell you about it over breakfast. Alexandria stirred up a lot of stuff last night. I don't know. I'm still trying to sort it all out."

Excitedly, she answered, "Oh, I can hardly wait to hear!"

As much as I loved Nan, I wasn't sure I was ready for her enthusiasm this morning. Every time I thought about last night and saw Alea dying in my mind, I wanted to cry again. In this condition, I was not anxious to go downstairs and see all the people with whom I'd spent the week. Under the circumstances, I couldn't be interested in their dreams with any kind of sincerity right now.

I pulled myself together and headed downstairs, avoiding eye contact along the way. I felt that my sadness was written all over my face. I kept worrying about Alea, afraid that she was dead now, as well as in the vision.

Nan was waiting for me at a table in the restaurant. She must have sensed my mood, because she was more subdued than she had been on the phone.

With a loving look, she said, "You look like hell this morning, Matt. What happened?"

I laughed in spite of myself and said, "Oh thank you! That's what I love about you, Nan; you have a way of making a guy feel so special!"

We both laughed. Then she took my hand and said, "Seriously, are you okay?"

I looked her in the eyes and said, "I had to drag myself down here this morning. I feel like I could start crying at any minute. Whatever Alexandria did to me last night, boy, it opened the floodgates to my past with Alea."

Nan's mouth dropped. "Did Alea come back?"

"No, not exactly. Instead I went back in time—I think—to when she and I had been in love. I saw her die, Nan. I saw her on her deathbed all dressed in white, and it seemed like it was all my fault."

My voice started to crack as I talked, and I felt that stinging surge in my nose that happens when you're trying to hold back the tears. She looked at me and said, "Do you want to go back upstairs to talk about this?"

I took a deep breath and drank some water, letting go of some of the energy that was building. "No. Let's stay and have breakfast. If I go back up there, I'll go through the whole thing again, and I really don't want to."

She responded supportively, "Okay, if you're sure. I'll keep people away if they try and join us. I'll tell them we're in a meeting."

I appreciated her understanding and protection. Fortunately, because this was the last day of the seminar, it wasn't as structured as the other days. The official classes were over, and everything offered today was optional except for the closing ceremony that night. Even this early, networking meetings were going on all over the place. I looked around for Alexandria, but she didn't appear to be in the restaurant. I wanted to ask her about what had happened.

Nan listened intently as I shared with her the sequence of events. I explained why it seemed as though it had been my fault, and how terrible I had felt seeing Alea die and, even worse, being responsible.

She said, "Wow, that is like a regular *Romeo and Juliet* tragedy—the kind you wish you could reverse, because it just isn't right."

I added, "Yeah, you know, Nan, I felt in that other world that Alea was someone really important, like royalty, or a goddess of some sort. I think that was part of the problem. I felt like it was my job to protect her or serve her, and instead we fell in love, sharing a love that was sacred, but forbidden."

All the while I was talking, in my mind I was right back at the temple. I went on, "Here I was supposed to be protecting her, when I was the very reason she was being harmed. I sure wish I could talk to Alea now."

A woman walked over to our table and said, "Hi," then turned to Nan to ask her when they could meet. Nan set up a time, then introduced me to the woman. "Matt, this is Jessica. Jessica—Matt."

I managed to smile and say, "Nice to meet you," even though I was wondering why Nan was introducing me instead of protecting me as promised.

Jessica said, "I didn't mean to interrupt your meeting. Before I go, I just have to tell you, Matt, that my gift, or my miracle, is the ability to see people's angels. Then I paint them. Someday I'd really like to paint yours, because you have all kinds of angels around you."

With that, she smiled, looking around my head as if she were seeing someone else, and then turned and walked away.

Nan and I looked at each other and started laughing. I said, "If she only knew! See Nan, this just doesn't ever stop. My poor head is having a hard time keeping up with all this airy-fairy stuff."

We both laughed some more, and then Nan added, seriously, "Well, Matt, I'm sure you wouldn't be attracting all this mystical input if there wasn't a pretty grand reason for it. After all, most of the folks here are regular people doing real business. You must be a strong magnet right now." Pausing for a moment, she added, "My sense is, and has been all along, that before you know it you will be speaking to thousands, making a huge difference on the planet."

"I forgot to tell you! I've been invited to speak to the United Nations!"

"Oh, Matt! That is great! When?"

"In just about two months."

After breakfast and talking with Nan, I felt more grounded, less on the edge. I managed to pull myself together and went back up to my room and made my daily call to Jessie. She wasn't home, so I left a message and then went back downstairs to network. I decided to get involved for the day, so I wouldn't have to think about Alea or the temple or what had happened.

The day went by relatively smoothly. I kept an eye open for Alexandria but never saw her again.

The time of the final closing ceremony arrived. Nan and I sat together as one of the class instructors debriefed our week and shared some tips on how to reenter the "real" world. As I listened to the instructor, I could hardly believe that only a week had passed. It seemed as though I had been here for at least a year.

They then announced that we were going to end the week with a dance of universal peace, a Sufi dance. Having never done one before, I didn't know what to expect as they had us form two concentric circles, the outer one facing inward, the inner one facing outward, so everyone had a partner. After teaching us the lyrics and the hand movements that went with them, we were instructed to sing the verse and go through the movements with our partner, then step once to the right and start again with a new partner.

The instructor explained the meaning of the hand movements; the final gesture, bowing to each other with the hands together at the heart as if in prayer, was to honor *Hu* in the other. He explained that *Hu* in the Sufi tradition meant *"The Spirit of God."*

Nan and I stood across from each other as initial partners, when we were given one last guideline. The instructor said, "Some of you are natural receivers, while others are natural givers. As you establish eye contact with the person across from you, be conscious to do both—give yourself and receive the other."

I thought of my definition in the hospital of inspire and expire. Here, face to face, eye to eye with another, the process was that of giving and receiving. Breathing spirit in and out.

Then the instructor said, "Let the dance begin."

With that, two hundred people began to sing:

May the blessings of God rest upon you.
May God's peace abide with you.
May God's presence illuminate your heart,
Now and forevermore.

We switched from person to person, singing the song of prayer and making the appropriate gestures, praying with our hands as well as our words. We gave this gift of blessing and received it at the same time. I was surprised at how close I felt to so many of them after just one week. One after the other they came, each one a new surprise. Some were crying, some were smiling, some were present and some were not. The intensity of being seen and being honored by another was overwhelming. The song just kept going and going, until it became like a mantra, as natural as the beating of one's heart.

The whole time I felt as if I were in love, in love with life, in love with hundreds of other people. I felt pain when I looked into the eyes of a few, and with that I sent them extra prayers. I understood how hard it could be to be treated like a soul deserving of God's love, joy and happiness, when you didn't have that same belief about yourself. As I sang the song and connected more deeply with these friends and strangers than I had with members of my own family, I felt full and complete.

When Nan and I were once again face to face as original partners, we sang the song again, one last time. I sang it this time with extra emphasis, as I deeply appreciated her influence and friendship in my life. *"May the blessings of God rest upon you. May God's peace abide with you. May God's presence illuminate your heart, now and forevermore."*

The love in the room was tangible. Many people were crying tears of both joy and sadness. We knew this would be the last time we would all be together and recognized what a miracle it was that just this exact combination of people had been in the same place on the planet at the same time. I wished that Jessie had been here, too. I would have liked to share something this affecting with her.

After hugging almost everyone, Nan and I escaped and went out for sushi. She said, "There was a guy in the class I went through who kept telling his wife the entire week that they shouldn't have come to class. Then on the last night, she dragged him into the closing ceremony still complaining, and that's when his heart opened and he really felt the meaning of this whole experience—the power of authentically sharing yourself with others in a give-and-receive exchange."

I listened, then commented, "I can imagine there are people who come here who aren't ready for this intensity, or who have no idea what to expect. It's certainly unlike any business class I ever dreamed of!"

We ate, shared our experiences and then returned to the hotel, where people were still networking. They looked as if they were on a roll and might be at it all night.

I said to Nan, "Well, I'm going to go call Jessie and try to find some way of explaining this whole experience adequately. It seems like an impossible task. . . ." I then added, "I'm exhausted."

As I spoke of my tiredness, I was flooded with a memory of why I hadn't had much sleep the night before, and a slight anxiety came over me; I wasn't sure what to expect when I closed my eyes. I took a deep breath and let it go, then wished Nan a good night.

She sensed my concerns and hugged me, saying, "Don't worry, Matt. The angels are with you. Sweet dreams."

I went up to my room and called Jessie. Somehow, after hearing about the events of her day, I managed to communicate the depth and multiplicity of experiences here. There were so many facets beyond the business benefits that it was hard to imagine if you hadn't been through it. While being very supportive of me, she made it clear that she wouldn't be interested in attending. She was happy that I was enjoying the experience and was missing me.

I was tempted to tell her about my experience with the alchemist and seeing Alea, but decided to wait until I got home. I didn't feel like it all made sense yet and wanted to think about it some more. I also didn't want her to hear all of this and think I was losing my mind, without her being able to see me face to face as an assurance that I was okay.

With sincerity, I said, "This has been an awesome experience that I wouldn't have wanted to miss. I'm really glad I came, but I sure have missed being with you. I'll be back tomorrow night, Jessie. I can't wait to see you."

"I can't wait to see you, too! How are you feeling, Matt? I keep forgetting to ask you, after hearing all about your adventures."

I answered honestly, "Right this minute I'm exhausted, but in general I've been feeling pretty good. This isn't a good place for recuperation, because there is constant activity from early in the morning until late at night, but I've managed pretty well. Thanks for asking, Honey. I'll see you tomorrow. I love you."

I hung up the phone, thankful to have her in my life.

I showered to wash the energy of the day off, in hopes that I would sleep more easily. Sitting down on the edge of the bed, I turned off the light and stretched, reaching my arms up toward the ceiling, feeling my muscles expand and relax.

Still with my eyes closed, I saw a bright dot of light in front of my eyes. My first thoughts, as I became aware of it, were that I must have looked at the light bulb too long. My mind stayed with the thought and I kept my eyes closed, looking at the bright dot, making a game out of wondering how long it would take for it to finally fade away.

Much to my surprise, the light didn't fade out and disappear as I expected it to and had seen many times before. Instead, it kept expanding and getting brighter. I watched as it began to spin, looking much like a galaxy complete with trailers of light generating out from it. Thinking that I must be really tired, I kept watching to see what kind of tricks my eyes would play on me next.

Slowly, the spinning light started to take form. I watched as it turned into an angelic figure, beautiful, delicate, complete with wings. I observed her for about a minute before deciding I had better stop playing this mind game. I opened my eyes, assuming that doing so would make it disappear, but the angel didn't go away! She was standing right in front of me. I couldn't believe my eyes. I blinked a couple of times to see if my tired eyes were malfunctioning, but the angel stayed constant, glimmering.

Strange as it was to be face to face with an angel, I felt no fear, only awe at the beauty of her essence. I was speechless. Tears streamed uncontrollably from my eyes as I felt the honor of such a rare and precious sight.

She said, in a tone of voice you might expect of an angel, *"I'm here to make sure of the healing of your heart."*

She reached over and touched my heart in the exact same place that Alexandria had anointed me the day before. She shimmered with a luminescence, and I marveled at how I could see right through her. She sparkled and shimmered for a moment longer, with her hand on my chest, and then, before I could say anything, faded away.

I couldn't believe what I had just seen. This was all more than my rational mind could take in during the course of twenty-four hours. All I could do was to sleep on it and hope for some perspective by morning. I sent a prayer of thanks and went to bed.

As I laid down, I slipped my hand under my pillow to fluff it up and there, as if left by the tooth fairy, was a golden Ring of Truth. My fingers wrapped around it, and I let out a huge sigh of relief, knowing in my heart that this meant Alea was still alive. I pulled it out, reached up, turned on my light and read the message out loud: *Accept a Miracle.* Holding it to my heart, I started to laugh.

Accept a Miracle! Suddenly, under the circumstances, that seemed to be asking an awful lot! The more I thought about it, the harder I laughed, until I was holding my sides and tears were running down my face. It felt good to enjoy the simple humor of it all and to release all the seriousness and tension I had been feeling.

After my bout of laughter subsided, I turned out the light and laid back down. Going through the same routine, I slid my hand under the pillow to make it higher. I felt another golden ring! I sat bolt upright in bed and turned on the light once more, lifting the pillow up to be sure I wasn't missing anything else. There, lying on the sheets, was another beautiful golden ring that read, *Give and Receive.*

I held one ring in each hand and leaned up against the headboard, meditating on seeing and speaking with Alea. I prayed short and listened long.

She was surprised to see him laugh so hard when he found the rings, pleased that he hadn't lost his sense of humor during the rather harrowing course of events. Not at all sure how he would respond to that past lifetime's remembrance and her death, she knew he had needed to know the truth in order to make sense of it all. She had called upon his guardian angels to assist with the healing, knowing the depth of the anguish he felt.

He had been through a lot in the last few days; it was time for her to come to him, to nudge the final pieces into place. He was ready to completely heal.

The two rings that he had just earned, Accept a Miracle and Give and Receive, together with Appreciation, were very closely linked. It was important that Matt recognize the value of all three of these aspects of resourcefulness, and that he help others to recognize their value as well.

Their differences are subtle. Accepting miracles requires both willingness to receive and an openness to the awe and wonder that surrounds us—the mystery! Mystery and mysticism are the common bond of all religions, or a common bridge if you will. Alea likened the idea to that of the hand. If all the fingers represent religions, the thing they have in common is where they root, in the palm, in mysticism . . . an aspiration to communicate with the Divine and to understand the ancient mysteries through internal illumination.

Children are natural mystics, enjoying with awe and wonder even the smallest of phenomena. As we grow up however, our rational mind seeks an explanation for everything and dismisses it as unreal if we cannot come up with a suitable answer. A willingness to "Accept a Miracle" allows one to be blessed without analysis, without understanding—without proof. It is a knowing of one's "deserve-ability" to receive.

Appreciation, by subtle variation, is the experience of deep gratitude for everything, miraculous or devastating. It requires surrender in trust, knowing that everything is always as it should be, acknowledging all circumstances as opportunities to practice the fine art of letting go and returning to resourcefulness—a state of gratitude in and of itself.

Give and Receive incorporates both the giving aspects of Appreciation and the receiving aspects of Accept a Miracle, but adds the dimension of giving of oneself and receiving of others—the breathing in and out of spirit, inspiring and being inspired—in the continuous ebb and flow of life. All three of these Rings of Truth are principles upon which one can build a joyful life.

She looked upon Matt as he sat in bed studying the rings and pondering their meanings. Upon his calling out for her, she drew forth the energy required to materialize yet another time, having determined that no time was better than the present to respond.

17

Union

Out of the corner of my eye, I saw something move across the room. My prayers had been answered. I could not hold back my tears at the sight of Alea, nor did I try; I was so relieved, grateful and full of joy that she was alive. I hugged her as if I would never let her go. Hesitantly, I released her while continuing to hold her hand, wanting to hang onto some physical evidence of her presence.

I didn't know where to begin, between my questions and recitations of what had happened since I had seen her last. I wanted to know so much. Who was she? What exactly did I do to cause her death? Where did the angel come from? The questions went on and on.

She helped me out by saying, *"I know you have many unanswered questions, Matt. That is why I am here—to help you with understanding, so you will be freed to go forward."*

I started with, "Where have you been? I've really missed you, Alea."

"Where do you think I go?"

I had hoped that she would just tell me the answers without making me work for them, but that never had been her style. I responded,

"Well, I don't really feel like you go anywhere, I guess. It seems as if you are always here, but you just aren't always available for my physical senses." Then I added, "You know, I have accepted you coming and going without knowing who or what you are, but now I really want to know. Ruling out what you are not has been easier than determining what you are."

Alea started laughing, amused with my struggle to understand. *"And what have you ruled out?"*

"Well, I have determined that you are not a ghost," I continued, in spite of the fact that her laughter had gotten louder. "I have also ruled out the possibility that you are an angel," adding with a bit of sarcasm, "because I am an expert on angels now."

Her laughter was contagious; I appreciated the lightness of the conversation. I then added, "For a while, I thought you were an aspect of myself, because you were always with me and knew everything I did, but that would mean I was hallucinating. You were too real for me to accept that option."

She seemed to enjoy hearing my thought processes, so I continued, "I figure you are a couple of things. I believe you and I were together in a past life and that you are now some sort of guide—assigned to me, if you will."

I glanced at her for visual signs of confirmation. She had stopped laughing and looked more serious as I spoke; I assumed this meant I was getting close. In my mind, I once again saw her on her deathbed, and tears came to my eyes. "What happened, Alea? Was I responsible for your death? I couldn't live with that; I never want to hurt you."

My brain flipped back and forth between the here and now and my vision of the past. It seemed silly to explain or apologize for something that apparently took place centuries ago, in some other place and time, but I needed to make amends, to clearly let her know how I felt.

She chose her words carefully. *"Matt, it wasn't your fault. It was our fault—actually, my fault. I allowed it. I was the forbidden one, not you. You see, as you have already gathered, my position was High Priestess, or Goddess of the temple, if you will. Your job was to serve and protect me. It was strictly forbidden that I be in love with one man as opposed to all of humankind. As you came to me each day, in service and adoration, it became impossible to resist your love and devotion.*

"Since we could not physically act on our passion, we spent hours and hours in meditation together, learning to entwine our thoughts and feelings. In the process, we discovered how to communicate telepathically and even to project ourselves out of our bodies so that we could be together. This activity was strictly forbidden. The power of our spiritual union scared my people even more than it would have if we had been physical lovers."

She had a faraway look in her eyes, as if she were reliving the past as she told it. *"We had kept our connection sacred—and a secret, but others of the temple were suspicious. I didn't fulfill my duties with a single-focused mind, distracted as I was by the love I held for you. To make the story short, we were discovered. Since I served in such an important position and had broken the sacred laws, I was sentenced to death. You were imprisoned for a time, but they knew that watching me die, and feeling responsible for it, would imprison you for eternity. There is no pain greater than feeling responsible for another person's death, especially that of someone you love. Of course, I too, felt responsible for your pain, for your grief. "*

She paused for a moment then said, *"However, these details are not important. The important truth is, I have come to set you free."*

The truth of her words seared my heart.

She continued, *"As soon as I was in a position to become your guide, I did, knowing that I could help you heal from this pain. I had to wait until you were ready, until you realized that the things that you used to numb your pain—things that only money could buy—were no longer what you truly sought. That was my opening, the window through which I could enter your consciousness and assist toward your healing."*

I didn't know what to say. My mind raced to put all the pieces together.

"But Matt, I can no longer come in this form. This is the last time I can visit with you in this way."

Tears poured from my eyes. I squeezed my eyelids together, as if by holding in the tears I could hold her here with me longer. "I don't want you to go, Alea. I don't know if I can bear it."

She smiled and said gently, *"Ahhh, yes you can. Besides, I won't really be gone; you just won't hear me or see me in the same ways. You can communicate with me all you wish, and if you listen to the whispers of life that come in many forms, you will hear my response."*

Feeling somewhat consoled, I asked, just for clarification, "So you came here to help me heal—do you think it worked?"

"Your heart is healing beautifully. Look at all you have gained, Matt. Do you see how far you've come?"

It seemed like such a long time ago—nearly a year—since she had first appeared. "I can hardly remember what I was like before, Alea. It seems like a lifetime has passed."

"It does seem as though ages have passed, but you still remember. What do you see as the significant changes? Or better yet, in what ways do you feel different?"

"I feel more balanced, you know, between my head and my heart. I also feel better balanced between my body, mind and spirit. I used to be mostly mind-oriented; now I honor my body and my spirit, as well."

"This is good evidence of growth and healing, Matt. Balance is an important attribute. What else do you notice?"

"It seems as if my whole life is in greater harmony. All the parts are working together to create a more beautiful whole. Also, since I learned about resourcefulness, I am less judgmental, which allows much greater harmony."

"Hmmm. Balance and Harmony. That has a nice ring to it!" She then added, *"The balance you speak of takes many forms—mind, body and spirit, as well as head and heart. You are also more balanced between the male and female aspects of your being."*

As a man, the concept of being more feminine was a little hard for me to accept. I had heard people talk about the feminine side of men but had never really understood it.

Alea saw the quizzical look on my face and said, *"Everyone has male and female qualities, as clearly as they have right and left hemispheres of the brain. Each aspect handles different realms of your being. The feminine, the nurturer, is in the domain of the heart, the creative spirit. The masculine, the provider, is in the domain of the head, the analyzing spirit. One is open to the mystical, one to the scientific. Both are needed—in balance and harmony. You were out of balance when I first appeared. Your heart was closed and your spirit was not in harmony."*

She added, *"Being resourceful requires a balance, Matt. When any aspect gets out of balance, all other aspects are affected as well. They are all connected, just as each person affects all the other people with whom they come into contact. You must respect this balance in order to maintain harmony."*

As she spoke of the masculine and the feminine, she handed me another of the beautiful golden rings and said, *"Let this serve to remind you, always, of the importance of this truth."*

I looked at the ring, with its inscription *Balance and Harmony*, and breathed deeply, then turned back to her and said, "Thank you, Alea."

I sat quietly in appreciation, reviewing the existence of these two principles in the life I now had. More questions began to surface. "Alea? I understand that these Rings of Truth serve as symbols and are beautiful reminders, but I get the feeling that there is something more to them—something they create together."

"You will remember when the time is right. Just keep them all safe; together they make up the Master's Key."

I sensed that she wasn't going to tell me any more; she had the mischievous twinkle in her eye that indicated, "I know something that you don't know—" as if we were playing a game of divine hide and seek. I decided to leave it and seek out other answers while I had the chance.

"Are you and Michael working together—in this case, on me? A male and female effort, if you will?"

"What do you think?"

"It feels as if, for some reason I have yet to determine, the two of you want me to be instrumental in spreading a message—in waking up his volunteers, but you had to wake me up first."

She said quietly, *"You are almost right, Matt—but I didn't wake you up. You had to wake yourself up before I could make myself known to you. I have yearned and waited for a long, long time to be able to appear to you."*

I acknowledged her response, then had to ask, "But why, Alea? I understand your wanting to heal what happened in our past, but why did both you and Michael come to guide me?"

She took a deep breath, obviously trying to find the right words and said, *"This is what you chose to do with your life. You volunteered. You see, we all have a choice as to whether we want each life to be a focused life, a playful life or a restful life. You chose to be a volunteer, to be a messenger of God, and*

Michael and I waited for you to wake up so you could fulfill your purpose. We are committed to helping you. You are a very powerful being and can make a huge contribution—if you choose to. You always have choice, which is why we had to wait until you expressed a clear desire before we could do our part. If a soul comes here and changes its choice, we must honor that. Even now, the choice is still yours. In order to find, one must first choose to seek."

Even though I already had pieced together some of this story, I had a hard time understanding why I would be the one to do this work.

As if hearing my thoughts, she said, *"You are not the only volunteer, Matt. Hundreds of thousands of them are here, each with varying degrees of ability, various methods of sharing the message, and each effective in his or her own way. One such volunteer is a little girl who came into this world with what some would call mental retardation, but she is constantly happy and effervescent, jumping around excitedly over the simplest of things. Her heart is huge, her smile wide and no one who encounters her gets by untouched. She makes people lighten up and see how beautiful pure happiness is in the moment.*

"Another special soul chose to come with some of her fingers missing or joined. While she is still young, we can see that she is already serving her chosen purpose of reminding people to love, rather than judge. As she walks through crowds, she kisses her altered little hand and blows kisses to people, smiling and twinkling with such joy that it melts their hearts. Her inner sparkle is so bright that many don't even see her 'handicapped' condition. Those who do, are doubly impressed with the sweet reminder of compassion. Her condition sometimes causes people to look twice, which gives her twice the opportunity to shine her light on them. She reminds the world that we are not just our bodies and that something much greater is within each of us. Despite any differences in her physical being, she shows the world that true perfection comes from a loving heart and soul."

As she spoke, different people who had touched my heart in some way popped into my mind—some whom you wouldn't ever realize were volunteers.

She then said, *"Soon, Matt, you will discover the Master's Key and with it, break the chain of pain, leaving in its stead a chain of love. You are ready to deliver this message to the world."*

A wave of anxiety washed over me as I thought of the dream I had had of all the people in the desert listening to me speak. My past flashed before me: living in a boxcar, picking cotton. . . . In self-doubt, I asked, "But, Alea, who am I to do this work?"

Showing her golden smile, she responded gently, *"Good question. Who are you to do this work?"*

A voice within me gave an immediate answer. It was more than I could bear; I squeezed my eyes tightly shut, trying to close out the immensity of what I had heard. I didn't say anything. Instead, I tried to avoid the question—and the overwhelming answer.

Just as the angel had done, Alea placed her hand over my heart and repeated the question, *"Who are you to do this work?"*

Still I struggled within myself, not wanting to know, not wanting to say. I felt as though I were in a cocoon that was just opening, suspended high above the ground; I wasn't sure I was ready to fly. In fact, I didn't even want to believe that I had wings.

She asked again and again, watching my internal battle without letting up or giving in to my resistance, *"Who are you to do this work?"*

The answer pounded in my head each time she asked, until finally, with a burst of energy and tears, I blurted it out, "I am a Human Being!"

Then again, louder and more confidently, I said, "I am a Hu-Man Being."

I remembered from the Sufi Dance that *Hu* was an ancient word for God. With this understanding, the translation of *Human Being* became *God-Man Being.* I then recalled having somewhere read that the word Man derived from the Sanskrit word *Manava,* which meant "one endowed with Mind, or Manas," giving *Hu-Man* the meaning, *God-Mind.* I was literally *God-Mind,* in a state of *Being!* My new awareness expanded to all Human Beings. In that moment, I saw us all, male and female equally, as *God-Mind Beings.* We just need to wake up to realize the Divinity that we really are—*Human*—and then *Be* that.

I looked at Alea, tears still streaming down my face, and she asked lovingly, *"Now do you see who you are—you and all the rest of the people on this planet? The difference is that you are now awake, and being awake means that you know you are a child of God, therefore a God-Man, or God-Mind. Once people wake up to that knowing, how they live and what they do seems to change. It is hard to be judgmental when you know that every person on the planet is simply walking the labyrinth of their lives, attempting to get to the center, their heart, where their soul will be illuminated—and their ego eliminated—at least the ego as most know it, the ego that separates us from everyone else.*

"The ego serves us well when it remembers who we really are; it is a matter of who is in the driver's seat. Once the recognition of each person's true greatness is revealed—his or her authentic power—then the ego can serve as a useful tool for promoting that knowing out into the world and sharing it. If the aspect of glory that you have been given is to sing, then sing your heart out and let others hear your song. If it is to write, then do so. If your soul's expression comes out in artwork, then share your art so other souls may be touched. If, along with the other talents open to us, your gift is to be a loving parent, then be that, and give the world the treasure of a child raised in loving support, cherished and held dear. Do all the things that call forth your passionate response, and the universe will support you."

She looked at me intently, her hand still on my heart, and said with emphasis, *"And if your gift is to speak and touch hearts and heads all at once, waking the world up through your words, then that is what you must do."*

I could not complain of obscurity or mystery; this time there was nothing subtle about the message she was giving me. I thought of the original question, Who am I to do this work? and had to laugh. Who am I *not* to do it?

As I looked at Alea, transcendent bridge between the angelic world and the human realm, I saw her transform before my eyes from how she had always *appeared* to how she truly *is*—a beautiful, shimmering Light Being. Much like the angel, Alea was now sparkling and luminescent. My tears were renewed as I sat, humbled and honored in her presence.

Within only moments, she returned to her more concrete human-like form. Blushing a little, as if she hadn't meant to reveal herself that way, she said, *"It is time for me to go, Matt. Once again, I will tell you this: I am always with you. I can hear you, I can see you and I love you. I will show you and Jessie signs, when I can, of my presence in your life, just as God continually shows you signs."*

Then, as if warning me, she said in what for her was a stern and very earnest tone, *"You must always remember to do your part. Just because you have guides and guardian angels and the Divine looking after you, doesn't mean that you don't have to look after yourself. Don't ask God to do for you that which you can do for yourself."*

On a softer note, she added, *"Matt, I am so proud of you. You have achieved great levels of self-mastery. I am honored to guide you. I am honored to know you, and I will treasure the love between us always."*

Just as our first encounter in my hot tub, she looked me directly in the eyes and a wave of unconditional love washed over me. Once again, I was absolutely sure that she knew everything about me, all I had ever done—and she loved me still.

I returned the look and the love, saying, "Thank you, Alea. God bless you."

She replied, *"And God blesses you!"*

Pointing to the golden ring of *Balance* and *Harmony* that I still clutched in my hand, she added, *"Keep the Rings of Truth alive in your life, Matt. They will serve you well."*

I wanted to beg her not to leave but opted just to say, "I'll be looking for signs of you."

She smiled and said, *"If you seek, you shall find."*

She touched my cheek with such a tender look that I started crying all over again. I had shed more tears in this brief visit than in most of my adult life. I felt in that moment such a mixture of emotions: hope, simultaneous despair and acceptance of her leaving, gratitude, humility at the gifts I had received from her, and most of all, love. Love at a level impossible to describe, of a piercing sweetness that reminded me of a sculpture I had seen in Italy of a saint whose heart was pierced by a spear in the hands of an angel. Her face was ecstatic, and the angel's face was both joyous and resolute. The spear, representing God's love, impaled the saint on what had felt to me to be the axis of the universe, around which all else rotates.

Looking straight through my eyes, into my soul, Alea whispered, *"May the blessings of God rest upon you. May God's peace abide in you. May God's presence illuminate your heart, now and forevermore."*

Without another word, she transformed once again into a luminescent glow of a million sparkling lights, then dimmed and disappeared.

I called out, "Alea, I love you."

As if I were in a canyon, I heard the words echo back at me, *"I love you, love you, love you . . ."* until they too faded away.

I sat there alone, thinking over all the events of the last twenty-four hours, feeling the honor of being Human, alive and awake.

Turning out my light, I set my sights on returning home to Jessie and telling her about all that had transpired. I slept soundly, feeling safe and well looked after, with *Balance and Harmony* in the palm of my hand.

She watched him closely as he slept, her heart full, relieved that his healing was now in place. She, too, would miss joining him in the physical realm, having enjoyed their visits as much as he—although, she acknowledged, being a guide had its merits. She was grateful for the honor of serving both the angelic and the physical realms.

She sat in prayer, offering thanks to God for the joy of being an instrument of peace. To be able to love, learn, laugh and serve was a great joy indeed. She silently wished everyone knew that they, too, held the rights to such blessings—even now, in this lifetime.

Alea continued her observations as Matt packed the next day, said good-bye to Nan and journeyed home. She watched with joy as Jessie and Matt embraced and happily shared all the events of their independent yet joined lives.

His enthusiasm beamed outward as he showed Jessie his new collection of golden Rings of Truth: Accept a Miracle, Give and Receive, and Balance and Harmony—and explained the importance of each.

Nineteen rings were now in place; only two more rings remained in the forming of the Master's Key. Once complete, Matt's work on the planet would serve to help awaken others, whose work would awaken others still—a ripple effect of a magnitude Matt had yet to realize, but which would shift millions of lives into a higher awareness of their true nature. While this work had already begun, now, with self-mastery well in place, the effects on others would be deeper and more lasting. No longer would the message be contained in just his words, but in the very essence of his being.

Alea knew that who we are speaks louder than what we say and do. If there is not a complete alignment between these, the integrity of the message is lost. She held such an alignment as sacred, knowing that through it, spirituality is caught, not taught. Rather, she amended, it is awakened. Once awakened, one's soul cannot go back to sleep, and it rouses others by its mere existence.

18

The Master's Key

I stood at the front of the room, looking out at the members of the United Nations. The courteous round of applause came to a close, and they looked at me expectantly.

Distilling all the things I taught into a short, concise, power-packed moment in time hadn't been as easy as I had hoped. I had spent weeks preparing exactly what I wanted to say. Having only twenty minutes to make an impact on the world was a great exercise in clarity. I decided to include the exercise in my future workshops as a homework assignment for my students, but for now this was *my* assignment, and it was most immediately due.

The air in the room was serious as I began my presentation. "There was a man who went out for a drive early one morning along a rural road. As he drove along enjoying the morning air, he noticed some activity out in the middle of a field under a tree. As he got closer, he saw that it was an apple tree, and there was a farmer running around the tree, chasing about two hundred tiny pigs. As he would catch one of the pigs, he would hold it up to the tree and let the pig eat an apple.

Then he'd set it down and repeat the process with another piglet, chasing it, catching it, holding it up to the tree and letting it eat an apple.

"Amused, the man finally walked out across the field to the farmer and asked, 'Excuse me, sir, I've been watching you for about an hour. Would you mind if I asked what you are doing?'

"The farmer looked at the man as if to say, 'Isn't it obvious?' But instead he answered politely, 'I'm feeding these apples to my pigs. They like apples.'

"'Pardon me,' the man said, 'but why don't you just pick all the apples off the tree, throw them on the ground, and let the pigs run around and eat the apples? Wouldn't that save a lot of time?'

"The farmer looked at the other man quizzically and responded, 'What's time to a pig?'"

Having caught them off guard, I was pleased to hear them let down the serious front and laugh a little. I went on, "I tell this to point out that, without perspective, we often take action that doesn't effectively serve our ultimate needs.

"Working together affords us the opportunity to see things differently, to combine our efforts and create a better outcome. When I face you, I have 180-degree vision in one direction. When you face me, you have 180-degree vision in the opposite direction. Together, we have 360-degree vision. In order for us to survive and thrive on this planet, we need the kind of vision that we can only acquire together, facing each other in cooperation—as united nations.

"I address you today, as leaders not only of your individual countries, but of the world—as representatives of more than your singular needs, of a common goal of unity, a common goal of peace and cooperation, a common goal of the continuation of the Earth and its creatures."

"What we need, in order to reach these goals, is to be resourceful—each of us individually and as countries collectively. You are all familiar with the necessity of the basic resources—food, shelter, commodities, water, air—but today I am talking about another kind of resource. I define *resourceful* as being *'once again full of Source.'* This is the most important resource we have, for without it, we will annihilate each other or, at the very least, create a planet where fear prevails and love is rare.

"When we, as individuals, take responsibility for becoming resourceful before we take action, then the action we take will be *solution-focused* and will benefit all of us, not just some of us."

I looked around the room and was almost moved to tears as I saw the multicolored, earth-toned faces looking back at me. I suddenly saw us each as a different aspect of the very planet we live upon, with each of us representing the different climates, lands and cultures, with attributes as varied as the Earth itself.

I added, "Look around. Go ahead, look at each other. We are the Earth's resources. She is depending upon us to be resourceful."

They looked around at each other, which caused them to smile and laugh a little bit, as if prior to this moment they had seen only each others' roles, and now before them were human beings. They returned their focus forward and listened intently as I explained the importance of self-observation and letting go as key steps in becoming resourceful. I illustrated how we must stop to observe ourselves before we make decisions or take action, in order to determine whether we were acting from a position of fear and our need to be in control, or from a place of love where we did what was right for everyone involved.

"Every action we take, as individuals or politically, takes us either closer to world peace or further away. Observe yourself, your actions and those of your country, and ask yourself, 'Do I, my actions and those of my country contribute to the problem, or do they contribute to the solution?' Ask yourself, 'Are my actions and those of my country moving us toward love or toward fear?'

"When we are not resourceful, we are motivated by fear rather than love. Decisions based in fear contribute to the problem rather than its resolution. Shift into recognizing fear as a gift that allows us to see that we need to let go. Learn to see fear not as a call for reaction, but rather as a reminder to return to a resourceful state and then, if necessary, take action from there. When we align with our fears, they become the fuel for our need to control. And when we have a need to control, we are then totally out of control. When we let go of our need to control, we can make intelligent, rational, compassionate choices for the harmony of all.

"If we analyze our historical patterns and then continue on the same path we have been on, inevitably we will end up with destruction. If we keep doing the exact same things, we are going to keep getting the exact same results. We have the ability to turn this around and create a different outcome.

"How? The solution must begin with each of us as individuals and then spread outward. Each of us must take 100 percent responsibility for world peace and restoration of the environment. Just as the United States' Pledge of Allegiance begins with 'I' and ends with 'all,' the solution must begin with us as individuals and end with us all, collectively.

"What does taking 100 percent responsibility mean? First, it means that we be courageous. It requires courage to be self-observant, to take responsibility for making the necessary steps toward change. It requires courage to stand up and declare resourcefulness, to do what is right for us all, to have compassion.

"Being responsible means that we align our actions with our most resourceful self, that every choice creates solutions that serve the higher good of us all, that our choices contribute to love.

"We say we value freedom, but in order to have freedom, we must take responsibility. Freedom cannot exist without responsibility."

I looked out at the sea of faces, then asked, "Do you know what sets us apart from other animals? It is the ability to imagine. We have the ability to imagine the possibilities. We have the ability to imagine the potential outcomes of our actions, the problems that may arise and solutions to those problems. That same imagination can create a vision of world peace and harmony. Once a vision is created, it holds the power to become a reality.

"Can you imagine if we, as countries, could let go of the past and take resourceful action in the present? Can you imagine how our future would be?"

I paused to let them form their own visions. I then continued, impassioned. "Can you imagine if we accepted others and allowed them their differences? Can you imagine if we all treated each other with respect and worked together to achieve our common goals? Can you imagine if we all aimed to leave every person we encountered feeling empowered? Can you imagine what we could create if we put our energies into cooperating with each other instead of into war? Can you imagine what would happen if every person were to let go of their non-resourceful feelings and instead sought to spread love and joy to others?"

With extra emphasis, I asked, *"What would the world be like?"*

Again I hesitated, to allow them an opportunity to consider the possibilities. The room was silent as they contemplated all I had said.

After a moment, I began again. "Right now there is a chain of pain around this planet, and it is spreading rapidly. You see it in the faces of your people. We hear about it in the news. It is evidenced in the crime and suicide rates, the statistics on substance abuse and the abuse of our children.

"This is the pivotal generation. If a shift does not occur immediately, we will surely see the devastation, perhaps the elimination, of life as we now know it. We must help this generation to turn the situation around, and restore the health on this planet and in the people—emotionally, intellectually, physically and spiritually.

"You, as the leaders, are in a prime position to break that chain of pain and create a chain of love in its stead. You are the healers. Leadership is not a position or an office; it is an action. It's the example you set; it's who you are. By taking personal responsibility for observing yourself, letting go, remaining resourceful and then taking inspired action, a link in the chain of pain is broken, and a new ring is added to the chain of love. Every time you do this, you show the way to others, giving them hope, vision and the inspiration to do the same."

Pausing for only a moment, I asked, "Do you know how many Elvis impersonators there are?"

The shift in topic shocked everyone out of their visions and back into the room. They laughed with quizzical looks on their faces.

I went on, "Ten years ago, there were two thousand Elvis impersonators. Now there are forty thousand. Do you realize that at that rate, in the next twenty years, we'll all be Elvis impersonators?"

Laughter burst out around the room. "If Elvis impersonation can spread like that—why can't love and resourcefulness?"

The room fell silent again. "Here is the key: Never approach or leave any situation without doing so with love in your heart."

After letting that sink in, I added, "If we each commit to taking responsibility to do this, the pain will disappear, the fear will disappear and all that will be left will be our True Source. Resourcefulness will be restored on Earth."

I wrapped up my presentation. "An interesting thing happened to me the other day. My friend and I were walking down the street in a big city. There was a fair amount of activity going on around us, and we were walking rather quickly, getting some exercise. Suddenly, I heard a couple of voices right behind me; at first I didn't think much of it because a lot of people were around. Then I realized that these people had to be right on my heels, because they were keeping up with us. I turned my head slightly to see what was going on, and I saw that it was only one guy, talking to himself, carrying on a conversation with two different voices.

"I heard one of his voices say, 'In the beginning, God created man.'

"And the other voice said, 'So? I know that.'

"The first voice added, 'Then God created woman.'

"The other voice said again, 'So? I know that, too.'

"Then the first voice said, 'Yes, but then God created fruit.'

"The second voice said, 'Fruit? What does fruit have to do with anything?'

"At this point I had to concur with the second voice, wondering myself what fruit had to do with it.

"As I listened on, the first voice explained, 'You see, inside the fruit there is a seed, and if you plant it, it will grow. If you don't, it won't.'"

Silence permeated the room. "You have the seed of resourcefulness right in the palm of your hand, a seed which, if planted, will allow your visions of peace, harmony and love to grow and become a reality. If you don't—they won't."

The silence was broken by a long round of applause and I was hopeful that they would take to heart the meaning of what I had said. As I turned to collect my notes from the lectern, there, on top of them, were two golden Rings of Truth. One was the same size as most of the others, while the second was much larger. As I looked at them, the sounds of clapping faded into the background. Knowing that I had to clear the podium quickly, I gathered the rings up with my notes and placed them in my briefcase without stopping to read what they said. Then everyone took a short break.

I joined Jessie, who was waiting for me off to the side. She hugged me and whispered, "Matt, that was wonderful! I am so proud of you!"

Several others came up to thank me and shake my hand. After exchanging cards and taking care of the business at hand, Jessie and I left.

Once in the cab, I sat quietly to let the miracle of what had just happened sink in. I was pleased with my presentation and so appreciative of the opportunity to do it.

Jessie reiterated how much she had enjoyed what I had said. "I loved the way you wove the Rings of Truth right into your presentation, Matt. I think the people were really moved. They certainly were an attentive audience!"

I appreciated her support and hugged her awkwardly in the back of the cab. Rerunning the whole presentation through my mind, I got to the ending and remembered the rings. In all the excitement, I hadn't even had a chance to see what they said.

Eagerly, I pulled them out of my briefcase. I knew these were the last two of the twenty-one rings Alea had told me about.

Jessie was as impatient as I was when she saw the rings in my hand. Her eyes grew large with excitement as she exclaimed, "Oh, Matt! Where did you get them? What do they say?"

I told her how I had found them on the podium when I finished the presentation. We looked at them together, with awe and appreciation. It still felt like an honor each time one appeared, even though I still didn't know exactly what the rings represented collectively.

The smaller of the two rings had the word *Responsibility* etched beautifully into its surface. I held it for a minute with my eyes closed, feeling the essence of its meaning. I knew that this represented validation for all I had just said to the members of the U.N. I felt strong in the knowledge that each of us must take responsibility for putting an end to violence, whether directed toward other humans, ourselves or the planet. I knew that, just as for everyone else, responsibility must begin with me. I took a deep breath and released it audibly.

I then held up the larger of the two rings. Jessie asked, "Wasn't the ring of *Resourcefulness* large like that one?"

I responded affirmatively, "Yes, it was considerably larger than the others, although I think it might be slightly smaller than this one. We'll have to put them all together to see."

Her patience was wearing thin. "Well? What does it say?"

The message was stated simply, yet clearly: *Love.*

I turned to Jessie and explained, "This one represents the concept of never approaching or leaving any situation without love in your heart."

I didn't know how I knew, I just knew. Then I added, "This makes the Master's Key, Jessie. Now we have them all!"

We made our way back to the hotel room, where I had the other rings in a special felt jeweler's bag. We sat on the bed, spreading the rings out before us.

Love was the largest ring, with *Resourcefulness* just slightly smaller. In hopes of making sense of them all together, we reviewed each of the *Rings of Truth.* I read them out loud to Jessie in the order I had received them. Each time I read one, I placed it on the bed, laying the rings out so that they overlapped in a circular chain pattern. *"Surrender, Live Each Moment, Observe Yourself, Be Courageous, Remember You Are God and I Am You, Let Go, Know You Are Not Your Ego."*

When I got to *Resourcefulness,* I placed this larger ring so that it surrounded the others in its center. Each time I picked up a ring and read its message, the circumstances that led up to the discovery of each truth flashed through my mind. It was almost as if I were quickly turning the pages of a child's flip book as the scenes passed before me, changing rapidly as they went.

I reminded Jessie that Alea had said the first seven, now surrounded by *Resourcefulness,* represented the *Seed of Life.* She commented on how the message changed from the *steps* offered in the first seven to the *qualities* offered in the rest.

I continued, explaining to her that Alea had said following the "directions" of the first seven Rings of Truth would bring about *Resourcefulness* and the remaining rings represented the many facets of resourcefulness that would result from the planting of the seed. *"Clarity, Follow Your Heart, Commitment, Intimacy, Acceptance, Compassion, Integrity, Appreciation, Accept a Miracle, Give and Receive, Balance and Harmony, Responsibility."*

I placed these rings with the others in the center of *Resourcefulness* and then picked up the largest of the rings, which was big enough to encompass all the rest, and *felt* its message as I read it out loud, *"Love."*

I placed it in the only position that made sense, for the ring of *Love* fit just perfectly around *Resourcefulness,* concentrically so *Love* and *Resourcefulness* surrounded all the rest. I figured they were larger because those two concepts were all-encompassing in their meaning, as well as their size. We sat there, simply looking at and admiring the rings, taking turns periodically adjusting the arrangement we had made on the bed.

Playing with the configuration, I moved *Surrender* to the center and then arranged the rest of the "Seed of Seven" around it, interlocking like a circular chain. Then, around the outside of the "seed," I laid the remaining rings, one overlapping and bisecting the next, in another circular chain pattern. It was pretty, looking much like a flower drawn with a compass in geometry class. Something about it looked vaguely familiar, but I couldn't place it in my mind.

Suddenly, Jessie's eyes opened wide and she gasped. Looking at her face, then back at the rings where she was staring, I tried to determine what she could see that I couldn't. I asked, somewhat concerned as to whether she was okay, "What is it, Jessie? What?"

She replied, "I'm sorry, I didn't mean to startle you. It's just that this formation with the rings—I've seen it recently."

I could see the wheels turning in her head, trying to recall why it was familiar. She then reached for the book on Egypt that she had on the nightstand. She had brought it to continue her research for our vacation and had been reading it on the plane.

She thumbed through it impatiently and then said with another gasp, "Look, Matt! Look!"

She pointed to a symbol on the page that was identical to the one we had laid out in front of us. Now I was the one gasping. I whispered, *"The Master's Key!?"*

We both stared in disbelief. I half expected something dramatic to happen and watched for them to magically vibrate or smoke or do something now that we'd discovered this configuration, but no such theatrics followed. I turned to the book in hopes of some answers.

The page showed two pictures. One was of some Egyptian ruins, and the other was *The Master's Key.* I took the book and read the caption below the symbol aloud, so that Jessie could also hear. "This Code of Creation is made up of nineteen interlocking circles, creating a flower-like design. The entire pattern is enclosed within two larger, concentric rings."

Below the picture, the text explained that the ruins were part of a temple complex outside the ancient Egyptian city of Luxor. The temple had once housed a Mystery School for the study of geometry, astronomy and mysticism. Inscriptions on the temple walls were said to contain certain "keys" to understanding various mysteries of human existence. Apparently, modern scientists themselves were mystified as to how the symbols were applied to the surface of the stones, for they appeared to have been inscribed through an as-yet-unexplainable "flash-burning" process.

The book went on to say that this precise geometrical pattern, this sacred geometry, represents the relationship that exists between light, sound and matter. This matrix puts mathematical form to the ancient mysteries of life. Contained within it are the patterns for all DNA—the genetic information contained in every cell of the human body and is replicated throughout all of nature, the solar system and the universe. Thus, *this intricate pattern forms the actual blueprint for all creation.*

Furthermore, similar symbols to the one pictured had been discovered at various places throughout the world. The pattern had come to be recognized as a universal symbol for Creation.

Since the book was on Egypt, not on sacred geometry, it didn't go into any greater detail, but rather went on to describe other nearby locations one might visit. Jessie and I looked at each other, speechless, then back at the symbol in the book and the symbol on the bed, knowing this could be no coincidence.

I couldn't help but wonder if the place mentioned was the temple where I had seen and known Alea. For now, I would have to wait and do more research in order to understand what all this meant.

Jessie and I sat in meditation; the mystery lay before us. Within my mind's eye, I held the vision of the flower-like pattern that the *Rings of Truth* formed. Asking for clarity, I simply listened in the hope of some greater understanding as to what this *Master's Key* meant, why it was given to me and what I was to do with it now.

Images came into my mind, clear and steady, as to the deeper meaning of this symbology. I had a sense, an inner knowing, that in its simplest form, wholeness was created out of the parts being set in place. The code is symbolic of society itself; each person, each race, each religion is represented by a ring. When each piece is resourceful and allows all the other pieces to be, to exist in harmony, they will see that they, together, form a bigger picture. *We are mirrors of the creation from which we are made, just as our creations are mirrors of us.*

As I meditated on it, I saw this pattern not only as twenty-one rings but as infinite, never-ending. I envisioned everything made up of these interlocking rings, every molecule of air—patterned and connected, every drop of water—patterned and connected, every cell, every substance—patterned and connected. Even what we considered to be empty space—nothing—became patterned. *The Master's Key* gave form to the formless. Strangely, I saw myself made up of this same design, as well as the air around me, Jessie sitting next to me, the bed under me—all was made up of the same divine stuff—connected. I felt as if my being could walk out onto this pathway between us, moving my consciousness from one place to another, as if astrally projecting myself outward supported by this matrix. I was *seeing* the underlying mathematics to miracles! With a true mastery of this—of which I did not yet have—I understood how one could connect with another telepathically, or even walk on water.

On a more subtle level, I could *see* how our feelings and thoughts affect others, even when we are not together. We truly *are* connected and the *Rings of Truth* are the conductors of our energy. When we hold onto anger or non-resourceful feelings, others are affected, as the Universal Energy Flow isn't able to travel freely along this intricate—

and beautiful—pathway. Unloving feelings create a block, a traffic jam of sorts, causing Internal Bodily Turmoil—causing this chain of interlocking rings to turn into the *chain of pain*, rather than the *chain of love* that it is meant to be. Each time we let go, each time we return to resourcefulness, we clear the pathway of debris, allowing love to flow, allowing all possibilities to exist.

The Master's Key puts mathematical form to the ancient mystery—as the equation that God uses to formulate his creations and that we, as *God-Mind Beings,* may also use to create our realities!

Shuddering as I breathed deeply, I felt as if I had just had a glimpse "behind the scenes" and was privileged with this vision. As I considered all I had just witnessed, I had a sense that understanding all the ancient meanings of the symbolism were not as important as mastering each of the concepts within the *Master's Key*—each of the *Rings of Truth.* With the mastery of each link, the pieces of the puzzle are set in place and the vision, the picture, becomes clear. It is not necessary to understand all the intricacies, all we must do is gain self-mastery, and the *Rings of Truth* serve the purpose of guiding us to this.

Alea overflowed with joy at how well Matt and Jessie had worked together to discover the Master's Key. While there was much more for them to know, she was sure they would not stop their search until they discovered the meaning of the symbology. She wondered if discovering the Master's Key would cause him to remember how they had learned to use the code, although it really didn't matter. It was just a sentimental thought on her part.

The code of creation encourages and supports each individual to find their unique connection with Source. It represents the balance between the male and the female—the coming together of which creates life. It represents the connection and interdependence of all parts in creating a powerful whole. Its focus is on bridging the gap of unconsciousness with love—loving acceptance of all life. It encompasses the qualities of integration, wholeness, self-responsibility, unity, compassion and understanding.

Alea considered the powerful changes that were to come about on the planet if the people of the Earth committed themselves to mastering the Rings of Truth. The love that would result could overcome all obstacles.

She knew that soon Matt would discover the deeper, hidden meaning of this sacred geometry, the Master's Key, the divine intelligence through which God creates.

Alea considered Matt's presentation at the United Nations and glowed with the power of his efforts. She could feel the shifting taking place in the people as they listened. When a soul wakes up, it creates an unmistakable sensation in the guide realm. Great bliss is felt as the recognition of the soul settles into place. It is often like a baptism or initiation, in which the person's guide acknowledges the being's new level of awareness in some way. The exact style of this ritual varies as much as personalities do. It is an honored moment to be sure, and this day, many such celebrations were taking place all at once.

Confident that Matt would continue on this path toward sharing love and resourcefulness, she knew that the Master's Key was in good hands. If the only thing he remembered was to approach and depart every situation with love in his heart, this alone would be enough to ignite this generation into inspired action, effecting great change.

19

Life Celebration

Jessie and I sat in the hot tub on our deck, relaxing. We were discussing the completion of my manuscript, *Authentic Power,* and looking forward to seeing it as a book in print.

Enjoying the dry, cool night air of the desert, we watched the sky in wonder. I shared my thoughts with her. "I'd like to have a celebration with Nan, Daryl and the boys. I'd really love to see everyone."

Jessie agreed. "Well, why don't you invite them all here?"

I thought about it for a moment and then said, "What do you think about getting together in the desert in California? I'm speaking at a retreat center out in Joshua Tree next month. What about bringing the boys and meeting me there for the weekend? I think they would love seeing someplace new, and it coincides with the Summer Solstice, which seems like a great time to celebrate."

"That sounds wonderful. Joshua Tree National Park is a really neat place. I'm game, if you can get all the other pieces in place."

Still in the hot tub, I moved closer and let her know how much I appreciated her. I thanked her for being so supportive and such a good friend, as well as my lover. She responded sweetly, and the perfect night became even more so.

In the morning, I called Daryl. "How are things going?"

He sounded happy to hear from me. "Everything is going really well. My people all over the country are talking about resourcefulness and letting go. It's about time we did another training!"

"Sounds good to me. Just let me know when."

He then asked, "How did your presentation at the U.N. go?"

"It went great. I've gotten a lot of interest in my work since then. Oh, and I've finished my manuscript! In fact, one of the reasons I'm calling is to invite you to a Life Celebration that Jessie and I are having in Joshua Tree a month from now, for the Summer Solstice. Any chance you can make it?"

He was quiet for a moment, and I assumed he was checking his calendar. "I don't have anything scheduled for that weekend. I'd love to come. Who all will be there?"

I answered, "Well, you are the first person we've asked, but my boys are scheduled to be visiting with me that week, so they'll be there. I'm going to call my friend Nan and see if she can come. I told you about her. She's the one who has joined us in our vow to stick around until everyone wakes up."

"Oh yes! I'm looking forward to meeting her."

I added, "I'm doing a workshop with a group down there. I thought it would be fun if afterwards we all got together to celebrate the turning of seasons—both literally and figuratively."

Enthusiastically he replied, "Count me in!"

We then went on for quite a while filling each other in on the details of our lives. It was good to talk to him.

After we hung up, I called Nan and went through a similar routine with her.

She was excited about it and said, "I'd love to! What a great idea! I'll see if Steve wants to come, too. You know, Matt, I think we should make 'The Summer Solstice Life Celebration' an annual event!"

I laughed and said, "Well, let's see how this one goes first!"

We set the plan in motion and hung up, happily looking forward to the gathering.

Time passed quickly, and before I knew it I was in Joshua Tree giving a seminar I had designed called "The Master Key." I referred to the final message of "Love" as the ultimate key because no matter how I looked at it, that seemed to sum everything else up. If we approach and leave every situation with love in our hearts, having also empowered the other people involved, then all the other pieces also fall into place.

Friday night, Jessie and the boys showed up. The usual initial awkwardness seemed to have been softened by their time with Jessie. She was so good with young people that she managed to melt any discomfort that either of them may have felt. By the time they got to me, everyone was ready for a great week.

That night we went for a walk and watched shooting stars. We sat on some big boulders that looked out across the valley and listened to the coyotes howling in the distance.

Jerry, no longer a boy but a young man, looked over and said, "Dad? Remember when we went camping in Oak Creek Canyon and we had that discussion about God?"

"Yes, I remember."

He went on, still staring at the sky. "Well, I think this is where God is the happiest, out here under the stars. You just can't help but think about him when you look up, you know?"

My heart swelled with love as I answered reverently, "Yeah, I know."

Tim added, "I know I'm happiest out here!"

Jessie chipped in, "Me, too, especially with all of you."

The feeling of connection between us all was as tangible as if we were holding hands. I sat happily watching the moonlight dance on my family and said a prayer of thanks.

The next morning, the Summer Solstice, Nan and Steve showed up, and then Daryl came in about an hour later. We all headed out to the park for a picnic and spent the afternoon exploring. We climbed on rocks and listened as Steve, who knew a lot about geology, explained some of the unique characteristics of the area. He pointed out that it seemed as if we were in the center of a large circular valley, with rock formations creating the boundary.

We found a hill made up of large, piled-up boulders and climbed up a ways; the boys settled on the largest one. The rest of us were not far behind and climbed into place to join them.

Tim pointed to an opening, possibly the entrance to a cave, and went ahead as a scout, then called the rest of us in. The opening was narrow, made of two huge rocks resting against each other. It then opened up into a small room, and light shone in through cracks and crevices. It was just large enough for all seven of us to fit. We stood in a circle and we went around, sharing one at a time, planting seeds for our dreams and goals, anticipating the upcoming season of growth.

Steve began by sharing that he had started a business in Santa Barbara leading hikes through the mountain range, educating tourists about the Chumash Indians who had lived there, the geology and the splendor of the area. His hope and vision was that through the summer months, the busiest tourist season, the business would prosper and he would contribute to his customers' experience and knowledge of the land they were visiting. He hoped that they would come away with a greater appreciation and respect than they had when they arrived.

Nan shared that her artwork had been accepted into some galleries in town, and she offered thanks for the joy of expressing herself and assisting others in expressing their creativity, as well. She also offered her appreciation for the gift of being able to guide and counsel others with clarity. She asked for the continued opportunity to be of service.

Daryl reiterated his convictions that his business contributed to the health, wealth and spiritual values of hundreds of thousands. He saw his nutritional products as a tool for empowering people around the world.

Jerry, who was a little uncomfortable with sharing his dreams with so many people, especially those he didn't know, hesitated. The silence in the valley was so peaceful and relaxing, however, that no one seemed to mind the wait.

He said, "Um, I am trying to decide what I want to do with my life. All I know is that this is going to be my last year in school, and I'm looking forward to graduating. While I want to look toward the future, I also want to be sure to really enjoy my senior year, because I know this is the last time all my friends are going to be together. I guess I just hope that what I am going to do next, after school is out, becomes clear, and that I make the right decisions."

Everyone smiled, remembering that age and stage of life and experiencing similar feelings. We turned our attention to Tim.

He said enthusiastically, "I'm going to be pitcher on my baseball team this year, and we are going to be state champions! I'm going to practice all summer long, so that I play my best when school starts."

We all laughed, enjoying his total clarity of vision. He left no doubt of his success in anyone's mind.

Jessie looked thoughtful, as if she weren't sure this was the right time and place to say what she wanted to say. Tears came to her eyes, but I could see that they were tears of joy, not sadness. I reached out and took her hand.

She looked at me and smiled, saying, "I'm asking for prayers and offering my love and appreciation to God for the blessing I have been given. This is the year of Motherhood."

I didn't think I had heard her right. Maybe she was just saying that she wanted to *become* a mother this year. I looked at her for clarification.

She returned my gaze and nodded, "Matt, I just found out—we're going to have a baby."

Everyone started talking at once, congratulating us excitedly. Somewhat in shock, I reached out and hugged her, whispering, "I love you, Jessie."

Jerry and Tim immediately put in their request for a brother, and Daryl told Jessie that she ought to be on his nutritional supplements. Steve wished us well, and Nan just smiled as if she already knew the child. I stood quietly, overwhelmed, taking in the information as if I had just been handed a gift far too precious to accept. It left me speechless for several minutes.

When the excitement settled, they looked to me, as it was my turn. Joking, I said, "It appears that I have already planted my seed for the year!"

Everyone laughed, and then I continued. "This year has been one of tremendous growth. I feel so awed by the wonder and miracles that surround me. Albert Einstein said, 'There are only two ways to live your life. One is as if nothing is a miracle. The other is as if everything is a miracle.' This year has proven to me that everything is a miracle, and I am so grateful.

"I look at this group gathered here now. The hopes and dreams we have shared today represent the balance of the mental, physical, spiritual, and . . . " I added with a look toward Jessie, "the emotional realms of our beings."

"We also represent a span of ages from the unborn through several generations, both male and female. My prayer is that this circle continues to grow, and that each year we continue to have a Celebration of Life in different places around the world, adding in people of many religions and races—all focused on a common goal. I see people joining us who are also committed to sharing their gifts and dreams with others, people dedicated to breaking the chain of pain and seeing to the continuation of the health of this planet and its creatures."

Pausing for a moment, I went on, "I offer thanks to God for the family and friends that I have been blessed with and ask for the continued strength and ability to be an instrument of peace, helping to spread love and joy around the planet, reconnecting people with Source. Today, I'm planting my book and teachings, looking forward to seeing what grows."

We stood looking at each other in silence. Everyone could feel the sacredness of the moment. Even the boys were in no hurry to leave the circle.

As if out of nowhere, I heard an enchanting voice; it echoed off the rocks, making its source hard to identify. Looking around, I saw that the singing came from Nan. She looked into each of our eyes as she sang the words, and soon we were all looking across the circle into each other's eyes as well.

The melody was heavenly:

"All I ask of you is forever to remember me as loving you.

"All I ask of you is forever to remember me as loving you.

"Ishq Allah mahbud lillah, Ishq Allah mahbud lillah.

"Ishq Allah mahbud lillah, Ishq Allah mahbud lillah."

The Arabic words meant, "God is Love, Lover and Beloved." She sang it through several times. As she did, there in the center of the circle, I saw something materializing.

The singing continued to echo throughout the cave:

"All I ask of you is forever to remember me as loving you.

"All I ask of you is forever to remember me as loving you."

As I watched, the forms of both Michael and Alea appeared, transparent and ethereal, but undeniably present nonetheless.

"Ishq Allah mahbud lillah, Ishq Allah mahbud lillah."

The singing sounded like angels.

"Ishq Allah mahbud lillah, Ishq Allah mahbud lillah."

Michael and Alea appeared only for a moment, but in the time I saw them, Alea smiled her glorious smile and reached out and touched Jessie's stomach, indicating her blessings for the baby. Michael no longer looked like an old man in overalls, but appeared now as the Archangel he truly was, a strong warrior, complete with rainbow-colored wings. He was so handsome that the beauty of the two of them was almost too much to behold.

As quickly as they appeared before me, they disappeared. Tears streamed down my face as I looked around to see if anyone else had seen them. By now, everyone was singing along with Nan; apparently no one had. I took the hands of those on either side of me, and they in turn took the hands of those next to them. With the circle complete, we sang one more round of the song and then grew silent.

Somehow the words seemed to echo on, even though none of us were singing. We all heard, as if sung in a duet:

"All I ask of you is forever to remember me as loving you. . . ."

Alea and Michael faced each other. He took his turn first, knowing the power of expressing one's vision in words.

"Now is my time to wake up all the volunteers and lead them to fulfilling their purpose. I will not quit until everyone knows their True Source and lives in alignment with their Divine Essence. I will make myself known around the

world through subtle yet unmistakable moments that remind people to follow their hearts and set this planet free of the chains that bind it."

Alea in turn stated her commitment. "I am an instrument of Thy peace. Where there is hatred, I shall sow love."

She smiled at Michael after alluding to the prayer of St. Francis and then continued, "I, too, firmly plant my commitment to serve as a bridge between God and the Hu-Man Beings now residing on Earth. My prayer is that love shall prevail and fear shall fade from their hearts."

She turned to look upon the gathering of friends and family. She bathed in the warmth of the moment and her honor in being a part of their circle.

Michael watched also, adding a glorious light to the scene of celebration. He then focused his blessings on Alea, saying, "You have done good work, Alea. You have guided Matt well. Now, I must go, as so many are ready to awaken—and what of you? How do you wish to continue your service?"

She considered all the possibilities, knowing that should she wish to change positions, now was her golden opportunity, for with the wave of Michael's hand another loving presence would step in as Matt's guide. She looked again at Matt and Jessie, then said clearly to Michael, "Thank you for offering this opportunity, but I wish to continue as a guide for Matt." She then added, "However, I would like to do it in physical form. . . ."

Michael answered, "As you wish," as he waved his hand in a sweeping arc, and they both disappeared.

To Be Continued

About the Authors

Jim Britt is considered one of the leading "scientists" in human behavior. His background includes all levels of experience, research and application. Jim devotes the majority of his time to sharing his breakthrough technology brought forth in the *Rings of Truth* book and retreats, and in his *Authentic Power* workshops and book, to be published by Health Communications in 2000.

Jim's work is designed to guide participants through a process of "letting go" of nonsupportive feelings, emotions and beliefs that keep them from living at their full potential. Regardless of your background, education or experience, Jim Britt's message is guaranteed to move you. Whether you are a reader of Jim's books or a workshop participant, it will be an indescribable, thought-provoking, emotional journey, leading to self-discovery and personal change. His unique combination of personal style and message content impacts everyone. He will ignite your imagination for becoming all you can be.

Jim has served as a trainer, marketing consultant and human behavior specialist for hundreds of companies throughout the United States, Canada and Europe.

In the past thirty years he has shared his life-enhancing realizations with more than *one million people from all walks of life.* He is more than aware of the challenges we all face in making adaptive changes for a sustainable future, both personally and professionally, as well as globally.

Eve Eschner Hogan, M.A., is an inspirational speaker and labyrinth facilitator. She is the author of *Intellectual Foreplay, Creating the Time of Your Life* and *The Way of the Winding Path.* Her specialty is in helping people to discover and expand their own inner resources and their awareness, strengthen their life skills and create healthy, joyful relationships. For information on Eve, her seminars and tools for self-mastery write Wings to Wisdom, P.O. Box 943, Puuene, Maui, Hawaii 96784, call 1-888-551-5006 or see *www.heartpath.net.*

For More Information About Jim Britt's Work

The *Rings of Truth* Retreat
The *Authentic Power* 3-4 Hour Seminar
The *Authentic Power* 1- or 2-Day Workshop
The *Authentic Power* Certified Trainers Programs
Keynote Presentations
Custom Training Programs

To order other tapes, books and programs,
schedule Jim Britt as your featured speaker,
or to receive a
free newsletter subscription,
please write or call:
P.O. Box 1743
Grass Valley, CA 95945-1743
1-888-546-2748
e-mail: *jimbritt@gv.net*

Check out Jim Britt's Web sites at:
www.personalgrowthtips.com for free on-line newsletters
or
www.jimbritt.com